Masculinities and Hong Kong Cinema

Hong Kong University Press thanks Xu Bing for writing the Press's name in his Square Word Calligraphy for the covers of its books. For further information, see p. iv.

Masculinities and Hong Kong Cinema

Edited by

Laikwan Pang & Day Wong

香港大學出版社
HONG KONG UNIVERSITY PRESS

Hong Kong University Press
14/F Hing Wai Centre
7 Tin Wan Praya Road
Aberdeen
Hong Kong

© Hong Kong University Press 2005

ISBN 962 209 737 5 (Hardback)
ISBN 962 209 738 3 (Paperback)

British Library Cataloguing-in-Publication Data
A catalogue record for this book is available from the British Library.

Secure On-line Ordering
http://www.hkupress.org

Printed and bound by Rainbow Graphic & Printing Co., Ltd., Hong Kong, China.

Hong Kong University Press is honoured that Xu Bing, whose
art explores the complex themes of language across cultures, has
written the Press's name in his Square Word Calligraphy. This signals
our commitment to cross-cultural thinking and the distinctive nature
of our English-language books published in China.

"At first glance, Square Word Calligraphy appears to be nothing
more unusual than Chinese characters, but in fact it is a new way
of rendering English words in the format of a square so they
resemble Chinese characters. Chinese viewers expect to be able
to read Square Word Calligraphy but cannot. Western viewers,
however are surprised to find they can read it. Delight erupts when
meaning is unexpectedly revealed."

— Britta Erickson, *The Art of Xu Bing*

Contents

Acknowledgements   vii

Contributors   ix

Introduction: The Diversity of Masculinities in Hong Kong Cinema   1
Laikwan Pang

Part I   History and Lineage   **15**

Chapter 1   Making Movies Male: Zhang Che and the Shaw   17
Brothers Martial Arts Movies, 1965–1975
David Desser

Chapter 2   Post-1997 Hong Kong Masculinity   35
Laikwan Pang

Chapter 3   Queering Masculinity in Hong Kong Movies   57
Travis S. K. Kong

Chapter 4   Unsung Heroes: Reading Transgender Subjectivities   81
in Hong Kong Action Cinema
Helen Hok-sze Leung

Part II   Transnational Significations   **99**

Chapter 5   Kung Fu Films in Diaspora: Death of the Bamboo   101
Hero
Sheng-mei Ma

Chapter 6   Obtuse Music and the Nebulous Male: 119
             The Haunting Presence of Taiwan in
             Hong Kong Films of the 1990s
             Shen Shiao-Ying

Chapter 7   Fighting Female Masculinity: Women Warriors   137
             and Their Foreignness in Hong Kong Action
             Cinema of the 1980s
             Kwai-cheung Lo

Chapter 8   An Unworthy Subject: Slaughter, Cannibalism   155
             and Postcoloniality
             James A. Steintrager

Part III   Production, Reception, and Mediation   175

Chapter 9   Bringing Breasts into the Mainstream   177
             Yeeshan Chan

Chapter 10   Post-Fordist Production and the Re-appropriation   199
             of Hong Kong Masculinity in Hollywood
             Wai Kit Choi

Chapter 11   Masculinities in Self-Invention: Critics' Discourses 221
             on Kung Fu–Action Movies and Comedies
             Agnes S. Ku

Chapter 12   Women's Reception of Mainstream Hong Kong   239
             Cinema
             Day Wong

Notes   261

Glossary   297

Bibliography   317

Index   333

Acknowledgements

We would like to thank the Hong Kong Polytechnic University, which funded this research project, and its General Education Centre, which provided the necessary technical and staff support. Our research assistant, Yvonne Leung Yee-man, provided research and editorial help to not only the editors but also many of the contributors. We are grateful for her prompt, accurate, and often creative work. We thank Mina Cerny Kumar of Hong Kong University Press who initiated this project, and we thank Colin Day, Delphine Ip and Phoebe Chan who followed up on this project with care and enthusiasm. Special thanks also to Fiona Ng who assisted our last phase of editing.

Chapter 2 is a revised and expanded version of Laikwan Pang's "Masculinity in Crisis: Films of Milkyway Image and Post-1997 Hong Kong Cinema" previously published in *Feminist Media Studies* 2.3 (Fall 2002): 325–40 (www.tandf.co.uk).

Contributors

Yeeshan CHAN is a film scriptwriter and Ph.D. candidate in the Department of Japanese Studies at the University of Hong Kong. Her Ph.D. dissertation focuses on the community of *zanryu-hojin*, Japanese civilians left behind in the former Manchuria after WWII, who since the 1980s have been repatriated with their extended Chinese families. She has written for multimedia in Hong Kong. She is also conducting research with a criminologist on Chinese organized crime in Japan, the results of which will be published in an anthropological paper on the subject.

Wai Kit CHOI is a Ph.D. candidate in the Department of Sociology at the University of California, Irvine. His dissertation is on proletarianization under Chinese capitalisms. His research interests are in social theory, economic sociology and political economy, and he is a contributor to an edited volume titled *Labor Versus Empire: Race, Gender and Migration* (Routledge, forthcoming).

David DESSER is Professor in the Unit for Cinema Studies and the Program in Comparative and World Literatures at the University of Illinois. He has published numerous books and essays on various aspects of Asian cinema and has edited, among others, *Ozu's "Tokyo Story"* and *The Cinema of Hong Kong: History, Arts, Identity*.

Travis S. K. KONG received his Ph.D. in sociology from the University of Essex (England) in 2000. He currently lectures at the Hong Kong Polytechnic University and teaches courses on topics such as sexuality, gender, media, and culture. His research interests focus primarily on the issues of gay men and lesbians, sex workers and people with HIV/AIDS. He has been published in journals such as *Body & Society* and *Sexualities*.

Agnes KU is Associate Professor of Sociology at the Hong Kong University of Science and Technology. Her research interests include cultural sociology, the public sphere, civil society, citizenship, Hong Kong studies, and gender issues. She has been published in such journals as *Sociological Theory, Theory, Culture and Society, International Sociology, The China Quarterly*, and *Modern China*. She is the co-editor of *Remaking Citizenship in Hong Kong — Community, Nation, and the Global City* (Routledge, forthcoming), and the author of *Narratives, Politics, and the Public Sphere — Struggles over Political Reform in the Final Transitional Years in Hong Kong (1992–1994)* (Ashgate, 1999).

Helen Hok-sze LEUNG received her B.A. in English from Oxford University and her M.A. and Ph.D. in comparative literature from the University of Wisconsin-Madison. She is currently Assistant Professor of Women's Studies at Simon Fraser University, where she teaches queer theory, film and cultural studies. She is working on a book on queer issues in Hong Kong culture. Her articles on Hong Kong cinema and queer politics have appeared in numerous journals and anthologies.

Kwai-cheung LO is Associate Professor of Humanities and English Literature at Hong Kong Baptist University. He is the author of *Hong Kong Transnational Popular Culture* (University of Illinois Press, forthcoming).

Sheng-mei MA is Professor of English at Michigan State University, specializing in Asian American/Asian diaspora studies and East-West comparative studies. He is the author of *Immigrant Subjectivities in Asian American and Asian Diaspora Literatures* (State University of New York Press, 1998). *The Deathly Embrace: Orientalism and Asian American Identity* (University of Minnesota Press, 2000) was completed under the auspices of the Rockefeller Foundation Fellowship for 1997–98.

Laikwan PANG teaches cultural studies at The Chinese University of Hong Kong. She is the author of *Building a New Cinema in China: The Chinese Left-wing Cinema Movement, 1932–37* (Rowman & Littlefield, 2002), and *Cultural Control and Globalisation in Asia: Copyright, Piracy and Cinema* (RoutledgeCurzon, forthcoming).

SHEN Shiao-Ying is Associate Professor in the Department of Foreign Languages & Literature at National Taiwan University. Her articles on Western and Chinese-language cinema have been published in *Chung-Wai Literary Monthly*, *Film Appreciation*, and *Post Script*. She is also co-editor of *Passionate Detachment: Films of Hou Hsiao-Hsien*, and is currently working on studies of works of a series of female filmmakers.

James A. STEINTRAGER received his doctoral degree in comparative literature from Columbia University and is an associate professor in the Department of English of the University of California at Irvine. He is the author of *Cruel Delight: Enlightenment Culture and the Inhuman* (University of Indiana Press, 2004) and is currently working on a study of pleasure and the semantics of liberation.

Day WONG received her Ph.D. in sociology from the Australian National University. She currently lectures at the Hong Kong Polytechnic University. Her research and teaching areas include gender and sexuality, feminist theories, and Foucault's works. She has written and co-written journal articles and book chapters on violence against women and sexual politics.

Introduction

The Diversity of Masculinities in Hong Kong Cinema

Laikwan Pang

MASCULINITY IN ITS PLURAL

Hong Kong cinema has recently been "discovered" as one of the most interesting and successful alternatives to Hollywood's dominant global, commercial film market. Many critiques of, and academic books on, Hong Kong cinema have been published in the past few years.[1] If American cinema is "Hollyworld," then the movie industry in this small corner of Asia is "Planet Hong Kong."[2] Both cinemas are celebrated and criticized for their long traditions, contributions to cinematic conventions, transnational appeal, and market ideology. If the wealth of scholarship and criticism has established the discursive coherency of Hollywood cinema as a unified body with its own ideology, tradition, and aesthetics, bountiful local and international critical efforts are similarly constructing a discursive Hong Kong cinema. The outstanding commercial success of Hong Kong cinema seems to have welcomed and cultivated scholarly criticism of and theorization about its film language, genre development, and audiences' (trans)national cultural identification. These critical efforts combine to construct a legacy of Hong Kong cinema that is increasingly taken for granted.

Hong Kong cinema has been particularly attractive to film scholars in two dimensions: its transnational commercial appeal and its local specificities. There seem to be many Hong Kong cinema followers around the world, which contributes to the impression that the commercial appeal of this cinema is universal and that there is negligible local specificity interfering with transnational entertainment. However, many movie fans and scholars also notice that the plots, characterizations, style, and "feel" of Hong Kong cinema are unique, which makes them hard to mistake Hong Kong films as productions of other cinemas. As Esther Yau declares: "Circulating in the far-reaching networks already established by immigrant business and economic diasporas, Hong Kong movies can appear provincial yet also Hollywood-like."[3] These seemingly contradictory transnational and local characteristics dialectically amalgamate Hong Kong cinema into a coherent entity that defines it as unique, and therefore "cultist." I find this discursive "coherency" of Hong Kong cinema particularly interesting in view of the discussions of gender in recent critical dialogues.

There may be scholarship on gender issues in Hong Kong cinema, but there is an implicit overall reading of the cinema as a unified collective: the auteur/genre dichotomy that such work often assumes leaves the commercial cinema untouched by, or unworthy of, gender analysis. While a handful of directors, such as Stanley Kwan (Guan Jinpeng) and Ann Hui (Xu Anhua), are singled out as gifted auteurs with feminine sensibilities,[4] most gender problems and nuances are taken for granted within the larger commercial framework. It is as though the sheer banality and shamelessness of mainstream Hong Kong cinema precludes it from complex gender analysis. Faced with an ultra-commercial cinema, instead of the more "sophisticated" Taiwanese or mainland Chinese films, most critics find it unproductive to impose a gender analysis on, for example, the outright sexist films of Wong Ching (Wang Jing). Individual auteur directors are praised particularly with reference to the surrounding "trashy" commercial films that demonstrate no gender ambiguities. Hong Kong cinema's overt commercialism, which often exploits gender stereotypes and hierarchy unabashedly, discourages us to come to terms with its gender issues in a complicated and sophisticated fashion. This selective (un)awareness is particularly evident in scholars' hitherto inattention to masculinity — a theme, ideology, and industrial structure that has ruled Hong Kong cinema for so many years.

Hong Kong cinema is famous for its action, and this long tradition of "male cinema," with its male stars and male stories, has won over millions of Chinese and other movie-goers around the world in the past few decades. But surprisingly few scholars have interrogated the complexity of this masculine tendency. Particularly during a time when Hong Kong cinema is in a slump, more are interested in investigating, explaining, and reclaiming its past commercial success than seeing that very success as symptomatic of a gender hierarchy.

Steven Cohan argues that a normative standard of a hegemonic masculinity is never stable or coherent or authentic; it has to exist alongside a range of alternative forms in representation. He defines hegemonic masculinity as "the configuration of gender practice which embodies the currently accepted answer to the problem of the legitimacy of patriarchy."[5] Cohan believes that while there are always multiple forms of masculinities existing simultaneously, a hegemonic gender normality dominates and accommodates others. While Cohan is right that different forms of masculinities are always fighting for control, in the case of Hong Kong cinema its volatility hardly allows any one to dominate. Maybe if we are really interested in studying the complexity and fluidity of Hong Kong cinema, not as a consistent body of work but a vigorous and contested cultural site that always contains disharmonious and contradictory ideologies and representations, we need to confront the diversity of masculinities underlined and represented in this cinema. To me and to the volume's contributors an interesting aspect of Hong Kong cinema is the cultural and theoretical complexity behind such diversity of masculinities. By confronting the multiple forms of masculinities contained in and interpreted by this cinema, not only can we understand the particularity of the cinema, but light can also be shed on general masculinity issues.

As the chapters in this volume demonstrate, even within a single genre and a single period in Hong Kong cinema we see multiple types and ideologies of masculinities interacting with each other. King Hu (Hu Jinquan) and Zhang Che developed and preached very different types of masculinity around the same time within the same genre (ch. 1). Jackie Chan (Cheng Long) is heroic and macho, but he can also be docile and domestic; his masculinity is so unstable and polyvalent that although he is considered an authentic Hong Kong hero he can be appropriated by mainstream American stereotypes of effeminate Asian men (ch. 10), and identified by female audiences as a gender-transcending model for self-empowerment (ch. 12). Stephen Chow (a.k.a. Stephen Chiau) (Zhou Xingchi) can play a clown and play God at the same time (ch. 11), so could the male filmmakers project their and the market's conflicted desires on the male characters they produce (ch. 9). Male ideologies might be fulfilled by female roles, even though they are often embarrassingly trapped between conflicting gender and racial discourses (ch. 4 and ch. 7). This wide array of masculinities that simultaneously exist is partly a result of the fluid and disorganized structure of the cinema, in which characters and stories are often created out of haste and by accident. Unlike precisely calculated Hollywood productions based on plenty of market research, Hong Kong cinema is famous for its lack of discipline, which is why alternative forms of masculinity can be created, as Yeeshan Chan documents in her chapter, simply out of the filmmaker's resentment about his own failures in life. The writing collected in this volume attests to the diversity of masculinities manifested and implied in this cinema, which is a vast resource within which we can re-interrogate the fictitiousness and diversities of male bodies.

If Chris Holmlund is right to argue that "visibility frequently translates to social acceptance,"[6] we are indeed seeing a rather open Hong Kong cinema industry and society producing and accepting such a diversified array of male bodies, naked or clothed, masculine or fragile, vigilant or limp, among and within which it is often difficult to find cohesive moral values or stable ideologies governing masculinity. However, we must not mistake such plural representations as ideal; seeing them simply as reflections of ideologies at odds with each other might not fully reflect the codependency, non-coherency, or even emptiness of these forms. While the production and representation of a masculine body are always woven by different forces, a single force can also shape a number of alternative masculine bodies and forms, and what they present is far from a romanticized picture of the congenial coexistence of different values and lifestyles. While I do not agree with Cohan that there is necessarily a "visible" hegemonic masculinity overruling or incorporating others, an invisible power structure, which operates not through a single masculinity but through many, is still intact. One of the most common pitfalls in studying masculinity in cinema is reflectionism, which assumes that one masculinity corresponds to one set of ideology. As the following chapters show, all forms of masculinity (if we can identify them as such) are so intimately related to other masculinities or identity structures that in the end it might be futile to locate or differentiate the dominant from the alternative. Each and every masculinity is at the same time too full of meaning and empty, but its transient nature should not rid it of the power it represents. I believe that different forms of masculinity are embodied identities and experiences, and at the same time discourses constructed for the sake of fulfilling people's fantasies and desires. Masculinity is a source of power, and a site where power operates, so that it is also subjected to power. Therefore, any simple political agenda that involves using one form of masculinity against another simplifies their ultimate interconnectedness, which is manifested in different ways under different social and cultural circumstances.

This complicated power network corresponds to the scenario depicted by Yeeshan Chan, whose chapter demonstrates that patriarchy approves and indeed derives pleasure from certain forms of female empowerment and alternative masculinities. The multiplicity of masculinities allowed in this industry is an effort to appeal to the market, whose power is not challenged but rather reinforced by such a happy coexistence of masculinities. Travis Kong's chapter also demonstrates a similar situation in Hong Kong cinema, in which the plurality of gay images allowed does not imply that they are not operated under a coherent set of powers determined by the market and heterosexual norms. As Kwai-cheung Lo pertinently points out in his chapter, "multiplicity or pluralization only helps make the ideology of masculinity even stronger and more powerful, turning it into a stable origin or foundation exempted from any radical deconstruction."[7] The heterosexual norm and the capitalist market are highly elusive and flexible structures of power that survive on, rather than are annihilated by, differences and crises.

The diversified forms of masculinity available in Hong Kong cinema are tempting texts to invite even more diversified interpretations; trying to engage critically with the wealth of possible meanings derived from these many male forms while always recognizing the specific discursive environments these meanings came from is the critical task our contributors have had to deal with. To avoid generalizing about a dominant Hong Kong cinema masculinity yet continue to investigate how power operates on various masculinities inter-relatedly, we must carefully situate masculinities at the specific time and in the specific space we want to investigate. David Bordwell describes this cinema as dynamic and full of kinetic energy,[8] which I think can refer positively to its vigor and negatively to its chaos. While the masculine Hong Kong cinema has been celebrated for its boundless actions and imagination, we can also describe it as a hysterical space, which stereotypically belongs to women. In turn, such volatility inevitably translates itself from representation to issues of identity and identification.

While we want to highlight, confront, and analyze in a sophisticated manner the diversity of masculine manifestations and ideologies before rushing to any conclusive statements about masculinity in Hong Kong cinema, "differences" are not our only concern. We are in fact committed to exploring issues related to identity, in spite of our critical distance against simple identity politics. As Helen Leung and James Steintrager demonstrate in their chapters, the hastening efforts of some queer and postcolonial critics asserting a certain identity are often based upon misunderstandings, bias, and stereotypes. Identity, if taken seriously, should be seen as a negative concept built on differences and negations, not as an uncritical endorsement of something ideal.[9] While the various cinematic masculinities explicated in this volume are by no means natural mirrors reflecting social facts, critically engaging in various forms of masculinities inevitably brings us back to the complexity of identity politics, as many chapters of this volume document. In spite of their different approaches, many chapters are ultimately concerned about Hong Kong or Chinese identity. The chapters of Shen Shiao-Ying, Sheng-mei Ma and Kwai-cheung Lo investigate and theorize the discursive formations of the Hong Kong-Chinese identity through the construction of a certain otherness, while Steintrager's and my chapters focus rather on the difficulties theoretically and cinematically in the project of postcolonial Hong Kong identity. Other chapters, like Travis Kong's, Helen Leung's, and Day Wong's, are committed to investigating the identity politics and subject formations of non-heterosexual male gender and sexual subjects in Hong Kong. Many contributors here show that to understand the Hong Kong identity at large is to confront first the alternative masculinities or gender forms posited as others, as accomplices, or as that which simply refuses interpretation. What this anthology shows is that only through careful and respectful readings of differences can we come to a complex scenario interpellating any form of identity; this is particularly so in the case of masculinity, which has claimed too much power while at the same time been rendered too vulnerable.

Issues of identity are also connected to the theoretical and practical predicaments of identification, which, regardless of its sex, is never simple but always involves many forms of desire; desire is always mobile, fluid, and constantly transgressing.[10] How critics and audiences read and appropriate the different masculinities captured on screen is also a deeply-felt concern shared by many of this volume's contributors. As many of the following chapters show, audiences and critics establish diversified relationships with films, and with the complication of racial, ethnic, and sexual differences involved in Hong Kong cinema, masculinity is bound to be received in multiple ways according to different reception contexts and dynamics. As Wong demonstrates, the receiving end of these masculinities can be very unstable, contrary to earlier feminist spectatorship studies that suggest a unified male identification as opposed to dis-unified female identification.[11] But claiming the seemingly politically correct position of articulating differences by no means makes the task easier for the contributor, because we in fact face the more difficult project of analyzing and providing ethical responses to these differences.

Avoiding the study of masculinity is to make it invisible and therefore to reinforce its omnipresence and omnipotence. But aggrandizing masculinity as a grand, monolithic, and hegemonic structure ruling over the entire film scene also prevents us from studying the complex ways in which genders and sexualities manifest and interact. We hope this volume can present us with a set of sophisticated studies balancing the dynamics of identity and differences, gender and culture, so that we can avoid running into the trap of either ignoring transcultural gender dynamics or privileging and glossing over the cultural and social specificities of Hong Kong cinema.

ABOUT THE BOOK

This anthology has two major objectives. First, we investigate the multiple meanings and manifestations of masculinities in Hong Kong cinema that compliment, contradict, and complicate each other. Second, we analyze the social, cultural, and theoretical environments that make these representations possible and problematic. Therefore, respecting the originality and uniqueness of each film text, we study gender representations beyond the representations themselves, and emphasize the intimate relationship between text and context. We want to provide a comprehensive picture of how Hong Kong mainstream cinematic masculinities are produced within their own socio-cultural discourses, and how these masculinities are distributed, received, and transformed within the setting of the market place. To address these complex problems in a comprehensive and organized manner, this anthology is divided into three interrelated parts: the local cinematic tradition, the transnational context and reverberations, and the larger production, reception, and mediation environments. We hope that a combination of these three perspectives will reveal the dynamics and tensions between the local and the transnational, between production and reception, between theory and practice, and between text and context that construct and constantly self-revise this very colorful and complex tradition of male representation.

In Part I, we argue that to critically assess the particularities of the representations of masculinity in Hong Kong cinema, it is vitally important to situate them in their unique historical and cultural environment. Looking back at the history of Hong Kong cinema, there was a phasing out of female-audience-oriented productions from the 1960s to the 1970s and a phasing in of those reflecting prominent male tastes and ideologies. This film trend of spreading overt male power and chauvinism has since played a dominant role in the development and success of Hong Kong's commercial cinema.[12] As most Hong Kong movie fans well know, not only are the action movies of Bruce Lee (Li Xiaolong), King Hu, Jackie Chan, and John Woo (Wu Yusen) clearly male-oriented, but the extremely popular comedies of the Hui Brothers, Cinema City, Wong Ching, and the early Stephen Chow from the 1980s and 1990s also show very little intention of attracting female audiences. The important Hong Kong new wave that began in 1979 was heavily slanted toward action films. Starting in the 1970s, when Hong Kong cinema was beginning to gain local and international fame, it produced very few melodramas and romance comedies, and no female performers could enter the first tier of the star division. Instead, action and comedy reigned, and these genres were almost always male-dominated.[13]

This extensive tradition that has produced so many diversified types of male bodies and masculine models by no means invites a simple-minded, generalized criticism of sexist gender representations. Instead of simplifying the criticism into an opposition between two genders, we should read more carefully the nuances and complexities of these male representations within their historical context to investigate how they produce different, or often unstable, meanings of maleness. David Desser, in "Making Movies Male: Zhang Che and the Shaw Brothers Martial Arts Movies, 1965-1975," provides a detailed and careful reading of the development of 1970s male cinema within a complex cultural context. Comparing the two martial arts movie masters, Desser argues that by any standard it was Zhang Che who had the more profound impact on Hong Kong cinema, although the female affinities of King Hu's movies are more critically attractive and would have made a stronger impact on Hong Kong films in the 1980s and 1990s. As the anthology's first chapter, Desser's argument sets up the historical context of the emergence of the dominating masculine tradition that this volume analyzes and questions. It also makes the bold statement that within the specific historical environment, King Hu's female sensibilities were residual while Zhang Che's masculine style was emerging and progressive. My chapter

"Post-1997 Hong Kong Masculinity" brings us to the end of this tradition and offers a close study of the genealogy and the corpus of Milkyway Image — an important Hong Kong film studio that emerged around 1997 — in its depiction of masculinity with reference to the dominating masculine aesthetics of Hong Kong cinema, as suggested in Desser's chapter. I focus on the studio's representation of masculinities in relation to Hong Kong's cultural environment and the film industry's concerns of recent years. I argue that the homosocial male bonding and the female characters depicted in Milkyway Image films are both characteristic and exceptional in the context of Hong Kong cinema, and that these changing representations witness the difficulties of a declining industry trying to come to terms with its own male traditions.

The homophobia of Hong Kong cinema, in which gay men are usually stigmatized as bitchy and campy sexual perverts, provides the impetus for two chapters investigating alternative masculinities. Travis Kong's "Queering Masculinity in Hong Kong Movies" presents a comprehensive picture of a diverse representation of gay men that has emerged since the 1990s. Many films have included images of ambiguous gender blending and an implicit homosexual subtext under a "homosocial overcoat." Some have even directly addressed homosexual love. But Kong explains how the logic of capitalism and heterosexual norms governs this proliferation of "gay visibility." He concludes that although homophobic and masculinist definitions are dominant in Hong Kong movies, they are constantly being subverted, which has thus allowed a visual queer space to grow. Helen Leung continues the examination of queerness in Hong Kong cinema in her chapter "Unsung Heroes: Reading Transgender Subjectivities in Hong Kong Action Cinema." Instead of revelling in the politics of destabilizing gender identity, she shows us the limits of queer theory in understanding transgender subjects. Her focus is on the butch lesbian characters in the films *Swordsman II* (Xiao'ao jianghu II zhi Dongfang Bubai) (dir. Ching Siu-tung, 1992) and *Portland Street Blues* (Hongxing shisan mei) (dir. Raymond Yip, 1998). She meticulously demonstrates that if these characters are read only as symbols of gender subversion, as typical queer criticisms would read them, they lose the agency to desire a gender of their own. Leung's chapter invites us to detect the subtle and deviant homoeroticism portrayed in the films beyond the queer discursive boundaries, and she believes that such explorations can help us unpack the complex discursive networks set up between mainstream masculinity and its repressed homoerotic roots typified in the respective genres.

The chapters in Part II focus on the different meanings of masculinity that Hong Kong cinema has produced within a transnational environment. Hong Kong cinema would fail to be what it is today without the enthusiastic support and contribution, both financially and conceptually, of transnational markets and audiences in the past six or seven decades. As I mentioned earlier, the transnational appeal of Hong Kong cinema is a key discussion topic in international film criticism. The chapters in the second part of the book investigate why and how Hong Kong cinema can or cannot anchor transnational identification, and more specifically discuss the ways in which such transnational identification is constructed around gender to raise our awareness of the underlying masculine ideologies that function nationally and transnationally.

Sheng-mei Ma's "Kung Fu Films in Diaspora: Death of the Bamboo Hero" discusses the adaptation of Hong Kong kung fu films migrating from Hong Kong's Chinese cultural context to the global market. In a careful textual analysis of *Crouching Tiger, Hidden Dragon* (Wohu canglong) (dir. Ang Lee, 2000) and a number of recent kung fu films, Ma demonstrates how certain filmic elements inherent in traditional martial arts movies — bamboo, traditional martial arts forms, and bodily exudation — are suppressed or reshaped to cater for the new audience. His analysis of the three thematic components also demonstrates how the polyphonic and loaded symbols bring a diverse Chinese-speaking global audience together through Hong Kong films and how they have to be sacrificed to forge a new global audience. In "Obtuse Music and the Nebulous Male: The Haunting Presence of Taiwan in Hong Kong Films of the 1990s," Shen Shiao-Ying calls our attention to the "Taiwan factor" in Hong Kong cinema. She demonstrates that while Taiwan has always been a major market for Hong Kong cinema, it is also often deliberately ignored. However, the elusive Taiwan factor both contributes to and frustrates the Hong Kongness constructed. Interestingly, as Shen demonstrates, this Taiwan factor is often represented by effeminate or lyrical masculinities that echo or struggle with China's paternal call. The Greater China saga can only be told with the dismissible but extant presence of Taiwan.

Through a close reading of *The Untold Story* (Baxian fandian zhi renrou chashaobao) (dir. Danny Lee, Herman Yau, 1992) in both its cinematic text and its reception in the West, James Steintrager presents us with a true nightmare of postcolonial critics: Western men viscerally enjoying a trashy Hong Kong film in which a Hong Kong man brutally rapes female victims and eats their flesh! If a postcolonial critic works so hard to find a "worthy" Hong Kong subject for its new postcolonial stage, Steintrager asks, how should the critic deal with a situation in which both the subject of the film (a male Hong Kong rapist and cannibalist refusing any cinematic identification) and the viewer of the film (the white male fan who cares nothing about Hong Kong people but obscenely enjoys their animality) are so "unworthy"? Steintrager presents a theoretical enigma yet also sheds light on current postcolonial discourse, which often repudiates its own claims by constructing an ideal non-subject. While Ma and Shen believe some sort of transnational male Chineseness, however distorted, is established through male subjects in Hong Kong cinema, Steintrager takes the position that, from the perspectives of Western film-goers and Western theories, there may never have been a transnational understanding of Hong Kong films, particularly when a subject turns object. Also focusing on the issue of Hong Kong cultural identity, Kwai-cheung Lo asks whether female fighters in Hong Kong cinema only reveal the impasse of Hong Kong masculinities in particular and Hong Kong identity in general. Similar to Helen Leung's strategy, Lo's "Fighting Female Masculinity: Women Warriors and their Foreignness in the Hong Kong Action Cinema of the 1980s" focuses on masculinized female characters to elucidate the politics of masculinity in Hong Kong cinema. Yet, in the context of the construction of Hong Kong identity, Lo adds the dimension of race to complicate further the unstable gender meanings in martial arts films that feature women fighters. In his careful analysis of several films featuring female fighters, he demonstrates how certain characters, particularly those played by Michelle Yeoh (Yang Ziqiong), dis-identify with the men around them only to convert themselves into "copies" of their opposite gender. Meanwhile, others, such as those played by Cynthia Rothrock, are presented as conventional asexual kung fu artists whose female masculinity, in making up for what's lacking in the colonized Hong Kong male subject, helps ease their desires.

While the chapters in the first two parts of this anthology explore the multiple significations of masculinities in Hong Kong cinema, the third part is more socially oriented. We believe that a pertinent study of Hong Kong cinema must have a comprehensive contextual perspective that takes into account not only the city's cultural, political, and economic milieux, but also the industry's structure as well as the specific reactions and responses of the audience; thus the interdisciplinary approach of this volume. Part III focuses on the dynamics among reception, production, and mediation. Although Hong Kong cinema has been celebrated for its commercial success, studies of its commercial setting are scarce. Those very few existing studies are relatively empirical and uncritical.[14] Some scholars are beginning to interrogate the hegemonic nature of Hong Kong cinema in other Asian markets,[15] but more thorough and in-depth discussions of its production environment and marketing network are urgently needed. We believe the industrial structure of Hong Kong cinema is as culturally unique as it is institutionally pre-determined. In a cinema industry where government and labor union regulations are minimal, the irregular working schedules, physical rigor, and high mobility structurally limit most positions to men and directly encourage sexism. Therefore, while many authors in this anthology take the film texts as sites of contestation to discuss the representations of masculinities in their complexity and nuances, we also want to study the masculine domination of Hong Kong cinema as not only a cultural but also an industrial and market symptom. The last part of this anthology is designed to provide extra information, insights, and critical analysis from the perspectives of the industry and the audience not only in Hong Kong but also in the United States to allow greater understanding of Hong Kong cinema's problematic gender disposition.

In "Bringing Breasts into the Mainstream," Yeeshan Chan asks how and why a recent group of comedies featuring female breasts was so widely accepted by local female audiences. Chan demonstrates that the films strategically re-package women's breasts for entertainment consumption through elegant clothing, a sense of professionalism, and quasi-feminist semiotics to appeal not only to male audiences but also middle-class Hong Kong women. Drawing on her experiences as a female script-writer in Hong Kong and her personal interviews with many filmmakers working in the field, she shares with us how the experiment of "upgrading" sex was motivated by the decline of locally made pornographic films and of the industry at large. Her thought-provoking chapter shows how "female empowerment" can be used to benefit patriarchy and the market. While Chan investigates the local industry, Wai-kit Choi's "Post-Fordist Production and the Re-Appropriation of Hong Kong Masculinity in Hollywood" asks whether the crossover of Hong Kong film professionals into Hollywood signifies that there is now greater multiculturalism in the U.S. film industry. Why did U.S. film producers decide to incorporate Hong Kong masculinity into the U.S. film market? Choi argues that despite the migration of Hong

Kong film professionals to Hollywood, the dominant social groups in the U.S. maintain their cultural hegemony in the film industry, and their (mis)perception of other groups continues to reign in cinematic representation.

Agnes Ku, in her "Masculinities in Self-Invention — Critics' Discourses on Kung Fu–Action Movies and Comedies" meticulously identifies three common reading strategies — reflectionism, deconstruction, and hermeneutics — adopted by film critics in their study of Hong Kong's action and comedy heroes. While she finds some criticisms more gender sensitive and vigilant than others, she demonstrates that all fail to explicate fully the domination of masculinism in Hong Kong cinema. With regard to action heroes, many critics connect in a coherent framework elements of masculinity in action movies and nationalist discourses, thus reinforcing both masculinity and nationalism. With regard to comedy heroes, critics' celebration of Stephen Chow's images of typical Hong Kong men encourage us to take them as a-gendered subjects and ignore the gender dynamics involved. Both discursive efforts naturalize and reinforce the deeply embedded masculinist norms in our culture. Like Chan, Day Wong studies Hong Kong cinema by combining in-depth interviews with pertinent cultural observations. In "Women's Reception of Mainstream Hong Kong Cinema," however, her emphasis is on those on the receiving end. Wong examines how local female audiences communicate with mainstream melodramas and action movies. Rather than assuming women are passive receivers of media content, Wong examines the selective and creative ways in which women engage with images of gender in mainstream Hong Kong cinema. While many women consider Bruce Lee, not Jackie Chan, to be the real hero, they prefer to take their family to watch Chan's, not Lee's, films. Through various interviews she compares and contrasts the diverse ways in which women interpret the films and derive pleasure from them, and argues that even in the supposedly shallow and sexist films of Jackie Chan, meanings are produced and mediated by the discourses surrounding the female audiences, as well as their lived experiences of being female at different times. Wong's chapter concludes the anthology, and leaves a reverberating call for a reconsideration of many of the issues raised in earlier chapters.

This anthology is not simply a collection of writings with a focus on gender and Hong Kong cinema. Through this interdisciplinary collaboration we want to introduce a specific framework and setting within which to understand the complex interrelations of popular cinema and masculinities in today's global cultural economy. We stress local uniqueness as much as transnational context, and reception as well as production. Hong Kong cinema provides a wonderful case study in this regard because it manifests unique and diversified depictions and narrations of masculinities with a broad local and transnational appeal. Through the particular and commercially successful representational politics of masculinity, the authors in this anthology demonstrate that gender issues and representations can intimately and in a complex way demonstrate the values and everyday embodied experiences of filmmakers, audiences, and critics, and they reveal also the commercial logic of Hong Kong cinema. The authors argue against the assumed equation of commercial cinema with a monopolizing, naïve, and tyrannical masculinity. A close study of the gender complexities of Hong Kong cinema once again proves that the word "masculinities" can no longer be rendered singular in our complex world. We hope this anthology shows how the simultaneous concerns and sensibilities, in practice and abstract theorization, can be brought together in an interdisciplinary collaboration.

Part I
History and Lineage

1

Making Movies Male:
Zhang Che and the Shaw Brothers Martial Arts Movies, 1965–1975

David Desser

It is a cliché of Hong Kong film history that Zhang Che and King Hu (Hu Jinquan) revolutionized the martial arts movie at Shaw Brothers in the 1960s. Here is a typical recitation, along with the now also-familiar differences between the two directors: "In the 60s and 70s, it was the Shaw Brothers studio which advanced a new century in film chronology with the 'New Style Martial Arts Pictures.' Leading the trend were the directors Zhang Che and King Hu … Zhang directed on the precept of *yanggang* (masculinity) and he employed a stock company of male actors for this purpose. King Hu utilized the features of Peking Opera, adding in elements of classical Chinese aesthetics."[1] Hu's "classical Chinese aesthetics" are typically said to revolve around Chinese (Beijing) Opera and various classical painting techniques. Similarly, his self-proclaimed lack of interest in real martial arts has entered the canon: "I have no knowledge of kung fu whatsoever. My action scenes come from the stylized combat of Peking Opera. In fact, it's dance."[2]

I will not argue here that King Hu's aesthetics do not come from Beijing Opera and other forms of classical Chinese art and aesthetics. Nor will I claim it was not the Shaw Brothers Studio that propagated the New Style Martial Arts film. Indeed it was. What I contend is that King Hu's early, and best, works had no immediate influence on the development of the martial arts film. It was, in fact, and almost exclusively, the film style, themes and motifs apparent in the works of

Zhang Che that shifted the martial arts films away from the style, themes
and stars of both the Cantonese and Mandarin martial arts film in the
years leading to Zhang's *Tiger Boy* (Huxia jianchou) (1966) and,
especially, *One-Armed Swordsman* (Dubi dao) (1967).

That King Hu is perhaps the only genuine cinematic genius of the
martial arts movie before and after the Hong Kong New Wave of the
late 1970s should not blind us to the fact his films had virtually no lasting
impact on the Shaw Brothers' movies and the subsequent martial arts
films that came to dominate the Hong Kong cinema and which entered
world film markets in the early 1970s. A remark by Tony Rayns in a 1980
article is instructive:

> [King Hu's] films *Come Drink with Me* [Da zuixia] (1965) and *Dragon
> Gate Inn* [Longmen kezhan] (1966) undoubtedly pioneered a certain
> style of action choreography derived from Peking Opera acrobatic
> stagecraft, and that style was widely imitated, especially in swordplay
> movies. But it is true that the genre as a whole was much more
> dominated by blood-and-guts fight scenes — such as those seen in the
> films of Zhang Che — than by Hu's flights of fancy, and that the
> appearance of the Bruce Lee [Li Xiaolong] film *The Big Boss* [Tangshan
> daxiong] in 1971 curtailed what small influence Hu's style had had.[3]

Rayns's claim has been all but forgotten; perhaps, writing in 1980,
he was closer to the truth than were contemporary historians who have
rewritten King Hu back into a mainstream that he had only temporarily
entered. Hu's considerable influence on Hong Kong martial arts films
cannot be denied, but that influence was not apparent until Tsui Hark
(Xu Ke), a Hu protégé, began his career with *The Butterfly Murders*
(Diebian) (1979) and *Zu: Warriors from the Magic Mountain* (Xin
shushan jianxia zhuan) (1983). Yet neither of these films inspired a
swordplay revival or sparked renewed interest in King Hu. (In the ten
years from 1965 Hu directed six feature films; in the sixteen years from
1976 he directed seven.) In fact, I would argue that Hu's real legacy does
not return until Hu and Tsui worked together (albeit not well) on
Swordsman (Xiao'ao jianghu) (1990). Its sequel in 1991, along with Tsui's
Once Upon a Time in China (Huang Feihong) the same year began a
new cycle of martial arts films that revealed Hu's legacy and impact. Not
surprisingly, then, in 1992 we find a remake of *Dragon (Gate) Inn*
(*Dragon Inn*), which also helped revive interest in Hu's original film.

AN OVERSTATED LEGACY

Contemporary historians of the Hong Kong cinema have misstated, misapprehended and vastly overrated Hu's immediate impact in the 1960s and 1970s. Thus, consequently, his legacy has been exaggerated. (Again, I take nothing away from King Hu's artistry and talent. That I think he is the finest director ever to work in Hong Kong should not influence my own judgment about where and how his impact has been manifested.) A few factors might account for this historical overrating. One revolves around the interest contemporary historians have in issues of gender representation. That King Hu's films so prominently feature women as martial artists (actresses Cheng Pei-pei and Hsu Feng especially) and that the swordplay films in the wake of *Swordsman* similarly foreground both women and issues of gender (e.g. the remake *Dragon Inn*, *Swordsman II* and *III [The East is Red]*) have led feminist-influenced contemporary film theory to prize these films greatly. As the (seeming) forerunner of feminist-influenced martial arts, Hu took pride of place in a new generation of female-centered filmmaking. Furthermore, even Hu's male stars hardly fit the pattern of heroic musculature so prominent in the US action cinema of the 1980s and 1990s. Shih Jun (Shi Jun) and even Bai Ying hardly look fearsome or particularly athletic. Thus, Hu's films implicitly and even explicitly allow for the centrality of women and raise intriguing issues of gender (especially his 1969 masterpiece, *A Touch of Zen*). Because academic film studies are female-centered and feminist-oriented, Hu's films and the return to his legacy in the 1990s make him a focus of interest today.

Perhaps no less a contributor to Hu's overstated impact has been the desire to construct a "Chinese" aesthetic and to anoint Hu its avatar. In Chinese-language scholarship and in Western-language scholarship sympathetic to this project this amounts to a rejection of Western-centric criticism and an insistence on the Chinese essentialism of Hu's works.[4] Thus the invocations of Beijing Opera and classical landscape painting construct Hu as a Chinese classicist. In addition, Hu is proclaimed as an auteur, a genuine creator who weaves together classical Chinese aesthetics to reinvigorate a classic Chinese genre. Comparisons with Japan's Kurosawa Akira are frequent, partly to acknowledge influence but more significantly to claim comradeship and equivalence, and to grant auteur status to a Chinese director where previously none had been acclaimed. As has been the case with John Woo (Wu Yusen) and Wong Kar-wai (Wang Jiawei) — both overrated in scholarly writing on Hong

Kong cinema at the expense of other filmmakers — the status of auteur lends legitimacy to the academic interest in a filmmaker. Hu's own insistence on his debts to Chinese aesthetics and the need to construct an auteur for pre-1980s Hong Kong cinema similarly combine to overvalue Hu's contributions to Hong Kong cinema after 1967.

By any standard — style, theme, characterization — it was Zhang Che's films and stars that proved immediately influential. Zhang's legacy can be traced directly to the films of Bruce Lee and the works of another influential and talented, albeit male-oriented, director, Lau Kar-leung (Liu Jialiang). These filmmakers, in turn, influenced John Woo and Ringo Lam (Lin Lingdong), not to mention Jackie Chan (Cheng Long), all of whom thereby perpetuated the legacy of male-oriented films and stars. In the mid- to late-1980s a shift away from male dominance took place in Hong Kong movie-making, though there was never a return to the almost all-female cast of box-office champions.

As women returned to prominence, especially in the martial arts genre, King Hu's films and influence were truly felt. At the same time, we must remember, English-language historians and critics started turning their attention to Hong Kong cinema and here the dominance of feminist-oriented theory and criticism gave pride of place to woman-centered/gender-bending films. As Chinese film historian Zhang Zhen notes, as far back as the late 1920s: "… there existed a visible subgenre that situates the female knight-errant at the center of dramatic tension and visual spectacle. This female-centered subgenre … is the precursor of a similar phenomenon in the later Hong Kong martial arts film. The legendary Michelle Yeoh [Yang Ziqiong] … is not a miracle woman with a 'pair of lethal legs' born in a postmodern vacuum. Rather, she is a descendant of the pantheon of female knight-errant stars … in a rich, if hitherto repressed, cinematic tradition."[5] This tradition, and the invocation of Michelle Yeoh, leads us directly to *Crouching Tiger, Hidden Dragon* (Wohu canglong) (2000), which, as director Ang Lee (Li An) freely admits, was largely inspired by King Hu. King Hu, then, far from inaugurating a tradition of female knights errant, participated in and resurrected the tradition, although it did not come to be fully appreciated until the 1990s. When Hu reinvigorated the tradition in the 1960s, there were factors that conspired against its taking immediate hold. We can account for the lack of Hu's immediate impact by recourse to a historical irony: it was precisely Hu's continuation of the legacy of Mandarin movies prizing female stars that prevented his continuing impact in the mid-1960s. That is, the idea that Zhang Che directed on the precept of *yanggang* (masculinity) and that he employed a stock company of male actors for this purpose, is exactly what the new Mandarin-language cinema required. Ironically, again, the Cantonese martial arts film also provided Hu with a model, this time of the average, even effeminate, male that would also be rejected in the New Style Martial Arts movie. In other words, the immediate *similarities* of Hu's films to previous works, rather than his divergences and breakaways, prevented his having a full impact until film history recycled its way back to his particularities.

Let me clarify this. Until the mid-1960s, female stars dominated Mandarin-language films. Hu largely continued this tradition. Though stars like Li Li-hua, Linda Lin (Lin Dai), Lucilla Yu (You Min), Betty Loh (Le Di), Grace Chang (Ge Lan), Jeanette Lin (Lin Cui), and Julie Yeh (Ye Feng) hardly, if ever, made martial arts films (opera films and historical dramas notwithstanding), they enjoyed virtually a total dominance of Cathay (MP & GI) Company and Shaw Brothers movie screens. The case of Ivy Ling (Ling Bo) is instructive here. She had her start playing the male role of Liang Shanbo in *Love Eterne* (Liang Shanbo yu Zhu Yingtai) (dir. Li Han-hsiang, 1963) a film about gender impersonation. King Hu is variously listed as assistant director, associate director or co-director of this film. Ivy Ling became the Shaw Brothers' top star thereafter, all the while playing the male roles in opera-derived films or overtly appearing as a male impersonator, as in the 1964 *Lady General Hua Mulan* (Hua Mulan; dir. Yue Feng). Meanwhile, Zhang Che started his career as a screenwriter at Shaw Brothers. He specialized in opera films and historical dramas, scripting a number of films for Ivy Ling, but also for Li Li-hua and Julie Yeh. That is, Zhang was at the center of the Shaw Brothers female-dominated film production. King Hu, at this time getting his chance to direct, unsurprisingly utilized a female star, Cheng Pei-pei (Zheng Peipei), for *Come Drink with Me*. Simultaneously, the Shaw Brothers invigorated the martial arts film with the talent of now-forgotten director Chui Chang-wang (Xu Zenhong), whose films of 1965 to 1967, like *Temple of the Red Lotus* (Jianghu qixia) (1965), *Twin Swords* (Huoshao hongliansi zhi yuanyang jianxia) (1965) and *The Sword and the Lute* (Huoshao hongliansi zhi qinjian enchou) (1967) feature female stars Chin Ping (Qin Ping) and Ivy Ling. It is in this strand of sword films — opera-like period pieces — that King Hu would make his presence felt thereafter in the Taiwanese films *Dragon Gate Inn* and *A Touch of Zen*. But both Hu and Chui would fade from influence in the wake of Zhang Che's breakthrough hit, *One-Armed Swordsman*, in 1967. The seeds of Zhang's revolution had already been planted, if we look at the male co-stars of Chui's films: Wang Yu, Lo Lieh (Luo Lie), Tin Fung (Tian Feng) and Wu Ma. These names were soon to be central to the New Style Martial Arts films. Though Chui Chang-wang regularly directed until 1972, and King Hu continued to produce in the 1970s, their lavish, colorful, female-centered movies lost in popularity to raw, hard-edged, tough-guy pictures.[6]

A MALE SCREEN

Zhang Che began a new tradition in Hong Kong movies by breaking away from the female-centered star system of Cathay and Shaw Brothers. The same system was largely true for the Cantonese cinema of the 1960s where, as discussed, women stars were dominant.[7] Such actresses as Josephine Siao Fong-fong (Xiao Fangfang), Connie Chan Po-chu (Chen Baozhu), Patrina Fung (Feng Baobao), and Nancy Sit (Xue Jiayan) made literally countless films in the 1960s, but their careers had come to a halt (at least temporarily) by 1970, owing to the triumph of Mandarin-language cinema — a triumph brought about by the assertion of a new type of male star.

Zhang Che, who had worked on numerous films for the Shaw Brothers' female-dominated talent list, was aware of Mandarin cinema's appeal. Sek Kei notes, "Mandarin cinema was initially aimed at the large female audience. Productions derived either from Mainland cinema (opera films) or from Western film."[8] In this respect for the audience, Hong Kong cinema differed from the West. Claims Zhang: "Hong Kong cinema was different. Its popularity was built on female stars, and stars like Ling Bo and Yam Kim-fai played male parts. Insiders in Hong Kong were obstinate about this tendency."[9] Zhang noted that in the rest of the world things were different: "I felt that in movies around the world, male actors were at the top. All the important parts were played by men. Why is it that Chinese movies didn't have male actors? If male actors could stand up, the audience would double … That's why I advocated male-centred movies with *yanggang* as the core element."[10]

Zhang was right about the male-centered nature of movie stardom. In 1973, when the kung fu craze swept the American box-office, there was only one "bankable" female star: Barbra Streisand. Indeed, throughout the 1970s, only a handful of female stars were thus considered and three of them were on the top-ten box-office lists only once each. Elizabeth Taylor made the list at the beginning of the decade, and Ali McGraw and Tatum O'Neal once each on the basis of just one film each later in the decade. Both stars are barely remembered today. Meanwhile, the likes of Paul Newman, John Wayne, Steve McQueen, Clint Eastwood, Sean Connery, Dustin Hoffman, Robert Redford, Burt Reynolds, Charles Bronson and Jack Nicholson made the list five, six, even eight times. Moreover, in the 1970s there were never more than two female stars in top-ten box-office lists until 1978, when there were three.[11] This is to say that the turn away from female stars in favor of male stars on the part of Zhang Che was in keeping with the triumph of male stars in the increasingly dominant Hollywood cinema. This turn to male stars by Hong Kong cinema is one of the reasons it could, and did, make its presence felt on international screens.

But why did this move take such an immediate hold on the Hong Kong imagination? For critic Sek Kei this is somehow related to the needs of the local audience: "By the mid-1960s the local audience was demanding films more in keeping with local feelings and ambitions. This gave rise to the so-called New Style Martial Arts film. Mandarin cinema turned from melodrama to action. The violence in the new films coincided neatly with a global emphasis on sensory stimulation in films of the late 1960s."[12] Implicitly then, the key was action, which provided for greater sensory stimulation and, implicitly, we suppose, male-dominated films could best supply this need.

Zhang Che himself makes the case that the New Style Martial Arts film reflects the contemporary zeitgeist: "The rise of *yanggang* was a requirement of the market and not discrimination against actresses … The age of love tales was past. The masses were striving ahead in a rebellious mood and the colonial administration was receiving a shock to the system. *Yanggang* and the martial arts pictures represented this spirit of the times. After I made *One-Armed Swordsman* (1967), riots broke out in Kowloon. Then, during the riots, I made *The Assassin* [Da cike] (1967)."[13] I'm not sure Zhang wants to claim that because of something inherent in *One-Armed Swordsman* riots broke out or that *The Assassin* reflects somehow the political turmoil of the time; however, it *is* undeniably about political turmoil. Rather, I think the word "spirit" is what he means. And this spirit was very much in evidence because political turmoil within mainland China must also be reckoned a part of the spirit of the times.

Critic Sek Kei notes that "the resurgence of the martial arts film in the 1960s coincided with China's Cultural Revolution. Hong Kong also experienced violence and social upheaval, and the fights on screen mirrored those on the city's streets." [14] Although a simplistic contention, this notion of desires for increased sensory stimulation amid social upheaval, taken with other developments, coincides with the rise of new male stars in action-oriented stories in tandem with the spirit of rebellion in the territory.

But, again, why this spirit should be reflected in such obviously, even over-determinedly, masculinist forms, is something to be more fully explored perhaps at a later date. Here I will suggest a few things as predominant: the youthful nature of the local audience by 1967, but especially by 1970; the rise of other youth cultural forms in which cinema is implicated; and the aging of the once-dominant stars. Alongside these factors we must also implicate the rise of television, generally acknowledged to have taken place around 1967 in Hong Kong.

As the generation of actresses who so dominated Cathay and Shaw Brothers a decade earlier began to retire, older audiences found even less to attract them to the movies. As with the Hollywood cinema, it was the youth audience that became the dominant market. This youth audience, too, had begun to coalesce around other forms that would affect cinema's content and themes. In particular, the "sensory stimulation" that Sek Kei finds in the cinema was also to be found in *manhua* (Chinese-language comic books), which began in this period to draw on the popular martial arts films and to reveal the influence of American comics and Japanese manga.[15] The graphic nature of *manhua* (in both senses of the term — as an art and in its content) reflects the youthful audience's appetite for violence, sex, technology and speed. The importation of British rock and roll of this period similarly indicates the ever-increasing audio-visual appeals to youth, particularly young men. Though manga has a vast and widespread appeal in Japan, in the US and in Hong Kong, comic books and *manhua* lean heavily toward the masculinist, as does rock and roll.

But it wasn't simply male stars that Zhang and Shaw Brothers brought to the fore: there had been male stars all along in Chinese cinema, even if they were less crucial to the film industry as a whole. Here Zhang's notion of *yanggang* must be brought back into the picture. Zhang: "So I took up the slogan of *yanggang* (masculinity) in my film column 'My Views on Cinema.' ... But in the film industry at the time, the realisation of *yanggang* would have to wait until the resurgence of a new martial arts movie style — a resurgence guided by the moguls Run Run Shaw [Shao Yifu] and Raymond Chow [Zhou Wenhuai]."[16] This *yanggang* was something brought about by the physicality of the new stars at the Shaws studio, but it was Zhang Che's particular talent and interest that emphasized it and brought it to the center of attention and attraction. By the early 1970s, then, athletic and often muscular male stars came to dominate Hong Kong screens, the likes of Wang Yu, Lo Lieh, Ti Lung (Di Long), David Chiang (Jiang Dawei), Lau Kar-leung (Liu Jialiang), Lau Ka-fai (Liu Jiahui), Alexander Fu (Fu Sheng), Chen Kuan-tai (Chen Guantai), not to mention Bruce Lee (Li Xiaolong), achieving the popularity and success previously confined mostly to women. Cheng Pei-pei, Xu Feng, Chia Ling (Jia Ling), and Angela Mao (Mao Ying) kept women on the screen, but in numbers more comparable to the Hollywood cinema of the present than to the Chinese cinema of the past.

It is possible that these highly masculine male stars, most of them fairly young (Wang Yu was born in 1943, Ti Lung in 1946, David Chiang in 1947), were attractive to Hong Kong audiences for reasons less to do with political activism and more to do with sensory stimulation of a different sort. On the one hand, critic Lau Tai-muk believes it reflects social reality in a different way than youthful rebellion: "The well-built male characters in the films, bare to the waist, satisfied the want of the middle class to gaze at 'healthy' bodies, and realized their subconscious need for worshipping muscular beauty. Wealth is a precedent to health as you are then able to spend time to 'keep fit.'"[17] For Taiwanese critic Peggy Chiao Hsiung-ping, on the other hand, it is even more basic and simple than that: "Those Chang Cheh [Zhang Che] films are all about male bonding. He worships the male body. All those muscles, all that nudity. It's all very sexual. I think it's his vision of male paradise. Very interesting."[18] (See also my earlier essay on the rise of Mandarin movies and the subsequent Cantonese-language martial movies for other explanations.[19]) It is likely, then, that some combination of all these factors led to the dominance of male stars: a younger generation of stars more in tune with its audience's demographics and desires; physical prowess as representing health and wealth in an emergent Hong Kong; homosocial desires on the part of the young audience, and the pleasure of women audiences in gazing at the male body.

Of course, the martial arts themselves may have something to do with the pleasure derived from these New Style Martial Arts films. The focus of these films came increasingly to rest on unarmed combat (kung fu), or in close fighting with knives and short swords. King Hu's preference for opera-style combat and the edited construction of his combat scenes was far afield from the use of longer takes to demonstrate more realistic combat. "King Hu's action aesthetics is of a high standard and he never faltered from his methods of the swordplay film. I gradually became interested in the Hung fist and the Wing Chun style which belonged to the southern school ... Though Kwan Tak-hing [Guan Dexing], Sek Yin-tsi [Shi Jian], Lam Kar-sing [Lin Jiao] propounded the Shaolin name, their kung fu had nothing to do with that school. The development of kung fu had to await stars like Bruce Lee, Chen Kwun-tai, Alexander Fu, etc."[20] Indeed, almost all the Zhang Che stock company were trained in the martial arts, with some achieving a mastery that compared with that of Bruce Lee and Jackie Chan, such as Chen Kuan-tai and Lau Ka-fai, while David Chiang, Lo Lieh and Wang Yu had extensive martial arts training before turning to film (or simultaneously in the case of child-star David Chiang). Moreover, the reliance on a group of martial arts coordinators, instructors and choreographers upped the stakes of fight sequences. But here, again, it depends on the type of star and the proclivities of the director. Take the case of actor/fight instructor Han Yingjie. King Hu credits him with many of the martial arts innovations of *Come Drink with Me* and *Dragon Gate Inn*. A highpoint in this regard would be *A Touch of Zen*. Yet Han also choreographed the fighting, along with Bruce Lee, in *The Big Boss* and *Fist of Fury* (Jing wumen) (1972). Yet Hu's interest in martial arts is quite different from Bruce Lee's and few films could be farther apart in style and tone than *A Touch of Zen* and *The Big Boss*.

FISTS OF (BOX-OFFICE) LEGEND

Whatever appeal lay behind these New Style Martial Arts movies their triumph in Hong Kong is unquestionable. Using box-office and production lists from 1970-1972 as a basis for analysis (top ten grossing films and studio releases taken from *A Study of Hong Kong Cinema in the Seventies*), it is clear that the combination of studio-star-genre-director in the form of the Shaw Brothers martial arts films directed by Zhang Che and starring David Chiang and Ti Lung ruled the roost in Hong Kong theatres. First of all, martial arts films were triumphant, making up twenty-five of the thirty movies that comprised the top ten lists of 1970, 1971, and 1972. In each of those years martial arts movies were in first and second place and no more than two non-martial arts movies made the top ten in any given year. Of these 30 films, the Shaw Brothers Studio produced 70%, contract director Zhang Che making 11 of the 30.

Combining the films of Zhang Che and Lo Wei (Luo Wei), who began at Shaw Brothers and then went on to direct Bruce Lee, more than 50% (16 out of 30) were directed by these two filmmakers alone. Out of these martial arts films, almost 85% of them star in some combination of Wang Yu, David Chiang, Ti Lung, Bruce Lee, and Chen Kuan-tai, precisely the new, young masculinist stars favored by Zhang, and all of them, save for Bruce Lee, were contracted to the Shaw Brothers. Of course it is true that Cheng Pei-pei, who was also working at the Shaw Brothers Studio, kept the candle burning for the female tradition in the Chinese Martial Arts cinema. Three films in which she stars appear in the top ten lists, one in 1970 and two in 1971. Interestingly, she is one of the stars who worked with both King Hu and Zhang Che (each of them in their own way establishing her stardom); Hu with *Come Drink with Me* (1965) and Zhang with *The Golden Swallow* (Jin yanzi) (1968), something of a sequel to Hu's film. Perhaps most revealing, however, is the fact that, though a contract player at Shaw Brothers, she worked numerous times with Lo Wei and Hoh Mung-wa (He Menghua) but only twice with Zhang Che. As Zhang's box-office ascendancy asserted itself, he was able to work strictly with the boys.

These box-office figures must be put into perspective to see how clearly Shaw Brothers and the masculinist martial arts films came to dominate Hong Kong screens.[21] Although Shaw Brothers produced 70% of the top ten box-office champs, the studio produced only 36% of the total number of films in those years. In 1970 Shaw Brothers had nine of the top ten films (90%), while rival Cathay had just one. Yet Shaw Brothers produced only 28% of the films that year, while Cathay had 17%. Clearly, Cathay had lost touch with its audience — it did not turn so resolutely to martial arts and it was starring women and the older-style male figures in its martial arts movies. In 1971 Shaw Brothers had 70% of the top ten biggest-grossing movies, while making only 41% of the total number of films. The studio slipped to 50% of the top-ten champions in 1972, but again produced only 41% of the films released that year. However, in 1972, not all of Shaw Brothers' top grossers were martial arts movies. Thus the studio continued to do well even if the martial arts films slipped a little, at least in terms of the year's highest grossers.

By 1973 this particular trend of the box-office dominance of the masculinist martial arts movie was over. Six out of the top ten films were non-martial arts movies and Zhang Che had no films on the list. But Shaw Brothers kept up their domination via the films of veteran studio director

Li Han-hsiang, who put four films on the list. Li's success was part of a trend toward soft-core pornography that arose in 1972 with his *Legends of Lust* (Fengyue qitan) and Chor Yuen (Chu Yuan)'s *Intimate Confessions of a Chinese Courtesan* (Ainü), also produced by Shaw Brothers. It was in 1973 that the Cantonese dialect started making a comeback in Hong Kong cinema, courtesy of Chor Yuen and Shaw Brothers with the mega-hit *House of 72 Tenants* (Qishi'er jia fangke). But within the martial arts genre itself, the masculinist movies continued to dominate and by 1975 Zhang Che protégé Lau Kar-leung began placing films in the top grossing lists, peaking with two films in 1978. It was at this time that martial arts also made a comeback in Cantonese with the rising popularity of Jackie Chan. In 1978 and 1979 half the films in the top ten were martial arts movies, with Jackie Chan showing a prowess (on the screen and at the box-office) not seen since Bruce Lee half a decade earlier. Once again there was a powerful combination of star and genre.[22]

Box-office success affected production practices in another way in this period, and that was in a clear and notable shift in the martial arts genre itself. An examination of the movies made in the period from 1967 to 1972 reveals a distinct shift away from swordplay in favor of kung fu. Until 1970 virtually all the movies made by King Hu and Zhang Che were costume swordplay films. Kung fu films in these years (and previously) were confined to the Cantonese cinema, especially the continuing series featuring Kwan Tak-hing as Wong Fei-hung (Huang Feihong). When the Cantonese cinema was (temporarily) extinguished in 1970, so, too, was the Wong Fei-hung series (not forgetting the occasional later incarnation of Wong Fei-hung by Kwan Tak-hing starting again in 1974, when Cantonese cinema was revived). Kung fu implies a focus on unarmed combat (notwithstanding the frequent use of knives in such films) to emphasize the actual martial and athletic prowess of the heroes and villains. With the introduction of more athletic and muscular stars like Lo Lieh and Ti Lung, Zhang Che recognized the utility of kung fu for enabling greater bodily and athletic displays. At the same time, there arose a tendency to make manifest the youthful rebellion and social criticism apparent in society by setting kung fu films in modern or contemporary times. This is to say that the introduction of kung fu in contemporary settings, such as Lo Wei's Bruce Lee vehicle, *The Big Boss* (1971), and Zhang Che's *Duel of Fists* (Quanji) (1971), starring David Chiang and Ti Lung, served multiple functions, including greater social relevance and greater opportunities for bodily and athletic display. That both films were set in Thailand and released almost simultaneously (Zhang's film on 2 October, Lo's on 31 October) seems more than coincidental. So, too, something more than coincidence marks the use of the Republican-era settings of Zhang's *The Duel* (Da Juedou; released April 1971) and *The Boxer from Shantung* (Ma Yongzhen) (released February 1972) and Lo's Bruce Lee follow-up, *Fist of Fury* (released in March 1972).

That *The Big Boss, Duel of Fists*, and *The Duel* all appear in the top five box-office hits of 1971 certainly speaks of the success of kung fu in a modern or contemporary setting. Thus, to capitalize on this stunning success, in 1972 no fewer than 23 kung fu films were released compared with the seven of 1971 and the six in 1970. This is not to say costume films were entirely replaced by modern-era stories; rather it is to note the replacement of swordplay by kung fu. In fact, period films in the 1970s were still more common than modern-day settings, and would become even more dominant after 1975 (though some films manage to confound any sense of specific time or even place, such as *The Bloody Fists* [dir. Ng See-yuen, 1972]). The point, rather, is that the turn to kung fu and away from swordplay, combined with the tendency to utilize Republican or modern-era settings, further alienated King Hu from the mass audience in the early 1970s, as he continued to make swordplay films in period settings. Recognizing this, Hu himself attempted to move toward a greater use of kung fu in films like *The Fate of Lee Khan* (Yingchunge de fengbo) (1973) and *The Valiant Ones* ((Zhonglie tu) (1975) both featuring fight choreography by Sammo Hung (Hong Jinbao). But Hu's marginal appeal was sustained by his outsider status and insistent use of stars Xu Feng and Bai Ying. Zhang Che was clearly more in touch with the youthful audience as his kung fu fighters struggled on the violent and mean streets of Bangkok or Republican-era Shanghai.

FROM BOYS TO MEN

In Zhang's tradition of making movies male, not only did he utilize a new generation of male stars — athletic, muscular, trained in the martial arts — but he also geared his films around specifically male and masculinist issues. First we may note the "strong emphasis on phallic weaponry, bodily penetration and even disembowelment in many of Zhang's films."[23] In woman-centered films, the primary trope for female vulnerability is rape, and the stripping of clothes from the woman represents the female body's display and weakness simultaneously. Zhang, as noted, frequently managed to show off the male body — a deliberate display without the trope of rape — while at the same time stressing its vulnerability to piercing weapons. (Bruce Lee would take this bodily display to new heights, though without quite so much of the phallic weaponry and disembowelment.) There appear to be two reasons for Zhang's preference for disembowelment. First, one can survive a gut wound. Lau Kar-leung claims Zhang told him: "A disemboweled man, even with his guts out, can still move, can't he? Anyway, the bloodier it gets the better!"[24] Second, Lau notes that "this hero, who while he was holding his guts in one hand, was still fighting anyways! The audience loved these heroes who didn't die. The mood was very Japanese."[25] The influence of Japanese sword movies on both Zhang Che and King Hu has long been claimed. Here Lau Kar-leung points to another such influence.

Aside from phallic weaponry and a Japanese tone, we might say more substantially that the major recurring motifs in Zhang's films all coalesce around issues in male psychology. Predominant among these are: Oedipal conflicts revolving around the death and replacement of the father; master/disciple relationships, which often have a father-son character (e.g., adoption into a family or school, marriage to the clan's daughter, etc.); male camaraderie and male-bonding; betrayal by the "brother" figure; revenge for the death of the father/*shifu*/master; phallic injuries (especially the loss of limbs); the uneasy status of women (often absent in Zhang's films or a cause of the hero's injuries); heroic sacrifice and death. Obviously, except for the hero's death, I have outlined the basic characteristics of *One-Armed Swordsman*. Here, let us briefly recall, a servant sacrifices his life for his master and begs him with his dying breath to take in his son. Thus Fong Kong (played by Wang Yu) becomes both a student of and a surrogate son to his master. Jealousy on the part of his "brothers" in the school and resentment by the master's daughter lead to his loss of a limb. He is rescued by a woman (a non-martial artist). They live relatively peacefully until Fong is reminded of his "impotence." As rivals are killing off the "father's" students, Fong learns the art of one-armed swordsmanship and rescues his school, thereby becoming the "master" and thus replacing the father. Though he seems to reject the martial world at the film's end, sequels and remakes would return this figure, or a variation of him (e.g. *One-Armed Boxer* [dir. Wang Yu, 1971]), to the same situations. Except for male camaraderie, which Zhang would stress over and again in the pairing of David Chiang and Ti Lung two years later, *One-Armed Swordsman* contains most of the major motifs that distinguish the masculinist films. While we can easily relate these masculinist motifs to Zhang's particular authorial characteristics, I am less insistent on an auteur analysis than in showing how these features became generic and not just authorial.

It is well known that Cheng Chang-ho (Zheng Changhe)'s *Five Fingers of Death* (Tianxia diyi quan) (a.k.a. *King Boxer*, 1972) inaugurated, with the help of Bruce Lee's films, the kung fu craze in America.[26] And I have made the claim that it was Zhang Che's masculinist turn — male stars in male-dominated films — that enabled the Hong Kong cinema to broach the previously denied borders of American mainstream movie screens. Now we will see that the film reproduces those masculinist motifs.[27]

Set in a mythical town and at an indeterminate time (paper lanterns are used at night and people travel by horse-drawn buggy, yet houses have electric lights with switch-plates on the wall to turn them off and on), *Five Fingers of Death* tells the story of Ji Hao (played by Lo Lieh), an orphan who has become the favored pupil and future son-in-law of Sung Wuyang (played by Goo Man-chung). Thus the twin motifs of the father figure and the orphaned hero are in place, father figure as both future father-in-law and *shifu*/master. When Sung Wuyang is attacked, thus revealing the weakness of the father (he will later be killed), the father sends the orphan to another school, where he will interact with a new father figure and with potential "brothers" in the form of the other students at the school of Shen Chin-pei (played by Fong Min). Along the way Ji Hao meets up with the "bad woman," the potential femme fatale Yen Ji-hung (played by Wong Gam-fung). The generic penchant for father-figures in Zhang Che-inspired martial arts films also extends to the "bad father," the corrupt clan or school leader who has his own set of followers. Here the bad father is Ming Dung-shun (played by well-known character actor Tin Fung), leader of the rival martial arts school. His corrupt son Ming Tien-hsiung (played by Tung Lam) will soon emerge as Ji Hao's main rival at the all-important martial arts tournament. Here and afterward, Ji Hao will have to seek revenge — Zhang Che's primary plot motivator — for the killing of his father-figure, Sung Wuyang, the wounding of his other father-figure, Shen Chin-pei, and the killing of his schoolmates at the hands of Ming Dung-shun and his hired (Japanese) henchmen. Interestingly, the actual killing of Ming takes place at Han Lung's hands, with the help of the "bad woman." To prove his mastery and his ascension to master-status (replacing the father by marrying the daughter and defeating the villains the father could not), Ji Hao will kill the Japanese villains, thus asserting not only his rise to mastery (fatherhood), but to Chinese nationalism as well.

This kind of over-determined Oedipal crisis and rise to masculinity are hallmarks of not only Zhang's films, but also so much of the martial arts genre in his wake, as *Five Fingers of Death* demonstrates.

Other typical motifs of Zhang and, subsequently, the genre, are revealed in the frequent display of Lo Lieh's muscular build and the emphasis on the severe physical trauma he experiences (the near loss of his hands), his chasteness, his natural goodness, his need for father figures and his instinctual trust of his brothers at the school, as well as the male bonding that transforms Chen Lang (played by Gam Kei-chu), a Ming henchman, into Ji Hao's supporter.

It is in the very typicalness of this film, then, that we see the triumph of Zhang's style and concerns, and how it was this mode, and not King Hu's, that introduced Hong Kong cinema to the world.[28]

Yet we should not rest with a simple or simplistic binary of Hu vs. Zhang. Further analysis of mid-1970s and early-1980s Hong Kong films reveal how Zhang's and Hu's legacies worked their way into the stylized yet masculinist films of Chor Yuen, who is perhaps as underrated a director in Hong Kong cinema as one could find. His Mandarin-language films produced in the wake of the return to Cantonese dialect (a return he helped bring about) reveal a cinema struggling to find an aesthetic that could return Hong Kong cinema to world prominence (both Hollywood and the Japanese cinema began to compete with Hong Kong for the martial arts audience in the mid-to-late 1970s) while keeping its domestic and regional audience satisfied. Chor's films like *The Magic Blade* (Tianya mingyue dao) (1976) clearly anticipate the works of Tsui Hark (Xu Ke), just as they reveal some of the influence of King Hu. Just how extensive is the influence of King Hu remains to be determined, but the way in which his style and themes in films like *The Sacred Knives of Vengeance* (Da shashou) (1972) and *Killer Clans* (Liuxin hudie jian) (1976) carry on and extend Zhang's seems clear enough. The full story of the thematic and stylistic range of Hong Kong cinema remains unwritten. Here I hope to have shed light on how the interests of the present have warped our view of the past while at the same time pointing the way toward further research that may reshape the tentative conclusions I have drawn.

APPENDIX

Top ten highest grossing Hong Kong films, 1970–1972

Title	Director	Stars	Studio
1970			
* *The Chinese Boxer*	Wang Yu	Wang Yu	Shaw Brothers
* *The Twelve Gold Medallions*	Ching Gong	Chin Ping	Shaw Brothers
* *Brothers Five*	Lo Wei	Cheng Pei-pei Lo Lieh	Shaw Brothers
* *The Heroic Ones*	Zhang Che	David Chiang Ti Lung	Shaw Brothers
The Singing Killer	Zhang Che	David Chiang	Shaw Brothers
* *Vengeance*	Zhang Che	David Chiang Ti Lung	Shaw Brothers
* *From the Highway*	Cheung Chang-chak	Peter Yang	Cathay
* *Lady of Steel*	Hoh Mung-wa	Cheng Pei-pei	Shaw Brothers
* *The Wandering Swordsman*	Zhang Che	David Chiang	Shaw Brothers
Valley of the Fangs	Cheng Chang-ho	Li Ching Lo Lieh	Shaw Brothers
1971			
* *The Big Boss*	Lo Wei	Bruce Lee	Golden Harvest
* *Duel of Fists*	Zhang Che	David Chiang Ti Lung	Shaw Brothers
* *New One-Armed Swordsman*	Zhang Che	David Chiang Ti Lung	Shaw Brothers
* *The Lady Hermit*	Hoh Mung-wa	Cheng Pei-pei	Shaw Brothers
* *The Duel*	Zhang Che	David Chiang Ti Lung	Shaw Brothers

* = Martial arts film

Title	Director	Stars	Studio
* The Anonymous Heroes	Zhang Che	David Chiang Ti Lung	Shaw Brothers
Legends of Cheating	Li Han-hsiang	Chen Chen	New Guo Lian
* The Shadow Whip	Lo Wei	Cheng Pei-pei	Shaw Brothers
* The Invincible Eight	Lo Wei	Patrick Tse Angela Mao	Golden Harvest
* The Deadly Duo	Zhang Che	David Chiang Ti Lung	Shaw Brothers
1972			
* The Way of the Dragon	Bruce Lee	Bruce Lee	Concord
* Fist of Fury	Lo Wei	Bruce Lee	Golden Harvest
The Warlord	Li Han-hsiang	Michael Hui	Shaw Brothers
* The Fourteen Amazons	Ching Gong	Lili Ho Ivy Ling	Shaw Brothers
Legends of Lust	Li Han-hsiang	Booi Dai	Shaw Brothers
* Boxer from Shantung	Zhang Che	Chen Kuan-tai David Chiang	Shaw Brothers
* The Bloody Fists	Ng See-yuen	Chan Sing Chen Kuan-tai	Empire
* The Water Margin	Zhang Che	Ti Lung Wu Ma David Chiang	Shaw Brothers
* The Good and the Bad	Ng See-yuen	Chan Sing	Empire
* Black List	Law Ma	Chan Sing	Kai Fa

2

Post-1997 Hong Kong Masculinity

Laikwan Pang

Contrary to local and international predictions in the 1980s and 1990s, 1997 was not the end of Hong Kong's history. But looking back at the seven-year "postcolonial" period, most Hong Kong people would agree that the new Hong Kong did not evolve as expected. Self-governance, which Hong Kong people yearned and fought for before 1997, became the greatest source of frustration. Questions were raised about almost everything Hong Kong people were proud of in the colonial system — like the efficient civil service, laissez-faire economy, flourishing real-estate market, and even the public housing and public healthcare systems. Pride disappeared, to be replaced by fervent and often futile discussions about finding a future. Although I do not believe cinema simply and directly mirrors society, a highly successful commercial cinema like Hong Kong's does organically intertwine with the collective emotions of local society, and the industry's abrupt changes are often triggered by changes in the social environment. In this chapter I will try to tackle the impossible: delineate and unwrap the complex relationship among society, cinematic representations, and the cinema industry.

Here I analyze the work of a new Hong Kong film company, Milkyway Image, to illustrate its male representation in the period immediately after 1997. In his study of the Hong Kong films of John Woo (Wu Yusen) produced before 1997, Julian Stringer concludes that Woo's movies are apocalyptic and despairing because under the current political situation, "Hong Kong action cinema ... cannot provide the system within which any new masculinity can be reconsolidated."[1] While I agree with Stringer that there has been a sense of crisis observed in recent Hong Kong cinema, particularly in its representation of masculinity, this is not purely a political product. It is also internally constituted by a masculine cinematic tradition, which seems to have exhausted itself. I chose Milkyway Image as the focus of my study because it is one of the very few film studios to have been established during a recession and prospered. Secondly, Milkyway Image has a unique history, with two distinct periods showing a sudden change in production orientation, which demonstrates an interesting gender shift in recent Hong Kong cinema.

In an interview, the studio's director Johnnie To (Du Qifeng) reveals that entrapment and powerlessness are two crucial themes in the early Milkyway Image films, which reflect the gloomy economic environment Hong Kong people experienced in 1997 and 1998.[2] Many people felt despair about the future as their multimillion dollar apartments became negative equity overnight or their previously secure jobs suddenly came under threat. The early Milkyway Image films were made to reveal this feeling of dejection and these films chose to deal with this crisis by analyzing and explicating male representation. In the films made during this period, male characters were often put under the spell of some omnipotent forces; slowly and brutally the male protagonists were made to struggle and look, often in vain, for ways out of their predicament. These films no longer exhibited male confidence and aggressiveness so often seen in earlier Hong Kong gangster and action movies. The man's world portrayed was full of anxiety and disturbance, and the characters were often in a state of insecurity and fear. Not only were they deprived of full confidence with regard to the opposite sex, but the relationships among the males were also often unsettled and complex. These films established a self-reflexive and intertextual world calling attention to a specific cinematic masculinity established in Hong Kong cinema, whose underlying mechanisms were revealed and problematized. Entering its second phase of development, the productions of Milkyway Image abruptly turned such male insecurity into male sacrifices for the self-fulfillment and actualization of women. Men were no longer caught in traps because they were already depraved, hopeless, or dead. These new films no longer mourned the vulnerability and impotence of the male characters because they had all turned into comical figures: they were overweight or childishly ignorant, or they had maternal instincts and were sissies. Some of the key ideological assumptions and representation politics of masculinity established in Hong Kong cinema were overthrown. Women now embodied the future of Hong Kong.

Every masculinity has its own history and forms its own discursive structure so the construction of masculinity is as otherly-defined as self-referential, in the sense that male representation is relative not only to those of the other sexes/genders synchronically but also to its own history and tradition diachronically. Tania Modleski has claimed that "male power is actually consolidated through cycles of crisis and resolution."[3] Some even claim that crisis is a condition of masculinity itself.[4] I am skeptical of the assertion that patriarchy, like the capitalist machine, is equipped with a self-expansion mechanism that can constantly overcome and incorporate its own crisis.[5] But I do believe masculinity, like other social configurations of practice, seeks refuge and breakthroughs from its own history when under threat. What I am interested in, therefore, is how masculinity in Hong Kong cinema deals with its own crisis, and whether these self-defense/self-interrogative mechanisms open up new space for both the male subject and Hong Kong cinema to confront themselves.

A BRIEF ACCOUNT OF MILKYWAY IMAGE'S DEVELOPMENT

Wai Ka-fai (Wei Jiahui), the most popular local TV producer in the early 1990s, and Johnnie To, whose 1992 *Justice, My Foot!* (Shensi guan) is one of the highest grossing Hong Kong films of all time, founded Milkyway Image in 1996. Hong Kong cinema at the time was deteriorating rapidly in terms of box-office records and production numbers. In 1997 Milkyway Image made its name known on Hong Kong's film scene with its first four remarkable films: *Too Many Ways to Be Number One* (Yige zitou de dansheng; dir. Wai Ka-fai), *Final Justice* (Zuihou panjue; dir. Derek Chiu), *The Odd One Dies* (Liangge zhineng huo yige; dir. Patrick Yau), and *Intruder* (Kongbu ji; dir. Tsang Ken-cheung). Although all were commercial genre films, they also attempted to experiment with the established formula.

For example, *Too Many Ways to Be Number One* and *The Odd One Dies* portray their leading male gangster heroes as timid, weak, and dim-witted. In *Final Justice* and *Intruder*, on the other hand, social order is no longer clearly defined by right and wrong, righteousness and betrayal — demarcations that can hardly be confused in many mainstream Hong Kong features. The film most acclaimed by critics among the four is *Too Many Ways to Be Number One*, a film dazzlingly experimental and witty. Stephen Teo calls it the "most striking" local production released in 1997. "The film's level of experimentation was always likely to divide critics (it has) and confer on its director, Wai Ka-fai, a sort of maverick status in Hong Kong cinema."[6] When commenting on the film, along with other

Hong Kong gangster films produced around the same time, David Bordwell also proclaims that "these and the other genre efforts show more experimental ambition than many of the U.S. 'independent' films of recent years."[7] As the first production of Milkyway Image, *Too Many Ways to Be Number One* earned the company a reputation for boldness and creativity.

Milkyway Image gained wide attention from both critics and audiences in 1998. *The Longest Nite* (Anhua; dir. Patrick Yau) grossed HK$10 million at the local box-office (about US$1.3 million), an impressive record in view of the sluggish film market. In keeping with the style and mood of the earlier four Milkyway Image films, *The Longest Nite* is a Hong Kong film noir that recounts how the hero embraces his own death. Together with *Expect the Unexpected* (Feichang turan; dir. Patrick Yau) and *A Hero Never Dies* (Zhenxin yinxiong; dir. Johnnie To), these three films form the Milkyway Image Trilogy, which is widely considered one of the finest trilogies in Hong Kong cinema.

Wai Ka-fai was mainly responsible for developing ideas for the seven Milkyway Image films in 1997 and 1998, while Johnnie To took care of production. As To himself admitted: "In our company, [Wai] is the creative driving force. Wherever he goes, we follow. He provides the concept and we shoot it, to realize the spirit of his ideas."[8] Johnnie To finally reclaimed the Milkyway Image director's chair in 1999 and directed three films that year — *Where a Good Man Goes* (Zaijian alang), *Running Out of Time* (Anzhan), and *The Mission* (Qianghuo) — all of which, again, fell into the gangster/action genre. *Running Out of Time*, a crime story framed as a cat-and-mouse plot, was a big commercial hit. *The Mission*, a unique and fascinating combination of Hong Kong gangster and Japanese samurai films, won Johnnie To almost all the best-director awards in Hong Kong and Taiwan in year 2000, defeating strong competitors like Ang Lee (Li An) for *Crouching Tiger Hidden Dragon* (Wohu canglong) and Wong Kar-wai (Wang Jiawei) for *In the Mood for Love* (Huayang nianhua). In the depths of one of the industry's most disheartening recessions, Milkyway Image established itself as the leading Hong Kong film company in three years.

Milkyway Image took a dramatic turn in year 2000, departing from the film noir and embracing the audience with light-hearted comedies. Starting in the new millennium, Milkyway Image merged with new company One Hundred Years of Film, financed by Hong Kong film tycoon Charles Heung (Xiang Huaqiang), whose plan is to rebuild a film kingdom almost destroyed by the financial crisis. *Needing You* (Gunan gua'nü), an overwhelming critical and commercial success co-directed by To and Wai in 2000, is a touching romantic comedy filled with local jokes and sensibilities. This was the first time since the early 1970s that light romantic comedy was the highest earner of the year at the box office. The same crew and talent made *Love on a Diet* (Shoushen nannü) the following year, breaking the box-office record of the previous film and grossing more than HK$40 million in Hong Kong alone. It was the second most popular film in 2001, beaten only by the magical *Shaolin Soccer* (Shaolin zuqiu; dir. Stephen Chow). *Love on a Diet* was followed by another great commercial hit, *My Left Eye Sees Ghosts* (Wo zuoyan jiandao gui), featuring Sammi Cheng (Zheng Xiuwen) as the heroine. These films were co-directed and co-produced by To and Wai. The auteur sensibilities of the two filmmakers shown in their earlier films were completely toned down, and these films very clearly scored higher box-office records than the earlier productions. Milkyway Image has now become the most commercially successful Hong Kong film company, and this new production strategy will seemingly continue.

THE FIRST PHASE

Milkyway Image's early productions, from 1997 to 1999, constituted an eccentric stage of the company's development. These films made the studio's name at a time when Hong Kong cinema was sinking into a deep depression, yet they reflected depth and creativity seldom seen in Hong Kong commercial cinema even at its peak. Among the eleven films produced by Milkyway Image in those two years, eight were produced under the direct supervision of Wai and/or To, and this collection of films was unique in its unification of themes and forms.

All eight films clearly belong to the masculine genre of gangster and action movies, and they feature the struggles of the leading male characters and a look at their psyches. There are almost no important female figures in the films, and the narratives are all initiated by the heroes and developed in line with the way they think. Together these "Wai-To" films represent a film collage that reflects and comments on Hong Kong cinema's representation of masculinity. Not only do they provide us with a window for examining the politics and internal contradictions of an overtly masculine tradition, but the collection of films can also be seen as an interesting case study of how masculinity deals with its own crisis.

Too Many Ways to be Number One is a peculiar first film for the company because it is precisely about beginning and starting again. The films opens with Wong Ah Kau having his palm read and being told that he will have to make a crucial life-changing decision on his forthcoming thirty-second birthday. His decision will determine how he will end up: exiled in disgrace and killed, or living in affluence and glory. The film presents both possible outcomes and invites the audience to experience the two adventures with the protagonist himself. In the first half of the film Ah Kau smuggles stolen cars from Hong Kong to the Mainland with his gangster friends; all, however, are eventually killed by the Chinese army. The film then brings the characters and audience back to the beginning, and there Ah Kau decides not to follow the gang to China. Instead, he is persuaded by another mobster, Matt, to go to Taiwan. There he scrambles for a bloody way to success, and in the end he becomes a godfather in his own right.

Despite the political interpretations of some critics,[9] I would argue that the film's China/Taiwan choice carries no real meaning. China and Taiwan could be replaced, and the distinct style and color schemes assigned to the two parts swapped around, but the development of the plot and characters would not be altered. The semantic structure of the film would be completely unchanged. There is no mention of ethics or morality in Ah Kau's decision and outcome; the film affords an existential exploration of individual freedom of choice. Seemingly the film emphasizes Ah Kau's ability to choose and to be the master of his own life, his fate the result of his own will. However, reading the film more closely we discover that the decisions he makes and the events that later take place are the consequence of situations over which he has no control. Whether it is the environment controlling him or Ah Kau taking charge of the environment, the film makes both options contingent and possible.

In the two versions of his life, Ah Kau is two separate individuals and his different personalities simply make the decisions for him. Contrary to what the film superficially suggests, it is not easy to figure out if Ah Kau is indeed in control of his life. Although the palm-reader tells Ah Kau that "the key to success is whether you can find yourself or not," who indeed is this self? In the first half of the film he is a cowardly character incapable of remaining on his own and refusing Matt and the gang. However, in the second half of the film, Ah Kau becomes a different person: he is confident and determined. Even Matt changes in the different parts of the film, transforming from a sturdy and decisive brother to a flimsy and craven petty crook. Therefore, although Ah Kau is making decisions for himself, the decisions being made seem predestined and he has no control over the consequences. Because of the fleeting representation of the male subject(s) neither the audience nor the character in question knows who is the real Ah Kau.

Why is Ah Kau so different in the two parts of the film? The film provides no absolute answer, but it does present two different environments in which Ah Kau is embodied. While the same Matt performs very differently in the two parts, the film simply provides two different women for the protagonist in the two sections. In the first half, when Ah Kau chooses the path of destruction, the film arranges for a mysterious "Sister-in-law" to appear on the Mainland to take charge of the gang's activities. This "woman in red" picks up Ah Kau to be her sex object, and allows him no sexual gratification while enjoying all she wants from him. At the end she orders the gang to rob the bank and indirectly pushes them to their deaths. Not only is Ah Kau controlled by Matt and the gang in the first part of the film, but most importantly he is also completely subordinate, mentally and sexually, to this mysterious woman. However, in the second part of the film, Ah Kau's partner is the devoted and beautiful massage girl Number Two. She desires him in a completely opposite way to that of "Sister-in-law." Number Two yearns for his protection and therefore his dominion throughout the story. Although the two women occupy little narrative space in the film, they are crucial in molding whom Ah Kau becomes and how he makes his life-or-death decision.

Too Many Ways to Be Number One is widely considered a mockery of the popular *Young and Dangerous* (Guhuo zai) series, to which six sequels were produced during the short period from 1996 to 1998.[10] At a time when John Woo's romantic and sophisticated male heroes were becoming too mature, and sometimes too dull for young audiences, the teenage and uneducated, yet more upbeat and trendy, delinquents in *Young and Dangerous* quickly became legendary. The films were so successful that a surge of imitations and satires was released in 1997 and 1998, among which *Too Many Ways to Be Number One* is considered one. Ah Kau, especially in the first part, can easily be read as the opposite of Ho-nam (Haonan), the protagonist in *Young and Dangerous*. Ho-nam is dominant and smart; he is also devoted to his love, and he is willing to sacrifice himself for his master, brothers, and girlfriend — in general, he has all the features of the stock hero found in hundreds of earlier Hong Kong male movies, including John

Woo's films, against which *Young and Dangerous* was supposed to provide a fresh and different contrast.

Too Many Ways to Be Number One very consciously challenges this hero-making. The film often uses low angle shots with 360-degree camera movements to represent the point of view of Ah Kau, stressing a sense of entrapment and impotence. Its background music is always light-hearted and funny, even when dangerous encounters, including a brutal killing, take place. The challenge is also posed structurally. R. W. Connell argues that there is always more than one kind of masculinity available in society; the dominant masculinity subordinates others and organizes itself at the top of a hierarchy through various hegemonic means.[11] Steven Cohan uses Hollywood films of the 1950s as examples to demonstrate this struggle, because they bear witness to the transition of one form of dominant masculinity during wartime to another in post-war America.[12] Although *Too Many Ways to Be Number One* also displays two forms of masculinity, the film does not necessarily favor the takeover by one form or the other — it does not legitimize the transition as a certain rite of passage for Ah Kau to attain manhood. The film does not provide ideological endorsement of the hero's "final triumph." Unlike Ho-nam, whose character is unified in all situations, Ah Kau is trapped between two completely opposing forms of masculinity. We witness a contradictory male subject who is at the same time powerless and powerful to the extreme, and each case is as legitimate and as possible as the other.

Although in the end one form of masculinity is defeated by the other, this oppression is made so clear that we are reminded of the hyperbolic construction of Ah Kau's, and probably Ho-nam's, subjectivity. When Ah Kau establishes his own gang and the title of godfather is conferred on him, he is in a wheelchair and strapped in a corset of bandages from head to toe. The scene is as comical as it is sad, because it seems to ask both Ah Kau and the audience: "Was it worth it?" The fierce brutality Ah Kau had to endure before gaining male power bears witness to the underlying violence of hegemonic masculinity. Here we observe an action hero trapped in a tug-of-war between the random violence of two kinds of masculinity, and he ends up as much a victim as a winner, although he does become "number one." And, most interestingly, the crisis of masculinity depicted in the film is not socio-political but cinematic, referring both to the industry and its mainstream gender representation. Although Ah Kau's world changes drastically in the two parts, the uncertainty suggested in the film is not so much about the empirical reality as the very existential question of who he is and the performativity of his gender identity. This strong sense of anxiety suggested in this first Milkyway Image film sets up the overall ambience for the following films, which continue to show that the Milkyway Image puts its films at stake to hold on to, yet also challenge, the male tradition of Hong Kong cinema.

Milkyway Image continues its exploration of the theme of fate in its later films. Among them, *Expect the Unexpected* is the most despairing and somber, commenting more directly than *Too Many Ways to Be Number One* on the vulnerability of individuals: they are often set up by fate and have no control of their fragile lives. Once again, however, the despair refers as much to the social environment as intertextually to a cinematic tradition. Following the plot of the classic cop movie, the film recounts how an outstanding police team arrests a group of fierce and brutal bandits who rape and torture women and gun down passers-by with machine guns.[13] But the genre formula is somehow twisted by the interference of another group of criminals, who are fresh-off-the-boat Mainland illegal immigrants wanting to rob banks. They are portrayed as stupid, ignorant, and clumsy country bumpkins who are no comparison to the sophisticated local criminals. In the film, both the audience and the cops focus on the local bandits, and ultimately our heroes succeed in capturing them. However, at the end of the film, when the protagonists are celebrating their victory, the group of Mainland robbers appears, and all the heroes and bandits are brutally killed by each other in this final confrontation.

The Mainlanders depicted as country bumpkins in the earlier parts of the film suddenly turn into Rambo at the end: they have a full load of heavy weapons in their cars and reveal themselves to be trained and sophisticated killers. Audiences are not prepared for this abrupt and almost surreal change, and neither are our hero cops. They have been wearing bulletproof vests throughout the film, and the vests have prevented them from being killed by the local bandits several times. Only at this time do they take them off, and it ultimately costs them their lives. The cops are fooled by their own prejudices against the Mainlanders, yet the audience is doubly vulnerable because recent Hong Kong commercial films seldom portray Mainlanders as threats to Hong Kong people.

Starting in 1982, when discussions between China and Britain on the future of Hong Kong began, Mainlanders in Hong Kong movies have often represented the conscious expression of filmmakers of the political contours of the city. The few Mainlanders portrayed in Hong Kong films in the 1980s, such as those in *Long Arm of the Law* (Shenggang qibing) (dir. Johnny Mak, 1984), were almost always politically symbolic, articulating the yet-to-be-crystallized anxiety of Hong Kong people towards the 1997 event.[14] This politics of representation underwent dramatic changes after the Tian'anmen Square incident. Many more Mainlanders appeared in local cinema after 1989, yet many of them were Chinese cops assuming their duties in Hong Kong.[15] It is easy to connect this type of representation with Hong Kong people's political anxiety, but interestingly the Mainland cops are almost always morally upright, and they are in Hong Kong to maintain order. Direct depiction of their corruption, as seen in *From China with Love* (Guochan linglingqi; dir. Stephen Chow, 1994), is rare.

The Tian'anmen Square Incident in 1989 aroused contradictory emotions in Hong Kong people, who realized that their destiny was forever tied with that of China, no matter how unwillingly they were. These intertwined emotions were indirectly revealed in the Hong Kong mainstream cinema in the 1990s, in which almost all the Mainlanders are portrayed as police, while the lawbreakers are the locals. Despite their positive and righteous images so laboriously forged, these Mainland cops bring forth and embody heavy symbolic violence. The Hong Kong people, like Hong Kong cinema, might have been too overwhelmed to grapple directly with their political distress: they feared the Mainlanders yet at the same time saw them as a blessing. The embedded political helplessness is indeed more compellingly revealed in the representations of Mainlanders as police rather than criminals.

In view of this intertextual reference, a remarkable aspect of *Expect the Unexpected* is the reversed stereotype: the Mainlanders are represented directly as people who want to rob Hong Kong. But unlike *Long Arm of the Law*, in which the perspectives of the Mainlanders are featured in order to show the complexity of border crossing,[16] *Expect the Unexpected* stays with the Hong Kong police throughout almost the entire film. The film does not render "subjectivity" to the Mainlanders; they are simply the fantasized objects of both the cops and the audience. The film calls our attention less to Hong Kong people's political despair than to a history of representation politics that governed the violence both on and off screen. The bloodshed depicted in the final scene of the film is therefore doubly echoed, reflexively punishing the characters for their self-confidence (developed diegetically within the narrative), and the audience for their ignorance (developed intertextually in Hong Kong cinema in general).

Placing the film in its own cinematic tradition, we discover that Hong Kong action cinema often constructs its masculinity through all sorts of self-deception and decoys. This cinema might have produced the most sophisticated and devoted police force in world cinema, personified by such charismatic stars as Jackie Chan (Cheng Long) and Danny Lee (Li Xiuxian). But the more marvelous the Hong Kong police becomes, the more anxiety is embedded. In the case of *Expect the Unexpected*, the film presents the police as agile, bright, and refined, yet the film also shocks us with their vulnerability, which has been built up by prejudices, stereotypes, and insecurity. In the film, all the members of the police unit are anxiety ridden, yet the film allows all these anxieties to be shaded to construct their hero status. Only when the cops are killed is the aghast audience reminded that these nuisances have never been settled.

Both *Too Many Ways to Be Number One* and *Expect the Unexpected* demonstrate a fragile post-1997 Hong Kong male subjectivity, which is seemingly autonomous but at heart vulnerable and incoherent. The death scene in *Expect the Unexpected* can be read as an allegory of Hong Kong cinema's politics of representation, a tradition that has relied on violence to cover up violence. Susan Jeffords refers to Hollywood masculinity in the Reagan era as a vicious circle of mutual reinforcement: "more and more spectacular film productions, larger and larger national deficits, increasingly demanding claims about U.S. military power, greater pressures for masculine success and appearance."[17] There was also a tendency towards intensifying violence in Hong Kong mainstream movies in the 1990s.[18] But I do not want to posit a direct mirroring relationship between Hong Kong cinema and Hong Kong society, as Jeffords does in her study of Hollywood. What I want to stress, instead, is that in dealing with the violence of Hong Kong cinema, which might or might not have anything to do with real social violence, all the Milkyway Image filmmakers can do is respond to the violence by offering more violence. The mutual concealment and refuge between the insecurity of fury and the insecurity of masculinity has defined mainstream Hong Kong commercial cinema in the last two or three decades. In the films of Milkyway Image, this conspiracy is made extreme to the limit of collapse.

The film concluding the first phase of Milkyway Image is *The Mission*, which begins with an unsuccessful assassination attempt on the gangster godfather Big Brother Lung. To protect Lung, Second Brother Nam finds Curtis, Mic, James, Roy, and Shin to act as Big Brother's bodyguards. After several soul-stirring ambush battles and escapes, the five finally figure out the conspiracy: it is Lung's own uncle who wants to kill him. But after they receive payment and are disbanded, Curtis obtains an order from Nam to kill Shin because Shin was found having an affair with Big Brother's woman. Curtis is devoted to Big Brother, yet Roy is more loyal to his own brother and demands Curtis not carry out this second "mission." At the end of the film, Curtis intelligently sets up a phony execution and secretly lets Shin go.

The Mission is Johnnie To's hitherto most artistically acclaimed work. The major difference between this film and the earlier Milkyway Image films is its simple narrative. There is little plot progression, and the major body of the film is focused on the several ambush battles to show off the suave action designs. When discussing The Mission, the famous local film critic Jitao proclaimed: "It is impossible to make this film without a deep understanding of Hong Kong cinema."[19] What Jitao was referring to, I believe, is a tradition of Hong Kong action cinema that features elaborate action designs and camera work to produce aesthetically appealing visual effects. Bruce Lee (Li Xiaolong) is one of the few exceptions who conceptualized martial arts in his films as forms of real fighting rather than performances. Most Hong Kong action films are instead indebted to Chinese opera and other forms of traditional arts/philosophy, developing a cinematic style emphasizing the beauty and performativity of violence more than its destruction and brutality. As some scholars demonstrate, this kind of aesthetic was adopted and developed in King Hu's (Hu Jinquan) and Zhang Che's films in the 1970s, which profoundly influenced the later generation of filmmakers like John Woo and Tsui Hark (Xu Ke).[20]

Aesthetics emphasizing choreography design, dexterity of action, and editing craft impregnate a specific type of male representation that displays fanciful actions and a refined body, which can be contrasted with Hollywood's standard hard-boiled representation of masculinity. Jillian Sandell describes John Woo's choreographed action sequences as constructing a "masculinity which celebrates both strength and intimacy, and where male bonding can suggest an erotic charge without the associated anxiety such relationships often trigger within the Hollywood action genre."[21] Sandell is accurate in pointing out a fundamental difference between the male representations of Hong Kong cinema and those of Hollywood, but she misses, I believe, a problematic gender ideology underlying this aesthetic. If we call Hong Kong action films suave, the accompanying sensation often reinforces and is reinforced by the films' homosocial bonding because masculinity is culturally characterized as clean and sober, as opposed to devious, clumsy, and confused femininity. Hong Kong's cinematic masculinity is often suggested and legitimized by an aesthetic mode of appeal and legitimization, relying on "non-rational" means to support an allegedly "rational" mandate. If the spectators of Hong Kong action movies experience the films' homosocial world as a form of pleasure, this pleasure is often induced by a sense of beauty and the sublime, and the order and harmony represented in turn justify the subordination of other genders/sexualities.

If all the earlier Milkyway Image films are male-oriented, *The Mission* is masculine in the extreme. Not only is the film's content focused on the male characters, but its sophisticated choreography is also always intimately designed according to a certain male homosocial structure. For example, in the astonishing "shopping mall" sequence, the actions are designed not only to create a visual spectacle but also to support an underlying ideology. The five bodyguards escort Lung to their cars from a meeting. As they travel through the closed shopping mall on an escalator, gunshots are fired but no one knows from where. They quickly find their protective shields in the mall's architectural structures, and everything becomes still except for the movement of the camera itself. The tension is balanced, but at the same time it is heightened by the silence and stillness, punctuated by the sudden action introduced by the moving escalator. The tension built up is brilliantly visualized and rhythmized in the overall design. The film's tempo is poised between movement and inertia, yet the tautness is also made possible by the assumed mutual understanding among the five gangsters. They have to rely on exchanged looks and mutual understanding to arrange an escape, because speech would immediately reveal their locations to the enemy. When they eventually escape, apart from being relieved of the tension, the audience is also stunned by the sublimated homosocial bonds that have developed among the five bodyguards.

Homosocial bondings are intimately revealed in small gestures or the mise-en-scène. For example, there is a scene showing Big Brother Lung making coffee for the bodyguards, and this small, humble gesture in the film alone is enough to justify the unyielding loyalty of the latter to the former. The film also shows plenty of mutual understanding/ respect between the two opposing gangs. When the guards finally locate the headquarters of the assassins, the film highlights a gun battle between Mic and the chief of the other gang in which they engage in a one-on-

one long-distance shooting competition performed in complete darkness. They do not see each other's faces, but the sound and light of their gunfire become alternative forms of communication, and their mutual respect and hidden bonding are articulated in the symmetrical wounds inflicted on their faces.

However, while *The Mission* is clearly a direct descendant of Hong Kong's male cinema, it also reveals some structural blind spots, which pop up at the end to startle the audience. According to Eve Sedgwick, the homosocial relationship is built upon homophobia and the domination of the heterosexual relationship: together they form the backbone of the patriarchal ideological structure.[22] While *The Mission* does not hint at any homosexual relationship, the film features only one female among the dozen male characters: Lung's anonymous woman. The five bodyguards come from different backgrounds; this "mission" brought them together, converting them from strangers to comrades sharing the same destiny. Yet the intense male friendship is placed in crisis when the subjugation of the opposite sex is revealed, and the entire homosocial structure is destroyed as a result of one small insurrection performed by a nameless woman, a *femme fatale*. She is beautiful and mysterious, yet unlike Hollywood's *film noir* this film seldom allows her to speak and always puts her a great distance from the camera. She has no name and passes by the gang only once in a while. All we know is that she is always in a hurry to get out of the elegant house. It is the seduction of this woman that smashes into pieces the male bonding so laboriously built up in the narrative. In other words, when woman-trafficking and heterosexual relationships are not completely tamed by and controlled by the patriarchy, the seemingly sublimated homosocial structure soon collapses.

This female insurgency immediately strips naked the core of the power structure. At the end of the film, James decides to seek mercy from Lung for Shin because he believes it the only way to settle the crisis. Just before he reaches Lung, James unintentionally witnesses the execution of the woman, and it is at this point the five brothers and the audience are made aware of Lung's tyranny and his absolute power. We are always reminded of the benevolence of Lung in the film. Only when a woman rebels are his sexual ability and dominion over the woman challenged, and the entire homosocial structure he reigns over put into crisis. Lung's kindness is quickly replaced by brutality, with the result that both his wife and his devoted follower must be killed with no mercy. At the time of the woman's execution everybody recognizes immediately that order has been re-established, and this brutality mocks all the sublimated aesthetics so assiduously constructed to support a supposedly humane homosocial structure. The woman's adultery signals the destruction of the power structure headed by Big Brother. It also jeopardizes the homosocial bonding among the five brothers because they are put in a dilemma between loyalty to authority and loyalty to brotherhood. Only when the woman and the traitor are executed can Lung's power, and the entire homosocial structure, be reinstated. It is also at this moment, when the patriarch fights back, that all the deceptions legitimizing the tyranny are exposed.

THE SECOND PHASE

These stylized and self-reflective gangster films brought To and Wai critical acclaim but also heavy debts. Before the public release of *The Mission*, To confessed that he had decided to depart from his artistic exploration and concentrate on producing money-making commercial films to improve the dire financial situation of the company.[23] To has always been a successful commercial filmmaker, and in his pre-Milkyway Image films he managed to package his films with a high-concept commercial formula, mixing big stars, heart-breaking emotions, and heated topics. *Running Out of Time*, although screened prior to *The Mission*, can be seen as the transitional film between Milkyway Image's first and second phases. Andy Lau (Liu Dehua) is cast as a dying hero-bandit constantly being injured and taking pills. But he finally manages to escape from the police and lead a free life. The hero may die at the end but he is able to fulfill his wishes and, therefore, has control of his life, a stark contrast to the storylines of earlier Milkyway Image films. But the real turning point in the company's development took place with *Needing You*, when Wai and To decisively left the male gangster genre and embarked on women-oriented light romance comedy.

In the film we are introduced to the life of the ordinary and sometimes spooky office lady Kinki (Sammi Cheng), who has to choose between the young, handsome, and rich Silicon Valley tycoon and her petty and lecherous, although as handsome, supervisor (Andy Lau). Symbolically, the heroine finds her true love in her own city and chooses not to leave Hong Kong for the then potent "dotcom fantasy." She decides to stay with her now unemployed ex-boss hoping to build a new life of her own.

To a relatively small studio with hitherto very clear and defined production orientation, this abrupt change from gangster film to light romance was both bold and inevitable at a time when producers were frantically looking for new commercial formulas. In highlighting woman's agency *Needing You* clearly differentiated itself from earlier Milkyway Image films. Not only is the heroine choosing between men, but she is also choosing between futures. The film is clearly tailored for a typical Hong Kong female viewer of average looks, not outstanding in any way and determined to lead her own life. I believe this film should have a special place in the history of Hong Kong cinema because its commercial success marked the cinema's collective turn to women genres and female audiences after decades of ignoring this market.

Since 1996, when the industry began to suffer from a rapid decline in attendance, there has been an increasing number of films specifically made for female audiences. New director Joe Ma (Ma Weihao) was the first to impress on the industry the significance of the large female market. His low-budget light romance *Feel 100%* (Baifenbai ganjue) stunned the industry in the summer of 1996 with its $20 million box-office record, and was ranked as the ninth most popular film that year. His subsequent *Feel 100% Once More* (Baifenbai "ngam feel" [Cantonese]) made another HK$15 million at the box office, which officially started the light romance trend. This new genre is preferred in times of recession because most traditional male genres like action or gangster films fail during these times, and secondly, it is much cheaper to make women's films because female stars demand much lower acting fees than their male counterparts. But among all the romance comedies made in 1996 and 1997, *Needing You* was the first to be hugely profitable. It can be seen as a turning point in Hong Kong cinema, which, along with some television productions, suddenly turned to "office ladies" for creative incentive and revenue. The film's box-office success turned Sammi Cheng from a declining singer to the most sought after female actress in Hong Kong cinema; it also turned romance comedy from an almost forgotten genre into a money-making machine. Suddenly Hong Kong filmmakers were reminded that female audiences were a great source of revenue. This abruptly reversed the gender disposition of Hong Kong films made in the following years.

To and Wai continue to make more gangster movies, like *Fulltime Killer* (Quanzhi shashou, 2001) and *Running Out of Time 2* (Anzhan 2, 2001). But the studio's biggest commercial hits hitherto are light-romance and melodramas. *Love on a Diet* was made more or less as a sequel to

Needing You. Although the stories and the characters of the two films are completely different, the underlying commercial formula is similar — the heroine Mimi chooses the fat and uneducated Hong Kong salesman instead of the handsome and talented Japanese violinist. Again it is the woman's choice and her dedication that are being highlighted. But while *Needing You* still emphasizes the career success of the male protagonist, this film simply strips him of charisma. Compared with the smart and gorgeous bachelor in *Needing You*, anti-hero Andy Lau in *Love on a Diet* runs wild. He represents the least attractive type of Hong Kong man: fat, poor, and lacking in good taste. Lau, simply named Fat Guy in the film, is a plain loser, albeit a happy and contented one. His self-confidence is so low that he cannot profess his love for Mimi. He even takes to street fighting to save money for her weight-control program so she can return to her ex-boyfriend with a slimmer figure. As expected, Mimi and the Fat Guy reunite, on a street corner, after they return to being slim and beautiful. But most importantly we see that this happy ending could not have been achieved without the Fat Guy's giving up all he has in the first place to give Mimi a new life. Although it is Fat Guy who makes the sacrifices, hope for the future is clearly placed on Mimi's shoulders: at the end she is the one who writes the book on starting a new life with a slim body. After all, weight loss is still largely a woman's issue in Hong Kong. More obvious than *Needing You*, *Love on a Diet* explores female psychology and asserts their identity, no matter how problematically. Its great commercial success is a reflection of its ability to touch the general female viewer.

My Left Eye Sees Ghosts helped take Sammi Cheng to the highest point in her career. Milkyway Image got rid of Andy Lau — arguably the biggest male star in the current local cinema — in this film in order to highlight Cheng's stardom. In fact, the male protagonist is dead even before the film begins: he was killed in a diving accident during his honeymoon. As a ghost he turns himself into the image of his wife's primary-school classmate, performed by Lau Ching-wan (Liu Qingyun), to keep her company. The dead husband hopes this naughty and kind-hearted childhood friend can bring his wife out of her grief and self-destruction and give her new incentives to live. A relatively simple story, the film is basically about the dedication and unyielding love of the wife to her dead husband. The heroine is also subtlely praised for her devotion to and care for her mother-in-law, sister-in-law, and even the ex-girlfriend of her husband. She eventually becomes the head of the household and takes care of not only the family members but also the business left behind by her successful husband. She replaces and becomes her husband through the deep and long mourning period. Once again, she embodies the hope for the future, and she is the one to be trusted in leading the dejected family to find a new beginning.

Milkyway Image's abrupt but successful changes in its production strategies afford us significant insights into Hong Kong cinema specifically, and cinema as a popular art generally. As Peter Krämer concludes in his study of Hollywood's pro-male marketing orientation, most film executives are convinced that male audiences are more determined and important customers than their female counterparts, although films with strong female appeal are cheaper to make and more profitable when they are successful.[24] As some studio executives themselves have admitted, most executives are male, so naturally they are more comfortable with male-oriented products.[25] In other words, female audiences are always an important market, but film studios tend be reluctant in catering to them when male movies are successful. It takes drastic changes in the commercial market to remind the studios of the presence of female audiences. Seeing the popularity in Hong Kong cinema today of Sammi Cheng and some of her imitators, like Miriam Yeung (Yang Qianhua), it becomes difficult to recall the long period in the 1980s and 1990s when most female performers could only be beautiful vases waiting to be admired, grasped, and broken. Milkyway Image's second-phase films might be stylistically and thematically less interesting than those made in its first phase because these films are clearly made with commercial objectives and precise market calculations. Although they are women-oriented productions, their underlying gender ideology is still packed with patriarchal assumptions. Romance is still the ultimate meaning of life, and women's self-identity and esteem can be obtained only through love of or for men. *Love on a Diet*, for example, does not question women's weight control as a patriarchal value. Nor does it endorse it. But the real significance of these films resides in their awareness of the female mass audience. These second-phase Milkyway Image films at the very least address women as valuable customers with their own specific emotions and needs.

As I have delineated, Milkyway Image is the film company that has been most devoted in recent years to the examination of the masculine tradition of Hong Kong cinema. Its self-reflexive efforts are so clearly documented in early productions that these films have become crucial meta-texts for the interrogation of the gender politics of recent Hong Kong films. While Wai and To have found themselves exhausted in this exploration of the representation politics of masculinity in Hong Kong cinema, the commercial disappointment of these films also forced them to give up the genres and issues they are familiar with and commit to exploring the other segments of the market. Their earlier painstaking and futile efforts in looking for a new beginning for Hong Kong male movies led to an unsurprising re-beginning in female genres. Milkyway Image is, I would say, the most successful local film company to produce women-oriented romance and melodrama in Hong Kong cinema in recent years partly because it has invested the most in investigating its past male legacy.

This interesting development of Milkyway Image provides us with one model for understanding the complicated relationship between society and cinema. It is widely agreed that cinematic representations can by no means be treated as simple reflections of social reality, but rejecting any relation between them is unproductive. The mutual influence between society and cinematic representation is always heavily mediated, and in this case I show how the industry and a male aesthetic get in the way. As mentioned at the beginning of the chapter, since 1997 Hong Kong has been undergoing a difficult search for a socio-cultural-eco-political identity of its own. There are heated debates about the benefits of having a non-interfering government or a welfare state; a free-market economy or strategic development of chosen industries; national identity or global identity, etc. All these noisy discussions were triggered by the recent economic crisis, and the interesting self-interrogation efforts of Milkyway Image were also the result of a slump in Hong Kong cinema not seen in the last thirty years. Both the city and the cinema have been hit hard by the recession, but from the experience of Milkyway Image we discover that only through such an ordeal was it able to get through the hitherto Hong Kong cinema gender blind spot and rediscover the commercial presence of women spectators. Let us keep our fingers crossed and hope Hong Kong benefits from the economic crisis, which, I think, can be guaranteed only by a serious re-examination and interrogation of its past successes.

APPENDIX

Milkyway Image Productions, 1996–2002

《攝氏32度》 *Beyond Hypothermia*. 1996. Patrick Leung (dir.). Johnnie To (prod.). Hong Kong Box Office: HK$2,621,660.

《一個字頭的誕生》 *Too Many Ways to Be Number One*. 1997. Wai Ka-fai (dir.). Johnnie To, Wai Ka-fai (prod.) Hong Kong Box Office: HK$3,154,303.

《最後判決》 *Final Justice*. 1997. Derek Chiu (dir.). Johnnie To, Wai Ka-fai (prod.). Hong Kong Box Office: HK$788,316.

《兩個只能活一個》 *The Odd One Dies*. 1997. Patrick Yau (dir.). Johnnie To, Wai Ka-fai (prod.) Hong Kong Box Office: HK$1,717,565.

《恐怖雞》 *Intruder*. 1997. Tsang Ken-cheung (dir.). Johnnie To, Wai Ka-fai (prod.). Hong Kong Box Office: HK$487,050.

《暗花》 *The Longest Nite*. 1998. Patrick Yau (dir.). Johnnie To, Wai Ka-fai (prod.). Hong Kong Box Office: HK$9,962,090.

《非常突然》 *Expect the Unexpected*. 1998. Patrick Yau (dir.). Johnnie To, Wai Ka-fai (prod.). Hong Kong Box Office: HK$5,359,800.

《真心英雄》 *A Hero Never Dies*. 1998. Johnnie To (dir.). Johnnie To, Wai Ka-fai (prod.). Hong Kong Box Office: HK$6,792,090.

《再見阿郎》 *Where a Good Man Goes*. 1999. Johnnie To (dir.). Johnnie To, Wai Ka-fai (prod.). Hong Kong Box Office: HK$3,804,320.

《暗戰》 *Running Out of Time*. 1999. Johnnie To (dir.). Johnnie To, Wai Ka-fai (prod.). Hong Kong Box Office: HK$14,659,574.

《鎗火》 *The Mission*. 1999. Johnnie To (dir.). Johnnie To, Wai Ka-fai (prod.). Hong Kong Box Office: HK$4,618,946.

《甜言蜜語》 *Sealed with a Kiss*. 1999. Derek Chiu (dir.) (prod.). Hong Kong Box Office: HK$1,498,075.

《無人駕駛》 *Spacked Out*. 2000. Lawrence Lau (dir.). Johnnie To (prod.). Hong Kong Box Office: HK$1,358,108.

《孤男寡女》 *Needing You*. 2000. Johnnie To, Wai Ka-fai (dir.) (prod.). Hong Kong Box Office: HK$35,214,661.

《辣手回春》 *Help!!!* 2000. Johnnie To, Wai Ka-fai (dir.) (prod.). Hong Kong Box Office: HK$14,219,885.

《天有眼》 *Comeuppance*. 2000. Derek Chiu (dir.). Johnnie To (prod.). Hong Kong Box Office: HK$243,650.

《鍾無艷》 *Wu Yen*. 2001. Johnnie To, Wai Ka-fai (dir.) (prod.). Hong Kong Box Office: HK$27,241,696.

《愛上我吧》 *Gimme Gimme*. 2001. Lawrence Lau (dir.). Johnnie To (prod.). Hong Kong Box Office: HK$211,560.

《無限復活》 *Second Time Around*. 2001. Jeff Lau (dir.). Johnnie To (prod.). Hong Kong Box Office: HK$4,006,900.

《瘦身男女》 *Love on a Diet*. 2001. Johnnie To, Wai Ka-fai (dir.) (prod.). Hong Kong Box Office: HK$40,435,886.

《全職殺手》 *Fulltime Killer*. 2001. Johnnie To, Wai Ka-fai (dir.). Johnnie To, Wai Ka-fai and Andy Lau (prod.). Hong Kong Box Office: HK$25,682,414.

《男歌女唱》 *Let's Sing Along*. 2001. Matt Chow (dir.) (prod.). Hong Kong Box Office: HK$1,272,185.

《暗戰2》 *Running Out of Time 2*. 2001. Johnnie To, Law Wing-cheong (dir.). Johnnie To (prod.). Hong Kong Box Office: HK$5,900,000.

《嚦咕嚦咕新年財》 *Fat Choi Spirit*. 2002. Johnnie To, Wai Ka-fai (dir.) (prod.). Hong Kong Box Office: HK$19,200,000.

《我左眼見到鬼》 *My Left Eye Sees Ghosts*. 2002. Johnnie To, Wai Ka-fai (dir.) (prod.). Hong Kong Box Office: HK$20,700,000.

3

Queering Masculinity in Hong Kong Movies

Travis S. K. Kong

In the history of Hong Kong movies it has been possible only to hint at homosexuality or to pathologize it. However, since the 1990s more diverse representations of gay and lesbian culture have slowly emerged. *Happy Together* (Chunguang zhaxie) (dir. Wong Kar-wai, 1997) features a gorgeous gay couple, Leslie Cheung (Zhang Guorong) and Tony Leung Chiu-wai (Liang Chaowei), who, bored with their lives, embark on a trip to Buenos Aires to save their relationship. Resembling HBO's TV hit series *Sex and the City*, the Now.Com series *20/30 Dictionary* features To Man-chat (Du Wenze), one of the protagonists, as an "out, loud and beautiful" type gay man. Apparently there is an increasing appearance in movies of major or supporting gay, lesbian or other characters from sexual minorities (i.e., glbt[1]). For example, *Oh! My Three Guys* (Sange xiang'ai de shaonian) (dir. Derek Chiu, 1994); *Boy's?* (Jianan jianü) (dir. Hau Wing-choi, 1996); *A Queer Story* (Jilao sishi) (dir. Shu Kei, 1997); *Intimates* (Zishu) (dir. Cheung Chi-leung, 1997); *Bishonen* (Mei shaonian zhi lian) (dir. Yonfan, 1998); *Portland Street Blues* (Hongxing shisan mei) (dir. Raymond Yip, 1998); *The Map of Sex and Love* (Qingse ditu) (dir. Evans Chan, 2001); *Lan Yu* (dir. Stanley Kwan, 2001); *Peony Pavilion* (Youyuan jingmeng) (dir. Yonfan, 2001); *Night Corridor* (Yaoye huilang) (dir. Julian Lee, 2003).

Does this mean increased "gay visibility" is providing an unbiased representation of the glbt community, offering new cultural icons for glbt youths, enhancing tolerance in society or even increasing the growing recognition of demands for civil rights for glbt? Or is this increasing visibility of glbt characters merely a ploy of capitalism in which "sexual difference" is commodified and glbt characters simply absorbed into straight culture, which in turn transforms subversive resistance to mere consumption?

In this chapter I attempt to understand the meanings and significance of the growing "gay visibility" in Hong Kong movies since the 1990s. In particular, I will focus on discussing gay men or gay male cinematic images in relation to masculinity, although references will be made to other sexual minorities where appropriate. Based on my theoretical standpoint of post-structuralism[2] and queer theory,[3] I will first argue that gay male identities have always been subordinated to the disciplinary notion of heterosexuality and hegemonic masculinity, but that the social construction of straight male sexuality has never been fully established. I will ascertain that popular culture is a contested terrain in which dominance is never securely held but must constantly be won. My theoretical reservoir enables me to view text as polysemic and subject position as heterogeneous. This thus allows me to demonstrate how gay male images are being represented, disciplined and policed under the logic of heterosexism and capitalist consumption, rather than offering a "correct" queer reading of these films from the viewpoint of a queer academic, or the "queering" of Hong Kong films from the perspective of a member of the glbt community.

Second, I will argue that Hong Kong movies always have a dual, contradictory nature in terms of homosexuality. Governed by the logic of heterosexism and hegemonic masculinity, Hong Kong movies are saturated with homophobic ideology and male homosexuals are stigmatized as deviants, campy sexual perverts, victims or villains. At the same time, however, a trend of homophilia has been operating in partial resistance to the hegemony of homophobia. Different forms of gay visibility — ambiguous gender-blending, the implication of a homosexual subtext under a "homosocial overcoat," or even the direct addressing of homosexual love — will be discussed. However, I will ascertain that this rise in "gay visibility" should not be seen as overturning the ideological tenets of heterosexuality, but rather as working along the parameters of the logic of hegemonic masculinity and heterosexism, and the commodity logic of capitalism.

MASCULINITY, REPRESENTATION AND QUEER THEORY

The conventional uses of the term masculinity arise from a series of explicit and implicit premises. First, the notion of masculinity is based on a rigid gender system of two sexes (male and female), in which masculinity is defined in opposition to femininity. Gendered identities (man and woman) with "appropriate" attributes are derived from this gender regime. For example, the alleged masculine attributes of men are physical prowess, virility, independence, aggressiveness, competitiveness, objectivity, rationality and emotional controllability; the alleged feminine attributes of women meanwhile are passivity, fragility, non-aggressiveness, non-competitiveness, sensitivity, nurturance, intuitiveness and emotional liability.

Second, the notion of masculinity is defined along the axis of sexuality, which presumes that "normal" sexual orientation and identity is heterosexuality. To be a "man" is to be a heterosexual (straight) man. The common-sense logic of homosexuality is thus simple: under the confines of the gender/sex role regime that conflates heterosexual orientation with masculine identity, being gay means lacking masculinity. If someone is attracted to the masculine, that person must be feminine, if not in body (the biological explanation), then somehow in the mind (the psychological explanation).

By assuming a unifying logic of the male (the biological), maleness (the sexual) and masculinity (the social), the idea of masculinity is essentialised and universalized. The result is the notions of "real men," "natural men" or "deep masculinity" that exist across cultures and historical periods. Thus, masculinity appears as "an essence or commodity, which can be measured, possessed or lost."[4] This essentialist conception of masculinity has come under attack from many disciplines as well as political forces.[5]

Drawing from Gramsci's original concept of hegemony in the context of class relations, Connell[6] provided a powerful account of how we can incorporate power into an analysis of gender and sexual relations by articulating the notion of hegemonic masculinity, which, as he argued, refers to a cultural strategy that some people (mainly men) are required to use in order to inhabit positions of power and wealth and to legitimate and reproduce the social relationships that generate their dominance. This successful strategy not only guarantees the subordination of women in a society, but also defines other masculine styles as inadequate or inferior. Connell refers to these other masculine styles as "subordinate variants." Just as women, "by default," are excluded in the first place, there are numerous men who comprise the subordinate variants. They include, for example, young working-class men without regular jobs who thus fail to perform the traditional role of breadwinner. Male homosexuals, according to the traditional definition, "lack" masculinity altogether. Hegemonic masculinity tends to place gay masculinity at the bottom of the male gender hierarchy.

Hegemonic masculinity is closely related to heterosexism. While homophobia is a deep antipathy, disgust or dislike of homosexuals, heterosexism is:

> *a diverse set of social practices* — from the linguistic to the physical, in the public sphere and the private sphere, covert and overt — *in an array of social arenas* (e.g. work, home, school, media, church, courts, streets, etc.), *in which the homo/hetero binary distinction is at work whereby heterosexuality is privileged.*[7]

Heterosexism, or in Adrienne Rich's term "compulsory heterosexuality,"[8] is a social system like capitalism or racism in which our sexual preference has never been a "free choice" but "something that has had to be imposed, managed, organized, propagandized, and maintained by force."[9] In *Gender Trouble*, Judith Butler[10] offers a strong critique of the system of "compulsory heterosexuality," which normalises a bipolar sex/gender system. She contests the very notion that gender originates from sex and argues that gender is produced by a ritualised repetition of conventions, and that this ritual is socially compelled, in part, by the force of compulsory heterosexuality. The performance of gender is produced retroactively by the illusion that there is an inner gender core or natural sex, the effect of some true or abiding sexual essence or disposition. Women and men are forced to conform to a binary men/women or masculine/feminine opposition (what she calls "heterosexual matrix") that appears to be natural.

Lesbians and gay men identify homophobia and heterosexism ("compulsory heterosexuality," "heterosexual matrix," or more generally, "heteronormativity") as the main forms of oppression from masculine and heterosexual society. There is wide evidence of the domination by heterosexual men of lesbians and gay men; for instance, in political and cultural exclusion; legal and street violence; economic discrimination and personal boycotts.[11] Oppressive structures not only abuse lesbians and gay men on a personal level but also define a boundary around "real" sexuality by the negation of homosexuality.

Masculinized and heterosexist practices are thus accompanied by a whole conglomerate of connected institutions. Gay masculinity is subordinated under the construct of hegemonic masculinity, while gay identity is also subordinated under the regime of heterosexism. Thus, the Hong Kong gay male identity is doubly subordinated under these gendered and sexed institutions.

In popular culture gay men are always represented as "hysterical men." They are usually alleged to be "fashion victims," almost always over-dressed and expected to hang around in highly westernized places such as Lan Kwai Fong.[12] Furthermore, popular culture enjoys this violent voyeurism and administers a heteronormative form of discipline in the framing of its homophobic reports and stories. Under this kind of voyeurism, gay sex is the focal point of "examination." Anal sex, group sex or public sex in the gay lifestyle is always exaggerated, and gay men are alleged to be promiscuous and thus responsible for the spread of AIDS. By positioning heterosexuals and homosexuals in two antagonistic and oppositional positions, popular culture successfully stigmatizes the latter as deviant.[13]

Roland Barthes[14] has persuasively argued that popular myth normalizes ideological meanings and ratifies the social status quo. Likewise, Bourdieu[15] employed the notion of *habitus* to refer to social power, which causes us to.regard the status quo as inevitable and natural, and thus justifies our taste and class distinction. We are living in a world of "social games embodied and turned into second nature."[16] Similarly, Foucault[17] argued that the subject (e.g., the "homosexual") is constructed "as an effect" through and within the rules of formation, and that discourses employ "modalities of enunciation" under professional "regimes of truth" (e.g., psychiatry, medicine and biology). Originally discussing how prisoners learn to internalize the idea of spectacle in terms of discipline, Foucault's discourse of power/knowledge[18] in effect culminates to assure us that individuals internalize specific values, and that this can be related more widely to experiences of other "docile bodies." Bartky[19] has argued that the subjectivity of women has been formulated under the process of social "surveillance" and objectification, just as in the case of the prisoner who is being watched. Fanon[20] made a similar observation of black people and their internalized self-hatred that has resulted from racism, in the way they negatively frame their experiences. Likewise, the administration of a heteronormative discipline seems to have been internalized into the lives of some gay men in the form of internal homophobia.[21]

However, no matter how explicit political leanings, sexuality or agendas might be, the social construction of sexuality has never been fully installed. If Foucault is right, "power is tolerable only on condition that it masks a substantial part of itself. Its success is proportional to its ability to hide its own mechanism."[22] Ideology is the winning and securing of hegemony over time. As suggested by Hall, "It is crucial to the concept that hegemony is not a 'given' and permanent state of affairs, but it has to be actively won and secured; it can also be lost."[23]

This is where the whole gay and lesbian movement challenges heterosexism and emphasizes the notion of community building, personal identity and lifestyle.[24] Counter-hegemonic tendencies not only inhere solely in social resistance, but also happen in text.

Barthes later argued that texts are indeed polysemic.[25] They are open to more than one reading, and there is no necessary correspondence between the message encoded by the film or programme maker and that decoded by audiences. Audiences are seen as producers of meaning, rather than just consumers of media. We decode or interpret media texts in ways that are related to our social and cultural circumstances and to the ways in which we subjectively experience those circumstances. The structured field (e.g., patriarchy, racism, sexism, heterosexism, hegemonic masculinity, etc.) constructs our viewing positions and identities, and reveals nothing but the will of power. However, it is deemed to be open since it is constantly being subverted by practices, writings, speech and *habitus*.[26]

Traditional cultural readings tend to overlook the dynamics of sexual preference. The ability of power to mask itself ironically is also the mechanism that produces pleasure. Pleasure is never innocent or neutral.[27] Although gay men and lesbians may internalize the heterosexual codes they nevertheless actively "queer" the straight codes for their own purposes and even find "secret" pleasures in texts that may appear ostensibly heterosexual. This practice of "reading against the grain" — "any text is always already potentially queer" — is one that recognizes the preferred meaning of the text while realizing the possibilities of alternative pleasures.[28]

The practice of "reading against the grain" has been widely discussed by cultural theorists (e.g., Benjamin[29]), feminist film critics (e.g., Kotsopoulos[30]) and in subaltern studies (e.g., Spivak[31]). However, this practice tends to assume that identity is a homogenous entity and favors the perspective of an essentialised spectatorship or readership (in this case, a "gay spectator."[32]) Post-structuralist and queer theory enables me to take the view that any social group (including the so-called glbt community) is heterogeneous and that even a single individual occupies multiple subject positions. Without an analysis of the glbt community, this chapter is not an attempt to "queer" the straights from the glbt community; nor is it a "correct" queer reading from a queer academic. Instead, I will discuss from a queer perspective how gay images are represented, disciplined and policed. The question becomes not whether gay men find pleasure from the proliferation of gay images in Hong Kong films, but rather how one might read and understand such pleasure.

The term "queer," nevertheless, needs clarification. The traditional terms "gay" or "lesbian" suggest that there is a polarized division between hetero- and homo-sexuality. These terms are often referred to and used by people who are white and middle class. By contrast, the term "queer" embraces a multiplicity of sexualities by including people of other "non-conventional" sexualities such as bisexuals, transvestites, pre- and post-op transsexuals; it also recognizes other "outcast" positions along racial, ethnic and class lines. Thus, "queer" includes "deviants" and "perverts" who may subvert hetero/homo divisions and go beyond conventional delineations of sexual identity as well as other non-sexual normative practices. As opposed to the more fixed meaning of terms such as homosexual (a medical description), or gay/lesbian (a white and middle-class description), queer is an identity always under construction.[33]

Queer theory means post-structuralism/post-modernism as applied to sexualities and genders. A post-structuralist understanding of identity suggests that the identity of an object or a person is always implicated in its opposite; i.e., the logic of identity is a logic of defining boundaries, which necessarily produces a subordinated other. In terms of sexuality the heterosexual identity that is taken for granted is produced at the expense of its subordinated Other, a binarized and stigmatized homosexual identity. Mainstream homosexual theory views homosexuality as the property of an individual or group. This property, or identity, is explained either as being natural (the essentialist position, which claims there is some "essence" within homosexuals that makes them that way; i.e., some gay "core" of their being, their psyche or their genetic make-up) or social (the constructionist position, which claims that "homosexual," "gay" or "lesbian" are just labels created by cultures and applied to the self). Queer theorists argue that both approaches have favored a view of homosexuality as the condition of a social minority. Queer theory, however, treats the heterosexual/homosexual binary as a master framework for constructing the self, sexual knowledge and social institutions. This binary sex system, or power/knowledge regime, creates rigid psychological and social boundaries that inevitably give rise to systems of dominance and hierarchical organization.[34] However, as argued by Butler, the social construction of sexuality is never fully recognised. The rigid dualism of men/women or masculine/feminine is constantly being disrupted and undermined by people who do not conform to the simple binary opposition of women and men (e.g. hetero, gay, lesbian, and bi sexualities). For example, a butch dyke who dresses like a man or a drag queen who masquerades as a woman is neither a chimerical representation of originally heterosexual identities nor "the pernicious insistence of hetrosexist constructs within gay sexuality and identity … gay is to straight *not* as copy is to original, but, rather, as copy is to copy."[35] The idea of gender as a regulatory ideal is no more than "a norm or a fiction that disguises itself as a developmental law regulating the sexual field that it purports to describe."[36]

As argued by Hennessy,[37] it is necessary to distinguish the various uses of the term queer as a newly emerging theory in the realm of cultural studies (i.e., queer theory), as an avant-garde gay and lesbian subculture, and as a new form of radical sexual political activism (e.g., Queer Nation). Rather than discussing the reception of queer — gay, lesbian, bisexual, transsexual, etc. — "communities" in Hong Kong, this chapter will deal with only the first sense of the word queer; i.e. I will discuss how academic queer theory helps us to look at issues of representation (gay male images in Hong Kong movies). As argued by Raymond[38] in her discussion of gay images in U.S. television, if the homo/hetero schema is "written into the cultural organization of Western societies,"[39] then the primary question is not so much the question of identity but rather "the homosexual/heterosexual matrix."[40] Such a perspective would be less about the question of how many gay/queer characters populate Hong Kong movies or even how sympathetically they are portrayed but "rather about the ways desire and meaning are structured, even in the absence of such images."[41]

It is thus the aim of this chapter to argue that the increasing proliferation of gay images and those of the far less threatening homosexuals since the 1990s might suggest the possibility of new normative understandings of sexual difference, even though most of these images are largely normalized within a heterosexist matrix.

This proliferation can be accounted for by two factors. The first is the decriminalization of homosexuality in 1990 (i.e., the removal of criminal penalties for homosexual acts committed in private by two consenting men older than twenty-one). The decriminalization of homosexuality not only protected people legally but also triggered first the mushrooming of gay and lesbian organizations and the establishment of different venues of entertainment for gay men (such as night clubs, saunas, karaokes, etc.), both of which provided meeting places for the constitution of a gay "community."[42]

Second is the commodification of identity (and the male body), a development originating in the West that has spread through the process of globalization and been driven by the commodity logic of capitalism.[43] In contrast with Western aesthetics of masculinity the Chinese ideal has always been the desexualized male body. In mainstream popular culture in Hong Kong the naked male body is seldom exposed. When a stripped man appears it is usually in a comedy.[44] From the 1980s onwards the naked male body has been increasingly displayed and sexualized in Western (and thus Hong Kong) popular culture.[45] As argued by Chang,[46] this new trend of queering or appealing to gay and lesbian communities is "a process of appropriating queer subcultural codes for commercial purposes or a way of baiting the queer consumer group."[47] Some advertisers even deploy a dual market strategy, which is "to attract the queer consumer in a way that will not offend heterosexist society."[48] Popular culture such as depicted in MTV (e.g., Madonna's *Justify My Love* and George Michael's *Fast Love*) and in magazines (e.g., *The Face, I-D, Wallpaper*) tends to market both sexes and produce "polysemic" imageries of pop stars and fashion models. This, in turn, allows the spectator the possibility of multiple sexual identifications. As argued by Evans and Gammon, "They gave readers 'permission' to be promiscuous with images, and they permitted images to function ambiguously, and thereby to speak to a range of different subject positions."[49]

This commodification of identity and the male body is having two significant effects. One is the increasing integration of the dual moments of "queering the straights and straightening the queers."[50] That is, a new trend of eroticizing men's bodies and even "homoeroticizing" the tastes and styles of straight consumers has been increasingly featured in films, advertising and fashion. At the same time, there is also another trend of assimilating gay men into the mainstream. As Sinfield argues, this is "the 'good homosexual' — the kind, who, unlike the 'dangerous queer,' makes him — or herself — indistinguishable from heterosexuals."[51] It is through these dual moments that sexualities are commodified and sexual difference is "dissolved."

Second, as noted by Kellner, "Difference sells. Capitalism must constantly multiply markets, styles, fads and artefacts to keep absorbing consumers into its practices and lifestyles."[52] hooks[53] was right to point out that the commodification of difference functions to silence resistance and transform subversive potentials to consumption. Like tourists, a straight audience views a gay character in a film as if they were "visiting" glbt communities without necessarily changing their straight minds.

In contrast to the new queer cinema of the West in the early 1990s (e.g., *Poison* [Todd Haynes, USA, 1991]; *Swoon* [Tom Kalin, USA, 1992]; *Rock Hudson's Home Movies* [Mark Rappaport, USA, 1992]; *The Living End* [Gregg Araki, USA, 1992]; *Desert Heart* [Donna Deitch, USA, 1985]; *Go Fish* [Rose Troche, USA, 1994]; *Mala Noche* [Gus Van Sant, USA, 1985]; *The Hours and Times* [Christopher Münch, USA, 1991]; *The Attendant* [Isaac Julien, UK, 1993]; *Garden* [Derek Jarman, UK, 1990]; *Edward II* [Derek Jarman, UK, 1991]), which is primarily the product of self-identified gay or lesbian independent filmmakers consciously committed to a radical politics, Hong Kong films that touch on the issue of homosexuality can hardly be considered "independent." Rather, these films are made for and consumed by the mainstream audience.[54]

QUEER AS FOLK

Hong Kong movies, especially popular action/comedy films, are full of sexist, even misogynistic, as well as homophobic, dialogue and content. Male homosexuals are always ridiculed as "sissies," the underlying idea being that they are a "woman's soul trapped in a man's body." Examples are numerous, Simon Loui (Lei Yuyang) in *The Sting* (Xiasheng) (dir. Wong Man-wan, 1992), Simon Yam (Ren Dahua) in *Full Contact* (Xiadao gaofei) (dir. Ringo Lam, 1992), Cheng Dan-shui (Zheng Danrui) and Chow Man-kin (Zhou Wenjian) in *Tom, Dick and Hairy* (Fengchen sanxia) (dir. Peter Chan and Lee Chi-ngai, 1993), Michael Wong (Wang Minde) in *I'm Your Birthday Cake* (Budaode de liwu) (dir. Raymond Yip, 1995), Wyman Wong (Huang Weiwen) in *Killing Me Tenderly* (Aini aidao shasini) (dir. Lee Lik-chi, 1997), or Eason Chan (Chen Yixun) in *Lavender* (Xunyi cao) (dir. Yip Kam-hung, 2000). In addition, homosexuals are mocked as if they were a kind of sexual pervert, or even a psychopath like Hu Jin-gwan (Xu yanjun) in *Crazy* (Siji sharenkuang 2 chi nanfeng) (dir. Hau Wing-choi, 1999). A gay man is always equated with AIDS and anal sex (e.g., *Pantyhose Hero*, dir. Sammo Hung, 1990). A Hong Kong gay man is usually stereotypically portrayed as a bitchy, campy, over-dressed and Westernized young man who hangs around the alleged gay "ghetto," Lan Kwai Fong. These characters usually appear in a minor role as victims or victimizers, and are killed off at the end of the film.

Parallel to this, however, is a new trend. Homosexuality in popular culture has become increasingly visible since the 1990s. This visibility takes different forms: ambiguous gender-blending, an implicit homosexual subtext under a "homosocial overcoat," or even the direct addressing of homosexual love.

Gender Blending

In Chinese traditional folktales, many characters, whether they are human beings, deities or ghosts, exhibit gender ambivalence because they can change, reverse or even transform their genders.[55] Inspired by these folktales Chinese operas constantly display this trans-gender tradition. In fact, in traditional Peking Operas, both male characters (*sheng*) and female characters (*dan*) were usually played by male actors. The most successful and famous actor who dressed and played as a woman onstage was Mei Lanfang.[56] In Cantonese operas both characters were usually played by females. Perhaps the best-known actress, Yam Kim-fai, spent her life playing men both on and off screen. Popular folktales, which tell of gender ambivalence, might increase people's tolerance of transgenderism. The traditional constructs of Chinese masculinity might also contribute to acceptance. Chinese masculinity has been constructed around two intertwining ideals — the *wen* ideal ("cultured behavior, refinement, mastery of scholarly work") and the *wu* ideal ("martial prowess, strength, mastery of physical arts.")[57] Yam Kim-fai, typical of the first type, always portrayed Chinese men who were weak, bookish, elegant and also asexual.

Hong Kong movies in the 1950s and 1960s were largely dominated by melodramas in which, unusually, the leading characters were females rather than males. It was very common at the time to watch actresses (e.g., Yam Kim-fai, Lung Kim-sun or Connie Chan Po-chu) play the leading male character. Although the popularity of Chinese operas has subsided in Hong Kong in the past two decades, the pattern of gender reversal (male characters played by female actresses or vice versa) has occasionally been repeated in popular media such as TV soap dramas or in films. In the early 1990s, some films seemed to be bringing back the tradition of crossing genders.[58]

The film *Swordsman II* (Xiao'ao jianghu II zhi Dongfang Bubai) (dir. Ching Siu-tung, 1992) was adapted from an action-fantasy novel. Asia the Invincible (*Dongfang Bubai*; played by Brigitte Lin) is a wicked man who wants to control the world. Indeed, in the novel, he is the metaphorical figure of China's former chairman, Mao Zedong. In order to learn superb kung fu from the Sacred Scroll (葵花寶典), he castrates himself and becomes more and more feminine. He then falls in love with the major male character Linghu Chong (played by Jet Li). Using his mistress to cover up his true sexual identity, Asia the Invincible has a one-night stand with Linghu Chong. But when Linghu Chong later finds out he is a man, Linghu Chong is shocked and keeps asking if he had sex with him or with his mistress. Asia the Invincible never tells Linghu Chong the truth and, at the end of the film, he is defeated by Linghu Chong and falls off a cliff.

Apart from its political metaphorical intent, the tale is basically a love story between two men. When the film was released in 1992 it was a hit in the gay and straight communities. The story of a gay man (especially a closeted one) who has a crush on a straight man but whose homosexual infatuation is doomed to failure resonates with a lot of gay men.[59] Nevertheless, the film operates under the logic of homophobia and heterosexism. At the end of the film, when Asia the Invincible is defeated and falls off a cliff, Linghu Chong tries to rescue him but keeps asking if he was the one with whom he slept. Linghu Chong's worry can be accounted for by his fear that he has messed up his life by sleeping with a man or by his repressed homosexuality. What is more important is that this direct expression of homosexual love does not offend a straight audience. This is because Asia the Invincible assumes a feminine role, and thus the rigid gender binary (a masculine/feminine pair) has not been challenged. In addition, Asia the Invincible is played by the stunning actress Brigitte Lin (Lin Qingxia), and even though we know "she" is supposed to be a "man" in the film, what the audience watches on the screen is a flirtation between two heterosexuals. Using cross-gender as a camouflage, the film creates a space for the visibility of gay sexuality on screen.[60]

Following the capitalist logic of profit making, many films have followed this punch line and have produced many similar gay and lesbian characters using gender-reversal roles. Such roles take many forms, as discussed in the following.

Men in drag always appear in comedies (e.g., Tang Gei-chan, Sun Mak-tse) and the gimmick seems to be performed at the expense of sexual fantasy. *Farewell My Concubine* (Bawang bieji) (dir. Chen Kaige, China, 1993), on the other hand, is a serious film based on a novel written by the Hong Kong author, Li Bihua (1986). It tells the sad story of a gay Beijing opera performer (Cheng Dieyi) who falls in love with his long-time stage partner (Duan Xiaolou), who is a straight man. The two never get together. Cheng was played by Leslie Cheung, who had not yet come out to the public at the time he played the role. However, he had always been alleged to be gay and his "delicate sensitivity"[61] ensured an elegant performance in drag.

In *Boy's?*, one of the three gay protagonists, Joey (played by Chan Kwok-bong), meets a straight man, Edmond (played by Leung Hong-man), when he is in drag. They fall madly in love but after discovering that Edmond is homophobic, Joey decides to terminate the relationship.

Living under the dominant ideal of heterosexual intimacy implies that Hong Kong gay men engage with a hegemonically embodied masculinity in which the "ideal" man is one who is physically fit, straight-acting, macho, non-feminine and economically secure. Meanwhile, the popular "ideal" gay man, a derivative of Western gay masculinity, is one who acts straight, and is young and physically fit. Therefore, both hegemonic masculinity in the straight world and hegemonic gay masculinity in the gay world determine the objects of desire of gay Hong Kong men and their possibility of forming a relationship.[62] If falling in love with a straight man is a fantasy held by gay men, dragging as a woman is a solution. If Cheng in *Farewell My Concubine* represents a traditional gay man's futile attempt at "loving the impossible," Joey in *Boy's?* might represent a modern gay man who searches for his new love by rejecting the traditional view that a gay man is a would-be woman and asserts the new erotic logic of a "man loving a man."

Men in drag always perform a comedic function; however, women in drag seem to suggest the opposite. We have a long history of female cross-dressing. In the past, we had Yam Kim-fai, Lung Kim-sun (Long Jiansheng) and Connie Chan Po-chu (Chen Baochu). In traditional martial arts it is convenient for women to cross-dress in order to fight; e.g., Cheng Pei-pei (Zheng Peipei) in *Come Drink with Me* (Da zuixia) (dir. King Hu, 1966), Shangguan Lingfeng in *Dragon Gate Inn* (Longmen kezhan) (dir. King Hu, 1967) and *18 Bronze men* (Shaolinsi shiba tongren) (dir. Kuo Nam-hong, 1976) or even Zhang Ziyi in *Crouching Tiger, Hidden Dragon* (Wohu canglong) (dir. Ang Lee, 2000). After *Swordsman II*, Brigitte Lin constantly played in drag on screen, and suddenly became Hong Kong's Marlene Dietrich; e.g., in *Deadful Melody*

(Liuzhi qinmo) (dir. Ng Min-kan, 1994), *Handsome Siblings* (Juedai shuangjiao) (dir. Eric Tsang, 1992), and *The Three Swordsmen* (Daojian xiao) (dir. Wong Tai-loi, 1994). Long before *Swordsman II* she also cross-dressed in *Peking Opera Blues* (Daomadan; dir. Tsui Hark; 1986). Other obvious examples include Pat Ha (Xia Wenxi), who played the role of Kawashima Yoshiko (Chuandao Fangzi) in *Flag of Horror* (Fenghuo jiaren) (dir. Ding Sin-saai, 1987), and Anita Mui (Mei Yanfang), who played Kawashima Yoshiko in *Kawashima Yoshiko* (Chuandao Fangzi) (dir. Fong Ling-ching, 1990).

A common comedic plot involves a woman masquerading as a man who creates homosexual tension when she befriends a man. The classical example is *The Lovers* (Liangzhu) (dir. Tsui Hark, 1994), based on the traditional story, "The Butterfly Lovers."[63] No matter how "stupid" or "closeted" Liang might be, the story is a great tragedy because both characters finally die. *He's a Woman, She's a Man* (Jinzhi yuye) (dir. Peter Chan, 1994) tells the story of a girl (Lam Chi-wing, played by Anita Yuen) who disguises herself as a man and wins a singing contest. She then moves in to her producer's apartment and the producer Koo Ka-ming (played by Leslie Cheung) and his lover, the famous singer, Rose (played by Carina Lau Kar-ling), both fall in love with her. Wing then tells Rose she is a "gay man" and thus transforms their relationship into one of "sisterhood love," while Ka-ming worries about his homosexual attraction to Wing. Even the recent *Chinese Odyssey* (Tianxia wushuang; dir. Jeff Lau; 2002) tells a similar tale. Based on a legend, a princess of the Ming Dynasty bored with palace life escapes with her brother. They head south and reach a village. The princess (played by Faye Wong), disguised as a man, meets a trouble-maker (played by Tony Leung Chiu-wai) and his boyish sister (played by Chiu Mei). The boyish sister has a crush on her but the princess is attracted to the brother, who also has a crush on her but is fighting his feelings so he doesn't run the risk of entering a homosexual relationship. Although these films have different endings, all the male characters (Nicky Wu, Leslie Cheung, Tony Leung) *resolve* their homosexual infatuations by finally coming to the realization that the object of their love is female. Moreover, the three female characters disguised as men are all beautiful women (Yeung Choi-nei, Anita Yuen, Faye Wong). Even a straight audience would not find this offensive.

Likewise, the story of a woman masquerading as a man and developing a crush on a woman is basically a lesbian love story. A classic example is Yam Kim-fai and Baak Suet-sin (Bai Xuexian). Recent examples include Anita Mui (Mei Yanfang) and Anita Yuen (Yuan Yongyi) in *Who's the Woman, Who's the Man?* (Jinzhi yuye) (dir. Peter Chan, 1994) Joey Wong (Wang Zuxian) and Brigitte Lin in *Swordsman III: The East is Red* (Dongfang Bubai zhi Fengyun zaiqi) (dir. Ching Siu-tung and Lee Wai-man, 1993), Josephine Siao Fong-fong (Xiao Fangfang) and Woo Wai-chung (Hu Huizhong) in *Fong Sai Yuk* (Fang Shiyu) (dir. Yuen Kwai, 1992). Judging by our long tradition of females in drag as men, this seems to be what most audiences are most "comfortable" viewing.

Other interesting cross-gender examples can be seen in *All's Well Ends Well* (Jia you xishi) (dir. Ko Chi-sum, 1992), in which an effeminate man (played by Leslie Cheung) and a butch woman (played by Teresa Mo) are a couple with reversed roles. In *A Chinese Ghost Story* (Qiannü youhun) (dir. Ching Siu-tung, 1987), Lau Siu-ming (Liu Shaoming) plays the androgynous Tree Demon (Laolao), while in *Ashes of Time* (Dongxie xidu) (dir. Wong Kar-wai, 1994), Brigitte Lin plays the androgynous and schizophrenic Mr Murong Yan and Ms Murong Yan.

Although these various forms of camouflage — whether a man in drag infatuated with a man, or a woman in drag generating homosexual tension in another man (or similarly, a man in drag attracted to a woman or a woman in drag with a crush on another woman) — open up a space for homosexual identification from various view points and subject positions, homosexual passion is still forced to hide behind rigid sexual and gender roles.

The logic behind this seems to be that a biological male (or female) should acquire masculine (or feminine) attributes and so should also be attracted to the opposite sex. Combining sex (male/female), gender (masculine/feminine) and sexuality (heterosexuality/homosexuality) in a formula not only stigmatizes other sexual "non-conformers" (e.g., a butch woman or an effeminate man) but also limits the fluidity of our sexualities.[64] Sedgwick is right to point out that "when something is about masculinity, it is not always 'about men.'"[65] Rather than treating masculinity and femininity as two opposite poles, Sedgwick argues that it is perhaps better understood in terms of threshold effects; i.e., "places where quantitative increments along one dimension can suddenly appear as qualitative differences somewhere else on the map entirely."[66] So how is it possible to recognize the dynamic struggle between, on the one hand, the biological absolutes of what we (more or less) always are and, on the other hand, the notion of free play in that we are made up of femininities and masculinities, as most constructionists remind us? To overcome this is to ask bluntly, "Would you be able to love me if I … ?"

Men to Men — Homosocial Overcoat[67]

Homosexual love seems to be "normalized" when masculine and feminine gender roles are sustained by a performance of gender reversal.[68] Is there, however, any room for love between two masculine men in popular culture?

Although there are different ideological connotations between a homosocial man and a homosexual man, or being "a man's man" and being a man who is "interested in men,"[69] a space for the male homosocial/homosexual imagination is opened up in popular culture, especially in some Hong Kong action films that emphasize male bonding.

The most obvious movies to turn to, those of Bruce Lee (Li Xiaolong), usually focus on the thesis of how nationalism relates to Chinese masculinity. As argued by Chan,[70] contrary to most James Bond movies, Bruce Lee's heroic characters are not overtly sexually intimate with the female characters. Instead of using any technologically advanced gadgets (e.g., guns, the typical phallic symbol of the West) to aid him, he uses his own abilities (his own body) to defeat his opponents. In addition, Lee's films are also interesting cases for examining homosexuality and masculinity. As noted by Chan, "On the one hand, his masculinity is defined in contrast to the traitorous gay characters in the film (e.g., Mr Woo in *Fists of Fury*, 1971). On the other hand, his characters do not demonstrate an outright rejection of homosexuality because he does not show any overt objection towards the sexual objectification of his body by gay men."[71]

Zhang Che, a major filmmaker of martial arts in the 1970s, might be right to point out that the traditional hero, following the *wu* ideal of Chinese masculinity, does not show any explicit sexual intimacy with women, and is more concerned with his male friends. Zhang's films (e.g., *The Heroic Ones*, 1970; *Blood Brothers*, 1973) focus largely on men and male friendships, and there is a strong emphasis on phallic weapons (e.g., swords), bodily penetration and even disembowelment.[72]

His successor may be the internationally acclaimed filmmaker, John Woo (Wu Yusen). As noticed by Stringer,[73] Woo's films usually repress sexuality rather than place it at the forefront. Like Lee and Zhang, Woo refuses to assert phallic power through the spectacle of a pumped-up hard body. He tries to redefine a new model of masculinity that celebrates both strength and intimacy. He shows relationships where "male bonding can suggest an erotic charge without the associated anxiety such relationships often trigger within the Hollywood action genre."[74]

The action films of John Woo, who is well known for his Hollywood hits *Broken Arrow* (1996) and *Face/Off* (1997), always highlight intense emotional bonding among men. For example, *The Killer* (Diexue Shuangxiong) (dir. John Woo, 1989) tells the story of a killer about to carry out his last assassination. He accidentally blinds a female cocktail singer in a shoot-out, for which he is very regretful (thus showing he has a conscience). With a police inspector constantly trailing him, the cop-and-killer pair form a special and intimate relationship and finally team up in a massive shoot-out. The inter-cut of their faces (deployed and largely developed in *Face/Off*), their fidelity (to the extent that each could die for the other) and an intimacy not shared even with their girlfriend/wife afford an erotic homosexual imagination under a homosocial overcoat.

Most Hong Kong action films, in fact, talk about underground secret societies, that is, triad societies. Bound by particular membership rituals, numerous identification signals and signs denoting rank, triad society apparently offers a very rigid schooling in moral solidarity among men. In reality, triad gangsters seem to be responsible for a number of serious crimes. In films and TV programmes, they are usually depicted in a sympathetic manner, or even glorified by presenting their personalities as heroic (e.g., possessing a strong sense of fidelity) and moral (e.g., killing only those who deserve to die). Therefore, most of these gangster pictures reveal some kind of psychological conflict and dilemma in the cop-and-gangster dichotomy and convey the message that some triad gangsters could be morally superior to policemen, thus directing the audience's sympathies towards the former rather than the latter. A triad society is basically a man's world. By celebrating the same-sex bonding of men and even sometimes displaying physical intimacy, these triad pictures open up a space for the homosexual imagination under homosocial relationships. Notable examples of coupled pairs include: Chow Yun-fat (Zhou Runfa) and Ti Lung (Di Long) in *A Better Tomorrow* (Yingxiong bense) (dir. John Woo, 1986), Andy Lau (Liu Dehua) and Cheung Hok-yau (Zhang Xueyou) in *As Tears Go By* (Wangjiao kamen) (dir. Wong Ka-wai, 1988) and Alex Fong (Fang Zhongxin) and Chan Kam-hung (Chen Jinhong) in *Cheap Killers* (Yue duoluo yue yingxiong) (dir. Clarence Fok, 1998).

A recent interesting example can be found in *Jiang Hu: The Triad Zone*. The bodyguard (played by Cheung Yiu-yeung), believing he is about to die, reveals his secret love to his "big brother" (Tony Leung Ka-fai), for whom he sustained injuries while trying to protect him. This blunt and direct expression of homosexual love is not glorified or treated as a joke. Rather, the "love that dares not speak its name" is simply ignored. This secret love just comes and goes as if it is a dream. When Cheung asks whether he can still be his bodyguard, Leung hesitates and says, "We'll talk about it later when you recover." He then adds, "But I would never go to a sauna with you anymore." Under the logic of hegemonic masculinity, Cheung lives successfully in a macho and homophobic underworld by acting straight but he failed to perform as a straight man during this life-and-death incident. But for Leung, Cheung's abrupt cry for love has had no effect on him at all. This short episode is never incorporated into Leung's understanding of his identity and sexuality. The possibility of bisexuality, a more fluid identity, is completely excluded. Maybe its "weight" cannot be consumed by the lightness of this comic straight film, which seems to suggest that it is better to keep such a love secret. If it is hard for a gay man to masquerade as a woman in order to express his love — as discussed — it would be much harder for a gay man to assert his maleness but still express his homosexual desires. A man's world is tough, for the straight and gay alike. A very similar example is *Sausalito* (Yijian zhongqing; dir. Lau Wai-keung; 2000). Eric Kot Man-fai (Ge Minhui) is openly gay and expresses his love to his business partner, Leon Lai-ming (Li Ming). Rather than rejecting him, Leon simply treats him as a good friend. Eric, like Leung, is thus forced to perform one function: to be almost always there (and thus almost always invisible) and give the main straight character unconditional love and support.

Mainstreaming of Gayness

There is an increasing appearance of major or supporting glbt characters. Even the recent film *Truth or Dare: 6th Floor Rear Flat* (Liulou houzuo; dir. Barbara Wong; 2003) features one main gay male character, whose girlfriend dumps him, although there is hardly any in-depth analysis of his sexuality. The presentation of such a gay character seems to be a cliché; in the culture of the hip, politically correct post-colonial film, such a character ought to be there. Films that feature "pretend gays" (e.g., Leon Lai who pretends to be gay — only by wearing an earring [!] to protect Sammi Cheng in *Killing Me Tenderly* [dir. Lee Lik-chi, 1997]) or "straight-mistaken gays" (e.g., Tony Leung Ka-fai in *The Eagle Shooting Hero*, [dir. Jeff Lau, 1993]) are numerous. They have less to do with the actual diversity of the glbt community, and more with how gayness itself is being understood and metaphorized.

However, there is a large number of films that directly addresses the issue of homosexuality, or at least feature it as a major theme: *Oh! My Three Guys*; one story in *Conjugal Affairs* (Xin tongju shidai; dir. Sylvia Chang, 1994); *He and She* (Jiemei qingshen) (dir. Cheng Dan-Shui, 1994); *Boy's?*; *A Queer Story*; *Happy Together*; *Bishonen ...* ; *Hold You Tight* (Yue kuaile yue duoluo) (dir. Stanley Kwan, 1998); *The Accident* (Xinyuan yima) (dir. Julian Lee, 1999); *The Map of Sex and Love*; *Lan Yu*; *Night Corridor*.

The most prominent themes of most of these so-called gay films are the classic issue of gay identity and coming out and the issue of AIDS. *The Wedding Banquet* (Xiyan) (dir. Ang Lee, 1992) is a Taiwanese film. It is very significant in Chinese film history because it was the first to address directly the issue of homosexuality (e.g., gay identity, coming out and the struggle with the iron law of marriage and the continuation of family bloodline in a neo-Confucian Chinese family setting). The story (in Chinese it is called *Happy Banquet*) revolves around a gay Taiwanese man, Wei Tong, who has a white American gay partner, Simon. The two live together in New York. To avoid upsetting his parents, he decides to marry a woman from Shanghai, Wei Wei, who is desperate for an American passport. On the night of the false wedding Wei Tong and Wei Wei have sex by "mistake" and Wei Wei becomes pregnant. The film then goes on to ask whether Wei Wei should have an abortion and whether Wei Tong should come out. At the end of the film Wei Tong's parents fly back to Taiwan. Wei Tong and Simon, as well as Wei Wei, decide to keep the baby and live in a fake nuclear family (a queer family?). Although Wei Tong's parents "know" he is gay (without explicitly talking about it), they are "happy" because Wei Tong has fulfilled his responsibility of continuing the family bloodline. Wei Wei is "happy" because she is attracted to Wei Tong and now has their baby, plus she gets her passport. Wei Tong is "happy" because he has not upset his parents and is still able to be with Simon.

The Wedding Banquet seems to be the most successful and well-known film about homosexuality in Chinese film history. Its popularity, however, seems to be owing to its conformity to traditional Chinese values (for instance the gay character pleases his parents by carrying out a fake marriage and having a baby with a woman, and then living with her and his own partner). It seems to tell a comforting story that pleases everybody. This film best illustrates the dilemma of gay Chinese men who have to negotiate their sexuality within the institution of the neo-Confucian family.[75]

Because gay characters are portrayed as heroically suffering or offering resistance in an oppressive world, coming out seems to be the focal point. For example, *A Queer Story* tells the tale of a closet forty-year-old gay man (Law Ka-sing, played by Lam Chi-cheung) and his boyfriend, an openly gay and flamboyant young man (Sonny, played by Jordan Chan). To fulfill family obligations, Law is forced to enter into a fake marriage, although he decides to face his true identity at the last minute. *Oh! My Three Guys* tells of three gay friends who live together — a feminine gay man (Gau Goo-leung, played by Eric Kot Man-fai) who dreams of becoming a star (a typical drama queen); a gay playwright (Ah Fa, played by Wong Chi-wah), who always works with his misogynist colleagues; and a straight-acting gay man (Yu Hoi, played by Lau Ching-wan), who falls in love with a woman at the end of the film. The film centres on the issue of coming out, and on the potential for social discrimination when one's gay identity is exposed. Even the recent *The Map of Sex and Love* is an autobiographical story of a gay man\searching for his cultural identity (as a Macau-born Chinese) and gay identity.

Moreover, these films usually assume that sexual orientation is innate, part of a biological make-up. The notion of an essential gay identity is frequently told in the narration of their sexual histories. Perhaps the only exception is Yu Hoi in *Oh! My Three Guys* when he struggles with his "straight" feelings towards a woman. Although in his final "turning straight" he might be criticised for having surrendered to the dominant heterosexist belief that sexual orientation can be "cured," it could also be read as his own awakening of a more fluid sexuality — the possibility of bisexuality.

Finally, perhaps owing to the myth that "gays = AIDS," AIDS is another key issue in these films. A side story in *A Queer Story* is Law's gay friend who dies of AIDS, while the most daring character (Gau Goo-leung) in *Oh! My Three Guys* is diagnosed HIV positive, and commits suicide as a result.

Another theme of these films is the depiction of gay lifestyles and a more diverse representation of gay men. *Boy's?* and *Bishonen* seem to be a kind of kaleidoscope of the lives of Hong Kong gays and lesbians.

Boy's? tells the story of three gay characters. The first, Joey (played by Chan Kwok-bong), meets a straight man, Edmond (played by Leung Hon-man), when he is in drag but pulls away because he is afraid of telling Edmond the truth. The second, Jaffe (played by Cheng Ka-wing), is a good-looking guy who screws around. The third, Juek Juek Gai (played by Siu Kwok-wah), is always looking for his Mr. Right. *Bishonen* is narrated by a woman, Kana (played by Shu Qi), who is the friend of a closet-gay policeman, Sam (played by Daniel Wu), who later commits suicide because his sexual identity, which he has repressed, has been discovered by his beloved father. The other main character, Jet (played by Fung Tak-lun), is a rent boy and befriends Sam, but tries hard to hide his identity as a prostitute.

Bars, discos, the gay "village" and other "scenes" all contribute an important cultural force to the gay movement because its participants can identify with one another through sexuality, language and values.[76] Most of these films (e.g., *Boy's?*, *A Queer Story*, *Bishonen*) feature the "communities" where gay characters go to bars and clubs to meet friends and cruise, and these "scenes" mainly take place in Central (Lan Kwai Fong as the gay "ghetto"). In addition, public sex (e.g., cruising in a public area, cottaging, saunas), radically disrupting the distinction between public and private, is a contested site of sexual visibility.[77] While cruising in public is seen as something done out of pain (e.g., Lai Yiu-fai, who goes cottaging or has sex in a gay cinema in *Happy Together*) or curiosity (the best friend of the three gay characters, Fanny's younger brother, experiments with homosexuality in *Boy's?*), it can also be seen as simply a fact of gay life, as in *Hold You Tight* (in which Eric Tsang plays the gay real-estate agent Tong), *Bishonen* (Jet cruises in a toilet), or *The Map of Sex and Love* (Victor Ma plays the gay dancer).

Although these films also typically feature gay men as sissies and campy drama queens (e.g., Gau Goo-leung in *Oh! My Three Guys*; Ah Keung, played again by Eric Kot Man-fai in *Conjugal Affairs*; Joey and Juek Juek Gai in *Boy's?* and Ah Gai, played by Tong Leung Ka-fai in *He and She*), there are numerous representations of straight-acting gay men: e.g., Daniel Wu in *Night Corridor*, Lau Ching-wan in *Oh! My Three Guys*; the gay couple Tony Leung Chiu-wai and Leslie Cheung in *Happy Together*; and Ng Ngai-cheung and his acquaintance Wong Hei in *The Accident*. This is not to say that a straight-acting gay man is (politically) more "correct" than a campy drama queen but to suggest that representations of gay men are more diverse and "real." Finally, as Rainer rightly asks, "If the intriguing solidarity between 'straight' and 'gay' men brought about by commodity culture signals a new hegemony, then it must produce its own exclusion and fringes. What are they?"[78]

It is women who are placed at the margins of this hedonistic homosocial world; these "fag hags" who play the "supporting" role are always good friends of the gay characters, and they are supportive, understanding, and even offer unconditional love.

Fok May (played by Wu Qianlian) in *Oh! My Three Guys* and Ah Yee (played by Anita Yuen) in *He and She* both win the love of a gay man, while Wei Wei (played by May Chin) lives with Wei Tong and Simon in *The Wedding Banquet*. They are lucky, but others are not so fortunate. Tam Lei-chuen (played by Ng Wing-Mei), falls deeply in love with Law Ka-sing in *A Queer Story* and helps him hide his sexuality from his family; while Mi Mi (played by Cheri Ho) becomes the best friend of both halves of the gay male couple in *The Map of Sex and Love*. In *Farewell My Concubine,* Juxian (played by Gong Li) is the wife of Duan Xiaolou, who tries without success to compete with Cheng Dieyi for the love of Duan Xiaolou. In *Boys's?*, Pauline (played by Pauline Chan) fancies Jaffe and even attempts to seduce him one night, but fails.

Moreover, cult gay hegemonic masculinity privileges gay men who are young, well-built, manly, straight-acting and emotionally in control. Conversely, the hyper-feminine body, the elderly body, the disabled body, the poor body and many others are all seen as subordinate gay variants or as "failing bodies."[79] Most of the films feature this cult gay hegemonic masculinity. Only *A Queer Story* touches on the issue of old age: one of the protagonists, Law Ka-sing, is a 46-year-old gay man who has to face his sexuality and the fact he is ageing. *Happy Together* is a story of exile in which the two gay characters struggle for survival in Buenos Aires. *Boy's?*, featuring Juek Juek Gai, is unusual, because the character's ugliness has always been emphasized to explain his constant failure to find a boyfriend.

CONCLUSION

Hong Kong movies always have a dual nature in terms of homosexuality. On the one hand, gay men are usually represented as sexual perverts and sissies, or as victims or villains under heterosexual and masculine frames of reference. The representation of such a gay character is nothing more than a gimmick. This administration of heteronormative discipline might structure our identities, which will in turn negatively frame our experiences. Parallel to this disciplinary surveillance, however, is a new trend in the development of the queer. Although gay men and lesbians have always known how to "twist" straight readings for their own purposes, even in texts that are ostensibly heterosexual there has been an increasing proliferation of glbt characters in Hong Kong movies since the 1990s. This apparent increase in queer visibility may suggest that a new "queer space" of desire has opened in Hong Kong movies. In particular, three forms of queer visibility can be seen: first, homosexual love seems to have been "normalized" when masculine and feminine gender roles are sustained by the tradition of transgenderism and the *wen* ideal of Chinese masculinity. Second, a space for the male homosocial/homosexual imagination has emerged in films where the *wu* ideal of Chinese masculinity and male bonding is emphasized. Third, films that directly address homosexuality are numerous. They feature gay men as heroically suffering from or offering resistance to the straight oppressive world. Issues such as gay identity, coming out, struggles with the family, AIDS, etc. are usually the focal point. Moreover, these films also exhibit a more diverse representation of gay lifestyles and gay characters. However, the real impact of the dual moments of "straightening queers" and "queering the straights" is a new hegemony in these films, in which women and subordinate gay masculinities such as those represented by ageing bodies, ugly bodies, poor bodies and so forth, are again being marginalized. Although these characters can help to increase the "visibility" of queer culture to the public, a straight audience could easily distance themselves from them and thereby return to their comfortable position as part of the dominant culture. We may believe that popular culture can disrupt the ideological tenets of heterosexuality and hegemonic masculinity, and in turn have a real impact on the glbt community and on society in general, but these films do not seem to represent a substantial critique of Hong Kong's heterosexist and masculinistic cultures. Therefore, I would like to ask: when can we watch a film that does not feature homosexuality as involving conflict and tension, but celebrates the view that being "gay" can really mean being "gay" (happy!), and in which AIDS is simply portrayed as a potential danger for everyone? When can we watch a film that views a homosexual life as an alternative, or questions whether a straight (especially married) life can be boring and mindless rather than treating it as a standard to which everyone is obliged to adhere? When can we watch a film that deals more honestly with the sexual desire of the characters, which in turn gives us more room to imagine the possibility of the fluidity of our sexuality rather than be confined to a rigid sex/gender regime? What we need might be more "queer" films to "challenge and confuse our understanding and uses of sexual and gender categories"[80] in order to give birth to new meanings of queer sensibility.

4

Unsung Heroes:
Reading Transgender Subjectivities in Hong Kong Action Cinema

Helen Hok-sze Leung

TRANSGENDER THEORY AND HONG KONG CINEMA

In her introduction to the "transgender issue" of the journal *GLQ*, Susan Stryker offers a definition of *transgender* that captures the nuance and complexity of the term:

> ... I use *transgender* not to refer to one particular identity or way of being embodied but rather as an umbrella term for a wide variety of bodily effects that disrupt or denaturalize heteronormatively constructed linkages between an individual's anatomy at birth, a nonconsensually assigned gender category, psychical identifications with the sexed body images and/or gendered subject positions, and the performance of specifically gendered social, sexual, or kinship functions.[1]

In Stryker's formulation, *transgender* is not a single identification or embodiment. It is an umbrella concept that refers to all "bodily effects" that trouble the assumed coincidence between our anatomy at birth, the gender assignment imposed on us (i.e. the "M" or "F" on the birth certificate), and our own subjective identifications. *Transgender* includes transsexuality in its rubric but is not reducible to it. The emergence of transgender theory — a growing body of knowledge that deploys *transgender* as a descriptive, analytical, and deconstructive category — has significantly reconfigured the debates on gender and sexuality.[2] It has challenged feminist theory to examine its history of transphobia, while igniting a resurgence of interest in the sexed body and its vexed relation to gender.[3] For gay and lesbian studies, transgender theory has complicated the discourse of sexual orientation and the notion of same-sex desire, both of which rely on a categorical distinction between male and female bodies. At the same time transgender theory has inspired new critical intersections with gay and lesbian work on alternative gender practices and with theories of bisexuality.[4] Most importantly, the academic presence of transgender theory, which would not have been possible without the continuing activism of transgender advocates in legal, social, and medical battles, is also starting to challenge the hitherto exclusive authority of medical expertise on transgender lives.[5] At the very least, no consideration of transgender issues can now go unchallenged without a recognition of the diversity of transgender experiences and the agency of transgender subjects.

More recently, there has been increasing recognition that more research on transgender phenomena outside the Euro-American context is needed. This is the result of an anxiety in the field that the notion of "transgender" itself may be in danger of reifying into an exclusionary narrative rooted only in the experiences of Europeans and North Americans. The response to this call for diversity has been especially keen in Asian Studies, resulting in the recent establishment of the Transgender Asia Research Centre and a growing number of works by emergent scholars from a variety of disciplines.[6] The recent release of films with transgender themes from locales as diverse as Singapore (*Bugis Street*, dir. Yongfan, 1997), Thailand (*Iron Ladies,* dir. Yongyoot Thongkongtoon, 2001), Sri Lanka (*Flying With One Wing*, dir. Asoka Handagama, 2002) and China (*Enter The Clowns*, dir. Cui Zi'en, 2001) also attests to the vitality of transgender cultural expressions in Asia. Hong Kong cinema similarly provides a rich source of material for the consideration of transgender issues. From Stanley Kwan (Guan Jinpeng)'s 1996 documentary *Yin ± Yang: Gender in Chinese Cinema* (Nansheng nüxiang: Zhongguo dianying de xingbie) to the recent works of critics such as Yau Ching (You Jing) and Natalia Chan (Luo Feng), there has not been a lack of insight and critical interest in issues of gender variance and gender transgression in Hong Kong cinema. Yet, as I will argue in this chapter, there is a tendency in critical works to view cross-gender expressions largely as symbolic subversion: as a disruption of the binary gender system, as queer destabilization of gendered spectatorship, or as a vehicle for dissident sexuality. Not enough attention has been paid to the formation of transgender *subjectivity*— i.e. the conditions in which transgender subjects may emerge on screen, not as symbols but as agents of his or her specific narrative of transgender embodiment. In this chapter I would like to trace the contours of two possible transgender subject positions through a re-reading of two films in the action genre. What does the hitherto invisibility and now intelligibility of these subject-positions signify for the gendered structure of the genre? In particular, what would the recognition of transgender subjects mean for the coding of masculinity in these genres, so commonly assumed to be the exclusive expression of genetically male bodies? By the same token, what implications does such recognition have for the coding of the male-born body that wilfully gives up its access to masculinity or even its embodiment of maleness?

TRANSSEXUAL EMERGENCE: *SWORDSMAN II* AND THE TRANSFORMATION OF DONGFANG BUBAI

Swordsman II (Xiao'ao jianghu II zhi Dongfang Bubai) (dir. Ching Siu-tung, 1992) is the second instalment of a series of films loosely adapted from Jin Yong's 1963 novel, *The Smiling, Proud Wanderer* (Xiao'ao jianghu). The film features one of the most memorable villains in Jin Yong's *oeuvre*: Dongfang Bubai, an ambitious swordsman who has castrated himself in order to acquire an awesome form of martial art. There is a dramatic difference between the novel's and the film's treatment of this remarkable character. Within this difference, it is possible to locate the emergence of a transsexual subjectivity, one that has critical implications for the status of masculinity in the martial arts genre.

In the afterword to the 1980 edition of *The Smiling, Proud Wanderer*, Jin Yong recalls the anxious political climate during which he wrote the serialized novel. The intense power struggle between warring factions in China, which at the time was on the brink of the Cultural Revolution, inspired some of the major themes in the novel.[7] The character Dongfang Bubai, whose name literally means "undefeated in the East,"[8] is a cunning parody of Mao Zedong's self-appellation — "red sun in the east" — and a pointed allusion to his megalomaniacal appetite for power. The critical force of Jin Yong's allusion, however, derives from a transphobic understanding of the gendered body. In the novel, the extremity of Dongfang Bubai's thirst for power is marked by his willingness to castrate himself. This trope of castration-as-desire-for-power recalls a historiographic cliché: the contention that many of the political disasters in imperial China can be attributed to the usurpation of power by eunuchs.[9] Jin Yong stretches this symbolic equation even further. The monstrosity of power corruption is symbolized not only in the fact of castration but in the very process of bodily transition from male to female. When Dongfang Bubai appears in the novel for the first time, her enemies are confounded. They remember *him* as "an awe-inspiring and fearsome fighter" who has "usurped the leadership of the Sun-Moon Holy Sect and reigned supreme in the martial world for twenty years" (1282). *She* now appears in front of them, "beardless, rouged, and wearing lurid clothes that appear to be neither masculine nor feminine" (1282). She sits embroidering in a perfumed chamber, "having lost all previous appetite for women" and become completely devoted to a man and obsessed with becoming a woman (1291). Dongfang Bubai has become, in the words of the novel's heroine, Yingying, "not a human, but a monster" (1293). The novel disposes of Dongfang Bubai within one chapter but its anxiety about the "monstrosity" of sex change continues. One of the most important narrative developments hinges on the secret of an elder swordsman and his son-in-law, both of whom have self-righteously persecuted the novel's hero, Linghu Chong, who is being wrongfully blamed for a series of crimes. The novel subsequently reveals the two men to be the real criminals. Hungry for power, they have been practising the same dark art that has transformed Dongfang Bubai. The physical changes in the elder swordsman are described through his wife's observations. She chillingly starts to notice the change in the pitch of her husband's voice, the shedding of his beard, and the loss of his (hetero)sexual appetite (1468). These are not, of course, medically accurate symptoms of castration or literal descriptions of transsexual transitions. Rather, the horror of power corruption is projected, through the wife's terrified observations, onto a sex-changed body. The novel allegorizes transsexuality, likening the somatic transition from male to female to a process of moral degeneration. Such transphobic understanding of ultimate villainy as a form of literal emasculation reveals the novel's own anxiety about the free-spirited and hermetic masculinity it celebrates in its hero Linghu Chong.[10] In the afterword, Jin Yong suggests that Linghu Chong never achieves the true freedom he desires, *not* because of worldly political struggles that have entangled him throughout the novel, but because of his committed love first for Yue Lingshan and later for Yingying. According to Jin Yong, Linghu Chong is "imprisoned" when he returns a woman's love, and most free in "Yilin's unrequited love for him" (1690). Apparently, a man is free in a relationship with a woman only if he does not return her love and thus escapes the "prison" of her influences! Jin Yong's remarks betray an acute anxiety about feminine sexuality and its constricting effects on the masculine freedom he envisions for Linghu Chong. Jin Yong's anxiety becomes *literalized* on the villainous male bodies: Dongfang Bubai and the other corrupted swordsmen are portrayed to be literally and monstrously bound by their feminizing bodies. Ironically, it is exactly at the moment these swordsmen are becoming feminized that they lose their sexual desire for women, thus escaping from the very influences that Jin Yong identifies as constraining for masculine freedom.[11] In this light, the novel's transphobia actually reveals an underlying crisis in the genre's conception of masculinity and freedom. On the one hand, an idealized masculinity is perceived to be vulnerable to the constraints of heterosexual desire. On the other, the ultimate freedom from heterosexual desire is inevitably coded in metaphors of castration (which, in this novel, is further imagined as a form of sex change) and, by implication, the *loss* of masculinity. This contradiction may explain why Jin Yong, even as he laments Yingying's constraining influences, does not end the novel differently, with Linghu Chong wandering free and unfettered by heterosexual desire. To do so would, I suspect, bring Linghu Chong too monstrously close to Dongfang Bubai, who in fact represents what is most abhorred and most desired in the novel's conception of masculinity and freedom.

If such a critique of the novel simply reveals the ideological limits of its times, then the dramatic transformation of Dongfang Bubai on the screen in 1992 owes something to the first stirrings of queer politics in Hong Kong. The debates about the decriminalization of homosexuality throughout the 1980s had resulted in not only the emergence of gay and lesbian identities and organized activism around those identities, but also a new discursive space where issues of sexual and gender transgressions could be openly voiced.[12] *Swordsman II* fed the public's newfound fascination with queer subject matters while reinvigorating a gender-bending tradition that has arguably always existed in Chinese cinema.[13] One of the film's most glaring departures from the novel's treatment of Dongfang Bubai is the centrality it accords to the novel's villain. Although Dongfang Bubai dies within one chapter in the four-volume novel, she occupies the most prominent role in the film, usurping even Linghu Chong (played by Jet Li), not unlike the way she usurps the leadership of the Sun-Moon sect in the novel. The film also invents an erotic relationship between Linghu Chong and Dongfang Bubai, further blurring the line between hero and villain. Most unexpectedly, Brigitte Lin (Lin Qingxia) was cast in the role of Dongfang Bubai. The box-office success of the film would later revitalize Lin's sagging career and instigate a trend of gender-bending roles that distinguish the careers of actors such as Leslie Cheung (Zhang Guorong), Anita Yuen (Yuan Yongyi), Anita Mui (Mei Yanfang) and, most prominently, Lin herself. The casting of Lin, an actress famous for her beauty, is significant. No longer represented as a castrated half-man, Dongfang Bubai remerges on screen as a (transsexual) woman. The film's inclusion in the Netherlands Transgender Film Festival in 2001, almost ten years after its initial release, completes Dongfang Bubai's remarkable transformation. Conceived as a symbol of masculinity-under-threat by a transphobic imagination during the 1960s, Dongfang Bubai is emerging in the new millennium as a transsexual icon.[14] However, the film has not always enjoyed such enthusiastic critical reception. In fact, it was routinely criticized in the first wave of queer critical writing to emerge from Hong Kong in the 1990s. This critical gap in the film's reception reveals an interesting contradiction between queer theorizing and transsexual subjectivity.

In the introduction to *Second Skins: The Body Narratives of Transsexuality*, Jay Prosser calls our attention to queer theory's foundational reliance on the figure of transgender. As a body of knowledge that takes as its point of departure the "queering" — i.e. the destabilization and displacement — of established categories of gender and sexuality, it is no surprise queer theory finds the trope of crossing and traversing genders immensely valuable to its theoretical enterprise. Prosser suggests, however, that the queer appropriation of transgender privileges only a particular segment of the conceptual umbrella represented by the term *transgender*: "Crucial to the idealization of transgender as a queer transgressive force in this work is the consistent decoding of 'trans' as an incessant destabilizing movement between sexual and gender identities."[15] Prosser argues that the formulation "transgender = gender performativity = queer = subversive" results in a conceptual split between queer and *transsexual*. The transsexual subject position, as Prosser shows, does not necessarily value fluidity, movement, and performativity but rather "seek[s] quite pointedly to be nonperformative, to be constative, quite simply to *be*" (32). Prosser's subsequent articulation of a theory of transsexual embodiment delineates a specifically transsexual experience of the body that is not easily reconciled with the queer imperative. While queer theory celebrates disruptions and instability as transgressive forces, the transsexual subject in Prosser's formulation is invested in gender transitivity not in and of itself, but as a process that eventually *arrives* at a more stable form of gendered embodiment. It is not surprising, then, that critics who turn to *Swordsman II* for a queer reading are often disappointed. In one of the earliest pieces of queer criticism on Hong Kong cinema, Chou Wah-shan (Zhou Huashan) offers a scathing critique of the film. He takes issue in particular with the casting of Brigitte Lin: "Dongfang Bubai and Linghu Chong are clearly homosexual lovers. Casting the beautiful actress Brigitte Lin in the role completely takes away the shock and anxiety a male actor would inspire in playing that role."[16] Chou is especially irked by one scene: Dongfang Bubai asks her concubine Sisi to act as a substitute for herself while making love to Linghu Chong in the dark. Chou interprets this scene as the film's final reinscription of heterosexuality: the only sexual scene in the film takes place unambiguously between a man and a woman. In a much more complex and nuanced reading, Yau Ching shifts the interpretive focus and locates queer pleasure in the spectatorial gaze. Yau argues that the film in fact offers its spectators "layered and diverse paths to project their desire" and the character Dongfang Bubai "allows us to refuse identification through sexual difference."[17] For Yau, the spectator's simultaneous recognition of the actress's female body and the character's male body means that identification with the character demands a (temporary) suspension of seamlessly gendered identification. Thus, as the gender discrepancy between actress and character becomes less intelligible — i.e. as Dongfang Bubai's transition progresses — the queer pleasure of the film also diminishes: "When Dongfang Bubai becomes more and more like a woman, the spectatorial pleasure of the female audience also becomes less radical and more conservative, until they finally only see the reflection of their own gender identification."[18] Both critics, in their very different readings, view Dongfang Bubai as a subversive character only in so far as s/he remains a symbol of gender instability. Chou prefers to see Dongfang Bubai played by a male actor, thus displaying a feminized male body and serving as an object of homosexual desire for Linghu Chong. Yau relishes the casting of Brigitte Lin, as long as a queer discrepancy is maintained between Lin's (meta-textual) female body and Dongfang Bubai's (textual) male body. Both critics become disappointed when they are confronted with what is arguably Dongfang Bubai's subjective emergence: i.e. as a transsexual woman who challenges

Linghu Chong's (and our) demand to *tell the difference* of transsexuality. In this light, the scene that has appeared so *un*queer to critics can be re-read as an inscription *not* primarily of heterosexuality, but of transsexual agency.

Prior to the seduction scene Dongfang Bubai has just told her concubine Sisi about her somatic changes, citing them as the reasons for their recent lack of physical intimacy. At that moment, Linghu Chong enters the compound and asks Dongfang Bubai, known to him only as a beautiful stranger, to run away together from the turmoil of worldly affairs. Dongfang Bubai extinguishes the lights and asks Sisi to substitute for her. She then pushes Sisi into Linghu Chong's arms and the two make love in the dark. Later in the film, Linghu Chong discovers the true identity of Dongfang Bubai and fights alongside his allies against her. Yet, when she is about to die, he tries to save her life, repeatedly asking if it was really *her* with whom he spent that memorable night. Dongfang Bubai neither confirms nor denies it was her, telling him that he "will never know, and will always regret this moment." She then lets herself fall to the bottom of the cliffs, leaving Linghu Chong none the wiser. Why does Dongfang Bubai offer Sisi to Linghu Chong? And what is her motive for continuing her "deception" of Linghu Chong until the very end? Chou, who insists on reading Dongfang Bubai as "rightfully" a gay man, argues that it is the film's way of "avoiding an explicit male-male sex scene."[19] Yet, Chou has already critiqued the casting of Brigitte Lin as a heterosexualization of the relationship between Dongfang Bubai and Linghu Chong. Why would her recognizably female body be in danger of suggesting a homosexual scene? The substitution in fact only makes sense as part of a transsexual narrative. In his discussion of transsexual embodiment, Jay Prosser theorizes the transsexual subject's relation to his or her transitioning body through Didier Anzieu's notion of the "skin ego." Anzieu's reworking of psychoanalytic theories departs from the emphasis that Lacan and his followers place on language as the defining structure of ego formations. Instead, Anzieu returns to Freud and the importance he attributes to the body, especially its surface, in the formation of the ego.[20] It is from this *tactile* origin of the psyche that Prosser derives his theory of transsexuality:

> Writing against the grain of most poststructuralist theories of the body informed by psychoanalysis, Didier Anzieu suggests the body's surface as that which matters most about the self. His concept of the "skin ego" takes the body's physical skin as the primary organ underlying the

formation of the ego, its handling, its touching, its holding — our experience of its feel — individualizing our psychic functioning, quite crucially making us who we are.[21]

Prosser goes on to explain the untouchability, or "stoneness," of the pre-transition body — a recurrent motif in transsexual narratives — as a feeling of a non-coincidence between "the contours of body image" and the material body, a "description simply of the refusal of body ego to own referential body."[22] Dongfang Bubai's refusal of sexual intimacy, both with Sisi and with Linghu Chong, can be explained in Prosser's scheme as precisely this wilful non-recognition of the (transitioning) body that is not (yet fully) her own. Furthermore, as Prosser suggests, it is this "dis-ownership of sex ... [that] maintains the integrity of the alternatively gendered imaginary."[23] In other words, Dongfang Bubai's refusal to be sexualized during physical intimacy as either "not quite man" (by Sisi) or "not quite woman" (by Linghu Chong) is her means of maintaining her subjectively gendered imaginary of being a woman. However, she does not simply stop there. She literalizes this alternative gendered imaginary, through Linghu Chong's desire for her, *on* Sisi's body. Prosser deploys Oliver Sacks's work on neurology to draw a parallel between the way amputees feel and animate their prosthetic limbs through a phatasmatic memory of their real limbs and the way transsexuals experience their post-surgical bodies. In place of actual memory, Prosser suggests that transsexuals experience their surgically transformed bodies through *nostalgia* for an idealized body that *should* have existed:

> The body of transsexual becoming is born out of a yearning for a perfect past — that is, not memory but nostalgia: the desire for the purified version of what was, not for the return to home per se (*nostos*) but to the romanticized ideal of home.[24]

Sisi's body represents for Dongfang Bubai the idealized gendered body that she longs to become/ return to. In substituting for Dongfang Bubai, unbeknown to Linghu Chong, Sisi is serving as a phatasmatic extension of Dongfang Bubai's body. By denying Linghu Chong the power to tell the difference, Dongfang Bubai has in effect closed the gap between her subjectively embodied gender and Linghu Chong's actual experience of her body. The price of Dongfang Bubai's subjective emergence in this erotic encounter is, of course, the erasure of Sisi. In this scene, she is disowned from her own body, which has become a phantom limb possessed by both Dongfang Bubai (through identification) and Linghu Chong (through desire). It is thus fitting that the figure of the concubine returns with a vengeance in the film's sequel, *The East is Red* (Dongfang Bubai zhi fengyun zaiqi) (dir. Ching Siu-Tung, 1993). In the latter film one of Dongfang Bubai's former concubines, Xue Qianxun (played by Joey Wong), refuses to be abandoned like Sisi. In a scheme to lure Dongfang Bubai (not dead after all) out of hiding, she impersonates her former lover and embarks on a killing spree, thus sending the entire martial arts world on a search for the real Dongfang Bubai. Xue's scheme is similar to Dongfang Bubai's deception of Linghu Chong in one important way: successfully disguised as a transsexual woman, Xue challenges the world to "tell the difference" of transsexuality, confident that they, like Linghu Chong (and the audience), will be unable to do so.

My reading of Dongfang Bubai as a transsexual subject does not mean to suggest that she presents a "positive image" of transsexual femininity. After all, she is a brutal, cunning and power-driven villain. What I appreciate in the film, in contrast to the character's treatment in the novel, is the intelligibility of Dongfang Bubai as a transsexual woman, who is moreover an agent of her own actions. Her power, though awesome and terrifying, is worthy of her enemies' respect. Most of all, she is no longer a symbol of damaged masculinity, to be conquered by Linghu Chong's free-spirited heroism. Instead, she has fully emerged into her self-chosen subject position as a woman. Unlike the novel, the film is not primarily about masculinity under siege. Rather, it offers a spectacular display of transsexual femininity that has successfully eclipsed the centrality of masculine heroism in the genre.

TRANSGENDER BUTCH BLUES: HEROIC MASCULINITY AND HOMOEROTICISM IN *PORTLAND STREET BLUES*

The transsexual narrative that I trace in *Swordsman II*, through Jay Prosser's theory of transsexual embodiment, is by no means the only possible articulation of transgender identity. While the transsexual trajectory tends to be marginalized within queer theory, it is by contrast the *dominant* expression of transgender identity within the medical discourse of gender dysphoria, which views transgender people pathologically as patients in need of treatment. The "treatment" offered is a rigid process of sex reassignment that follows strict medical protocols, prescribed and monitored by medical and mental health professionals. A "cure" is understood to be the patient's successful reassignment from one sex to another.[25] Until very recently, narratives of transgender embodiment that do not conform to, or consciously *reject*, this grammar of binary gender transitions are viewed with suspicion and hostility by the medical community. Since the 1990s, thanks to the continual efforts of transgender activists, the medical establishment has been relinquishing some of its exclusive claim to expertise on transgender lives. With the increasing input and participation of activists, academics and cultural producers who are themselves the consumers of transgender care, a much more complex and diverse picture of the experiences and needs of transgender people is starting to emerge, both in the medical community and in mainstream culture.[26] Leslie Feinberg's 1992 novel *Stone Butch Blues*, for instance, has brought a new visibility to transgender narratives that explicitly departs from the transsexual trajectory. The protagonist Jess has first lived as a butch lesbian, then taken hormones and undergone surgery and lived as a man, while finally realizing that neither of those identities fully encompasses who s/he is. Toward the end of the novel, Jess asks this poignant question:

> I felt my whole life coming full circle. Growing up so different, coming out as a butch, passing as a man, and then back to the same questions that had shaped my life: woman or man?[27]

The novel deliberately refrains from answering the question. In the end Jess stops passing and resolves to live as s/he is: neither man nor woman but transgendered in hir (Feinberg's preferred pronoun) own way. All of Feinberg's subsequent writings, as well as the works of authors such as Kate Bornstein and Riki Wilchins, are committed to a sustained critique of the binary conception of gender at the same time that they demonstrate the diversity of transgender lives.[28] In my reading of *Portland Street Blues* (Hongxing shisan mei) (dir. Raymond Yip, 1998), I would like to trace, in the protagonist Sister Thirteen (Shisan mei), a form of transgender subjectivity that does not conform to the transsexual trajectory. The possibility of reading Thirteen — previously overlooked by critics — as a transgender character also has critical implications for the debates on homoeroticism in the gangster genre.

Portland Street Blues is the fourth instalment of the *Young and Dangerous* (Guhuo zai) series, which comprises blockbuster films adapted from a comic-book series about young Hong Kong triad gangsters. The film documents how Sister Thirteen (played by Sandra Ng), leader of the Portland Street branch of the Hung Hing Triad, rises to power. From her first appearance in the opening scene where she is dressed in a classy black suit, her hair slicked back and a cigarette between her lips, Thirteen perfectly embodies the heroic masculinity made famous by Chow Yun-fat (Zhou Runfa)'s characters in John Woo (Wu Yusen)'s films from the 1980s. In the *Young and Dangerous* series, this tradition of heroic masculinity is modulated and reinvented through the youthful characters played by Ekin Cheng (Zhen Yijian) and Jordan Chan (Chen Xiaochun).[29] What is Thirteen's subjective relation to this/ her masculinity? The first flashback sequence in the film is initiated by a scene of mourning. While Thirteen burns incense in front of a portrait of her late father (played by Ng Man-tat), she explains to her triad brother: "I've always thought of myself as a man. Do you know why?" A dissolving shot cuts from the late father's portrait to the past where the father is playing mah-jong with triad bosses who use him as a pawn in the game. The narrative of Thirteen's transgender identification is thus visually linked to her father, a man who has never been able to live up to the heroic masculinity glorified in the genre. As a result, he is harassed and bullied and eventually dies in brutal humiliation. Thirteen's masculine identification thus also signals her identification with triad power. However, the desire for triad power alone does not explain Thirteen's transgender identification, only the *type* of masculinity she embraces. Her masculinity is not simply "functional": it is not just a means to gain triad power. Subsequent flashback sequences show that long before her triad ambitions, Thirteen was already a tomboy in her youth. Scenes of Thirteen and her girlhood companion A Yun (played by Kristy Yeung) playing, smoking, joking, and cuddling in bed together consciously echoes what would be recognized in the Hong Kong lesbian lexicon as a TB/TBG (literally "tomboy/tomboy girl" and signifying butch/femme) relationship, even in the absence of any explicit sexual relations between the two. Thirteen is what Judith Halberstam would call a "transgender butch." Halberstam first formulates this category in order to challenge the overlapping, often blurry but frequently contested "borders" between butch and FTM (female-to-male transsexual) identities:

> There are real and physical differences between genetic females who specifically identify as transsexual and genetic females who feel comfortable with female masculinity. There are real and physical

differences between female-born men who take hormones, have surgery, and live as men and female-born butches who live some version of gender ambiguity. But there are also many situations in which those differences are less clear than one might expect, and there are many butches who pass as men and many transsexuals who present as gender ambiguous and many bodies that cannot be classified by the options transsexual and butch. [30]

The category of "transgender butch," which emphasizes a cross-gender identification (transgender) while retaining a reference to a masculine form of femaleness (butch) that is distinct from either "man" or "woman," provides a more flexible category for those who inhabit the borderland between butch and FTM. I describe Thirteen as a transgender butch to signify her masculine identification and masculine presentation as well as to underscore the fact that she does not seek to pass as a man or transition physically. This specificity is important to my reinterpretation of the film's sexual dynamics.

The romantic plot of *Portland Street Blues* is full of twists and turns and offers an especially interesting example of the way transgender theory complicates the discourse of sexual orientation. Throughout the film Thirteen suspects that A Yun is in love with Coke (played by Alex Fong), a hit man from the rival Dong Sing Triad. To Thirteen's surprise A Yun admits toward the end of the film that the true object of her love has always been Thirteen. Her apparent desire for Coke is, like her many scheming acts of seduction earlier in the film, simply a weapon of manipulation. In retrospect, it becomes clear that she seduces Coke in order to keep him away from Thirteen, who, in a further twist of the romantic plot, greatly admires Coke and later betrays an intense affection for the man. Thirteen also runs a prostitute ring, cruises young women, and is widely known to be a lesbian. Yet, the only emotionally charged and intimate encounter she has in the film is with Coke. As a result, many reviewers are puzzled by the film's sexual dynamics. The veteran film critic Sek Kei [Shi Qi], for instance, ends his review of the film with this question: "… moreover, is the Sandra Ng character [Sister Thirteen] actually homosexual or heterosexual? This was never made very clear."[31] Sek Kei wants to know, once and for all, whether Thirteen is "actually" lesbian or straight. What Sek Kei, or any other critic for that matter, fails to take into account is Thirteen's transgender identification and its implication for our understanding of her sexuality. If we read Thirteen not simply as a woman but more specifically as a transgender butch —

i.e. as a *masculine* figure — then her desire for Coke is neither lesbian nor straight, but *gay*. Admittedly, my use of the term "gay" here is tongue-in-cheek, because the word inevitably invokes a discourse of sexual orientation that categorizes desire according to the sex of the desiring bodies, regardless of their gender presentation. Yet, if we take transgender identifications seriously, then sexual orientation may be much more complex than the binary scheme of heterosexuality and homosexuality. Is Thirteen's desire for Coke still heterosexual if she does not identify as feminine? In fact, because she is attracted to Coke as a self-identified *masculine* woman, would it not be more accurate to describe this attraction as *homoerotic*? This latter suggestion makes particular sense in the scene where Thirteen and Coke show immense tenderness for each other. The two are reunited for the first time after many years. They reminisce and make sexual jokes in ways that are typical of male-male camaraderie. Then, all of a sudden, the mood shifts and Thirteen awkwardly asks Coke for a hug and he obliges, tentatively but tenderly. The film critic Shelly Kraucer has observed that during the exchange, the editing consistently violates the 180-degree rules, which means that from our perspective, the two characters keep switching position from left to right, continually replacing one another in placements.[32] The editing of the sequence recalls John Woo's famous manoeuvre in *The Killer* (Diexue shuangxiong) (1995). In a formal analysis of the film, David Bordwell describes the ways in which Woo "cuts across the axis of action" to make the two heroes, John and Li (played by Chow Yun-fat and Danny Lee), "pictorially parallel":

> Thereafter John and Li are compared by every stylistic means Woo can find: crosscutting, echoing lines of dialogue, and visual parallels ... He intercuts tracking shots in John's apartment to make Li literally replace John, and he will have them face off again and again in a dizzying series of variant framings, while telling the blind Jenny they're childhood friends. Woo violates Hollywood's 180-degree cutting rule in order to underscore graphic similarities between the two men.[33]

In the scene from *Portland Street Blues*, the "quotation" of Woo is significant in two ways: it anchors Thirteen's transgender identification in the mirror of Coke's masculinity at the same time as it represents an intense intimacy between two masculine figures. In a later scene, when Thirteen arrives at the place where Coke has been shot dead, she grieves for him in a highly masculinized gesture: she picks up three burning cigarettes, lays them on the ground together like three burning sticks of incense, and then kneels down to pay her respects to Coke. Furthermore, in another implicit romantic subplot between Thirteen and her triad partner Han Bin, who awkwardly tries to give her a ring to express his affection, the relationship is also coded in generic images of male-male camaraderie rather than heterosexual romance. The bonding scenes between the two show them getting drunk together while heading out to cruise women, expressing mutual respect for each other's abilities, and loyally watching each other's backs amidst triad power intrigue. All of these scenes typically occur between male characters in the genre. Thus, Thirteen never once steps out of her role as masculine hero, even — in fact, especially — in her romantic relations with men. What, then, is the significance of Thirteen's appropriation of this hitherto exclusively male homoeroticism (now understood as eroticism between two masculine-identified figures, regardless of their assigned birth sex)? In order to answer this question, it is necessary to turn, for a moment, to the debates on homoeroticism in Hong Kong action cinema.

In Jillian Sandel's analysis of John Woo's pre-Hollywood films, she suggests that the implicit homoeroticism in Woo's films signifies a repudiation of femininity, heterosexual desire and the burden of family, all of which threaten the hero's ideal of individualism and freedom.[34] However, this homoerotic tension is never allowed explicit expression in the films and is instead resolved in an aestheticized excess of violence inflicted on the male bodies. For Sandel, the homoerotic relationships in Woo's films are impossible to sustain because they articulate a form of freedom that the films associate with capitalism which, for Sandel, is an economic system that only permits competitive relations between individuals. Sandel's analysis is quite compelling but it is premised on an overly hasty identification of femininity and the family with Chinese tradition. Violently masochistic masculinity is, by contrast, linked to capitalism, with the unresolved homoerotic relations between men as its (impossible) fantasy of freedom. In another reading of the films' masculinity, Mikel J. Koven reverses Sandel's argument in an equally problematic move. Koven contends that the discussion of homoeroticism in gangster films is a Western "misreading" of "traditional Chinese masculinity," which he characterizes as more openly expressive of emotions. For Koven, the intense affective investment in honor, duty, and loyalty commonly experienced by Chinese men is misrecognized as eroticism by Western critics.[35] Both Sandel and Koven, in their rush to set up a Chinese vs. Western dichotomy, are unable to see the interconnections among homoeroticism, masculine freedom, and "traditional Chinese masculinity." While Sandel insightfully links the homoeroticism in Woo's films with the repudiation of femininity and family, she overlooks the possibility that the masculine freedom idealized in these homoerotic relationships is not necessarily an embrace of capitalist individualism and a repudiation of Chinese tradition. Rather, it is a nostalgic reconstruction of traditional masculinity, precisely in response to the competitive individualism of capitalism, which eclipses such relations. Kovel, by contrast, recognizes the action genre's investment in traditional masculinity but is unable, or unwilling, to understand it as anything but categorically heterosexual.[36] Contrary to Kovel's assumption, homoeroticism abounds in pre-modern Chinese culture and is far from incompatible with "traditional Chinese masculinity."[37] As I have argued in this chapter, there is a crisis in the conceptualization of masculinity in the martial arts genre. While heterosexual desire is perceived, on the one hand, to be a constraint on masculine freedom, the repudiation of heterosexuality, on the other hand, seems to lead dangerously to feminization and homosexuality. While Jin Yong alleviates this crisis with an expression of transphobia, Woo represses it by offering a homoerotic subtext that is forever deferred by outbursts of violence, and thus never in danger of developing into homosexuality.

Just as *Swordsman II* provides an intriguing variation on the theme of masculinity in Jin Yong's novel, so *Portland Street Blues* provocatively modulates the homoeroticism in Woo's genre films. The film attempts to imagine a male-female relationship that departs from the generic portrayals of heterosexuality. The "homoerotic" relationship between Thirteen and Coke is unfettered by the burden of family and free from feminine influences. It is built on loyalty and mutual respect. Yet, for such relationships to be intelligible within the gender dynamics of the genre, the film must fully articulate Thirteen's transgender identification as a masculine subject. This portrayal, which in effect concedes that masculinity is not the exclusive property of male bodies, is simply too threatening to be accommodated fully in a genre film. In a discussion of the cross-dressing opera diva Yam Kim-fai (Ren Jianhui), Natalia Chan argues that Chinese culture seems to have more tolerance for women who cross-dress as men than vice versa, because a cross-dressing female performer like Yam Kim-fai, who embodies a "tragic" version of feminized (*yinrou*) masculinity, does not pose a real threat to the tradition of tough, strong (*yanggang*) masculinity.[38] Thirteen's decidedly *un*feminine masculinity in *Portland Street Blues* certainly departs from this tradition of feminized masculinity exemplified by Yam. More importantly, unlike Yam's roles, that of Thirteen is not a cross-dressed performance. Sandra Ng (Wu Junru) is not playing a male character as Yam was in Cantonese operas. Rather, Thirteen *is* a masculine character who has announced her transgender identification and who embodies a masculinity that rivals that of any other male characters in the film. She even forges a homoerotic relation with another hero. As such, she represents a far greater threat to the gendered structure of power than the examples of cross-dressed masculinity in Chan's analysis. The film's concluding scene exposes the anxiety of the genre toward this threat, which ironically is the fruit of its own production. After Thirteen has avenged the death of Coke, a bunch of young gangsters led by Ho-nam (played by Ekin Cheng), the hero of all the early *Young and Dangerous* films, congregate around her. This show of mass collectivity is a signature scene in all the films in the series. As Thirteen grieves Coke's death, Ho-nam remarks coolly, "She is a woman after all." Here, Ho-nam speaks the anxious conservative voice of the genre in this sudden attempt to tame the transgender butch, who has until this moment been its shining star. However, his remark sounds oddly disingenuous as the sight of a masculine hero grieving for another man is commonplace in gangster films. For instance, Ho (played by Ti Lung) grieving (far more emotionally than Thirteen) for Mark (played by Chow Yun-fat) at the end of *A Better Tomorrow* (Yingxiong bense) (dir. John Woo, 1994), would not have shown him to be "a woman after all." Ho-nam's insistence on Thirteen's "difference" is the film's anxious last-minute disavowal of her transgender identification, but the remark also ends up undermining the film's own innovative reworking of generic masculinity.

UNSUNG HEROES

My analysis of the two films is meant to provoke future work on other unsung heroes who have been overlooked as transgender subjects in Hong Kong cinema. I also hope to have shown that insights from transgender theory can significantly complicate our understanding of sexual desire. Furthermore, exploring different forms of transgender subjectivity and the context of their emergence in these two films has revealed an intriguing crisis in the representation of masculinity in the martial arts and gangster genres. The most idealized forms of masculinity in these genres involve a repudiation of heterosexuality and feminization; yet such repudiation also threatens to expose the repressed homoerotic roots of this masculine ideal. In *Swordsman II* and *Portland Street Blues*, transgender portrayals are a means of resolving this crisis. Yet they end up reconfiguring the fundamental gender and sexual dynamics underlying the genres. *Swordsman II*'s bold transformation of Dongfang Bubai substitutes the novel's anxiety of emasculation with an abandonment of masculinity altogether. In the film, it is the heroic *femininity* of a transsexual woman that triumphs over the restrained masculinity of Linghu Chong. In *Portland Street Blues*, a butch woman's successful embodiment of masculinity and appropriation of homoerotic desire has disrupted the seemingly natural association of heroic masculinity with genetic male bodies. However, despite the box-office success of these films, they remain exceptional examples. There hasn't yet been another transsexual woman or transgender butch on screen storming the martial or gangster world in heroic glory. I believe a critical recognition of these characters *as* transgender subjects is a necessary first step toward their continual existence on the big screen.

Just as exploring transgender subjectivities in film can lead to reconceptualizations of generic formulations of gender and sexuality, so the social and political recognition of transgender subjects may lead to changes in public attitudes toward gender and sexual variance. At the time of writing, following the suicide of Leslie Cheung on 1 April 2003, there has been an unprecedented surge of public appreciation for his brilliant cross-gender performances on screen and on stage. On 7 May, just over a month after Cheung's death, the much less publicized but equally heartbreaking suicide of Lin Guohua, a transgender woman from Taiwan, also prompted much public reflection on the urgent need to respect, support, and protect transgender lives.[39] It is my hope that contributing to cultural work that respects the complexity of transgender experience and the agency of transgender subjects will, in its own modest way, contribute to the social and political struggles for gender and sexual diversity.

Part II
Transnational Significations

5

Kung Fu Films in Diaspora:
Death of the Bamboo Hero

Sheng-mei Ma

In our global village scholarly attention has turned increasingly to Hong Kong kung fu films, exported to the world via Tsui Hark (Xu Ke), Jackie Chan (Cheng Long), Jet Li (Li Lianjie), Yuen Wo-ping (Yuan Heping), and others. In the past decade or so, two strains of writing on what I call "Hongllywood" films have emerged: film orientalists who see in Hong Kong cinema a cultural alternative to mainstream Western productions; and film nostalgics who consider the Chinese/transnational identity as celluloid constructed. At their worst, such writings degenerate into fanzines' plot summaries or the fetishization of celebrities. At best, they not only map out an engaging art form specific to Hong Kong but also point to its global reach. Mostly of non-Chinese descent, the former group yearns for the non-self, an essentialized entity never part of Western-ness. Mostly of Chinese descent, the latter yearns for the "lost" self, an essentialized entity imagined to be part of Chinese-ness. The former is tinged with fresh-eyed, exotic longing, the latter with tired wistfulness. I belong decidedly to the film nostalgics group. In view of the nostalgic nature of Hong Kong kung fu films, as contended by Hector Rodriguez and others, I am apparently not alone.[1]

A disclaimer about the opening focus on Hong Kong: at least two filmmakers analyzed here are based partly in Taiwan: King Hu (Hu Jinquan) and Ang Lee (Li An). The fight scene in the bamboo grove in Hu's *A Touch of Zen* (Xianü, 1969) was filmed in central Taiwan; Lee, himself from Taiwan, shot most of *Crouching Tiger, Hidden Dragon* (Wohu canglong, 2000) on location in China. In addition, Taiwanese and overseas money and market play as pivotal a role in the filmmaking process as does the felt need for an essentialized Chineseness among the Chinese diaspora.[2] I consider Hong Kong more the epicenter than a confined geographical area for the nostalgia industry on Chineseness. Now that Hong Kong has returned to "the embrace of the Motherland," I see an even greater need to grant the island its due as the core for the network of celluloid fantasies.

Consequently, this chapter explores the stylization of Chineseness in the trope of kung fu masters, particularly when they — or their shadows — relocate across time and space to Southern California. As the trope of martial arts continues to wed masculinity with power within the context of the global market, the traditional "bamboo-like gentleman hero" falls out of favor. But first one must sort out the intricacies of *wuxia pian* (swordplay films) and kung fu films (using primarily fists and legs) in the evolution of Hong Kong cinema. The dominance of *wuxia pian* gave way to kung fu in the early 1970s, but the two never truly parted company: Jackie Chan's (Cheng Long) modern action thrillers continue to thrive on props and stunts, drawing from both traditions. Their merger is not surprising, in view of Hong Kong films' complex fountainheads: *wuxia xiao shuo* (novels of chivalry), Beijing Opera, Chinese *wushu* (martial arts or kung fu), and even Hollywood's entertainment industry, with its gun-toting action heroes and special effects. All these cultural strands contribute to the visual spectacle that is kung fu, which can be simulated as much by Jet Li, a martial artist, as by Jackie Chan and Michelle Yeoh (Yang Ziqiong), a Beijing Opera trainee and a modern-dance student, respectively.[3] Hence, "kung fu films" in this chapter also allude to *wuxia pian*. Despite the difference in fighting styles the two genres closely resemble each other in terms of their historical settings and escapism. The removal from the present makes possible the self-empowering fantasies. Action thrillers associated with such names as John Woo (Wu Yusen), Chow Yun-fat (Zhou Runfa), and Jet Li project identical, a-historical longing into a postmodern or futuristic setting, where gun-slinging, car-chasing, multiple explosions, and consciousness- and form-altering are justified by the same kind of distance from the here and now. Mutating in response to the global market, action thrillers in diaspora have skillfully cloned themselves, becoming replacements for the casualty list I am belaboring in these pages. I intend to study kung fu's afterlife at some future date.

A CASUALTY OF THREE

As kung fu films migrate from Hong Kong's Chinese cultural context to Hollywood's global marketability, creating the hybrid subgenre of "Hongllywood" films, kung fu's "Chineseness" is stylized to bring it more in line with consumer preferences. Granted that "Chineseness" has always been stylized, even in mainland Chinese or Hong Kong films, it takes on shared characteristics in Hongllywood "bastards." In this stylization certain filmic elements are suppressed, which I call "casualties," in accordance with martial metaphors inherent in this genre. Given the inevitable changes in the history of filmmaking, this chapter may be taken as a requiem of sorts, because disappearance or even extinction signals vulnerability and ill-adaptability. Specifically, I witness a casualty of three: in terms of film sets, the once-ubiquitous bamboo has disappeared; in terms of fighting, traditional kung fu and Beijing Opera forms and tableaux have been replaced by stunts aided by special effects, cinematography, editing, and computer wizardry; in terms of body exudation, the extravagance of blood, *qi* (breath), and traditional sentiments like *yi* (camaraderie) have been excised. This "trinity" of setting, stunt, and exudation, I contend, are the composites of any particular fight scene and the "essence" of the masculinist kung fu genre. The "bamboo-like gentleman hero" is one who possesses all three: the revered qualities of bamboo, exceptional fighting skills, and traditional values.

To illustrate the three components, imagine yourself the film editor working on the rushes in the editing room. You can freeze a fight scene and digitally erase the fighters, thus directing attention to the set and props. In this process, bamboo emerges as one of the favorite sets and props; it frequently transforms itself from part of the static set to a dynamic prop, even as the hero's weapons. A pioneer of kung fu films, King Hu's *Come Drink with Me* (Da zuixia, 1965) creates a *zuixia* or drunken master wielding a bamboo staff as a weapon and as an emblematic scepter to his gang of beggars. Similarly, the protagonist in Lau Kar-leung's (Liu Jialiang) *36th Chamber of Shaolin* (Shaolin sanshiliu fang, 1978) chances upon the concept for a new weapon, a *nunchaku* prototype, when he plays with a broken yet still attached bamboo stem. Bamboo, which interpellates Hong Kong kung fu films, is completely cut from Hongllywood productions.

Let's put back in the frame the fighters, the intended focal point of any martial arts sequence, and we soon discover that fight choreography has undergone drastic changes. Hollywood places far more emphasis on stunts than on traditional kung fu punches and kicks and Beijing Opera tableaux. However supple and acrobatic, and however elaborate the footwork and martial arts forms, the repertoire of the body is limited in comparison to a high-tech dream factory. As opposed to the longish takes from a single camera in early films such as *36th Chamber of Shaolin* and Jet Li's *Shaolin Temple* (Shaolin si) (dir. Zhang Xinyan, 1979), multiple cameras, brief shots, cinematographic innovation, constructive editing, and special effects have come to dominate Hong Kong films, as evident in Tsui Hark's oeuvre. I would also count John Woo's aesthetics of bullet- and explosives-riddled violence in the "stunts" category because of the simple fact that the next area of body exudation entails *immediate, direct* issuing from the human body rather than by means of such vehicles as guns or machines. By the same token, *anqi* (secret or concealed weapons like darts) in *wuxia pian* also belong to the "stunts" category. The oft-used playing in reverse of a flying-dart sequence in kung fu films testifies to *anqi*'s "technical" origin.

The last area of body exudation includes all that issues, unmediatedly, from fighters' bodies — body liquids of blood, especially the kind that spews forth profusely from the mouth, vomit, sweat; body parts, for example in the grotesque, sadomasochistic case of Zhang Che's *One-Armed Swordsman* (Dubi dao, 1967); and sounds emanating from the body, such as heavy breathing, grunts, moans, cries, last gasps, cracking of bones and skulls, cackles and variations of what I have come to regard as a quintessentially Chinese performance of mirth. The final point is intriguing: a Chinese kung fu laugh consists of a series of near-detached units similar in tone but in decreasing volume and intensity, each utterance punctuated by a slight pause, enough to give the laugh the appearance of "a sentence of monosyllables" like Mandarin and Cantonese. How one laughs is determined, I submit, by the language one speaks; a monosyllabic tongue engenders monosyllabic laughs. The most memorable duet in merriment are, on the one hand, the sonorous, deep-throated "Hah Hah Hah," signifying contentment or exultation and, on the other, the shrill, semi-insidious "Heh Heh Heh." Possibly, such stylization of laughs can be traced to the Beijing Opera's performance of Zhong and Jian, loyal and traitorous characters. To illustrate the likely origin of these stylized laughs one recalls Tsui Hark's *Peking Opera Blues* (Daomadan, 1986), whose opening and concluding credits roll with the image and distinctly "monosyllabic" laughter of a Beijing Opera warrior with a painted face. In addition to such body sounds, the typical kung fu soundtrack encompasses loud, often discordant music; the abrasive, aspirative contact noise of punching and kicking; and, of course, the poor, side-splitting dubbing in English. The formulaic performance of *qigong* (kung fu with *qi* or breath) is yet another kind of body exudation that never fails to give Western audiences the giggles. What appears to be a "supernatural" transmission of one's energy through palms into an ailing character is so unscientific and eccentric that it comes to confirm all the stereotypes Westerners harbor about the backward Orient. Yet in recent sci-fi films, *qigong* seems suddenly plausible, judging by the showdown between Yoda and Count Dooku in *Star Wars: Episode II — Attack of the Clones* (dir. George Lucas, 2002), in which colossal stone pillars are hurled with *qi* or energy emitted from bare palms.

Western audiences' giggles over the extravagance of kung fu exudation aside, fight scenes are key to kung fu's popularity in Hollywood, so long as they are properly repackaged. The secret of success for martial arts choreographers such as Yuen Wo-ping lay in the fact that kung fu, to borrow from Maxine Hong Kingston's concluding sentence in *The Woman Warrior*, "translated well." Primitive grunts, smashing sounds of human flesh, and metallic clanks of swords are not dialogue, presenting minimal obstacles for moviegoers from another linguistic system. Indeed, such non-lingual in fight scenes, including the whooshing of bullets, deafening explosions, and shattering of glass in a vintage John Woo, vie with English as the "lingua franca" of global cinema. Similar to dances in musicals, kung fu's balletic choreography requires minimal linguistic and cultural knowledge for it to be appreciated. Much of the culture-specific subtleties, however, are lost in translation. Bamboo is but one example.

First of all, the set, or the disappearance of bamboo in kung fu films: Bamboo is cut from kung fu films because it does not "translate well." The United States is a bamboo-less country and the rich symbolism inherent in bamboo in kung fu films would be entirely lost on an American audience. Nevertheless there is an association called The American Bamboo Society (ABS) formed in 1979, which became incorporated in the state of California in 1981. Today ABS, which is part of an international bamboo society, has more than 1,400 members living throughout the US and in 37 other countries. The ABS publishes a bimonthly magazine and an irregular journal. In 2001 the ABS had chapters in Southern California, Northern California, Texas, Northeast, Florida-Caribbean, Pacific Northwest, Hawaii, Southeast, Oregon, Louisiana-Gulf Coast, Tucson, Arizona, and Puerto Rico. However, most people in the United States know next to nothing about bamboo, which grows only in coastal areas, although the situation may be improving. Freer Gallery of Art and Arthur M. Sackler Gallery, part of the National Smithsonian Institute in Washington, D.C., feature monthly family programs called ImaginAsia, which hosted "Sacred Lotus, Symbolic Bamboo" in summer 2002. This program coincided with "The Silk Road," the theme of the thirty-sixth Festival of American Folklife at The National Mall, in late June and early July that year. Also, among the junk mail I received recently, I discovered a United Airlines brochure promoting its Mileage Plus frequent-flyer program to China, Hong Kong, and Taiwan. Printed prominently on the envelope and the brochure was fresh-green bamboo, along with an ancient coin bearing Chinese script and a classical arbor with upturned roof. Bamboo has become as recognizably Chinese as have Chinese script and classical architecture. In terms of fashion, bamboo has long been deployed to evoke the exotic in décor — lamp stands, kettle handles, even chinoiserie wallpaper. In a *New York Times* full-page advertisement on 19 May 2002, the clothing company Banana Republic featured its summer fashions protruding from a handbag with circular bamboo handles, displayed on a tabletop of thin strips of bamboo or rattan — a retro women's fashion look. The Travel section of Sunday's *New York Times* frequently features advertisements for Jamaica, with a long bamboo raft, two Caucasian tourist-passengers seated in the rear, and a dark-skinned man at the bow propelling the raft with a long bamboo pole.

In Chinese culture, bamboo is, for lack of a better expression, Chineseness itself. Similar to roses in the West, bamboo permeates Chinese culture, so much so that it requires exceptional mental rigor to think of bamboo as, for instance, river cane, tropical grass, or a "bamboo tree," as Judy Garland sings in *Meet Me in St. Louis* (dir. Vincente Minnelli, 1944). One of the "four gentlemen" (plum, orchid, bamboo, chrysanthemum), bamboo is said to stand for probity because of its straightness, flexibility because of its gently swaying and graceful stem, and humility because it is hollow inside. Beloved in Chinese painting, each part of bamboo — the long stem with knots, the finger-like leaves, the bamboo shoots — resembles a particular brush stroke in Chinese calligraphy. Since painting and calligraphy are the domains of the traditional literati, bamboo has long been dear to "keepers" of Chinese culture. At the other end of the cultural spectrum, a major gang in Taiwan, whose members are the descendants of mainland émigrés, is called *Zhu Lian Bang* (The Gang of Bamboo Union). Its leader, Chen Chi-li (Chen Qili), masterminded the 1984 assassination of Henry Liu

(Jiang Nan), a San Francisco-based journalist alleged to have defamed in his writings then Taiwanese President Chiang Ching-kuo (Jiang Jingguo). Chen Chi-li is believed to have acted at the behest of the Taiwanese government's intelligence chief.[4] With strong ties to the *Kuomintang* (the Nationalist Party), the Gang of Bamboo Union also feels itself exiled from China and claims, like its namesake, old-fashioned loyalty and camaraderie (*zhong* and *yi*). The practical and decorative functions of bamboo are boundless, including scaffolding used in construction work, building materials, clothes drying poles, broomsticks, furniture, chopsticks, calligraphy brushes, and so forth.

This contrast of the culture-specific symbolism of bamboo leads sadly to the conclusion that its richness in Chinese culture, like the Zen *koan*, cannot be transmitted or decoded in American culture. Stunts and body exudations have to be similarly contextualized. The various origins of kung fu films, including Chinese *wushu* (martial arts), Beijing Opera, and early Cantonese and Mandarin kung fu films in Hong Kong have two common threads regarding the human body running through them. First, the body is always made to undergo rigorous training and trials tantamount to torture to obtain victory, which often verges on the spiritual rather than merely the physical; the body, with all the pain it must endure, becomes a vehicle for higher goals. The staple of protagonists' arduous apprenticeship and combat should be predicated on a philosophy that emphasizes self-discipline, so much so that it appears to be "sadomasochism" to outsiders. On the other hand, absolute subjection to the master seems to run counter to the ultimate lesson of self-sufficiency, which defines kung fu. One's physical body, its materialist extension in the form of weapons, its transcendental reserve of *qi* or spirit, and its faith in nationalism and ethnic identity, make up the arsenal one might need to annihilate multiple enemies, at times a whole army. The abjection of blood, sweat, and grimaces of pain, comes to suggest the sublimity of the mind and ideology — an Eastern version of romanticism yoking the mundane and the sublime.

Body exudation, of course, pours out of this wedding of opposites: it could be the invisible, life-giving *qi*; it could also be the blood one vomits to forecast defeat and imminent death. In the worst case scenario, the former looks rather superstitious, the latter revoltingly uncouth. Given the blood, sweat, saliva, and auditory manifestations of yells, moans, and other sounds that permeate any fight scene, middle-class Western sensibility is prone to tuning out kung fu and dismissing it as kitsch. Be that as it may, kitsch reveals much about the "home" culture that engenders it and the "host" culture that receives it. Perhaps owing to the lack of scientific equipment as much as to anything else, traditional Chinese medicine and health-care practice place tremendous emphasis on physical symptoms — visual examination of the patient, taking of the pulse, and inspection of blood, phlegm and other forms of secretion. Hence, audiences of Chinese descent tend to accept the oft-seen scenario in which a diagnosis is made on the basis of brief pulse-taking. To non-Chinese, this seems ludicrous. In addition, the discrepancy between production and reception of filmic body fluids may well stem from the two cultures' drastically different environments. An island just south of the Tropic of Cancer, Hong Kong is unremittingly hot and humid, where sweating is spontaneous when one steps out of an air-conditioned building or automobile. The reek of perspiration wafts close-by; the sweat "maps" around armpits, back and waist are a common sight on men and women; tempers flare up, short and quick, demanding instant release, such as in kung fu's quick punches. Conditions in Southeast Asia, where Cantonese emigrants were once the major market for early Hong Kong films, are even more tropical. Like lush vegetation, the exuberance of bodily fluids comes across in the West as both exotic and repulsive, both life-affirming and chaotic. Following "editing room" protocol, an analysis of the "bamboo-like gentleman hero" will foreground the set, the stunt, and the body exudation respectively, whenever possible. In the vortex of action, however, one does not always discern lines of separation among the trio.

BAMBOO-LIKE GENTLEMAN HERO

Critics have repeatedly pointed out the nostalgic quality of King Hu's oeuvre. A Beijing exile in Hong Kong, Hu draws extensively from Beijing Opera and Chinese tradition. David Bordwell in *Planet Hong Kong* makes an observation about kung fu films in general and about King Hu in particular: "The alteration of swift attack and abrupt rest is characteristic of the Asian martial arts" — a style attributed to both martial arts and Beijing Opera conventions, whereby movements are punctuated with "moments of pure stasis, the technique of *liang hsiang* ('displaying'), often underlined by a cymbal crash,"[5] otherwise known as a clapper (*ban*). Undoubtedly, Hu's action sequence and the musical accompaniment owe an enormous debt to Beijing Opera. Hu's stylistic borrowing from Chinese culture also includes bamboo, which associates protagonists with righteousness. This bamboo lineage of the gentleman hero manifests itself in King Hu, Tsui Hark, and Ang Lee, among others.

Aesthetically framing a key fight scene halfway through Hu's classic *A Touch of Zen* (1969), bamboo links human bodies with mortality by the sword. The duel takes place in a bamboo grove, with the protagonists overwhelmed by their enemies. On the run, they cut down much bamboo, followed by their enemies engaged in the same "clearing" of the battleground. Yet the heroine abruptly doubles back and performs a flying stunt, alighting on top of a bamboo branch before hurling herself down to slash her opponent, a move made possible by the earlier clearing. Similar to bamboo felled by steel, the heroine reverses the fortune of war when she turns bamboo's fragility into flexibility. Faced with swords or adversity, human bodies are not unlike bamboo, bending temporarily but bouncing back in the end. Hu further ties bamboo to an essentialized Chinese rectitude in that the protagonists are persecuted by the Ming Emperor's chief eunuch. Nationalist paranoia intertwines with castration anxiety.[6]

Compared with swordplay films today, Hu's action sequence appears rudimentary and overly static by the standards of MTV and Tsui Hark: fighters frozen in preparation for the next move; swords locked in an awkward, arm-wrestling stalemate. Mediocre fights are, nonetheless, enlivened by the soundtrack and beautiful set, using what Bordwell describes as "constructive editing."[7] Fragmentary, elliptical shots showing characters leaping to the tops of bamboo trees and falling from them are woven together by the soundtrack's crescendo of bodies whooshing through air and a musical piece using traditional Chinese instruments. The scene rounds off perfectly when the male protagonist (played by Bai Ying), exhausted and spent, resheathes his sword at the very instant the music falls silent.

While Hu sets his film long before the arrival of the West in China, Tsui Hark's *Once Upon a Time in China* (Huang Feihong) series in the 1990s locates the nationalist hero squarely during the late Qing entanglements with colonialism. An increasingly complex symbol, bamboo resurfaces in fight scenes throughout the series. Toward the end of *Once Upon a Time*, the Cantonese Wong and northerner Yim duel in a warehouse filled with bamboo and, specifically, on bouncy bamboo ladders. Yim's northern "iron robe" kung fu — a legendary form of *qigong* — shrouds and protects him, even stopping a huge iron weight falling on him. Yet the southern kung fu practiced by the bamboo-like gentleman Wong prevails. Within the larger nationalist sentiment, Hong

Kong audiences would surely be gratified by the outcome of this north-south rivalry. Ever so calm and with a faint smile, Wong readies himself for any attack in an open-armed, welcoming tableau, in contrast to Yim's teeth-gnashing, animalistic rage. Wong does not even seem to breathe any harder during the fight, which is further "ritualized" by Wong Fei-hong (Huang Feihong)'s theme music. Since the 1950s, this music has been used in ninety-nine films about the hero, played invariably by Kwan Tak-hing (Guan Dexing). By contrast, Yim issues bestial cries, which are rendered hilariously in English captions as "EEE-YAH!" or "HEY-YAH!" Toward the end of their fight, Yim's disheveled hair, cut loose by his own *anqi* of a knife hidden at the tip of the queue, associates him with barbarians, according to Confucian ethos. Indeed, Yim's iron robe, steel-like moves, and *anqi* bring to mind modern Western weaponry; moreover, Yim is in cahoots with a gang that collaborates with Americans in smuggling coolies and women to the U.S. Although blinded by his ambition to reign supreme in kung fu, Yim is not the archvillain. His disciple, played by Yuan Biao, in fact, defeats the American henchman on the slave ship and practically lynches him on the mast. Witnessing Yim being cut down by a volley of musket shots, the disciple cries out "Master!", in effect acknowledging both Yim and Wong. Yim's ultimately benign nature is revealed by his dying words. In a pool of blood, he cautions Wong, "You can't fight guns with kung fu," hence evoking the history of gunboat diplomacy and Western imperialism in the late Qing era. Again, Wong exhibits Hu-styled trickery when he kills the American antagonist with a musket bullet finger-flicked like a traditional *anqi*. As resilient as bamboo, Chinese kung fu allegedly wins when it integrates Western technology.

As Hong Kong goes hi-tech and Hollywood, the filmic imagery of bamboo is replaced by a more general, contemporary code of flexibility and resourcefulness. For instance, at the end of the sci-fi Kato-esque *Black Mask* (Heixia) (dir. Daniel Lee, 1996), Jet Li destroys his enemy not by flinging a marble-shaped bullet but a computer disk at him. The final showdown of Jet Li and the demonic antagonist takes place in an underground chamber. The gloomy set appears vaguely post-holocaust in style, with bouncy boards over a pool of water conducting an electric current. Once stripped of the postmodernist trappings of computers, electric cables, and guns, the set resembles the rickety bamboo ladders from 1991's *Once Upon a Time*. The truncated electric cables spewing forth sparks are wielded much like the "cloth" whip in the 1992 *Once Upon a Time in China II*.

Bamboo serves both as the set and the prop in *Once Upon a Time II*. The finale comes as the corrupt Qing official (played by Donnie Yen) and Wong confront each other in a warehouse full of bamboo racks and baskets. Then Wong and his disciple are cornered in a narrow, dead-end alley. Donnie Yen's weapons associate him not only with Yim but with the West. Yen tries to gun down Wong and his disciple in the warehouse and, in the alley, twists a lengthy bed sheet, turning it perversely into a steel-like whip with his *qigong*. Although vulnerable, Wong's weapon of a splintered bamboo pole prevails yet again. As Yen tightens the steel-whip noose around Wong's neck, the cracked bamboo pole enables Wong to cut through the cloth and, with a single fiber sticking out of his pole, Wong slashes Yen's throat. In slow motion, a stunned Yen picks out the fiber in his throat and a thin line of blood oozes out and then explodes. Body exudation from Yen's throat brings about his violent end. By contrast, blood-letting via the normal orifice — the mouth — is less deadly, as Wong's disciple survives despite the copious blood he coughed up when he was whipped earlier.

Like Hong Kong itself, Tsui Hark is a cultural mixture; born in Vietnam, trained at film schools in the United States, and based in Hong Kong, he is restlessly innovative and unabashedly commercial.[8] For instance, Tsui Hark adroitly manipulates nationalist sentiment in his *Once Upon a Time* saga, varying the role of antagonists against the constant of Wong's heroism, providing the appearance of variation in what is essentially a banal formula. *Once Upon a Time I* pits the hero against Western imperialism, which takes the form of an American slave ship, whereas *Once Upon a Time II* locates antagonists in the nativist White Lotus rebellion. The U.S. Consulate in *Once Upon a Time II* provides a sanctuary for China's founding father, Dr Sun Yat-sen (Sun Chongshan), and his struggles to overthrow the Qing dynasty: Americans are now good guys. *Once Upon a Time III*, in turn, casts Russians as the evil force, complemented by Chinese thugs. As a whole, the *Once Upon a Time* series demonstrates that Chinese-speaking audiences accept shifting alliances with foreign powers and, more importantly, that racial/ethnic consciousness grows in conjunction with conflicts and interactions. *Once Upon a Time III* closes with a lion dance contest for a ball on top of a bamboo-erected dome. Notwithstanding the extravagance and "bang" (literally, of gongs and cymbals), notwithstanding the loaded "Chinese" symbols of bamboo and the lion dance, it proves to be an anti-climactic "whimper" to the trilogy.

Ang Lee's *Crouching Tiger, Hidden Dragon* is a belated tribute to *wuxia pian*; it revisits the sets and symbols of bamboo, but with unprecedented sexual tensions. Based *very* loosely on the fourth of Wang Dulu's five-part *wuxia xiaoshuo* (novels of chivalry), *Hetie Wubu Qu* (The Crane and the Steel), Lee's *Crouching Tiger* makes several major changes to Wang's plot. The narrative perspective is no longer that of Liu Taibao, a second-rate martial artist with the foibles of Everyman. Wang's focus on the young lovers, Jen and Lo (Yu Jiaolong and Luo Xiaohu in Chinese, played by Zhang Ziyi and Chang Chen), is balanced by Lee with the older pair, Yu Shu-lien (Yu Xiulian) and Li Mu-bai (played by Michelle Yeoh and Chow Yun-fat). To bring out the film's theme fully, far more passion and eroticism mark the young lovers' relationship, in contrast to their suppression by the older pair. Characterization and plot are similarly revised to intensify sexual transgression, especially with respect to the alleged affair between Li's master *Jiangnan He* (Southern Crane) and the witch-like Jade Fox (Yu Huli). Lee also magnifies Wang's Taoist tendencies, making the film more consonant with the contemporary "New Age" or alternative culture fad.

Like many novels in this genre, the story revolves around a precious sword, *Qingming* ("Green Destiny" but literally, "Bright and Obscure," a yin/yang Taoist union).[9] Because its Chinese name is highly suggestive, I elect to use the Chinese version in the following discussion. First of all, the sword is a phallic symbol, the exceptional aggressiveness of *Qingming* manifested in its effortless shearing of every other weapon. A patriarchal heirloom, it has been passed down by Southern Crane to Li Mu-bai. That Jen seeks to steal and possess it shows female subversion of patriarchy, an attempt no different from that of Jade Fox, Jen's "master," who, decades ago, tried in vain to gain access to the secrets of Wudang Pai (the Taoist counterpart of the Buddhist Shaolin) by giving Southern Crane the pleasure of her body. It is worth noting that a Wudang master violates the vow of celibacy while hypocritically upholding the Wudang interdiction against passing on its martial arts, and hence power, to women. Another way to think about the "obscure" or suppressed history of the sword is to reflect on the blood it has shed, not only virginal but of its enemies, all traceless now on the brightness of the sword.

While Li Mu-bai appears on the verge of changing the Wudang tradition and taking Jen as his apprentice, he remains staunchly traditional in his resolve to kill Jade Fox and avenge his master. Moreover, his interest in Jen is not entirely, shall we say, "professional." The master-disciple relationship across the gender line can be characterized by mastery and submission in such a way that it becomes fraught with sexual longing and repression. A heterosexual bonding is no longer "containable" by the family paradigm of filial piety and devotion. After all, the genesis for action lies in Li's unrequited love for Yu Shu-lien, with whom he has maintained a platonic relationship out of respect for her dead fiancé and his sworn brother. Li's discontent is so powerful that he decides to "*chuguan*" ("terminate or come out of retreat"). The retreat being the path to transcendence, Li wishes to embrace rather than abandon human passion. And yet his love for Shu-lien is derailed once he comes across Jen, the thief of his masculinity. As much as Jen's desire to usurp male power, Li subliminally satiates his sexual drive toward a younger, more attractive Jen by pursuing and subjugating her. The erotic entanglement of Li and Jen is buried under the two explicit pairings — Jen and Lo; Shu-lien and Li. Another secret of *Qingming*, the mutual attraction between Li and Jen is in fact a reprise of their respective masters' transgression. Whereas no film critic has mentioned the jealousy and tension in the triangular relationship of Li, Shu-lien, and Jen, it is readily apparent if we closely examine Shu-lien's anxiety, and Li and Jen's interaction, both taking place very close to or amid bamboo. Herein, Ang Lee transforms bamboo from King Hu's aesthetic objects and Tsui Hark's utilitarian items into "objective correlatives" for human desires.[10]

In the scene of the brief confession of love between Li and Shu-lien at a roadside rest stop, bamboo provides an idyllic backdrop through the geometric wall opening. In addition, their teacups are carved from bamboo stems. Asking her to be patient, Li fails to initiate an escape from the prison of human constructs, like the rest stop, and of social obligations to the dead. So close to the bamboo grove, they cannot bring themselves to venture into nature and answer the call of love. Instead, Li follows Jen into a much wilder bamboo grove later in the film. This turn of events is foreshadowed by Shu-lien's anxiety about Jen as a potential rival. In their duel Shu-lien proves a far superior swordswoman, yet Jen's *Qingming* sword cuts through all her weapons. Comparing this fight with Hu's *A Touch of Zen*, one is aware of how far martial arts choreography has come. Multiple camera angles, quick editing, acrobatic moves and stunts, and Tan Dun's Academy Award-winning soundtrack capture the action in an exhilarating flow. A brief skirmish involves a medium shot of the two women, followed by a shot from above, as well as one from behind a character (as if seen through her eyes and highlighting the opponent), and in reverse (as though through the opponent's eyes), and so forth. Ang Lee nonetheless paces the sequence with the time-honored kung fu film counterpoint of dynamics and stasis. There are pauses in the action, like inhalations, before one launches into another round of combat. Better still, such caesuras lie between exhalation and inhalation, a momentary void where life is suspended in uncertainty, hence making the life that continues all the more precious.

One caesura arrives when Jen complacently runs her fingers over the blade that has disenabled all of Shu-lien's weapons. Shu-lien shouts almost in hysteria: "Don't touch it! That's Li Mu-bai's sword!" "Come and get it if you can!" Jen dares in a battle of words over control of Li's manhood. Shu-lien's shout is out of character, as she manifests a composed, resolute demeanor throughout, in contrast to Jen's breathlessness and flustered look. (Zhang Ziyi's acting turns out to involve a great deal of heavy panting.) In fact, there is a note of desperation in Shu-lien's warning. Instinctively, she feels insecure. Halfway through the film, Shu-lien comments on Li's interest in Jen: "I know she'll intrigue you," a somewhat misleading translation of the line in Mandarin, "I know you'll be suspicious." The English version intentionally heightens sexual innuendo. When Li does pursue Jen, the matronly servant Wu Ma consoles an injured Shu-lien by saying perhaps "Li Mu-bai can do it [kill Jen]." Shu-lien's worried and doubtful look in response bespeaks her premonition of the emotional entanglements of Li and Jen.

Into the bamboo grove go Jen and Li. Courtesy of wirework, the two alight on waving bamboo stems.[11] Unbeknown to the godfather of human sexuality, Sigmund Freud, bamboo is phallic, as visualized by Ang Lee's cinematography. Bamboo bends and is soft at one moment, then straightens and erects itself the next. The drama of submission unfolds as a power play, the hypnotic eroticism written on Jen's youthful and almost translucent face as it flows across in slow motion. Bamboo leaves and her long black hair cast shadows like a veil over the face to accentuate the mystery of its desire. With her supine posture and facial longing captured in a high-angle close-up, with her near-perfect face occasionally occluded and completely controlled in the frame, this aesthetic gaze at Jen originates from Li's and the audience's dominating point of view. As Jen's bamboo swings back to loom above Li, he suddenly kicks the bamboo and Jen falls down, thus in effect denying any position of power for the woman. This is the first of Jen's three falls; all three have to do with loss, with Jen crashing down from dizzying ecstasies.

Li finally corners Jen on a boulder by a pool. In a classic Wudang move, Li points his fingers at Jen's forehead and subdues her. She nearly faints under his magnetic power. What Li accomplishes in that fleeting moment is transmission of *xinjue* ("heart secret": psychic and spiritual empathy and identification between master and disciple), a kind of mystical body emission involving, I imagine, *qi*. But Jen's expression of, in Georges Bataille's term, "little death"[12] when touched between the eyebrows seems a consummation of the erotic arousal started back on bamboo stalks. Jen gives in, promising that "if you can get the sword back in three moves, I'll follow you." The phrase "*wo jiu gen ni zou*" ("I'll follow you") brings to mind the misogynist Chinese proverb of "Follow the chicken if you marry a chicken; follow the dog if you marry a dog." Directly stealing the sword in an underhanded move, Li commands Jen to "*ba shi*" or "*pa shi*," translated as "kneel." Jen, for good reason, is unwilling to capitulate. Li then hurls *Qingming* into the pond, claiming that the sword is of no consequence, now that she is his disciple. Jen initiates the second fall in the film: she dives in to retrieve the sword and is rescued by Jade Fox. The crisis of submission to masculinity is averted, only for her to return to matriarchal oppression.

Li's cry of "*ba shi*" or "*pa shi*" is so poorly articulated that this critical turning point becomes a bewildering lacuna. This is not only because Chow Yun-fat's voice tends to be indistinctly high-pitched whenever he gets emotional but because, more fundamentally, his Mandarin is shaky. The initial reaction to the film shared by many Mandarin speakers is that Chow's and Michelle Yeoh's delivery of lines in Mandarin is so monotonous and stilted that it severely mars the film. (Chang Chen's is not much better by northern Chinese standards.) But in view of the global cinema and films festivals around the world that Ang Lee targets, the discomfort of native speakers matters little. Non-Chinese moviegoers are unlikely to notice the flatness of emotions in Chow's and Yeoh's voices. In view of Hong Kong films' tradition of dubbing for non-Cantonese speaking markets, performers have long been regarded as bodies and faces divorced of "authentic" voices — humans reduced to visual spectacles with no simultaneous dialogues and thus no interiority. As far as the global audience is concerned, Chow and Yeoh may as well have been pantomiming through the film. For that matter, the subtitles in English clearly package the product for the West. Other than the examples of sexual tension to which I have already alluded, subtitles are often simplifications to accommodate the West. A case in point: the northwestern province of Xin Jiang is translated as "the West," evoking the American West and the genre of Westerns.

In pursuit of Jade Fox, Li moves from his territory, the phallic bamboo, into hers, a dark, rain-soaked, womb-like cave. (The mouth of the cave reminds one of an underexposed image of Georgia O'Keefe's vaginal orchid.) Li enters the cave and finds a drugged Jen trying to rouse herself in a shallow pool. Jen turns to Li, her flimsy blouse so drenched that it hugs her breasts and protruding nipples. "Is it the sword or me you want?" offers Jen, while subconsciously tearing open her blouse. The scene borders on sexual foreplay. Li, supposedly one rung above his philandering master, remains unmoved and paternal. Li then proceeds to revive Jen with *qi* transmitted through his palms into her back. At this juncture, Li and Jen are caught "red-handed" by Shu-lien, who has tailed Jade Fox back to the cave. Shu-lien is momentarily taken aback, but quickly recovers when she realizes the lurking danger. Yet that fleeting moment of suspicion of the pair's subterranean "liaison" is intriguing. Shu-lien is the only "witness" to Li and Jen's repressed eros, from the theft of Li's "penis," to the stroking of it during the heroines' fight, and, in the cave, to the actual physical touch of the "lovers." Li touches two women in this film: he caresses Shu-lien in the rest stop and kisses her before he dies; he touches Jen on her forehead and, during the resuscitation, on her shoulder blades. Ang Lee fine tunes these scenes so they hover somewhere between classic heroism and decorum, on the one hand, and Freudian clashes of Thanatos and Eros, on the other.

Carnal desire also intertwines with death in the form of Jade Fox's *anqi*, poisoned needles propelled from her cudgel. One such needle finds its way into Li's neck and his blood stream, a masculine penetration delivering death. The duality of *Qingming* — its manifest and latent drives, its masculinity and femininity, its love and hate, its attraction and repulsion — self-destructs in a suicidal bloodbath. Ang Lee manages to pack in one more ambiguity in this double death scene. Li kills Jade Fox before his own demise. No blood spews forth from Jade Fox, which is atypical of the gruesome deaths of kung fu villains. On the contrary, Jade Fox confesses that her real target is Jen, her apprentice who, since age eight, has harbored the true poison because she withheld the subtleties of the Wudang martial arts manual from her illiterate master. This well-founded indictment implicates Southern Crane, who also withheld secrets; Li Mu-bai, who avenges Southern Crane; and the entire martial arts institution. Jade Fox articulates, in crisp, couplet-like Mandarin, the theme of paradox in *Crouching Tiger*. "Jen, my only family, my only enemy." Likewise, Jade Fox and Li destroy each other, members of an illegitimate family sired by Southern Crane.

Following Li's last wish, Jen travels to the mountains of the Wudang Monastery. She reunites with Lo for one night and, early the next morning, has Lo repeat the Xin Jiang legend that one who has "a faithful heart" can survive a fall from the top of the mountain — "*Xin cheng ze lin.*" As abrupt as in a dream sequence, Jen jumps off the cliff, to Yo Yo Ma's (Ma Youyou) elegiac cello. This is Jen's third and final fall. Religiously, this suggests a leap of faith in taking the vow to enter Wudang and leave the secular world and Lo. But the profound sadness in this fall recalls the pattern of plunges from the heights of bamboo, into the deep pool, and now through the clouds, all for the specific loss of Li Mu-bai — the first time an anti-climax to the orgiastic play with Li; the second time in search of Li's phallus; the third time the absence of Li himself. To read the leap not metaphorically, but literally, namely, Jen is jumping to her own death, demonstrates Jen's total surrender to Li and his last words. Refusing to save his last breath to elevate himself and reach eternity, as Shu-lien counsels in tears, Li instead confesses his thwarted love for Shu-lien. Rather than the enlightenment Taoism strives for, Li chooses human love, as ephemeral as it is. Now, in mourning for Li, Jen dies with her own unrequited love. The love-making with Lo the night before may well have been a last farewell, but the shot of a supine, grief-stricken Jen, with a blank stare past her lover's shoulder, does not divulge with whom she fantasizes herself having sex — Lo or Li or both.[13] Nor does Ang Lee foreclose this ambiguity. Even if a literal suicide, Jen's airborne suspension acquires a mythic dimension. Posited on romantic longings, kung fu films often locate finales in the expediency of deus ex machina, a reversal of the fortune of war through the intervention of a larger-than-life, otherworldly power. The monk savior in King Hu's *A Touch of Zen*, for instance, sacrifices himself and emits golden blood from a spot reminiscent of Christ's wound in his side. The vaguely apocalyptic tone of kung fu "endgames" permeates Ang Lee's closure as well.

Ang Lee's film, however, is an anomaly among the trans-Pacific careers of his fellow film practitioners. Jackie Chan, John Woo, Chow Yun-fat, and others carry various forms of their "Chineseness" into the genre of Hongllywood films. The symbolic capital of an exotic Orient begins to outweigh their early Hong Kong works, leading them further to commodify and universalize culture-specific performances for a global audience. In such contemporary, Westernized settings of post-Hong Kong films, there is no place for tropes exclusive to China. Ironically, bamboo and the bamboo hero, symbols of kung fu and the core of

Chineseness, are *bumped* from the cast or bumped *off*. When bamboo returns in *Rush Hour 2* (dir. Brett Ratner, 2001), it is to provide comic relief. Dangling from bamboo scaffolding bent into an "L," Jackie Chan reassures his partner Chris Tucker: "Chinese bamboo, very strong," before the pole breaks and they crash to the ground.

FADE-OUT

"Three" in Chinese suggests multiplicity. Among the many casualties of Hong Kong kung fu films in diaspora, I have identified only those bodies recognizable to me. Perhaps you can do the same for other remains.

6

Obtuse Music and Nebulous Males:
The Haunting Presence of Taiwan in Hong Kong Films of the 1990s

Shen Shiao-Ying

In the 2001 Taiwan Golden Horse Awards, many of the top honors went to Hong Kong films with strong narrative connections to China, for example *Lan yu* (dir. Stanley Kwan, 2001) and *Durian Durian* (Liulian piaopiao) (dir. Fruit Chan, 2000).[1] It seems, as we move into the twenty-first century, China's presence in Hong Kong cinema will become increasingly prominent, and ironically Taiwan's Golden Horse becomes more and more an arena which observes and highlights this trend.[2] As I write this chapter, news arrives about plans on how Teresa Teng (Deng Lijun)'s villa in Hong Kong is to be sold and a museum of the diva to be established in the port city of Shanghai. While Teresa Teng's iconic commercial legacy will be moving to Shanghai, a land she never physically stepped on, Hong Kong has already produced in recent years two films titled after Teng's songs, fully exploiting the metaphoric potential they hold for Chinese audiences.[3] Meanwhile, Taiwan remains the site of Teng's entombment, and as a place where the haunting nature of her death is still being probed.[4] Golden Horse's becoming the showcase for Chinese settings and actors, and China's becoming the display "home" of Taiwan-born Teng — these kinds of fascinating cultural symbiosis and shifts occurring among the different Chinese communities are what I would like to probe in this paper. The interesting evolution and entanglements of different Chinese communities and diverse kinds of "Chineseness" manifest themselves most seductively in the cinema of Hong Kong. Furthermore, the manifestation of this evolution can be linked to the curious choice of music to accompany several Hong Kong films, and their presentation of varying modes of masculinity.

I will focus on four Hong Kong films of the 1990s, namely *Farewell China* (Ai zai taxiang de jijie) (dir. Clara Law, 1990), *Chinese Box* (Zhongguo he) (dir. Wayne Wang, 1997), *Happy Together* (Chun'guang zhaxie) (dir. Wong Kar-wai, 1997), and *Ordinary Heroes* (Qianyan wanyu) (dir. Ann Hui, 1998), and analyse how they wrestle with Hong Kong's self-positioning as its relationship with China evolves, how Hong Kong's sense of self can be revealed in unexpected narrative sites, and how Hong Kong's self-image can be understood in gendered terms.

Writing from Taipei, I will specially highlight the haunting presence of Taiwan in these films. I use the word "haunting" to describe Taiwan's presence because the four cited Hong Kong films are not primarily concerned with any Taiwan issue; indeed in some cases there seems to be no trace of Taiwan at all. However, there is an elusive Taiwan factor to be detected and highlighted, and those films help tease out a kind of Hong Kongness that might otherwise escape our attention. Moreover, we shall also see how intricately Hong Kongness is linked to the gender structure embedded in the films, and when we unpack some of the films under a spectrum of different shades of masculinity, we will have a collaged picture of Hong Kong's self-reflection as it faced the last part of the twentieth century.

How does Taiwan exist and yet not exist, and haunt and help bring out a certain Hong Kongness in Hong Kong films? Let me begin with my viewing of Clara Law's *Farewell China* and Wayne Wang's *Chinese Box*. Hong Kong's struggle against and acquiescence to the fatherland — China, and its reaffirmation of its sense of self, can be detected and delineated in the musical space of these two films.

My first viewing of *Farewell China* was unremarkable until the film's end. The film was made around the time of the June Fourth Incident in 1989, and released a year later. The timing explains the obtrusive insertion of a goddess of democracy figure[5] at the end of the film. It was surprising and disorienting to witness the appearance of such a politically and historically loaded icon at the end of a heavy melodrama lamenting the Chinese obsession with migrating to the United States in pursuit of the American Dream. However, if it was unease one felt when spotting the goddess of democracy as the film closed, then what came after provoked a shock.

What comes after in *Farewell China* is the song "Ssu Hsiang Ch'i" (Sixiang qi) (To recall), an old Taiwan ballad made popular by Chen Ta

(Chen Da). Many have found it necessary to question or to comment on the arresting choice of music. Chinese film scholar Sheldon Lu, presenting his paper "Hong Kong Diaspora Film" at the Second International Conference on Chinese Cinema in 2000, explained that the song provided a nostalgic end to the film.[6] Taiwan film writer Lan Tsu-wei (Lan Zuwei) repeatedly inquired about the choice when interviewing the film's music editor, Shen Sheng-te (Shen Shengde),[7] who stated that the song expressed an all-encompassing Chineseness.[8] I myself felt the urge to ask the director about the song, when she visited Taipei during the 2000 Taipei Film Festival, to which she responded, the music simply felt right.

I agree with Shen Sheng-te that the initial impression of "Ssu Hsiang Ch'i" for many Chinese and non-Chinese might be its strong lyrical Chineseness; indeed that is exactly what one experiences when the song is first played at the beginning of the film. By the time we come to the film's tragic end, we have the sense that the raw and sad voice of Chen Ta does "feel right" for the picture. However, the reason I (and perhaps also Lan Tsu-wei)[9] found it necessary to question its selection involves that shock experienced when encountering this Taiwan ballad *in full force* at the end of a film about two Mainlanders. It is a shock of being jolted into a strange familiarity. As a Taiwan viewer one can maintain a "secure" distance when watching the disintegrating lives of the film's two Mainlander-protagonists, but the final song shatters that merely sympathetic distance. What is more, the song ends the film. As a Taiwan viewer I was left with an irreconcilable sense of disorientation.

To explore further my fascination, or perhaps obsession, with *Farewell China*'s "Ssu Hsiang Ch'i," let me first segue into Roland Barthes's "The Third Meaning: Research Notes on Some Eisenstein Stills."[10] In this 1970 article, as is obvious from its title, Barthes uses stills from Eisenstein's *Ivan the Terrible* (1945) and *Battleship Potemkin* (1925) to elaborate on his notion of "the third meaning." And it is my intention to borrow Barthes's notion of the third meaning to try to articulate how music can sometimes play out a muted aspect of a film's narrative. In line with his semiotic concepts, for Barthes, analysis can engage with the three levels of meaning of a text, the first two being the informational and the symbolic levels. Should I use Barthes's scheme to look into *Farewell China*'s "Ssu Hsiang Ch'i," on the informational level, I would then register elements such as its being a Chinese ballad, a song sung by a man, etc. On the symbolic level, considering the song's placement in the film's narrative, one could decide that it expresses lament toward the tragic state of Chinese people who have left their homeland, their homesickness, and their inner struggle with an alien culture. However, it is in the third meaning in which things become more interesting. Barthes finds the third meaning to be "persistent and fleeting, smooth and elusive," [11] and also a bit hard to name. Barthes first attempts to name the third level as that of *signifiance*, to differentiate it from *signification*, which is in the realm of the second level. If you find the term *signifiance* not immediately understandable, Barthes is not helpful in clarifying it, except to say that it is Julia Kristeva who first proposed it.[12] Barthes then drops *signifiance* and continues to use the terms *third meaning* and then *obtuse meaning* to explore what can constitute the third level of meaning. Is *obtuse meaning* any better than *signifiance*? Maybe not; but with the latter Barthes does elucidate:

> An obtuse angle is greater than a right angle: *an obtuse angle of 100°*, says the dictionary; the third meaning also seems to me greater than the pure, upright, secant, legal perpendicular of the narrative, it seems to open the field of meaning totally, that is infinitely. I even accept for the obtuse meaning the world's pejorative connotation: the obtuse meaning appears to extend outside culture, knowledge, information; analytically, it has something derisory about it: opening out into the infinity of language, it can come through as limited in the eyes of analytic reason: it belongs to the family of pun, buffoonery, useless expenditure. Indifferent to moral or aesthetic categories (the trivial, the futile, the false, the pastiche) it is on the side of the carnival. *Obtuse* is thus very suitable.[13]

So, what is *obtuse* about the final "Ssu Hsiang Ch'i" in *Farewell China*? The placement of the downsized model of the goddess of democracy must be related to it. For Clara Law, a filmmaker who has proven her capacity for stylization and coolness in her films — *Autumn Moon* (Qiuyue) (1992), *Temptation of a Monk* (Youzeng) (1993), *The Goddess of 1967* (Yushang 1967 de nüshen) (2000) — the final appearance of the democracy goddess is certainly sudden, over-the-top, and aesthetically out of place. And then comes "Ssu Hsiang Ch'i." Paired with images of under-developed China, the plaintive tones of "Ssu Hsiang Ch'i" further direct one toward a longing for a China that is nowhere — rural, divorced from landmarks, with its humble young and old. Such emotional maneuvering leaves one adrift between derision and reluctant submission.

For a Taiwan audience "Ssu Hsiang Ch'i" also evokes other

associations and sentiments: the song is at once old and modern, nostalgic, full of lament, and yet assertive and awakening. "Ssu Hsiang Ch'i" is an old song, but it was rediscovered during the 1970s, and inseparably identified with the plain singing style of Cheng Ta. During the time of Taiwan's economic growth and modernization, the singer and the ballad came to be associated with a moment of cultural awakening and the plain folkish singing of the very rustic Chen Ta was then considered "the true voice of Taiwan."[14] Thus, as one sits with the song in the end, there is not only the lingering unease of being confronted with the goddess statue and being enveloped by a sense of sadness, nostalgia, and mourning in the singing; what is more remarkable is that the song is also accompanied by an excess of meaning — the "baggage" of a sense of awakening, self-assertion, and protest. Coming immediately after the democracy goddess, "Ssu Hsiang Ch'i" is no longer merely a sentimental closing, but can ironically also be obtusely political. In the end "Ssu Hsiang Ch'i" does feel right, albeit awkwardly so, for *Farewell China*, a product of the emotional aftermath of June Fourth.

Barthes himself was aware of the problem in using film *stills* to locate possible third meanings in *motion* pictures, and devotes a segment in his "The Third Meaning" essay — 'The Still' — to defend his views. In it Barthes proposes that the "movement" in motion picture might not be "animation, flux, mobility, 'life,' copy, but simply the framework of a permutational unfolding."[15] Whether one agrees with or questions Barthes' proposition, one can still appreciate his attempt to locate the filmic, the essence of film if we must, not in the familiar motion, montage, photocopy, or diegesis, but in the elusive somewhere else. In fact, in a note in his article, Barthes suggests that the third meaning might well be in the third of the classical five senses — hearing; he further highlights this by disclosing that his probing of the third meaning is very much inspired by his consideration of Eisenstein's remarks on sound in film.[16]

It might well be that in many films, the moment of interest, of shock, of repulsion, and of affect happens in one smooth and fleeting frame or in one persistent and haunting tune. For me *Farewell China* finally becomes interesting at the moment "Ssu Hsiang Ch'i" begins to infect the democracy goddess. Just when the feminine statue establishes itself as a rather crass emotional and historical statement, Chen Ta's masculine singing soothes such a narrative break with a call for that eternal land, a gaze back at that "China that is nowhere." Just as one escapes China — landing in a park in New York, basking in a Taiwan ballad — the final quiet images of China pull one back to that insistent homeland.

Just as one considers the film as a feminine melodrama, about the pathetic disintegrating life of the female protagonist shackled to the land of liberty and opportunity, the film's awkward close gestures toward masculine allegorical possibilities. *Farewell China* does have its China connection (in the figure of Tony Leung Ka-fai) hysterically killed off (by Maggie Cheung) in its narrative, but ultimately, in its final montage and male vocal it relents to the quiet, firm, and unchanging call of China. This final sequence works like the filmmaker's last glance at China, a love at last sight, a tearful farewell to China. In the 1990s Clara Law and her screenwriter husband Eddie Fong began their gradual move to Australia.[17]

If the title *Farewell China* points to the film's oblique political stance in 1990, its Chinese title, *Ai zai taxiang de jijie* (Love in the season of another land), embodies the more melodramatic tone of the film. This incorporation of the different urges of a film through its different language titles is demonstrated in another film shot in Hong Kong in 1997, about the territory's handover to China: *Chinese Box*, or *Ch'ing-jen he-tzu* (Qingren hezi) (Lovers' box).[18] The English title of this Wayne Wang film highlights the film's Chinese connection; its Chinese title used in Taiwan, on the other hand, erases China and stresses the picture's romantic content. If one of the urges wrapped within the melodrama of *Farewell China* is an attempt to break away from the strong grip of parental China, then lodged within the love story of *Chinese Box* — whose title sequence opens with an actual Chinese box displaying oriental curios — is its urge to freeze or to "antique" Hong Kong into an exotic fetish, caressing it this way and that, before surrendering it to its rightful owner.

Chinese Box, another work grappling with formidable China, is a film about which Hong Kong reviewers at the time of its release found very few good things to say.[19] Even one of its stars, Maggie Cheung (Zhang Manyu), carefully admitted in an interview, "Wayne's view of Hong Kong kind of stayed in the 70s, or whenever he left."[20] Some have also commented on how "heavy-handed" Wang's metaphors are in this film.[21] The basic premise of the film is perhaps too obviously and neatly allegorical: the British Jeremy Irons as the dying colonial, longing for and losing his long-time Chinese object of desire; the Chinese Gong Li as the woman from China who desires to be the proper wife of her Hong Kong businessman boyfriend; and Maggie Cheung as the scarred Hong Kong local incapable of forgetting her former British lover.[22]

Chinese Box, through its actors, images and languages, shows us the different peoples related to Hong Kong's modern identity: the British, the Cantonese, the Mainlanders. However, *Chinese Box* seems to have, perhaps rightly, no trace of Taiwan. Does Taiwan then occupy no place in this tale, which tries to cohere and envision Hong Kong's state of being at a symbolically critical time in Chinese history? Well, not exactly, when we *listen* carefully. And when we do pay attention, the elusive Taiwan presence helps elucidate a Hong Kong that might otherwise easily be relegated to the background of *Chinese Box*'s Britain-China affair. In other words, in a tale where British Jeremy Irons and Chinese Gong Li predominate, the recurrent musical space in *Chinese Box* might be where an almost marginalized Hong Kong can be re-focused.

After many years of watching Hong Kong films through the filter of the looming handover, I was curious about how Wayne Wang, born and raised in Hong Kong but now a Chinese-American director, would picture his home city during 1997. In 1998, after viewing about twenty minutes of *Chinese Box* in a Taipei theatre, and hearing British Jeremy Irons urgently proposing to Chinese Gong Li, and when refused, self-righteously protesting, "What are you frightened of? I'm offering you something real, something now, something concrete. Don't be a coward, please!" I was worried about how much longer I would have to endure this suspiciously orientalist film. But then video images of Hong Kong and Maggie Cheung appeared, paired with a percussive and upbeat song that sounded familiar. The tune, which lasted only about twenty seconds: before I could register it, it was gone. As I puzzled over it the piece of music re-emerged with video close-ups of Maggie Cheung staring straight at the camera. This time the song played for twice as long. It was New Formosa Fun Park Band's funky "Song for a Jolly Gathering."

The excitement of hearing that song and my desire to hear it again helped me sit through the film. The reward was more than one minute of the song in the final segment of the film. Hearing it in *Chinese Box* had none of the shock that accompanied "Ssu Hsiang Ch'i." Encountering it was more like spotting a familiar and friendly face at a party of otherwise little interest. The spirited "Song for a Jolly Gathering" functioned more like an antidote to the film's thematic inclusion of the otherworldly, floating voice of Dadawa.

Dadawa's *Chinese Box* wailing theme song occurs almost ten times in the film, and accompanies the progressively consumptive male protagonist, John (the British journalist played by Jeremy Irons), as he slips into sleep at the end, beside Victoria Harbor, giving the impression that the whole film, or Hong Kong's colonial presence, is but a grand dream of an Englishman. Dadawa's wailings are exactly that — female vocal displays with no lyrics. From Changsha, Hunan Province, but born in Guangzhou as Zhu Zheqin, the very Han Dadawa likes to associate her New Age-like music with spiritual Tibet, with voices from the sky, with heavenly music, and with phrasings of a celestial spirit.[23] Dadawa's vocals seem to want to go beyond the earthly pull of language and the restraints of a restricted Chineseness; her voice soars into the ethereal. However, at times within the theme music, there is also background chanting by a child chorus, persistently reciting some Chinese mantra. Dadawa's wailing and the children's chants produce an eerie tension that also relays well John's complicated feelings toward Hong Kong and the Chinese woman for whom he's fallen. John, unlike many expatriates who prefer to keep a sanitary distance from the congested humanity of Hong Kong, plants himself in an old flat among the busy alleys and streets of Kowloon, breathing in market smells and tolerating the sounds of construction. But then, when life becomes too much (or death too near), he curses, "Oh God, I hate this city!" Paralleling his sentiments toward Hong Kong is his wrestling with his own Madonna-whore complex towards Vivian, his Chinese love (played by Gong Li). But ultimately, John's struggles and obsessions, like the persistent and ethereal theme music, and like the languid pace of the film, dissolve into a fade that evokes little weight and poignancy.

In this rather hollow Englishman's tale of Hong Kong, what injects it with a little bit of energy are the video montages of the plucky local Jean (played by Maggie Cheung) and of life in Hong Kong. These video images are paired with "Song for a Jolly Gathering." In contrast to Dadawa's vocal score, New Formosa Fun Park Band's song embraces languages, celebrates bastardized identity, and shakes listeners with an earthy stomping beat. "Song for a Jolly Gathering" begins with, "NA I YA LU WAN NA, I YA NA YA O HAY NA I YA LU WAN NA, I YA NA YA O" — not exactly familiar language. But most Taiwanese would recognize the phrases from the chants of our indigenous people (Taiwan aborigines, also called "mountain people" in the past, were driven into the mountains by the arrival of the mainland Han people). A male voice singing in Fukien comes next in the song, to be followed by singing in Hakka, interspersed with additional aboriginal chants by a female chorus. The song bids you "to remember to have a relaxed heart, to move your steps. Not to waste happy times." The song invites you — "whether Fukien or Mainlander, indigenous people or Hakka" — to love and celebrate the family on Formosa. This is almost too jolly to be true.

New Formosa Fun Park Band is very much identified with its lead male vocal, Bobby Chen (Chen Sheng), a singer-composer who can tackle both native folk ballads and urbane pop tunes, and whose laid-back and sometimes irreverent style adds an ironic twist to his work. Like the band's playful name, whether in its original Chinese (Xin baodao kangle dui) or translated form, the song is all about having fun reworking, subverting but not destroying the past or the status quo. The Chinese version of "fun park band" ("kang-le-dui") is usually associated with the military's very proper, and not very exciting entertainment corps. Bobby Chen appropriates the term, links it with the more inclusive "Formosa" = baodao (in relation to the lately more rigid and political "Taiwan"), and presents us with the very campy New Formosa Fun Park Band. "Song for a Jolly Gathering" manifests this carnival attitude; it also dismisses the grand Chineseness of the past (we hear no Mandarin in the song), is wary of the shackling Taiwaneseness of the present, and highlights difference but also celebrates the desire for a jolly partnership. In this upbeat song, there also pulsates an awareness of the fact that its jolliness might well be too good to be true; however, it beckons us "to pay attention to what surfaces within our hearts," that although we might want to hide our "sappy" tears when we hear the mountain song, we need to listen to "the primal call of the faraway" — "let's not argue NA I YA NA YA O HAY, you and I be mates NA I YA NA YA O HAY."

The pairing of Hong Kong video images with parts of "Song for a Jolly Gathering" total about two minutes of the 95-minute *Chinese Box*. These carnival pairings are out of tune with the frequent surfacing of the theme song performed in Dadawa's pure vocals. They are out of pace with the lethargic Englishman's tale and out of time with the film's weighty focus on the momentous handover. They seem to be set to their own temporality. They are flashes that escape the film, yet possess a poetic grasp of one angle of this triangular allegory, the angle represented by the character Jean, accentuating her disfigured, bastardized state of being a colonial subject, her relentless energy to survive, and her impossible desire for being one with her colonial master. Wayne Wang once commented that the Maggie Cheung character "is in some ways the most important character in the film. She is the one who comes closest to embodying the true spirit of Hong Kong, for me."[24] *Chinese Box* fills itself with the musings of a colonial, with John's trinkets, with ninety-odd minutes of this Englishman's dream of Hong Kong. Yet ninety minutes of languorous John and celestial Dadawa pale against, and cannot chant away, two minutes of quirky Jean or the earthly and punchy "Song for a Jolly Gathering."

One wonders why a ninety-odd minute film about Hong Kong hides and reserves the "true Hong Kong" in snippets of video montages. Perhaps that is where the film's obtuse meaning might lie. As Barthes claims, obtuse meaning often "has something to do with disguise;" it carries a certain *emotion* that, when caught up in disguise, is never sticky, "an emotion which simply *designates* what one loves, what one wants to defend."[25] In this allegorically thought-out picture of Hong Kong, in this "thinking picture" of Wayne Wang's,[26] what ultimately registers are those short bursts of energy that highlight Wang's emotion toward a city long lost to him, an emotion exposed when countered with the direct stare from Jean, an emotion bared in a cynically ideal song from Taiwan. Through "Song for a Jolly Gathering," one accesses the innermost drawer of Wayne Wang's Chinese box.

In that innermost drawer of *Chinese Box*, Hong Kong lurks as a scarred pearl, subsisting under the prominent stories of Britain and China. In the romantic historical narrative, the pale colonial master insists on a stoic and ceremonial bowing out; and the returning master, the seemingly reserved China, assuredly moves in. Appropriately at this handover moment, English switches to Chinese/Mandarin/Putonghua, alluring Gong Li takes over the Englishman's voice-over and coolly claims her say in the narrative. The sexy, potent and vocal presence of Gong Li seems to expunge and muffle out the waiflike Hong Kong local from this tale of the Orient. Hong Kong, however, counters its own obliteration through its video montages, confronting the smooth celluloid grand narrative with its fragmented, crude images of local life in the alleyways. As it stares back and exposes itself in video form, Hong Kong further shouts back with a "foreign" song, shaking the pure, ethereal, and eternal vocals of Dadawa with a clamor of Taiwanese, Hakka and aboriginal lyrics. Like the goddess of democracy and "Ssu Hsiang Ch'i" in *Farewell China*, *Chinese Box*, with its video montages and "Song for a Jolly Gathering," attempts to resist the inevitable, gesturing a stance before submitting to the overwhelming and determined course of history. The choice of songs in both films helps open an alternative space, an area where gender codes can be loosened slightly, a space where one can evade narrativized demasculinized males and scarred females, and where one pines for a Chineseness, a Hong Kongness that might elude staunch history.

Chinese Box begins with the British Jeremy Irons and ends with the

Chinese Gong Li; it plots the death of the Englishman while giving the woman from China a new start in Hong Kong. Wayne Wang's choice of actors from different backgrounds fits well his tale of Hong Kong, presenting the end of the British era and the beginning of Chinese rule. Other Hong Kong filmmakers have also used this kind of device in telling tales of Chinese destinies. Stanley Kwan (Guan Jinpeng), in his *Full Moon in New York* (Ren zai niuyue) (1989), used Maggie Cheung, Sylvia Chang (Zhang Aijia), and Siqin Gaowa to play three Chinese women in New York, each, fittingly, coming from Hong Kong, Taiwan, and the mainland. At one moment in the film, the three women carouse and start singing Chinese songs popular in each of their cultures. The next time they meet and drink, they earnestly toast their friendship. *Full Moon in New York* was filmed before the traumatic June Fourth incident, a time when it was still possible for Stanley Kwan to imagine a Greater China where different tunes can be embraced with the anticipation of a grand and friendly historical union. What was possible in *Full Moon in New York* certainly changed in Hong Kong films of the 1990s. *Chinese Box* clearly establishes China's assured presence in Hong Kong. *Happy Together*, another film made in 1997, and *Ordinary Heroes*, made in 1998, offer different variations on the theme of the China-Hong Kong connection. Unlike Gong Li powerfully representing China in *Chinese Box*, *Happy Together* and *Ordinary Heroes* respond to 1997 without representing China in their narratives in a prominent way. Instead, both films use Taiwan elements to articulate their sentiments toward Hong Kong's return to the fatherland. Both also rely on depictions of various forms of masculinity to convey a kind of alternative space in their post-1997 imaginary. *Happy Together* includes a Taiwan character and *Ordinary Heroes* uses a Taiwan actor to bring about a hopeful alterity to their sense of post-1997 Hong Kong.

Wong Kar-wai (Wang Jiawei)'s *Happy Together* presents us with a Hong Kong gay couple stranded and struggling in Buenos Aires. There is also a third character,[27] a young man from Taiwan, played by the Taiwan actor Chang Chen. In *Full Moon in New York*, each of the three Chinese women in the film occupies equal footing narratively and metaphorically. In *Happy Together*, basically an all-male film, there are Hong Kong and Taiwan roles, but no character representing China. Although Wong once was reluctant to admit that his 1997 film ponders Hong Kong's handover,[28] almost no writing on *Happy Together* accepts Wong's claim and would not acknowledge that connection. In the following part of this paper I would like to concentrate on Taiwan's role in relation to that connection, looking at how the Chang Chen character affects this tale of Hong Kong away from Hong Kong, and how Chang's kind of masculinity operates in a film that begins with a scene of gay sex.

Chang Chen (Zhang Zhen) plays Chang, a young fellow from Taipei who befriends the protagonist Lai Yiu-fai (played by Tony Leung Chiu-wai) at a Chinese restaurant in Buenos Aires where both of them work. The appearance of Chang about half way into the film brings a different tone to *Happy Together*. While Fai is somber and preoccupied with boyfriend Ho Po-wing (played by Leslie Cheung), Chang is carefree and unattached; while Fai and Po-wing speak Cantonese, Chang brings Mandarin into the scene. Fai and Po-wing's world is depicted either in saturated lurid hues or rough, grainy black and white; the restaurant kitchen where Fai and Chang meet comes through in a whitish blue, with a translucence that suggests a welcoming of future colors. In other words Chang catalyzes the film's change of mood, language, and color, modifying the tone of Fai's story. Furthermore, Chang also directly affects Fai himself — through their shared activities such as playing soccer in an alley, visiting and drinking at dancing bars. Chang helps usher in a social breathing space that helps Fai wrench himself away from his confined and claustrophobic relationship with Po-wing. The change becomes acutely palpable in the scene in which Chang and Fai say goodbye to each other. The scene's elusive freeze and slow-motion give poignancy to their farewell. Before their parting hug, Fai asks Chang to close his eyes, then tells him that he truly has the look of a blind swordsman. Projecting the image of the fantastical blind swordsman onto Chang, Fai associates the Taiwan Chang with an aura of romance (as in swordsman novels), of a hero with mysterious and extraordinary powers — powers that can perhaps help see him through the quandary in which he is mired.

Happy Together does bestow a special power on Chang — a capacity to hear beyond that which is possible for ordinary people. What does Chang hear? In Fai's voice-over, he wonders if Chang can hear his heartbeat when they hug farewell. As Chang reaches the end of the world — the lighthouse at Ushuaia — he listens to the tape onto which Fai has wept, and in his voice-over he nonchalantly says he can hear a "strange sobbing noise." The film gives Chang the power to hear but also furnishes him with youth and a lightness of being, suggesting that he might hear Fai's heartbeat but not necessarily grasp the depth of his heartache. Chang is like a swordsman who has not quite mastered his extraordinary power, or one who deliberately makes light of his gift. This somewhat nebulous quality in Chang is also manifested in his sexuality. Chang shows interest in and cares for Fai, but we are not exactly sure of the extent of his feelings. Whether apart or alone, Fai and Po-wing cruise the city's sexual ghettos of porn theatres and public toilets.[29] When Chang is alone, however, he eats and drinks by himself, and repeatedly refuses social invitations from females. Evidently, the film does not want to clarify Chang's sexual leaning; rather, it wants to highlight ambivalence. On a narrative level Chang's amorphous sexuality provides, for Fai, the intriguing possibility of an alternative kind of relationship, in contrast to his clearly gay one with Po-wing. On a meta-narrative level, Chang's ambivalence gives room to the existence of a different mode of interaction with that looming "greater home" — a paternal Chineseness from which both Chang and Fai seem to be escaping. In other words Chang's nebulousness exists in *Happy Together* to furnish space for more open forms of sexual and political identifications.

In the last segment of *Happy Together*, on his way back to Hong Kong, Fai comes smack upon this "greater home" as he transits in Taipei and is hit with news of Deng Xiaoping's death. The "greater home" is that euphemistic Greater China, the awkward link tying China, Hong Kong, and Taiwan. Both Fai and Chang travel to the southern hemisphere to get away from this home: Chang runs to The End of the World Lighthouse at Ushuaia, and Fai drives to the majestic Iguazu Falls, facing and basking in the waters of each site, cleansing themselves of the past patterns. Diegetically, home for Fai is his father in Hong Kong with whom he is at odds; allegorically, home for the Greater Chinese is China, and Deng Xiaoping was its father figure for the most part of the 1990s. Under the shadow of these two paternal beings, Fai's leaving home and his homosexuality become manifestations of his disinclination towards submitting to the laws and normativeness insisted by the Father.

By the end of the film, Fai does embark on a journey back home. As he stops in Taipei, Fai attempts to find traces of Chang in the city. Fai indirectly re-connects with his Taiwan friend when he visits Chang's family's modest business. Although the Hong Kong father and China father are mentioned but not visually represented in *Happy Together*, the film privileges Chang's Taiwan father, and shows him and his family members conducting their food-stand business with gusto at Taipei's boisterous night market. Contrasted with the alienating Buenos Aires, Taipei, together with its friendly father, welcomes Fai with its crowded old streets and its new slick MRT (Mass Rapid Transit System, Taipei's elevated railway). And it is after meeting Chang's affable family that Fai realizes the source of his Taiwan friend's ease and freedom — "there's a place where he can always return" — and only then does the film unleash the buoyant song on which the film's English title is based. Hearing about Deng Xiaoping's death and seeing Chang's affable father in Taipei, Fai faces the chance of a new beginning. Taiwan's affable father fosters Chang's nebulous maleness, and in that nebulousness resides the possibility of becoming. Much is possible for the "blind swordsman" who has yet to finetune the powers of his gift. And much is possible for Fai with this romantic Taiwan fellow. In the end the Taiwan young fellow, the third character, an afterthought in *Happy Together*,[30] has become the locus of Fai's displaced hope; Taiwan then emerges as a promising site in Hong Kong's diasporic imaginary.[31]

Happy Together employs elements of national identity, of romance embedded in film genres (e.g. love story, swordsman quests), and gradations of masculinity to unfold its tale of 1997. *Ordinary Heroes* (1998) uses many of the same elements to ponder post-1997 Hong Kong. An interesting twist, however, is how the Taiwan factor again plays a role — this time not through Taiwan but a Hong Kong character. In his "(In)Authentic Hong Kong: The '(G)Local' Cultural Identity in Postcolonial HK Cinema,"[32] Chu Yiu-wai observes that in many Hong Kong films of the late 1990s, directors used actors from Taiwan to play Hong Kong characters (e.g. Shu Qi in *City of Glass*, Lee Kang-sheng in *Ordinary Heroes*). These actors and their strange-sounding or dubbed Cantonese provide an interesting hybridity in those films. Indeed, sometimes Hong Kong filmmakers employ Taiwan actors not necessarily to represent Taiwan but to obtain a certain quality that would add complexity to their work. In the case of Chang Chen in *Happy Together*, Wong Kar-wai not only wanted him for his Taiwan affiliation, but also to shape and bring out a certain gender quality in him that would complement the film's sexual dynamic. In an interview, Wong told of how he sent Chang Chen to study boxing in Argentina for two weeks, to toughen and sharpen him.[33] It appears that Wong wanted Chang to embody gentle and hardy attributes — an interesting mixture of maleness. In the case of Lee Kang-sheng (Li Kangsheng) in *Ordinary Heroes*, Chu soundly points out that director Ann Hui (Xu Anhua)'s choice of Lee can be related to market and award considerations (with an eye toward the Taiwan market and its award aesthetics), and connected to the desire for a foreign quality.[34] In the last segment of this chapter, I would like to further Chu's analysis and consider the choice of Lee Kang-sheng in *Ordinary Heroes* from the point of how the "foreignness" in him might be linked to the kind of maleness with which Lee is associated, and what that can mean in a postcolonial Hong Kong film.

Taiwan or international audiences would probably know Lee Kang-sheng through the films of director Tsai Ming-liang (Cai Mingliang) (*Rebels of the Neon God, Vive l'Amour*, etc.). Lee had nothing to do with film before Tsai,[35] and, having had no dramatic training, is best at delivering minimal-acting performances. In this sense, although his Cantonese dialogue had to be dubbed, Lee fits well into Ann Hui's choice of the semi-documentary style in *Ordinary Heroes*. Another manifest quality of Lee Kang-sheng is the sexuality he has represented in Tsai Ming-liang's films. Perhaps one would immediately associate that sexuality with gayness, a sensibility Tsai is most skilled at probing.[36] But if we look at all four films in which Tsai and Lee collaborated in the 1990s, we find Lee involved in both homosexual and heterosexual acts (even in one role), making him an actor possessing a curiously fluid maleness. Thus, I propose that the foreign or outsider quality Ann Hui wanted from Lee does not only relate to his non-Hong Kongness, as pertinently analyzed by Chu, but also a kind of maleness that plays into the gender politics in *Ordinary Heroes*.

The foreignness of Lee's role is, of course, relative to the other figures in *Ordinary Heroes*. Among the leading characters of the film, Lee's Li Siu-tung is foreign in his reservedness and quietness. He is privileged with voice-overs, but they function more as expository aids than a device revealing his innermost thoughts; in contrast, Father Kam's (played by Anthony Wong) diary voice-overs reveal his personal regrets and repentances. While others actively engage in social protests and movements, Lee's Tung is more passive and observant. While another male lead, Yau (played by Tse Kwan-ho), has an affair with the woman to whom Tung is attracted, all Tung can do is offer her cigarettes, apples and chicken essence. On the two occasions the woman, Sow (played by Lee Lai-chen), actually asks for his affection, Tung literally runs away. The film wants to keep Tung unattached. Seeing *Ordinary Heroes* through the structure of gender, the film, typically, puts its females (Sow and the Mongoloid young woman) in positions of weakness and victimhood, its males (Yau, the fierce Mainland sweeper, the molesting market-produce peddler) in positions of aggression. What is interesting, however, is the existence of a third position — the position of the ascetic mediator, the pacifist, and the comforter. And this position is occupied by the celibate Father Kam and the unattached Tung. Father Kam is supposed to be of Italian descent and is played by Anthony Wong (Huang Qiusheng), who has a racially mixed background. Tung is partly educated on the Mainland and is played by the Taiwan[37] Lee Kang-sheng. Both possess that foreignness that sets them apart from the film's other Hong Kong characters, and it is through their cultural and sexual difference that the film distinguishes its true ordinary heroes.

The film further bestow halos on Kam and Tung by means of making them the possessors of music. Father Kam plays the guitar and passes the skill to Tung. Through music, the film appoints Tung the inheritor of Kam's idealistic and compassionate ways. This is most tenderly conveyed through Tung's repeated harmonica playing of Teresa Teng's song, "Ch'ian yen wan yu" (Qianyan wanyu) (Tens of thousands of words and utterances). Through Tung's plaintive playing of this Taiwan tune, the film recalls and soothes the disappointment of ideals lost and the pain of commitments betrayed — the social experiences of Hong Kong during the 1980s.

In *Ordinary Heroes*'s final slow motion and freeze, the camera pans by a couple with a baby and stops at Tung. With a beautiful young boy in tow, Tung seems to go beyond gender as he embodies both the fatherly and the motherly. Lighting commemorative candles at Victoria Park, Tung passes on the legacy of social commitment and compassion to the angelic boy. The soundtrack for this final scene is the very Chinese song "Hsieh-jan te feng-ch'ai," (Xue ran de fengcai) (Aura of the bloodstained),[38] which has the plaintive refrain, "Do not grieve ..." This combination of candle-lighting and song, in a way, ties the multiple Chinese communities together: we sense the sentiments of Hong Kong in this unmistakable act of commemoration, the China connection through the "bloodstained" song, and the subtle pointing toward Taiwan through the presence of Lee Kang-sheng. The tenderness and the nebulousness embodied by Lee open a space for the yet unknown, and his pairing with the angelic child suggests hope within that unknown. If nothing else the employment of the very un-Hong Kong and sexually nebulous Lee Kang-sheng inserts a hopeful openness in *Ordinary Heroes*, bringing something different to the cultural imaginary of post-1997 Hong Kong.

The above study of *Farewell China, Chinese Box, Happy Together,* and *Ordinary Heroes* affords us a sample of Hong Kong's struggles during the 1990s in relation to China's paternal call, and its resistance of, reluctance toward, and in the end resigned hopefulness about, the inevitable. These intricate and, at times, self-conflicting responses to father China manifest themselves in the elusive sites of the musical in *Farewell China* and *Chinese Box*, and the structuring of masculinity in *Happy Together* and *Ordinary Heroes*. In this new century, as Hong Kong filmmakers continue to probe the Hong Kong-China bond, Ann Hui's 2002 *July Rhapsody* (Nanren sishi) (Man at forty) offers a new twist in the Greater China saga. At the end of the film its Hong Kong male protagonist reclaims his midlife self by reaffirming his love for cultural China; at the same time he witnesses the death of his Taiwan-connected mentor (played by Taiwan actor To Tsung-hua). That is to say as Hong Kong finds itself at peace with great cultural China, the Taiwan factor becomes redundant and dismissible, but not eradicable. The illegitimate son of the Taiwan-connected mentor continues to live under the roof of, and is adopted by, the Hong Kong protagonist. And so continues the Greater China saga.

7

Fighting Female Masculinity:
Women Warriors and Their Foreignness in Hong Kong Action Cinema of the 1980s

Kwai-cheung Lo

Does maleness automatically produce masculinity?

Is there a kind of masculinity independent of the biological male?

Can the women who kill in action cinema occupy a position that has been historically thought of as exclusively masculine?

In her book *Female Masculinity*, Judith Halberstam argues that there exists a group of lesbians who see themselves as masculine females. Rather than a simple derivative, imitation or impersonation of male masculinity, "female masculinity," she finds, is actually a specific gender with its own cultural history.[1] Trying to remove the stigma of female masculinity so it has an empowering image and identity that give the male-identified woman a sense of pride and strength, she contends that the connection between homosexual woman and masculinity is by no means pathological.

Halberstam's study is inspiring because her argument urges us to rethink the presumption that there is always an essential relationship between masculinities and men; her work also shows that an analysis of masculinity is not necessarily at the expense of the study of women. The ideological implications of masculinity can be radically re-examined by not simply looking at men exclusively but also mapping and recognizing the culture of a certain female type. Scrutinizing that which is the sexual opposite of man instead of focusing solely on the male may sometimes reveal more of the nature of masculinity. Though challenging the conventional perceptions of masculinity and subversively alienating it from the biological male, Halberstam's analysis continues to regard masculinity as something that is real, substantial, and symbiotically tied to power. Multiplying or pluralizing masculinity in different alternative versions even by inventing "female masculinity" for women, I would say, would never really pose a significant challenge to the established notion that is fundamentally left unquestioned. Indeed, multiplicity or pluralization only helps make the ideology of masculinity stronger and more powerful, turning it into a stable origin or foundation exempted from any radical deconstruction. A gay masculine female, by the standards of the patriarchal norm, is far less intimidating and repulsive than a straight feminized male because the former differs little from the mainstream notion of masculinity.[2] Although Halberstam nicely dissociates maleness from masculinity, with reference to Judith Butler's concepts of gender performativity and constructivism, to my surprise she fails to examine — as well evinced in many popular-cultural products, especially action movies — that masculinity in a male may not be a given. Rather it is something that a man has to strive hard to gain to prove he is a "real man." It is a rite in action-adventure films that the hero, or sometimes the heroine, demonstrate that masculinity does not necessarily correspond with the sexed being but instead is the kernel of his/her unique identity that must be strived for. Hence, masculinity and men can sometimes be unconnected because it is never something that naturally belongs to the biological male (male characters, including "weak" ones, in action movies would otherwise have it too easy) but is that which comes from beyond to justify and legitimize the principles of inter- and intra-sexual hierarchy and subordination, and to assert the sexual division of labor under the patriarchal order. A man with so-called masculinity is always more respectable and admired than a biological male without or with relatively little masculinity, that is to say, a sissy.

However, having or not having "it" can by no means be consistently and objectively grasped or gauged. Representations of masculinity have already been reduced to a site of contest. To an extent, masculinity is an elusive entity that gives plenitude to the lives of men (and some women in the action genre) and sorts out sexual identification. Perhaps masculinity, as if the "Woman" in Lacan's notorious statement "there is no such thing as Woman,"[3] is an imaginary thing that does not exist in itself but is insisted upon as forms of ideology or fantasy that patriarchal society invents and develops to make sense of human lives for both men and women.[4] Ideas about what men or women should be are built around the hegemonic notion of masculinity that symbolically articulates the sexual differences and provides an anchor for social relations. In a way masculinity may function more or less like the phallus. It refers to an imaginary object men desire because it represents power; it also serves as a signifier with regard to the symbolic difference between the sexes. Modernity might have had a devastating effect on hegemonic masculinity and relentlessly subverted the traditional gender boundary and definition. But the liberal logic of the capitalist system advocating the value of sexual equality never really erases so-called traditional masculine qualities. Actually the new mechanism of capitalism further provokes the human desire to be "more equal."[5] The ideology of masculinity, though in unprecedented crisis, remains at stake for sexual politics and the struggle for power because it can convey symbolic values. It is merely turned into a contested domain within which different ideological groups repeatedly re-define its meanings for their own interests. Those who have "it" are those privileged and qualified to rule over those who don't. Therefore, though masculinity may become a signifier without its secured and steady signified, its appearance still has to be maintained. Even though that for which masculinity stands these days might be illusory or false (radically speaking, it has been false from the beginning), the human world could not do without such a measure of proper symbolic articulation for sexual difference. If we did away with the fake representation of masculinity, directly approaching so-called sexual reality, we would be in danger of losing reality itself because reality is supported by representation. We could not afford to lose the anchor for the symbolic expression of sexual and social differences. To use terminology from Deleuze and Guattari's *Anti-Oedipus*, that the deterritorializating forces of capitalism can persist depends on a fictitious ideological agency, that is a reterritorialization mechanism, which is to balance and stabilize its border-breaking operating system.[6] In other words the arrival of modernity, shaking up the traditional notion of masculinity, is also the very system rescuing it from destruction and helping it adapt to new social demands.

RECONSTRUCTING MASCULINITY WITH A TWIST

Because masculinity functions as a symbol to differentiate values and mark sexual categories in our modern world, I will follow this line of argument to find the reasons there are not a small number of women warriors featured at particular historical moments in Hong Kong cinema of the 1980s, though Chinese society conventionally has been perceived as male-chauvinist. These women fighters on screen might not be labeled "masculine females" in the way Halberstam describes them because they are usually depicted as very "feminine" in appearance, even though they can beat up men with spectacular combat skills. Remaining as objects to be looked at,[7] as many female characters are in mainstream cinema, these martial arts women's "female masculinity" — if we broaden the term from a sheer masculine outlook to some abstract qualities — constructs for them an ambivalent subject position quite different from that of the male leads in action movies. What I find interesting about the idea of "female masculinity" is not its uniqueness and separation from maleness to evolve into a specific gender. The real impact of female masculinity resides in its being feminine and masculine at the same time — a female who derives masculinity not from her own but from the patriarchal norm, her masculinity simultaneously supporting and transgressing the norm from within. King Hu (Hu Jinquan) is regarded in the West as the first Hong Kong director to cast actresses such as Cheng Pei-pei (Zheng Peipei), Hsu Feng (Xu Feng), and Angela Mao (Mao Ying) as prominent women warriors in martial arts films in the 1960s. But the championing of fighting heroines in Hong Kong cinema can be traced back as far as the 1940s, when renowned action actress Yu Suqiu — whose father, Yu Zhanyuan, was Jackie Chan's (Cheng Long) and Sammo Hung's (Hong Jinbao) Beijing opera teacher — was already in relatively parochial and low-budget Cantonese swordplay films. I do not intend to provide a comprehensive study of action heroines in Hong Kong cinema history. I would like to focus only on the women warriors reconstituted for a series of popular female-cop movies in the 1980s. Judging by today's standards, Hong Kong action movies in the 1980s may seem cheesy, technically backward and an excuse for non-stop action. In addition, their characters were thinly developed and their storylines generally boring and lacking in logic. But these are precisely the "unnecessary things" in Hong Kong action cinema I will focus on. Irrespective of the poor quality of the details, they are there to confer symbolic meaning. Had they been taken away, the action movie would have fallen apart. No matter how redundant they appear, they are inherent to the action genre — not unlike female masculinity in relation to hegemonic masculinity — revealing the contradictory nature of the kernel itself.

The 1980s were a prosperous decade for the Hong Kong film industry, during which local productions not only performed better than Hollywood imports at the box office but also succeeded in developing a universally translatable film genre that could attract transnational fans. The action genre evolved from traditional kung fu but had a modern setting, dominated the market and reinvented itself by continually integrating new elements. Jackie Chan, Sammo Hung, and John Woo (Wu Yusen) have since become household names. While most of the action performed in the male space and the spread of onscreen masculinity seemed overwhelming, Sek Kei (Shi Qi), the foremost Hong Kong local film reviewer, also points out that other than the fact women were becoming major social and economic players in society, "the sense of crisis and anxiety brought about by the 1997 problem had also 'humanized' Hong Kong people to the extent that it had made them more sensitive and susceptible to emotional feeling ... Action films with women as 'heroines' also became more popular."[8] In his studies of Hong Kong cinema, David Bordwell makes thought-provoking observations about the female action-film genre, whose emergence is understood not to be a simple reflection of social reality:

> It is always tempting to explain genre development as a reflection of social trends, but we get more pertinent and proximate explanations if we also consider the filmmaking practice and the genre's specific tradition. Take the female-cop movies that earn local critics' scorn but captivate Western fans, girls and boys alike. We might posit that *Yes, Madam!* [Huangjia shijie] [dir. Yuen Kwai, 1985], *Royal Warriors* [Huangjia zhanshi] [dir. Tsang Ken-cheung, 1986], *Angel* [Tianshi xingdong] [dir. Raymond Leung, 1987], *The Inspector Wears a Skirt* [Bawang hua] [dir. Wellson Chin, 1988], *She Shoots Straight* [Huangjia nüjiang] [dir. Yuen Kwai, 1990], and other girls-and-guns movies reflect the growing importance of women in the local economy. But there are more proximate explanations. First is the variorum nature of popular entertainment. Once a genre gains prominence a host of possibilities opens. Horror filmmakers are likely to float the possibility of demonic children if only because the competition has already shown demonic teenagers, rednecks, cars, and pets. Similarly, once the male-cop genre was going strong, someone was likely to explore the possibility of a tough woman cop. Local traditions could sustain the innovation: swordplay and kung-fu films celebrate the woman warrior, and in many 1970s erotic movies raped women take violent revenge. Moreover, energetic heroines might attract women viewers, who made up half the local audience, even for action pictures.[9]

The popularity of female action movies in the 1980s might not necessarily have had any social references, according to Bordwell. Rather than directly reflecting the gender conditions in social life, female masculinity in Hong Kong cinema may be nothing more than something that developed in line with changes in the movie genre itself. Woman warriors in the cop movie, or swordplay or kung fu genre are actually derived from their male counterparts. In other words they are spillovers of the excessive masculinity in Hong Kong cinema. The origin of these female fighter movies could be the creation myth of Eve, made of Adam's rib in Genesis: they are either copies or spin-offs of the founding genre itself. It is true that many local film critics consider the female-cop films "secondary" even though the sub-genre is categorized "alternative" by Western moviegoers. Attracting a cult following, these girls-and-guns features are always more popular with audiences abroad than in Hong Kong. For instance, some Western critics would like to believe that "Hong Kong cinema may be the only place in the world where men and women fight as equals."[10] "Contrary to the Western perception of Chinese culture as chauvinistic in the extreme, Eastern cinema has featured an extraordinary number of woman warriors compared to Hollywood. Tinseltown has long since relegated women to the stereotypes of victim, prize or queen bitch, whereas Hong Kong actioners have always featured fighting females doing battle with the menfolk on an equal footing."[11] Regardless of whether local and global viewers consider them secondary or alternative, these female-centered action films could only define themselves against the hegemonic meanings of masculinity in the histories of kung fu and cop flicks even though they might be particularly appealing to female viewers. Indeed, females attracted to violent action movies do not need the motivation of a predominantly female presence in such a sub-genre to go to the theater because, firstly, there are relatively fewer girl action flicks to cater to the demand, and secondly, male-dominated action movies are actually as appealing, if not more so, to female fans. On the other hand, action films with female leads do not necessarily lay any claim to women's rights, raising little or no feminist consciousness specifically to win over women audiences. To put it differently, by no means is the woman warrior excluded from Hong Kong action cinema or Chinese popular culture in general. The swordswoman and female fighter has been a recurring character in traditional Chinese literature and early Chinese cinema.[12] But her inclusion may merely efface her voice because, within the dominant conceptualization of masculinity in the film genre, her agency is always impossible to see. So it may be a strategic mistake to analyze whether women can speak for themselves in female action cinema.

I would argue that female masculinity, more a derivative than an independent entity, in female-cop films can be a constructive model for us to examine issues of masculinity. At first glance, female masculinity is only one of many versions of masculinity, albeit a relatively subordinate one, which is perhaps not much different to queer masculinity. Its existence is recognized but merely as one that is passive. Yet, female masculinity could have the potential to produce, through perverse reiteration, unconventional formulations of masculinity that expose its limited and exclusionary features at the same time that the female version mobilizes a new set of demands. Female masculinity should not be understood as a force of opposition to the masculine norm, because the very opposition is merely an instrument through which the power of the dominant masculinity operates. On the contrary, the supporting role of female masculinity or of gay masculinity in action films of the James Bond ilk, as Halberstam points out, can reveal "the absolute dependence of dominant masculinity on [these] minority masculinities."[13] Comparing the representations of the various masculinities in *Golden Eye* (dir. Martin Campbell, 1995), Halberstam finds that the normative heterosexual masculinity of James Bond is primarily prosthetic and most unconvincing vis-à-vis the female masculinity of Bond's boss, M, and the queer masculinity of Agent Q, who provides new gadgets to Bond. Without his supply of gizmos and accurate information about the secret-agent network, Bond could never prove his white masculinity and could be reduced to a hero without action or adventure. In the Hong Kong female-cop movies I will discuss, although women play lead roles, their "masculinity" is still constructed around the dominant male ones. But the female masculinity of these women cops always reveals a gap between masculinity and its representation. They don't look like men though they act like men: they are hard-fighting, weapon-wielding, independent, heroic and violent rather than sensitive, loving and nurturing. Though representation is never completely transparent about what it represents, it does not follow that masculinity is a perfect substance that could never be fully articulated. There is indeed never a so-called real meaning of masculinity hidden behind the representations. Masculinity *is* the representation through and through. The tough cop images assumed by the policewomen are only attempts to fill the structural ruptures of masculinity. In other words, the more masculinity has been imitated or represented in the female-cop movies, the clearer its inconsistencies and holes become.

WOMEN WARRIORS AND THE "LITTLE MEN"

In the usual Hong Kong woman-cop movie, the female inspector is always subordinate to a male boss who symbolizes a rigid, old-fashioned and authoritative masculinity and who is occasionally ridiculed as a "dinosaur patriarch." The female lead may develop a romantic attachment to a young male character (who appears sometimes in a group) still desperately searching for a heroic image of manhood. The woman always plays the mediating role in the relations between the two kinds or two generations of men. Other than functioning as a conduit for their male homo-social desires and a vessel to monitor the traffic of these men's heterosexual orientation, she moderates the inflexible, "antique" masculinity belonging to the traditional fatherly figure and stimulates the young male hero to achieve his ideal form of masculinity. In contrast to the good guys' surplus and surfeit of masculinity, the villainous men with whom the female protagonist battles always occupy the middle ground and are generally portrayed as the ones who always feel comfortable with their own manly identities. Ironically, action movie audiences, most of them men, usually do not identify with the most secure masculine positions belonging to the bad guys. Perhaps steady-going and unchanging masculinity is considered the least attractive and interesting. Viewers are, therefore, encouraged to identify with only those characters whose masculinity is at stake. In Yuen Kwai's *Yes, Madam!* (the first installment of the "Huangjia Shijie," literally "Royal Policewoman" or the commonly used English series title "In the Line of Duty"), it is not only the two female inspectors — Michelle Yeoh (Yang Ziqiong) (credited as Michelle Khan in all her Hong Kong movies of the 1980s) and Cynthia Rothrock — who have to work hard to show off their masculine power in order to earn the respect of their male opponents. There are also three con artists who have trouble defining their manhood.

Played by Mang Hoi (Meng Hai), John Shum (Cen Jianxun) and the renowned director Tsui Hark (Xu Ke), these three petty crooks remind audiences of those comic characters in the "Lucky Stars" (*fuxing*) slapstick series starring Sammo Hung (who produced *Yes, Madam!* and has a cameo appearance). Having neither combat skills nor courage in hand-to-hand fight scenes, but skillful at using tricks to gain the upper hand, especially in girl chasing, they are typical clowns, like the Marx Brothers or Monty Python, in Hong Kong action films. Their job is to crack jokes before the real kung fu fight kicks off. Brought up together in an orphanage, these three silly characters in *Yes, Madam!* are as close as brothers but always fight among themselves. They find themselves in big trouble when two of them steal the passport of a British agent killed by a hit man belonging to a crime organization. They soon find themselves being chased relentlessly by the police and the hit man and his gang because there is a microfilm hidden in the passport that carries incriminating evidence about the group's dirty business.

Weirdly named after pharmaceutical pain-killing products, "Panadol," "Asprin" and "Strepsil," these three criminal rogues probably stand for the other (or negative) side of the action hero, or the opposite of the ideal masculinity. They intentionally strip off the clothes of two women, exposing their brassieres but not for a sexual purpose (one happens to be the nurse in the pension house and the other is Michelle Yeoh in the police station). Although they do everything the hero won't and vice versa, they are portrayed as fun and lovable characters. Perhaps the masculinity model could be divided into an acknowledged part and a disavowed one to which the dumb and dumber trio of losers belongs. However, the disavowed part has never been seriously denied. It has only been displaced by the bodies of these clownish figures who represent men's sleazy fantasies violating decency and good taste.[14] They are really the "painkillers" for the seemingly decent but actually repressed kind of masculinity because, as proxies for the heroes, they can do the cheeky stuff the heroes can't. With encouragement from the women, however, these hopeless men can also transform themselves into "real" heroes, performing courageous deeds that are beyond the scope of even the female cops. Toward the end of the film, with Michelle Yeoh and Cynthia Rothrock unable to kill the mob boss — who may go unpunished because the microfilm has been destroyed — the handcuffed Mang Hoi suddenly becomes so angry he avenges the death of his buddy by grabbing a pistol from a policeman and firing it at the mob boss.

If a petty burglar could remake himself into a masculine hero, we should not be surprised by the transformation of Yeoh — a former beauty pageant winner and ballerina from Malaysia — from a decorative beauty in *Owl vs. Dumbo* (Maotouying yu xiaofeixiang) (dir. Sammo Hung, 1985) to a spectacular action queen who ignited the reinvented "girls and guns" sub-genre of Hong Kong cinema in the 1980s.[15] That was the industry's golden age for creatively mixing genres, bringing in new cinematic elements and breathing fresh air into the roles of women and foreigners. *Yes, Madam!* was a typical and rather successful mix-and-match attempt of the 1980s to crossbreed a Hollywood buddy-cop movie, a traditional Chinese kung fu genre, a slapstick comedy and an action thriller into a "woman" film with a Chinese and Western cast. Rothrock had no idea what the film would be like when she was cast as "Dirty Carrie" and made her first visit to Hong Kong. "When I flew to Hong Kong, I expected that I'd be making one of those old-fashioned, period kung fu films, with a black wig and pigtail. I was so surprised when I got there and we were in modern dress with guns and everything."[16] It was her blonde hair and Caucasian features, apart from her martial arts prowess, that led to roles in the new hybrid Hong Kong flicks of the time. Until the 1990s the production house of this female-cop film, D & B Films, owned by the Hong Kong tycoon Dickson Poon (Pan Disheng), who later married Michelle Yeoh, presented a steady flow of female fight flicks, such as the *In the Line of Duty* (Huangjia Shijie) sequels and *Black Cat* (Heimao) series.[17] But modernizing the kung fu genre and introducing (foreign) lady fighters in Hong Kong cinema were by no means D & B's sole pioneering act. Jackie Chan had already successfully transformed himself from being a traditional martial arts hero in imperial China (*Drunken Master*, dir. Yuen Wo-ping, 1978; *Dragon Lord*, dir. Jackie Chan, 1982) to a Chinese sojourner in the West (*Wheels on Meals*, dir. Sammo Hung, 1984), a modern cop (*Police Story*, dir. Jackie Chan, 1986) and an Indiana Jones-type adventurer (*Armour of God*, dir. Jackie Chan, 1986). Similarly, Sammo Hung, whose blockbusters in the early 1980s were kung fu comedies set in late Qing China, also used a modern Hong Kong urban setting for his action comedies, for example, *Winners and Sinners* (Qimou miaoji wufuxing) (dir. Sammo Hung, 1983), *My Lucky Stars* (Fuxing gaozhao) (dir. Sammo Hung, 1985) and *Twinkle, Twinkle Lucky Stars* (Zuijia fuxing) (dir. Sammo Hung, 1986). In these modern action movies, the opponents of Jackie Chan and Sammo Hung were no longer merely middle-aged Chinese patriarchs but also young, fashionable Westerners. There were also four leather-clad black muscular vixens in *Armour of God* and the Japanese woman bodybuilder, Michiki Nishiwaki, in *My Lucky Stars*.

In contrast to the aforementioned movies, female masculinity stands out particularly in *Yes, Madam!* not simply because it occupies center stage, but also because it is simultaneously highlighted and suppressed. The femaleness of Yeoh's and Rothrock's bodies is repeatedly emphasized in several scenes. When Yeoh's jacket comes off to reveal her brassiere, in a scene supposed to be comical, a male colleague confronts Rothrock by slyly commenting on her sexy feminine body. Whenever the two female protagonists engage in fights with their male opponents, they are called "bitch" or otherwise verbally insulted with such sexist jibes as "Go back to the kitchen!" But the kung fu battle between the women warriors and the hit man that takes place in the men's toilet of the nightclub may symbolize the relentless effort of women to break into the men's zone. When the hit man snatches John Shum and Mang Hoi and holds them in the men's restroom to coerce them to return the microfilm, the two women immediately intrude to rescue them. Halberstam interestingly argues that "men's restrooms tend to operate as a highly charged sexual space in which [homo]sexual interactions are both encouraged and punished."[18] The gesture the two women make is that they will not stop at the line drawn by the restroom to segregate the sexes and will not obey gender-conformity rules. For the woman fighter, nowhere, not even the men's restroom, is out of bounds, and it is not necessary for her to masquerade as a man to pass through the gender-bound door. Assertive and self-empowering though the women's intrusion to the men's restroom may sound, allowing them freely to enter the private place for men could also be interpreted as a mischievous fantasy of the "Lucky Star" characters to expose themselves to the girl whom they have never managed to bed. On the other hand, what the men's restroom scene signifies is that the phallic symbol the female protagonists do not possess is merely an instrument of urination and could never be used against women as an aggressive and powerful weapon of copulation.

THE FORMULA OF SELF-REPETITION

In *Royal Warriors* (written and directed by Tsang Ken-cheung), a sequel to *Yes, Madam!*, the female sexuality of Michelle Yeoh has been largely elaborated. Her sexuality comes through although she continues to play her tough female inspector character, Michelle, who joins forces with a Japanese cop, Yamamoto (played by Hiroyuki Sanada), and a half-Chinese and half-British security officer, Michael (Michael Wong), to foil a hijack attempt on her return from a vacation in Japan. Unlike *Yes, Madam!*, in which she is accompanied by another woman fighter, which may obliquely imply some inter-racial lesbian relationship, Yeoh here is the only female who is under the male gaze and who has to go between two groups of men — one good, the other villainous — both of which are similarly motivated by a desire for revenge. The two hijackers killed on the plane by Michelle, Yamamoto and Michael belong to a coterie of Vietnam veterans who pledge eternal loyalty and brotherly love to one another. The remaining members swear to take vengeance on Michelle and Yamamoto. It begins the real battle between the "loyal" warriors and the "royal" ones (Michelle works for the Hong Kong Royal Police Force in the British colony). Yamamoto's Japanese wife and daughter become the first casualties because they are blown to pieces by a time bomb set in Yamamoto's car by a fanatical gang member. Now it is the Japanese cop who does not care if he breaks all the laws to avenge the death of his wife and child and to make his enemies pay. Michelle remains sober and urges Yamamoto to stay cool despite the difficult circumstances. But the burning desire to get his revenge drives Yamamoto to use Michelle and Michael as bait to lure the villains. Not only is Michelle caught between helping the vengeful Yamamoto and fighting with her angry boss (played by Kenneth Tsang), who wants to constrain Yamamoto, she also finds herself trapped in a sort of "love triangle": Michael, who repeatedly tries to hook up romantically with Michelle, accuses her of developing a love interest in Yamamoto.

In the battle of the lone fighting femme, Michelle has four frontlines: she has to deal with her merciless police chief, calm the untameable Yamamoto, decline Michael's annoying romantic advances, and remain alert to the brutal attacks of the bad guys. Perhaps there are messages to be detected here, such as that "men and women handle things differently," or that "women may have better self-control in critical situations than men." However, Michelle's juggling with different men may not necessarily reveal any fundamental sexual differences, nor does it indicate the superiority of female masculinity over male masculinity, which relies on the former to recreate itself. The role conferred on Michelle as a policewoman who mediates with the men, differentiating them, and even differentiating herself from them, may actually give us a false picture of dis-identification with the ideology of male masculinity. Ideological domination is capable of creating an illusion that those under its control and influence believe they always have the freedom to act on their own.[19] Likewise, masculinist ideology works most effectively when it succeeds in constructing a space of false distance from the subject's interpellated position. The contrast between Michelle and other men reveals the shortcomings of male masculinity on the one hand, but it also expresses the subjective complexities of masculinity assumed by Michelle on the other. By showing her inner doubts about the masculine way of handling the situation (that is, an eye-for-an-eye approach), Michelle actually is more of an ideal agent for securing the ideological conformity than any naïve subject devotedly identifying with the traits of masculinity. Indeed her self-reflective distancing does not stop her from finally becoming those men. On the contrary, her dis-identification with the surrounding men creates a favorable condition to change herself into a "copy" of her opposite gender. When Michael is captured by the last villain and suspended by his feet from the roof of a high-rise building in order to lure Michelle to come to his rescue, Michael, refusing to put his beloved Michelle in danger, unties himself and, to Michelle's horror, plummets to his death. At Michael's funeral, Michelle promises to avenge her comrade. Ironically, it is usually women who play the objects to be mourned and avenged by heroes in action cinema. But the moment she declares "I'll kill him!" — a phrase she repeats several times — she transforms herself into one of those avenging "men."

This female cop film seems to tell us that masculinity will never die but continue to reproduce itself with numerous followers, imitators and copiers. On the side of the villains, at first, there are two men — one an extradited criminal, the other his "brother" from army days trying to free him — who die (for each other) in an in-flight confrontation with the heroes. Then a third gang "brother" swears vengeance, wiping out Yamamoto's family before dying in a nightclub shootout. Scarily there is a fourth who never gives up, insofar as he has the last breath, he hangs on to brotherhood, male bonding and comradeship around which the ideology of masculinity is built. Masculinity seems to be ghost that haunts all characters, good or evil. Almost exactly the same pattern is detected on the heroes' side. When Yamamoto sees his wife and daughter blown to bits, there is only vengeance on his mind. He will do anything to get even. And when Michelle sees Michael plunge to his death, she no longer sees herself as just a law enforcement agent but a comrade of a dead "brother" whose only mission is to settle "private" business with her rival. The film is fascinating because, although the bad and good guys look so different at the beginning, they are fundamentally facsimiles of one another. The appearances that manifest differences are actually false and illusory. Good, bad, man or woman — all are nothing but incarnations of the dominant masculinity.

Realizing that Michelle and Yamamoto will come after him sooner or later, the remaining bad guy steals Michael's coffin and hangs it from a giant crane in an abandoned mine field with dynamite planted everywhere. Then he sends videos to Michelle and Yamamoto challenging them to show up. Yamamoto arrives early, only to be wounded, leaving it to Michelle to combat the villain with a big armored vehicle, a spectacular prop that begs the question of how she got hold of such a thing when she has resigned from the police force. A brutal fight with the villain ends, of course, in triumph for Michelle and Yamamoto. But the last shot of the movie is horrifying: the victorious couple walk away from the deserted mine with Michael's coffin. Is the coffin their trophy? What do the hero and the heroine get after the battle? A dead man's body? The "reward" for the woman warrior who ultimately defeats all men is only a deceased male. Does it denote that, no matter how hard the heroine fights for a masculinity that stands for power and glory, she will end up with one that's deceased? Is masculinity, the real stuff, something woman can never obtain? Or is masculinity already dead, but made to seem alive by its exclusion or foreclosure to woman?

TRANSNATIONAL FETISHISM

Even if a woman possesses a certain masculine power, she remains outside the realm of masculinity. In other words the Chinese woman warrior may have the same lack of access as her non-Chinese female counterparts to the privileged masculinity represented in Hong Kong action cinema. In *Righting Wrongs* (Zhifa xianfeng) (also known as *Above the Law*) (dir. Yuen Kwai, 1986), Cynthia Rothrock is not only the female protagonist but also a blonde American woman among a cast of Chinese guys.[20] She plays an expatriate cop working for the Hong Kong Royal Police Force. Although the conspicuous presence of Westerners in the Hong Kong government was common during the colonial era, the casting of Rothrock in Hong Kong female-cop films conveys a special meaning. In contrast to the Chinese hero (played by Yuen Biao), a Westernized, yuppie attorney with overseas work experience, the Rothrock character, Cindy (whose voice is dubbed in Cantonese), finds herself more in tune with the locals and their lifestyle. When Cindy first appears in the movie, she goes to a mahjong parlor to arrest a suspect.[21] Because of the nature of her job, Cindy has to mingle on a daily basis with many low-class gangsters and hooligans. She also unwillingly becomes a mentor for a clumsy and untidy middle-aged loser, nicknamed "Bad Egg" (played by Yuen Kwai), who works as a junior investigator in the department. In short, her white woman's body is contained within a relatively parochial local space set apart by a strong sense of proletarian distinction. In contrast, the Yuen Biao character is a flamboyant upper-middle class yuppie living in a big mansion who has solid connections with powerful judges locally and in Europe. Even the villain, Sergeant Wong (played by Melvin Wong), a turncoat policeman, seems to have many international connections and can commission a black hit man, a Caucasian woman and many local thugs to kill for him in order to cover his crimes. The reversed social status of the Chinese and the Westerner in colonial Hong Kong is not necessarily a fantasy. Hong Kong's economic boom beginning in the early 1980s did produce many highly educated, newly rich Chinese who could afford a luxurious Western lifestyle and had money to hire Western employees. But casting Rothrock as a local working-class figure is more than a simple domestication of the Westerner or ridiculous mimicry of the Western supremacist discourse by substituting whites with Asians.

It is often said that the significance of the martial arts genre is rooted in the cultural tradition and the national character of Chinese cinema. Martial arts have always been regarded as a national symbol of Chineseness. Though inheriting many elements from traditional culture, Hong Kong martial arts cinema was determined to rejuvenate itself by asserting a modern Hong Kong self-awareness and creating an international fantasy. As David Desser observes, the action genre of Hong Kong "certainly derived features and resemblances from the Hollywood western, while in the 1960s it was hugely influenced by Japanese Samurai and gangster films (themselves influenced by American westerns and gangster films)."[22] The film industry of the 1980s became more and more conscious of the hybrid, transnational influences and origins of its martial arts movies and welcomed efforts to distinguish those traces. Action was the genre that constantly and consistently opened up its space to non-Chinese actors and actresses because its universal body language could overcome cultural and linguistic barriers.[23] Actually, Hong Kong cinema of the 1980s became so self-assured that Cantonese was the lingua franca used by all characters, foreigners included. No doubt Hong Kong audiences, whose pride about their city's modernization led them to think globally, found it doubly satisfying to watch a blonde Western woman performing traditional Chinese martial arts and speaking perfect Cantonese in a Hong Kong film. As a matter of fact, female warriors in Hong Kong cinema were far more multi-racial than their male counterparts, and non-Chinese women fighters had more opportunities than foreign men to play heroes (these parts for men were dominated by the likes of Jackie Chan, Sammo Hung, and Yuen Biao). Some of the foreign female fighters were: Americans Cynthia Rothrock (in *Righting Wrongs, Yes, Madam!*) and Karen Sheperd (in *Righting Wrongs*), Briton Sophia Crawford (in *Story of a Gun*, dir. Kirk Wong, 1991), Australian Kim Maree Penn (in *In the Line of Duty 5: Middle Man*, dir. Chris Lee, 1990), Eurasian Joyce Godenzi (in *Eastern Condors*, dir. Sammo Hung, 1987; *She Shoots Straight*), Japanese Michiko Nishiwaki (in *In the Line of Duty 3*, dir. Arthur Wong, 1988); and Yukari Oshima (in *Angel*); and Filipina Agnes Aurelio (in *She Shoots Straight*). Although these foreigners made the hybrid Hong Kong action movies look more international, they lost their "freshness" after appearing in about half a dozen movies. The issue probably is not what their shelf life was but how far they were able to help us understand the ideological constructions of masculinity in relation to the female version in action movies.

Casting Westerners such as Rothrock in action cinema of the 1980s was definitely a trend that highlighted Hong Kong's urban modernity and international flavor. The presence of the foreigners lubricates the ideological reproduction of racial otherness because fascination with the exotic image could produce a fantasy of power over and mastery of the other, especially Westerners. The most visible elements of racial difference represented by Rothrock are of course her blonde hair and white skin. Though only having a rather brief career in Hong Kong cinema and then moving back to Hollywood to star in a couple of action films, Rothrock, as Yvonne Tasker pointed out, "has become an important figure on the video marital-arts scene and has received publicity due to both her talent and the novelty attached to the fact that she is a white woman working in a genre associated with white men in the West and Chinese performers in Hong Kong."[24] The combination of her whiteness and her womanhood inscribed in the martial arts genre made her a prime target for fetishization. Indeed, the fear and anxiety projected onto the racial otherness of a white muscular man that always poses a threat to the Chinese hero in Hong Kong action cinema could be softened by the erotic investment in the petite and blonde Rothrock. Her eroticism was by no means offered as a "sexual spectacle" in the style of the fighting heroine in many Hollywood action movies, who is usually clad in few clothes so as to exaggerate her breasts, muscles and other outstanding sexual characteristics. Rothrock was fully clothed in all her Hong Kong action movies. Neither did she develop any romantic relations with the Chinese male protagonist in the films,[25] although it is always said that colonized ethnic men want to have sexual relations with white women in order symbolically to promote their social status and rid themselves of their humiliating experience of colonialism. Apparently, the white body of Rothrock did not carry such an explicitly "erotic" function for the colonized Chinese male. On the contrary, invoking images of traditional Chinese fighting heroes who are always sexual puritans capable of resisting feminine charms, and sometimes even misogynistic,[26] Rothrock is implicated in Hong Kong movies as a conventional asexual kung fu artist who observes celibacy as one of the tenets of martial arts training. But the cinematic objectification of her race and femininity as reflexive reference has helped to establish the Hong Kong spectator in the ideological position of the "Chinese male subject" vis-à-vis a Caucasian female object of the male gaze.

While Hong Kong cinema of the 1980s was craving a stronger sense of modernization, Westernization or internationalization, an appropriate Chinese identity was still necessary for the subject to position itself in the global scene. Given Western hegemony and its display of modernity, it is not unusual that in its attempt to catch up with the West, Hong Kong began to identify with it. Watching a Caucasian woman skilled in Chinese kung fu and fluent in Cantonese onscreen is like seeing a new Chinese self coming under the admiring gaze of the West to confirm Hong Kong Chinese cultural values and self-esteem. But the "Chinese self" incarnated by the American blonde is of course a reinvented Hong Kong cultural subject — a "Caucasianized" one — imagined in order to gain access to the West and recognition by the West. To understand how Rothrock occupies a certain fetish-object status in Hong Kong action films, we need to borrow psychoanalytical language again. As an American masculine woman fighter, her Caucasian image or her whiteness is a symbolic substitute for her missing penis. The "West" she stands for, a kind of leverage for Hong Kong cinema to elevate itself to an imaginary global scene, not only disavows that which is lacking from her female body but also denies for the Hong Kong Chinese male viewer his "absent symbolic phallus," that is to say his degrading colonized position and so-deemed inferior Chinese ethnic status.

This may explain why, unlike the heroine in many action movies, the Rothrock character is not supposed to be a romantic interest or a sex trophy for the hero. She is "untouchable" because she, with her Caucasian female masculinity, helps to cover up the vulnerable position of the Chinese male subject. Apart from being a center of action, Rothrock in *Righting Wrongs* is also a point of identification, but one that does not have much staying power in comparison to the real hero of Chinese origin in the film. At best, the whiteness and female masculinity of Rothrock represented in Hong Kong action cinema are merely secondary to real Chinese masculinity. No matter how powerful and masculine this white person might be, she is only a woman, and thus poses no real threat to the Chinese male audience. Her whiteness is used for the expansion of Hong Kong's global imagination and her female masculinity fills out what's lacking in the colonized Hong Kong male subjectivity. When she has served her function, she is dispensable (she is killed by Sergeant Wong near the end of the movie, so the finale is left to the Chinese hero and the super-villain).

At first glance, the female lead is not so much a woman as a "woman" in the female-cop genre of the 1980s. It is tempting to say that men continually re-inscribe male identity in their representation of female masculinity because all these movies are directed and written by males. The male filmmakers only find in "woman" a figure or a trope for representing the latent dimensions of masculinity or covering up its void. It is usually men or masculinity, not women or their femininity, that are the issue or the problem to be dealt with. To invest the elements of masculinity in these female bodies is a way to rebuild the sexual norm. Indeed norms, sexual or patriarchal, are never as static or stable as one generally believes. They incorporate and interpret features of changing realities in order to craft identification, or produce materials for tenacious sexual identifications and disavowals. On the other hand, even though these women fight like men and can be as strong as them, they are still women. In other words, heterosexuality and the ideal morphologies of gender division become "inevitable." At a different level, precisely because these women fighters are "just women," they are less threatening and more approachable for action-film audiences, which are largely constituted by men to project their, not necessarily sexual, fantasies.

8

An Unworthy Subject:
Slaughter, Cannibalism and Postcoloniality

James A. Steintrager

In the introduction to *Hong Kong: Culture and the Politics of Disappearance*, Ackbar Abbas claims that the space invoked in his title marks a particularly interesting conjunction of colonialism and postcoloniality, of multiple crisscrossings of global flows and local idiosyncrasies. Published in 1997, this study makes much of the impending handover. This is an event that looms so large on the horizon that it forces Hong Kong's citizens to take account of a cultural identity that has become apparent only in hindsight. The term Abbas coins for this situation takes the commonplace French expression "déja vu" and gives it a postmodern twist: the "déja disparu." It appears that the combination of uniqueness — there is no other situation quite like Hong Kong's at this time — and generalizability — are not capitalism and technology pushing all of us in a similar direction? — has produced a cinema that has a purchase on critical spectators everywhere: "The new Hong Kong cinema deserves attention because it has finally found a worthy subject — it has found Hong Kong itself as subject."[1] While Abbas is certainly not interested in some sort of reflective realism, there is nonetheless more than a kernel of just that in his account. That is, the most representative films from Hong Kong will in fact best represent the spirit of Hong Kong. (I choose such a humanistic term as "spirit" deliberately and somewhat mischievously.) What films or types of films are representative in this sense? Four out of Hong Kong's rather more sizeable offerings are selected as most suited to demonstrate the thesis of worthiness: Wong Kar-wai's (Wang Jiawei) *As Tears Go By* (Wangjiao kamen) (1988), Ann Hui's (Xu Anhua) *Song of the Exile* (Ketu qiuhen) (1990), and Stanley Kwan's (Guan Jinpeng) *Rouge* (Yanzhi kou) (1987) and *Center Stage* (Ruan Lingyu) (1992). Wong's films are also treated at greater length in a separate chapter; the director's openly avant-garde creations are a clear favorite with the critic as they are on the "global" art-film circuit. In this chapter I will not be concerned with deepening our understanding of such films and filmmakers. On this score Abbas's study contains many fascinating aperçus. Rather, my focus will be on what most academic accounts of Hong Kong cinema omit and therefore deem tacitly and sometimes expressly unrepresentative. Rejected, repudiated and largely hidden, we might call this something the postcolonial abject.

What is this thing that must be held at bay? Clearly, part of what Abbas wants to counteract is the widely held view, especially abroad, that Hong Kong cinema is "essentially a cinema of action" (17). What puts the works of Wong Kar-wai and company in a "privileged position" vis-à-vis Hong Kong's culture is that they engage with the complexity of the moment (17). In fact, the reason action films are unrepresentative is *not* that there is a paucity of them or that action genres have not historically taken up a significant slice of the pie. To assert the contrary would be mere wishful thinking. Action films in general are unrepresentative in that they are too simple — too simple either to grasp our attention for more than the time it takes to watch them and too simple to render adequately a situation that is itself complex. This is true, for example, of the works of John Woo (Wu Yusen), director of several action films that have enjoyed popularity in Hong Kong, elsewhere in Asia, Europe and North America. Concerning Woo's use of slow motion in the so-called heroic bloodshed genre (where guns take the place of swords and kicks), Abbas suggests that the technique is used to "romanticize or aestheticize" violence rather than used "analytically to study, to understand" as it is in Wong (35). I believe that this negative judgment partially has to do with a longstanding critical distrust of the spectacular that crops up even where the visual is otherwise being elevated over the diegetic as more appropriate to our postmodern world, but there is more to the matter than that.[2]

A second and not unrelated reason has to do with the perceived maleness of the action category.[3] In this respect, the kung fu genre in particular is read by Abbas as providing various definitions of "the ethos of (mainly) male heroism and personal prowess" in relation to the evolving colonial situation (29). Further, as far as so-called heroic bloodshed films go, John Woo is primarily concerned with violence, on the one hand, and, on the other, affection "usually between male friends"

(23).[4] And if the director with most favored status on the whole undermines easy versions of heroism, even he is not immune to the charge of indulging in a manly agenda: "One of the many interesting features of Ann Hui's film [*Song of the Exile*] is that it takes us away from the largely male concerns of Hong Kong cinema (Wong Kar-wai is not exempt from this charge in his earlier films)" (36). There is here I think a sort of equation between Abbas's two main criticisms that could be expressed vulgarly thus: men are stupid. If we want, however, to avoid the perceived oversimplications of the action genre itself, relying on such a reductive and ahistorical binary as male/female seems ill advised. In fact, the devaluation of "maleness" runs deeper than it appears. It is more or less a cover for a concern that has become ubiquitous in poststructuralist and postcolonial thought: the critique of the subject as autonomous and self-present. In this regard, the term "personal prowess" takes part in what we might call the subject code. The "personal" refers us to a stable identity; "prowess" to the power of this agent to will and act. As opposed to this manly subject, the good subject — the worthy subject of Hong Kong cinema that reflects Hong Kong as a cultural space — will be feminized, fragmented, spectral, and no *subject* at all.[5]

If the action genre as generally understood (kung fu, swordplay, gun battles) is often discounted in academe, what then to make of a film such as *The Untold Story* (Baxian fandian zhi renrou chashaobao) (dir. Herman Yau [Qiu Litao], 1993)?[6] This Category III thriller stars Anthony Wong (Huang Qiusheng), who has made a career out of playing outlandish villains.[7] The narrative thrust of this charmer is straightforward. It begins with a backstory set in Hong Kong: after an argument about gambling debts the protagonist, Wong Chi-heng, murders the disputant and torches the evidence. The action then jumps forward several years to Macau, where Wong, having thus far escaped the clutches of the authorities, is running the Eight Immortals Restaurant. Seen cheating at mahjong by a newly hired cook, Wong does in the employee with brutal insouciance. Then, suspecting that a female worker has told some suspicious police investigators too much, the hero is launched into yet another murderous frenzy. This involves a lengthy and particularly brutal rape scene that culminates in the worker being violated with a fistful of plastic chopsticks. One of the last shots of this sequence is filmed from under the table on which the rape takes place; the viewer sees the dangling legs of the victim, heaving with departing life, the legs and torso of the killer, and his hand, clutching the bloody implements. When the police do eventually apprehend Wong, he is tortured into confessing an earlier crime: the slaughter of the former owner of the restaurant and his entire family. This is the visual centerpiece of the film, and it is rendered in gut-wrenching detail. That this murderous rampage is revealed as a flashback also allows for a moment of mock-tragic *anagnoresis*: the police only realize in retrospect that the flesh of the victims has been used to make the delectable "pork" buns that have been so popular of late and that they too have been enjoying free of charge. Much of this is made quite clear in the Chinese title of the film, which translates as *The Eight Immortals Restaurant's Human Meat Roast Pork Buns*. The film ends with Wong's suicide in prison (sawing into his wrist with a pop-top lid from a soda can that he had secreted in his mouth). I should add that the film is loosely based on a 1986 murder case in Macau.

In many respects *The Untold Story* has not proved unique to Hong Kong production since the Category III rating was put into place in 1989. As Darrell Davis and Yeh Yueh-yu have shown in their essay "Warning Category III," films that fall under this rubric represent a sizeable portion of total Hong Kong output, and those that graphically commingle violence and sex are by no means marginal within the category (following Tom Wolfe, they suggest "pornoviolence" as a distinguishing label for such fare).[8] Of course, the rating system did not create these spectacles; it was put into place as a reaction to similarly violent, porno-violent and more straightforwardly pornographic products. On the other hand, ratings systems do in a sense hypostatize the perceived existence of categorical markers, simultaneously inviting transgression and limit-testing.[9]

As a film that carries several of these markers and which clearly pushes limits, it strikes me as uncontroversial to say that *The Untold Story* is representative of something in Hong Kong cinema — but of what exactly? For example, is the film representative in the sense that Abbas puts forward? Certainly we would not want to see in it a fractal of some supposed Hong Kong culture, nor would I grant it a privileged position from which to view the same (although one should always be careful not to scorn the underprivileged). Is it then representative in the same way that Woo's films are supposed to be and should it be marginalized on account of the same factors (perceived stupidity and maleness)? Certainly, some have seen in *The Untold Story* an apparently willful, perhaps malevolent, obtuseness. Hong Kong-based movie critic Paul Fonoroff remarks in his pan of the film that it "uses its intriguing subject matter [the real case] as an excuse for unfolding a *mindless* orgy of blood-letting" (my emphasis).[10] Furthermore, given the subject matter, we might be excused for assuming that the principal audience of *The Untold Story* and other films of its ilk has been male. There is evidence to suggest, however, that its reception in Hong Kong is more complex than this assumption would lead us to infer. Moreover, even in its reception abroad, where there is at least anecdotal evidence supporting the maleness of its primary viewers, I would assert that the situation of the film is still far from simple. Indeed, if at first glance it appears that there is little to learn from this grisly extravaganza, my goal in this chapter is to complicate such matters considerably. In particular, I will argue that we can perhaps learn more from an unworthy subject — a subject that in its very abjection reveals the horrific joys and sadistic miseries of identity formation in a postcolonial, global order — than from the productions of the deliberately *bien-pensant*.

DARKER THAN NOIR

When the movie critic complains of "mindlessness," the hidden premise is that spectacles in general and above all violent spectacles require legitimation. Thus Fonoroff notes in his review of *The Untold Story* that "anyone hoping for a bit of *Silence of the Lambs*-style psychological insight will leave this restaurant hungry" and that "the audience hasn't a clue — not even a superficial one — as to the underlying motivation for [Wong's] heinous acts."[11] To my mind, the contrast between the American *Silence of the Lambs* (dir. Jonathan Demme, 1991) and the Hong Kong work is somewhat specious. That is, I am far from convinced that either Hannibal Lecter or the serial killer he helps track is given depth or complexity. Lecter is supposed to be a genius, ergo criminally insane; the killer has gender-based identity problems. In both cases, the etiology of criminal behavior is sketched out superficially and stereotypically. The spectacular aspect of the film seems much more compelling (Lecter's prison chamber; the disorienting terror of the night-vision goggles sequence, and so forth). But let us nonetheless grant the terms of the comparison for a moment. The assumption is that the "high" film product presents the viewer with psychological depth of character, whereas the "low" is a mere sound-and-light show. This notion of depth is largely an inheritance from the formerly prevalent printed media (the development of the novel above all), and it hangs on as a survivor in middle-brow movie criticism. More theoretically inclined criticism has long since eschewed a naïve insistence on deep content, which is reduced to a surface effect, and focused our attention instead on matters of form and the specificity of the film medium. Take the case of one of the seminal works in the slasher/serial-killer genre, long since elevated to "high" art status: Alfred Hitchcock's *Psycho* (1960). Norman Bates's Oedipal problems — the character's motivation — are really quite unconvincing. On the other hand, film theory has correctly surmised that the camera work and editing are the true sources of the film's artistry and impact. The legitimacy of the shower scene, which would seem to require some sort of justification if it is not to appear as simply a woman being slashed to death, rests on these criteria.

I have no interest in formulating a qualitative comparison that would weigh Hitchcock's prowess against the directorial work of Herman Yau. Having said this, it does strike me as worthwhile to move beyond the matter of character motivation — I will return to it later in good dialectical fashion — and see whether *The Untold Story* has any claim to formal complexity. In particular, we might wonder whether the spectacle most in need of some justification offers anything more than gore. So what are the formal qualities of the central massacre sequence, in which a small son, a mother, a father and four young daughters are dispatched in that order? The sequence itself lasts approximately four minutes, from the time the camera first pans across the faces of the bound victims until the killer's hand reaches out for the last daughter and the camera, blackening the screen. In this period, there are seventy-one shots spliced together. The primary angles are as follows: high (seemingly shot from the ceiling, detached and voyeuristic); slightly lower (closer to the killer's implied point of view); eye-level (as if one were standing in the same room); low (apparently from the victim's viewpoint); and a worm's-eye view (as if shot from the floor). The list is not exhaustive, but does suggest the range and alternation of angles and viewpoints. Furthermore, while some of the camera work is from such a distance that characters fit entirely into the frame, much of it is so tight as to give the spectator only a fragmentary field of vision, inserting one claustrophobically into the action. The action itself is quite gruesome, and the constant accompaniment of the children's wails, which slowly decrescendo into plaintive sobs and then silence, adds to the sickening atmospherics. The son is stabbed in the neck with a piece of glass; the mother repeatedly in the stomach (after having a chunk of her face bitten out); the father too is stabbed in the neck; three of the daughters are decapitated with a cleaver; it is implied that the death of the fourth takes place in the same manner. I might note as well that the killing of the third daughter echoes the rape scene. The camera once again places the spectator under the table upon which the girl is pinned down; her head and a curtain of blood then drop and cascade into the frame.

What is one to make of these complex formal moves? Evidently, they cannot be sundered from either what is being shown or the spectators' reactions. No amount of dissection of camera angles and editing will get rid of the images of slaughter, dismemberment and gore, and only the truly inured to such visions — and the habitué does develop detachment — would not respond in a manner almost inevitably labeled "visceral." Response, however, does not reside in the stomach, even if the sight of disembowelment tends to induce nausea. The purport of the "visceral" is simple: it suggests that the mind is bypassed, that the impact of the spectacle is immediate, that the story ends there. In fact, where a critic such as Abbas rejects the notion that Hong Kong cinema is pure presence and spectacle as a primitivism indulged in by foreigners, his marginalization of "action" plays largely into the same impulse. It would appear, in fact, that one reason action films are eschewed by those who want instead to concentrate on films deemed more representative of the complexities of the postcolonial situation in Hong Kong is that they are treated precisely as having those attributes otherwise disdained: immediacy and presence. When it is a question of spectacular violence in particular, there is a tendency to fall back surreptitiously on these notions in order to define and celebrate what the preferred films are *not*. The worthy subject of postcolonial criticism, in other words, takes shape through a process of negation and rejection. Those films that at least appear to appeal to the stomach and not to the mind, that appear to feature the willing subject of masculine desire rather than a fragmented and feminized subject, must be simultaneously invoked and thrown away.

A citation from David Bordwell, whose omnivorousness does occasionally lead him to consider Category III, may help confirm these hypotheses and suggest a way out. Bordwell is discussing the technique of flashback and has just dealt with Jeff Lau (Liu Zhenwei)'s *Days of Tomorrow* (Tianchang dijiu) (1993). He writes:

> More viscerally, the key flashback in Herman Yau and Danny Lee's *The Untold Story* ... catches the viewer between sympathy and loathing. The film intercuts the exploits of the cannibalistic killer with the police squad's casual investigation. It is hard to attach feelings to anyone in this carnival of sadism and petty ineptitude. But when the killer is

captured and the police extract a confession under torture, we can hardly withhold some sympathy from a demented man who is suffering so much. Then comes the flashback to the crime we have not seen — the killer's relentless butchering of a family. We are left with no one to feel for; the killer commits suicide, his crimes disturbingly unexplained and unexcused.[12]

Bordwell's work is best known for its emphasis on form, and his *Planet Hong Kong: Popular Cinema and the Art of Entertainment*, from which the above citation is taken, fits the pattern: the evolution of the studio system, economic cycles and similar historical factors are brought into dialogue with largely formal concerns. But as the discussion of flashback in *The Untold Story* indicates, it is hardly possible to keep formal concerns from constructing an ideal spectator of popular entertainment. This spectator has by implication certain attributes, desires and expectations. Above all, what is posited as expected by the spectator is the establishment and continuity of sympathetic identification, i.e., the converse of what actually happens in *The Untold Story* according to Bordwell. Rather, what the flashback technique, in conjunction with what is shown in the flashback, does in Bordwell's account is disrupt this process. As a further mark of perversity, not only are we barred from identifying with the "hero," we are also barred from sympathizing with the cops, who come off as mean-spirited bullies as well as buffoons. The spectator does not engage emotionally with any of the onscreen subjects — at least not consistently — and is further discouraged from doing so by the lack of interest that the director shows in deep motivations. Finally, because it fails to reach the goal set by the construct itself, a negative judgment on the quality of the film can be inferred. That is, because the film does not engage sympathetic identification, it is simply no good. Ironically, this failure is more ideal than real, for as Bordwell notes elsewhere, *The Untold Story*'s popularity and sales figures are not insignificant.[13] Of course, sympathetic identification of this sort is usually only expected in entertainment as opposed to "high" artistic product. It is worth noting that the disruption of identification that so disconcerts in *The Untold Story* might well be considered engaged, political and progressive in other contexts. Think, for example, of Brecht's theory of alienation or *Verfremdungseffekt* in drama and similar tactics used in film (certain works of Fassbinder come to mind).

The importance of sympathy and cognates such as pity have, as is well known, both an ancient pedigree and a lengthy reception. I have no desire to return us to Aristotle's *Poetics*, the early modern reception of this text and its further adventures. It is an unavoidable fact in this context, however, that sympathetic identification and cathexis — the attachment of feelings to a character — have played a robust role in film criticism, with particular emphasis on the conjunction of formal analysis and psychoanalytic accounts of subjectivity. Thus identification with a given character has been explained as a process that takes place in film not simply thanks to some emotional affinity for someone shown on screen but rather through the structuring of shots. In classical Hollywood cinema, for example, a shot will first frame a character and then be followed by a counter-shot in which the camera suggests the same character's field of vision; the spectator is hereby stitched, as it were, to this character's point of view. It is through this process that the spectator also becomes ineluctably drawn into the film as an ideological product — a process all the more insidious because it is supposed to transpire by and large unconsciously.[14] In this regard, the process of "suture" has often been read in terms of gender and especially in terms of the indulgence and reproduction of the so-called male gaze (although recent critiques of the concept have pointed out aberrations, complications, points of resistance, etc.). Of course, this means that we also have to broaden the definition of "sympathy" to mean not simply compassion for suffering but potentially identification with misdeeds as well. This is the very possibility set up by the play of shots and editing. Slasher films may thus establish the spectator in the position of the killer, providing a sadistic thrill for the viewer (often presumed male) who watches the victim (probably female) suffer. Does *The Untold Story* confirm this scenario? The rape sequence does in fact tend to follow this highly problematic pattern. On the other hand, as my breakdown of the slaughter sequence should have made clear, the horror thereof is predicated on possibilities of identification tendered and then withdrawn. Indeed, the vacillation between "sympathy and loathing" that Bordwell sees as triggered by the flashback to the slaughter sequence — a vacillation that eventually derails identification altogether — is operative within the sequence itself as a disconcerting oscillation or sliding from one subject position to another.

The process of subject deformation that *The Untold Story* would seem to provoke looks very much like a reversal of the process of subject formation according to certain psychoanalytic theories. In particular, Julia Kristeva has proposed the term "abjection" to describe the repudiation of those things that blur the line between self and other — those things that must be disavowed if identification and subjectivity are to take hold. Kristeva has linked the abject above all to the mother's body as opposed to the father's image, which forms the basis of identification. Resurgence of the abject is accompanied by horror — the horror of the disintegration of the self.[15] Cannibalism, where the other is literally incorporated into the self, would be a sign *par excellence* that we are in the realm of abjection. Because the abject is clearly disconcerting, one should not be surprised to find it accompanied by sadistic attempts to master the threat of disintegration. In keeping with a theory that positions the mother as that which must be repudiated, moreover, there is little doubt that sadism is frequently played out on women's bodies. Similarly, in his seminar on ethics, Jacques Lacan proposes that *das Ding* (or "the thing") be used as a technical term for the horrific intimation of that which lies outside of the Imaginary (above all the register of identifications) and that which resists assimilation into the Symbolic (the register of language and similar semiotic systems). Behind sadism — and Lacan refers us directly to the works of Sade — is an attempt to hold at bay the mute, idiotic, undifferentiated matter of what he calls the Real.[16] Although their terminology differs, the theoretical positions of Kristeva and Lacan are largely in accord.[17] Given the subject matter of *The Untold Story* and given that "suture" is precisely what fails to take hold because it is technically withheld, an approach to the film via abjection seems entirely fitting. The disturbing part is that, while horrific, there must be also something alluring and enjoyable about this shock to the spectator. If this were not so, who would watch?

What should in any case be obvious is that we have moved beyond the simple binary of male/female and the critique of the subject embedded therein. While *The Untold Story* may at one level indulge in the shoring up of the ego as voluntaristic agency (the sadistic element), in the final analysis the film problematizes these constructs by foreclosing motivation (the demand for "deep" insight into a character) and above all by the subversion of identification. Here, we may be reminded of Abbas's celebration of Wong Kar-wai's *As Tears Go By*, an action film that is elevated to the status of postcolonial worthiness on similar grounds. Specifically, Wong's film does not engage in simplistic heroics but is rather a "special kind of film noir": "the *neonoir* of a colonial subject caught in the confusions of colonial space" (34). In this case, we are told: "Violence may always be threatening to erupt, but it is never straightforwardly celebrated as the voluntaristic act of an individual subject, as in John Woo's films; rather, it exists as a ubiquitous and unavoidable dimension of urban space itself, which offers the individual no choice" (34-35). It is the presence of such complications of the subject that leads Abbas back to the category of film noir, for it was in noir that "moral ambiguities," the reverse of simple male heroism, and urban space first came together on the screen (34). As should be clear by now, *The Untold Story* provides moral ambiguity in spades. And while I think we would rightly hesitate to celebrate *The Untold Story* without qualification, there is nevertheless something about its very literal "mindlessness" — the way it forces an encounter with the idiotic and abject — that is akin to the avant-garde product. Wong Chi-heng, the unworthy subject, is literally not worthy of the designation "subject." He is therefore a doppelganger of sorts of that worthy non-subject praised by the postcolonial critic. From spectrality and fragmentation, we have simply slipped one step down to horror and dismemberment. In short, it turns out that the "unworthy subject" of the postcolonial theorist — the manly, stupid subject, that reduced and simplified version of *the* subject that has become a longstanding target of critique — thought to be and, in fact, required to be present in action films is not even there in this Category III festival of gore. Further, the rather more disturbing discovery we have made is that, thanks to the formal techniques by which identification is barred in this repulsive and violent spectacle, *The Untold Story* appears in uncanny, if monstrous and deformed, proximity to its avant-garde others.

GLOBALIZATION AND THE QUANDARIES OF RECEPTION

If we read *The Untold Story* as the emergence of the abject — or better, as presenting a conjunction of form and content that imply a spectator cast momentarily into abjection — is our critical task over? That is to say, have we then understood the film? If we answer this question affirmatively — and I do think that the answer is a partial "yes" — then the question of representativeness is greatly simplified. *The Untold Story* will have tapped into a universal structure and will represent precisely this recurrence of abjection. In this respect, *The Untold Story* will be representative of a class of films — regardless of whether this class includes one or many members. Its pleasures and horrors will be part of what Bordwell, with respect to action films, has somewhat paradoxically called the "transcultural": forms and contents that have no need of *translation* because they are not in fact *cultural* at all.[18] Clearly, not all films are like *The Untold Story*. Then again, there are many that are. The rape scene is not untypical of other Category III films. Frequently, graphic display of sexual violation is compensated for by equally lurid revenge sequences. There is here a narrative disingenuousness so blatant that it makes a mockery of *mauvaise foi*. As far as novels are concerned, it was a favorite technique of Sade. In fact, neither is such fare specific to Hong Kong nor is it a historically recent occurrence. Sadistic-voyeuristic thrillers are widespread and commonplace. More specifically, "revenge for rape" films constitute a recognizable and well-represented sub-genre within the vast array of B-movie exploitation fare. In the United States, classics — if the term is apt — include *I Spit on Your Grave* (dir. Meir Zarchi, 1977) and Wes Craven's harrowing freshman effort *Last House on the Left* (1972). In Europe, prolific provocateur Jess Franco's soft-core "roughies" have never strayed too far from this territory. Moreover, unashamedly B-movies of the sort have their "high" counterparts in films such as Sam Pekinpah's controversial *Straw Dogs* (1972) and Ingmar Bergman's *Virgin Spring* (1960). The latter supposedly served as a model for Craven. As for slaughter and cannibalism — the abject side of the matter — the title of Herschell Gordon Lewis's seminal *Blood Feast* (1963) speaks for itself. Nor should we forget *Sweeney Todd, the Demon Barber of Fleet Street* (dir. George King, 1936), which boasts a plot remarkably similar to that of *The Untold Story* and became the basis for Stephen Sondheim's hit Broadway musical of the same name in the late 1970s. Lowly and campy cannibal tales too have an artsy double in Peter Greenaway's *The Cook, the Thief, His Wife and Her Lover* (1989). In the name of cosmopolitanism, we might also look to some of the more sexually violent and gory *pinku eiga* (pornographic films) from Japan, not to mention Italian *giallo* movies, the blood-splattered horror associated with directors such as Dario Argento and Lucio Fulci. Needless to say, we are just scratching the surface in terms of film history.

In addition, although the medium-specific aspects of spectacular abjection should not be discounted, we can also find earlier dramatic equivalents of *The Untold Story*. Consider, for example, Seneca's rhetorical bravura in *Thyestes*, where Atreus, a wronged husband, kills his brother's children with gruesome panache and then has the remains cooked up and served to his perfidious, gullible and unsuspecting sibling. Or again, Shakespeare's *Titus Andronicus* — which owes much to Seneca — where the eponymous hero exacts revenge on the wicked

Tamora by doing in her sons and serving them in pie form to her at a banquet. Similar examples could be culled from Baroque drama in Germany and France, and there are no doubt other cases as well.[19] In each instance, treacherous women, reeking gore and the ingestion of human flesh (often of family members) appear to mark the intermittent pulse of the abject. In each case, however, it would be a critical mistake to wrest such apparent universality from historical contingency. Seneca's blood feast is inseparable from the politics of imperial Rome (the playwright was Nero's tutor, no less, and was eventually commanded to commit suicide at his student's behest). Shakespeare's extravaganza of horror has a complicated relationship to both the evolution of the genre of revenge tragedy as well as to the pressing matter of monarchical power and its limits. It would likewise be wrongheaded to treat the emergence of the abject in *The Untold Story* without considering the historical context of its violent eruption.

In this regard, one of the most compelling aspects of Abbas's study is the way in which the specificity of Hong Kong's colonial situation as well as technological developments are brought to bear on his reading of local film history. The good-humored antics of Jackie Chan are thus keyed to the "relaxation of colonial tensions" during the 1970s (30). This period was to come to an end with the two defining traumatic experiences of the Sino-British Joint Declaration and the crushing of the Tiananmen uprising. As such events undermined appeals to "Chineseness" against colonization, a new investment in a transnational future would arise, expressing itself in novel configurations of the kung fu genre (notably the special-effects driven spectacles of Tsui Hark [Xu Ke]'s *Once Upon a Time in China* [Huang Fei Hong] series and Wong Kar-wai's *Ashes of Time* [Dong Xie Xi Du], both of which Abbas reads as gestures toward technology over the old forms of colonialism). We might see the steady rise of Category III-style violence in the years leading to handover as yet another reaction to the same events and situations. Indeed, if I pointed out the disquieting proximity of the good subject of postcolonial theory with the monstrous subject of *The Untold Story*, it was in order to suggest that this particular instantiation of the abject has much to do with the particularities of place and time.

What, then, might a reading of the film that takes socio-political context into account look like? Given the impact of the Tiananmen massacre on the citizens of Hong Kong, we could construe *The Untold Story* as a sort of political or psycho-social allegory. This is an approach that makes a good deal of sense when talking about another film from roughly the same period that also indulges in extreme displays of violence, both sadistic and masochistic: John Woo's epic *Bullet in the Head* (Diexue jietou) (1990). This film uses the anti-British riots in Hong Kong of the late 1960s and the Vietnam War as allegorical backdrops to probe political wounds and anxiously to work through the threat to Hong Kong identity posed by the coming of the SAR.[20] At one point in the film, a peace demonstrator on the streets of Saigon even stands down a tank. During the course of the action, it becomes clear that the Vietnamese stand in for the Mainland, and the brutality of the Vietcong soldiers in particular reflects the bloody denouement of the demonstrations of 1989. But while the allegory is quite well guided by the director in many respects, the moral of the film remains unclear. *Bullet in the Head* begins with three childhood friends; by the end, all are either dead or lie dying by one another's hand. What is one to do with such an apocalyptic and ultimately nihilistic response to violence and fear? It would appear that the threat to Hong Kong identity explored by Woo's work provokes simultaneously a sadistic attempt to master the situation and an excuse to wallow in abjection. *The Untold Story* is nothing if not more ambiguous in this regard. We might assume that, given the fact that he massacres a family, Wong Chi-heng is the allegorical figure — conscious or not — of the killers at Tiananmen. On the other hand, it seems even more plausible that the Macau police are imaginary stand-ins for stereotypically backward, unsophisticated, inept and cruel Mainlanders. This development would even suggest that the monstrous protagonist occupies the place of Hong Kong itself! We might see in the loathsome actions of Wong an outburst of "freedom" in the face of freedom's possible demise, and, taking a cue from Laikwan Pang's exploration of the thematization of death in less sanguinary cinematic fare, we might consider the violence perpetrated by the hero as a way of working through questions of identity and its loss in Hong Kong's cultural space.[21]

These matters of freedom and identity resonate, moreover, in the reception of the film in Hong Kong. If there is something that truly stands out about *The Untold Story* as an ultra-violent Category III spectacle, it is that it enjoyed more official recognition than most of its type. Whereas the film has a cult audience in the West, Anthony Wong garnered the best-actor prize at the 1993 Hong Kong Film Awards for his nuanced performance (best picture went to the romance *C'est la Vie, Mon Chéri* [Xin Buliao Qing]). We might read this occurrence as a political gesture or, more crudely, as an act of perverse defiance confronting possible future repression. The reality is probably slightly more complicated. Above all, it is crucial to point out that the award mimics the perceived conversion of violent entertainment from "low" to "high" in *Silence of the Lambs*. The latter appeared two years before *The Untold Story* and had swept the most important categories of the Academy Awards (best actor, best actress, best director and best picture). In this respect, Paul Fonoroff's comparison of the two films is entirely apposite and of the moment. In fact, *The Untold Story* was not the only film to recall the Demme picture: 1992 saw Danny Lee's debut directorial effort with the gruesome chiller *Dr. Lamb* (Gaoyang yisheng) (co-directed by Billy Tang [Deng Yancheng]), another reality-based serial killer tale that pulls out all the stops. The rise and reception of Category III pornoviolence must in certain respects be seen not simply as an evolution of the film system, not simply as a response to local or otherwise pressing political contingencies, but also as a gesture toward Hollywood. Moreover, instead of regarding this gesture as mere emulation of the global entertainment hegemon, we might see it as the election of a deliberately cosmopolitan stance. A rejection of parochialism and of the imposition of a delimiting ethnicity, the appropriation of Hollywood would here mark an openness and flexibility to the world outside China and the East. Read in this manner, we are reminded that any theory that makes a film narrowly reflective of its political or social context is reductive. The rapid distribution of film and other types of information on a global scale mean that reception will henceforth always take us beyond the simplifying schema of concrete locale and ethnicity to more problematic — and ultimately more interesting — negotiations of identity and constructions of meaning.

The question of reception has opened up a potentially fruitful but perhaps troublesome avenue of inquiry. It appears that an insistence on the specificity of a work may lead to a surreptitious elevation of place over space, which would include the rapid flows of information supported by new media technologies.[22] Personally, it strikes me as premature to speak of the disappearance of place as some have suggested. We all still have bodies and tend to find ourselves specific locales. On the other hand, when the success of *Silence of the Lambs* sparks emulation in a film industry largely located thousands of miles away, then the role of space clearly needs to be addressed. Of course, postcolonial critics and other theorists of the present usually do try to balance these issues, but there is nevertheless a tendency to revert to place as a primary determinant. This reversion is, I think, a symptom of a deeper malaise: the simultaneously avowed and repressed realization that producers, product and consumers can no longer be bundled in the neat package that we have come to call culture. It is precisely this symptom, at work in postcolonial theory, that is analyzed and critiqued by Rey Chow in the final part of *Primitive Passions*, where she points out the unthought and insidiously nativist insistence that "Chinese" films have a "Chinese" audience, and examines the discounting of the works of Zhang Yimou or Chen Kaige on the grounds that they play to a "foreign" market and supposedly oversimplify, pander and ultimately betray ethnic purity.[23] What these directors do is blast apart the hermeneutic desire to "read over the shoulders" of another culture in anthropological fashion.[24] That is, rather than providing a fractal of their own culture, these producers communicate difference to consumers through the product (in this case, film) which acts as a sort of translation — but not a translation as some sort of pure or supposedly faithful transmission. What Chow remarks then is a certain, often horrified, resistance to giving up culture as that bundling of production, product and reception. Part of this resistance has to do with our academic habits of understanding: we have become used to "culture" as a way of underwriting the unity of the objects of our investigation. The horrific facet of this resistance has to do with the fact that with the disintegration of culture we feel the loss of that unity and object — a slipping away that leaves us in a state of undifferentiation and abject identity confusion. The success of a film such as *The Untold Story*, however, reminds us once more that there may also be something freeing and obscenely enjoyable in this situation. We may even glimpse a politics of abjection that refuses to submit to the sadistic imperative to behave in accordance with cultural norms and to take up the mantle of this or that ethnicity.

In this last phase of my argument, I want to use this questioning of hermeneutic desire to address another aspect of the reception of *The Untold Story* and films like it: the point of view of the overseas fan. This may seem like an extraneous concern because the study of reception abroad does not appear to help us understand the film. Certainly it has nothing to do with understanding the film by looking at its "native" context — if anything, it points us in the direction of the failure of translation rather than successful communication (unless we fall back entirely on the notion of the "transcultural"). In fact, it is the very nature of this failure that is instructive. To simplify the matter, I will stick to works published in the United States. I would also note that the writers whom I quote, publishers of guides directed at fans and clearly fans themselves, are all men. Consider the opinions, for example, of Thomas Weisser, editor of the fanzine *Asian Trash Cinema* and primary author of guidebooks of the same name. Weisser is unrepentant in his praise of Category III excess. On the film *Naked Killer* (Chiluo gaoyang) (dir. Clarence Fok [Huo Yaoliang], 1992), he writes: "This film is part of the new wave of *roughies* coming out of Hong Kong, filled with nudity, lesbian sex, ultra-violence, and gore. It deserves our unmitigated support."[25] While occasionally demonstrating a taste for classier fare, Weisser is generally derisive of the latter (on Wong Kar-wai's widely distributed *Chung King Express* [Chongqing Senlin, 1994]: "so slow and ponderous — so-o-o-o goddamn self important — it can't possibly be recommended"[26]). As for *The Untold Story*, it is "amazingly good" — obviously because rather than in spite of the massacre, described as "the most brutal you're likely ever to see."[27] *Dr. Lamb* receives a comparable assessment: "easily one of the best Hong Kong films around. Both vicious and stylish — at the same time."[28] Or take the case of Stefan Hammond and Mike Wilkins's guide *Sex and Zen & A Bullet in the Head*. They dedicate a separate chapter to "over-the-edge" entries, including *The Untold Story* and *Dr. Lamb*, and, in their own words, "salute the exploitative spirit — the 'ghoulie, roughie, kinkie' mantra."[29] This volume is also much more generous than others when it comes to the question of motivation and compassion, although these matters takes a back seat to the splatter: "*The Untold Story* is a pretty good character study, evoking sympathy for the murderer (at least at first) without ever asking you to like him. Anthony Wong's killer is repugnant and insane, but he still comes off as a human being."[30] The need to find the sentimental side to serial killing is itself almost touching.

In academic literature, such considerations are generally marginalized or eschewed entirely. David Bordwell comes closest to taking fans seriously. Thus, in his essay "Aesthetics in Action: *Kungfu*, Gunplay, and Cinematic Expressivity," he notes that *Sex and Zen & A Bullet in the Head* is "a hilarious read, and the peppy plot synopses play up the films as seedy, sexy, bloody, and nutty."[31] Bordwell remarks that the fan's state of excitement must be acknowledged, and then good-naturedly dismisses the fan's own dismissive attitude to attempts to intellectualize cinematic pleasures and proceeds to his intellectual analyses of the same (fair enough). While Abbas does not directly address fan literature, his disparaging remarks about how Hong Kong cinema is promoted overseas and his assertion that "foreign" rather than "local" critics are more likely to praise Hong Kong cinema — and praise it for action, effects and immediacy — suggest that fan literature is below dignity.[32] In this regard, the implied objection to the fan is that the enjoyment of the products of the other is not legitimate. Rather, the relationship is parasitic: the fan attaches himself to the host culture, lives off of it, perhaps even damaging it in the process.[33] For example, many fan guides tend to perpetuate racist and ethnocentric stereotypes even when — or rather especially when — they hold out the other product as the most worthy of attention (this will come as no surprise). A film such as *The Untold Story* puts us in truly discomforting territory: the idea of white men watching the rape and murder of a woman of color for their entertainment. This possibility, opened up by media that allow the easy reproduction and transmission of information, is hardly worthy of attention in so far as any critique would be practically self-evident. Yet there is still something instructive about this situation insofar as it leads us to infer that the fan's biggest crime is really that he does not care for the hermeneutic task of understanding the other at all. This is where we would be mistaken to see in the English title of *The Untold Story* simply a failure of translation. After all, it is not even an attempt at translation. The packaging of the videocassette and DVD in any case make abundantly clear the nature of the contents. By not translating the original Chinese-language title — *The Eight Immortals Restaurant's Human Meat Roast Pork Buns* — the marketers at Tai Seng did not tap into a desire on the part of fans to find out what really happened in Macau in 1986 much less the anxieties of Hong Kong's citizens circa 1993. Rather they cannily surmised that what a fan wants is an alternative to mainstream Hollywood fare. In the global marketplace this is the selling point of the product, advertised as the "original uncut Hong Kong version," and the fan's pleasure in large part stems not simply from watching mayhem but from knowing that this gore is not what he is supposed to consume.[34]

In a sense, the underground embrace of violent Category III films abroad is the strange counterpart to the Hong Kong gesture in the direction of *The Silence of the Lambs* and of the legitimacy bestowed on the latter by the Academy Awards. Both occurrences are subversive, and yet both might well make the postcolonial critic squirm. The overseas fan whittles away at Hollywood hegemony by locating and consuming a product deemed beyond the pale of local standards; the colonial subject turns toward the hegemonic force itself and embraces it as a way to deconstruct ethnicity narrowly construed. In both cases of reception, what we witness is a refusal to pay attention to the boundaries that have come to define identity in the modern world.

Above all, these boundaries are underwritten by the twinned concepts of culture and ethnicity. In this regard, if I have an objection to Bordwell's term "transcultural," it has less to do with the humanist universalism therein implied than with its tendency to reify the category of "culture" in the very act of negation. That is, the term suggests that all that is not universal is cultural. Logically speaking, we are here faced with the fallacy of false dilemma: illegitimately limiting options by posing the problem in the form of either/or.[35] Hybridity does not help us out much either, for it tends to suggest a negotiation between two or more cultures rather than seriously considering the possible desuetude or limitations of the term "culture" itself. Likewise with Abbas, where the insistence on keeping product, producer and consumer together in one place resurrects the category and the problem of the native.[36] Just like the movie itself, the North American fan of *The Untold Story* is very much akin to the abject of psychoanalysis: that which must be repudiated if the postcolonial subject as *worthy* subject is to take form. The fan's choice points to what is unworthy, problematic and troublesome about the "other," undermining the notion of the good native — for that is what the worthy subject of postcolonial theory often appears to be, poststructuralist trappings aside. On the other hand, the mimicking of Hollywood in Hong Kong provokes similar anxieties. Why won't the good native behave? Watch the types of spectacles that best represent the complex postcolonial subject that is Hong Kong? Of course, we might recur to the semantics of original purity and desecration. Perhaps Hollywood has infected the "other" with its products. If I were more of a humanist, I would find the temptation to go in this direction frankly dehumanizing. The truth of the matter is that the interplay of place and space, of local political concerns and global media flows, constitute a situation infinitely more complex than theory has generally been able to grasp.

As a step in this direction, I have tried to demonstrate in this chapter that a Category III thriller such as *The Untold Story* harbors just as much interest and complexity as many films that pass as avant-garde. Surprisingly perhaps, there is even a deep and troubling similarity between the refusal of identification and the dissolution of subjectivity in the "unworthy" film and that which is supposed to occur in more respectable vehicles. In the second half of my argument, I have gone on to claim that we might read the eruption of abjection depicted in and, in fact, induced by *The Untold Story* as an allegory of politics in Hong Kong — or at least keyed to the socio-political context of Hong Kong

— prior to handover. The reception of the film both in Hong Kong and abroad, however, suggests that we must couple any analysis of the importance of place with an analysis of space. In part, this means that we can no longer insist that the right types of people — the natives — must watch the right types of film: those that are deemed befitting the dignity of postcolonial spectatorship. In addition, as the example of fandom abroad was meant to show, we need to acknowledge and begin to theorize more carefully — rather than eschew — what is often held out as the wrong type of spectatorship. In this regard, I have tried to show some of the ways that film criticism, in spite of itself, can act as a sort of border patrol to keep the natives neatly circumscribed and keep the (Western) savages out. Most intriguing is the case of postcolonial criticism, which, deeply invested in de-stabilizing the subject and in showing that its borders are historically constituted, repudiates the former and constructs instead a feminized, spectral and fragmented non-subject as ideal. But what happens when hybrids turn out to be monstrous, fragmentation turns into dismemberment, and ghostly apparitions transmute into psychotics? What happens, that is, when we stare squarely at the abject, that something pulsating and barely hidden behind the "worthy" subject of the postcolonial critic? Concerning these final queries, I have suggested that one reason that abject entertainment might crop up both within Hong Kong and elsewhere at this particular time is that cultural and ethnic identity — even postcolonial identity — is increasingly difficult to maintain. Celebrate this situation as we might, there is still an understandable tendency to recoil before it and to fall back on well-worn, not entirely apt semantics and strategies. This critique of one aspect of postcolonial theory should be taken as immanent. It is an attempt to approach difficult and not always pleasant matters without reverting to value judgments of worthiness and unworthiness that are themselves evasions of political responsibility rather than the contrary. The task of grasping the abject may not be easy or obvious. Indeed, it may well be that in order for any discourse or critical theory to constitute itself, certain bits of reality will have to be discarded with disdain. On the other hand, it seems well worthwhile to look into the untold stories that this process of abjection inevitably produces.

Part III
Production, Reception, and Mediation

9

Bringing Breasts into the Mainstream

Yeeshan Chan

This chapter is an attempt to present, based on interviews and participant observation, the perspectives of Hong Kong filmmakers behind popular productions.[1] In line with the Hollywood experience, the worse the economy, the more profit there is to be made in comedies.[2] In Hong Kong, *La Brassiere* [Jueshi hao "Bra"] (dir. Patrick Leung, Chan Hing-kar, 2001) and *Beauty and the Breast* [Fengxiong mi "Cup"] (dir. Raymond Yip, 2002),[3] both made in an extravagant comedic style, were well received by the masses in the midst of Hong Kong's economic downturn.[4] The key reason for their success is that women's breasts are employed strategically as entertainment through elegant clothes with feminist symbolism, which effectively targeted middle-class Hong Kong women audiences. Clifford Geertz expanded on the point that culture is a matter of individuals suspended in webs of significance that they themselves have spun and in which they have become caught.[5] This cultural perspective postulates that semiotics and symbols are a logical way of delving into how images of gender in Hong Kong's popular cinema have been projected and exploited. Focusing on the two selected comedies, I shall discuss operational patterns and working styles among producers, directors, scriptwriters and production managers in the Hong Kong film industry.

BRIEF DESCRIPTIONS OF TWO MOVIES

La Brassiere [Jueshi hao "Bra"]

Category IIB; Produced in 2001

Director(s)	Patrick Leung [Liang Baijian]; Chan Hing-kar [Chen Qingjia]
Scriptwriter(s)	Chan Hing-kar; Amy Chin [Qian Xiaohui]
Cast	Lau Ching-wan [Liu Qingyun]; Gigi Leung [Liang Yongqi]; Carina Lau Kar-ling [Liu Jialing]; Louis Koo [Gu Tianle]

Johnny (played by Lau Ching-wan) and Wayne (played by Louis Koo) are hired by the Hong Kong branch of a Japanese company run by Samantha (played by Carina Lau Kar-ling), who has been assigned to design the world's best bra by making use of the creativity of male designers. The two men are excited about their new job, thinking that it will enable them to seduce every girl in the all-female office. Lena (played by Gigi Leung), the head designer, rejects the idea of male bra designers and through silly games forces them to learn what a bra means to women.

Johnny fantasizes about his success in seducing his lonely boss, Samantha, and decides to leave his girlfriend who lacks career ambition. Samantha regards the one night stand with Johnny as casual fun to heal her emotional pain. She believes that a male partner is equivalent to a bra. It is absurd to continue wearing the wrong bra, and sometimes wearing no bra is more fashionable. Johnny finally seduces Samantha with his submissive statement: "I'm a bra that keeps making you feel good and you ought to keep using this bra."

As for seducing the arrogant Lena, Wayne realizes he has to try harder. When a woman annoys Lena, Wayne evilly seduces the woman in order to punish her for Lena. When Wayne is accused of sexual harassment, Lena defends him in order to secure his job. At the same time, Lena is hurt by a man she has fancied for many years who decides to marry a woman with 36D breasts. She teaches Wayne what an ultimate bra means to her by inviting Wayne to feel her breasts tenderly: "It should give me a feeling like this, of being embraced, protected, warmed and respected."

Finally, the two men design the ultimate bra, having learnt to understand and respect women.

Beauty and the Breast *[Fengxiong mi "Cup"]*

Category IIB; Produced in 2002
Director   Raymond Yip [Ye Weimin]
Scriptwriter   Not A Woman [English pen name] (Bushi nüren)
Cast   Francis Ng [Wu Zhenyu]; Michelle Reis [Li Jiaxin]; Daniel
                  Wu [Wu Yanzu]

Yuki (played by Michelle Reis) joins a company that produces a breast-enhancement cream. Her womanizer colleague, Mario (played by Francis Ng), fakes a terminal disease to gain her sympathy. While the kind-hearted Yuki takes care of him, Mario flirts with two huge-breasted female colleagues and extends them unfair privileges. Angered by the special treatment, Yuki and Amy (played by Halina Tam) unite to fight against the injustice. Amy, who distrusts her lover, Daniel, because he is a close friend of the playboy Mario, often forces Daniel to reveal secrets about other men, including Mario, who has been cheating on Yuki.

Yuki's father, a Chinese-medicine doctor, has invented a secret formula for a super-effective cream to enhance breast size. Wishing to teach Mario and Daniel a lesson, the two girls use them surreptitiously as involuntary guinea pigs to test the new formula. Suffering the pain of growing breasts, the two men lose their jobs. Yuki, however, is promoted because she has created a marketable product for the company. She and Amy then team up with other small-breasted colleagues to humiliate the two huge-breasted women by proving their breasts are fake. Yuki offers Mario and Daniel jobs, and Amy urges the two to take the subordinate jobs by shouting: "Don't be a useless man!" Mario finally has a chance to win Yuki's love by amending his behavior. Yuki, moved by the change in him, gives him her beautiful breasts, enhanced by the new product she developed herself. Receiving such a surprising gift, Mario finds his male objective in life: meeting the right pair of breasts.

SEXUAL TALK, BODY IMAGES, AND HONG KONG WOMEN

It has been observed that, in general, Hong Kong's economically independent women have a relatively conservative attitude toward sex compared with their urban counterparts in Taiwan and mainland China.[6] Three structural factors seem to explain this sexual conservatism. First, primary and secondary education in Hong Kong is predominantly provided by Christian and Catholic schools as well as a number of Buddhist schools. The families of most religiously influenced school leavers usually imbue them with Confucian values. Thus, their mindset concerning sex is built on a dual ideological rigidity. Second, most young people live with their families in crowded apartments and have few opportunities to pursue sexual freedom. Third, Hong Kong women are faced with a harshly competitive marketplace for men because Hong Kong men have abundant choices when seeking lovers, wives, mistresses and prostitutes in mainland China or other less-developed areas. In serious relationships, Hong Kong women tend to make use of traditional gender values to cultivate feelings of responsibility in men. In return, women are expected to behave in an inward, passive and dependent manner. Consequently, it is considered degrading for women to talk about sex or to use indecent language, despite the fact discussing sexy body shapes is socially acceptable because it is done to please men. The socio-linguistic taboo against talking about the size of the male organ belies the impression generated by popular discussions about breast size that Hong Kong women are privy to a sexually liberated language environment. Colloquialisms referring to the penis are still considered profane, especially references to someone's "small size." Unlike swear words, the formal terms referring to the male organ have never been classified as Category III by the Hong Kong Broadcasting Authority,[7] and therefore talking about penis size should be permissible in a wide range of contexts as long as the terminology remains formal. However, cultural expectations tend to place different emphases on the intrinsic physical and psychological distinctions between men and women.[8] This polarization of men and women in the socio-linguistic area is explained by Nancy Bonvillain in her studies on cross-cultural linguistics. Women in general tend to be more sensitive about preserving the face and dignity of other people. When participating in cross-sex conversations, women talk more collaboratively, cautiously, correctly and politely than do men in order to avoid conversational blunders. In many languages gender differentiation is encoded in grammar, vocabulary and metaphor.[9] In view of how language profoundly reproduces and reinforces gender inequality, trying to eliminate discriminatory words from language has been a major task for the feminist movement. Yet such a movement has never prevailed in Hong Kong, which implies that the fear of making linguistic mistakes exists among local economically independent women. Thus, sexual talk that may be perceived as offensive to men is unacceptable and condemned by both men and women, while the opposite is not the case.

According to socio-linguists Bolton and Hutton, officially banned swearwords may have a powerful linguistic effect on speakers and listeners.[10] In this sense, because linguistic risk is involved, taboo talk about the size of the male organ can also have a corresponding potential to hurt and insult. When the dominant gender group faces such linguistic danger, a cultural taboo is required. Women are especially affected by this taboo because they are pressured by the consequence of being labeled "lusty" or "excessively interested in sex." As a result, talking about penis size is effectively controlled not by official condemnation but by the consideration women have for image. Enjoying greater rights to talk freely, men exercise their linguistic power to direct social conversations about women's bodies. Because discussions concerning the size of the male organ are taboo, discussions about breasts could be seen as a substitute for sex jokes.

Most women are sensitive about the size of their breasts, with few considering their biologically determined body shape perfect, or even adequate. Because of ubiquitous glamorous images of women professionally produced by the skillful use of make-up, cinematography, lighting, special effects and editing, most women are dissatisfied with their own appearance,[11] including "perfect" models, movie stars and celebrities. Advertisements constantly urge women to improve their appearance to build up their confidence. Erotic movies and pornographic magazines constantly enhance the aesthetic taste for the equation: sexy women = large breasts + slim body + conquerable wildness. This stereotypical image derived from the dominant gender group has been promoted through the uneven and one-sided exhibition of the bodies of the subordinate sex group. It has given birth to creative slang words targeting "unattractive" people. For instance the reference to fat women as *jueh paah*, which literally means pork chop, effectively urges them to consume a variety of keep-fit products. A recent socio-psychological survey reports that even nurses ignore their medical knowledge and take harmful medicines to control their weight.[12] No wonder slang expressions like *fei gei cheung*, literally meaning airport runway but referring to girls with flat chests, make Hong Kong women sensitive and aware of the size of their breasts. Women are exhorted to keep their bodies slim by starving themselves or taking dangerous medicines, and they compete with each other on bra-cup sizes. The focus is thus shifted from the fear Hong Kong men have of having "small" penises. The breast-centered jokes that function as topics for social conversation serve as a beauty standard for women, cultivate a profitable product line for Hong Kong cinema, and deflect from the critical question of women about why the size of Hong Kong women's breasts must be judged by the standard of sexy Western models, while Hong Kong men are spared similar treatment.

FEMINISM, MODERNITY, AND CONSUMERISM

There is a general assumption in Hong Kong that when women gain economic power they no longer rely on men, and the concomitant improvement in their status allows them to enjoy greater dignity. This assumption is accentuated in both *La Brassiere* and *Beauty and the Breast* through their idiosyncratic portrayal of modernity and feminism. Modernization relies on the expansion of consumerism supported by a system of financial credit, directed by advertisements and accelerated by the new technology of mass production. Products and services have to be made available everywhere for people to realize that they "need" them. The feeling of "need" is enhanced by the ideology that consumption shows individuals are hardworking and progressive. A modern feminine quality may be measured by the power to consume goods. Thus, women achieve a sense of worth by adopting a stylish appearance that tallies with the splendid images of the goods projected by advertisements and celebrities who also consume the products.[13]

Despite accentuating a feminist image by making its female characters strong and smart, *Beauty and the Breast* starts out with a male obsession: breasts, and how their shape determines a woman's personality. The strong and smart women in the comedy are not treated according to their work capability but are forced into sexualized roles. The comedy also shows a female fantasy, namely that women with small breasts can end their suffering by using "breast-growing cream" to increase their size. This image of victory is further emphasized by an ugly and miserable woman who gets what she deserves when she stupidly uses a lousy product to enlarge her breasts. While highlighting breast enlargement as a way of achieving harmonious gender relations, the comedy also panders to the popular resentment against fake breasts, condemning plastic surgery and insulting women with fake breasts. *Beauty and the Breast* thus sets a bizarre and contradictory standard for "good women": do not cheat your men by using "unnatural" breast enlargement products — nurture your breasts with the best-quality breast products.

Interestingly, these sexist scenes did not offend female audiences. Instead, they were cheered by the leading character Yuki, who was able to conquer the bigoted playboy. She was able to make him a loyal lover simply because of her smart choice to improve her breasts by using "Piggy Brand" cream. Her victory gave female audiences a sense that "we are all equal" in the consumerist world because such empowerment is available to everyone — if you work hard and consume smartly, you will overcome all natural disadvantages. *Beauty and the Breast* is aware of how people who believe in the merits of education and hard work feel about beauty bringing privileges. Its challenge is expressed through a supporting female character who smiles at an unattractive fat man for no specific reason and later discovers to her surprise that he is the company's top boss. Instead of showing contempt for the culture of "no beauty, no rights," the comedy teaches women that they should never judge men by their appearance, but should spend every cent to enhance their own appearance.

La Brassiere shows images of successful women who are bossy and sexy. The female boss of the bra company Samantha is a mature, attractive, single, hardworking professional who is always well dressed. She empowers herself by making sexy bras for fashionable female consumers who want to please their men. The chauvinist designer, played by Gigi Leung, is shown as professional and tough, although she lives in a ludicrous fantasy world of flowering meadows and party hats. This world resembles that of Hong Kong's future "strong women" who, before consuming sexy fashions during womanhood, are university girls attending graduation ceremonies with cute dolls and flowers. *La Brassiere* focuses on modernity and faithfully follows the spirit of consumerism. It presents a professional setting for bra production, and its bra philosophy appears like an exorbitant bra advertisement. Surprisingly, a seller of cheap bras delivers the following paradoxical line: "A low-priced bra has the ultimate use value because it never deforms the original shape of the breasts." This truism must be discredited in the comedy because brand-names strive to convey images of pride and individualistic merit, and Hong Kong women live in a culture that extols "earning aggressively and buying massively." *La Brassiere* thus carefully minimizes the value of cheap bras by making the seller appear stupid.

The producers, directors and scriptwriters of both comedies have a profound understanding of the relationship linking modernity, feminism and consumption in Hong Kong, and that is that economically independent women have been driven to play subtle but harsh body politics. As Michel Foucault observes, power is not a coherent or coercive force that is merely exercised through class/legal positions, but is realized through finer social and cultural institutions.[14] The bodies of independent women are inspected and controlled by an omnipresent visual media, by men's jokes, and by the judgmental comments of other women. Therefore, both comedies invest women's beauty with a modern quality of sexiness and a traditional quality of obedience. They offer a handy solution to the dilemma of women of how to gain success, happiness and control, which is that it all depends on how much a woman is willing to pay to improve her appearance.

OPTIONS FOR MASCULINITY

Following Bruce Lee [Li Xiaolong]'s popularization of the martial arts, Jackie Chan (Cheng Long) made kung fu comics fashionable in his portrayals of "authentic Chinese heroes" and "the Hong Kong superman." John Woo [Wu Yusen] uses intense brotherhood loyalties to portray spectacular choreographed gunfight sequences, sentimentally combined with heroic honor in a ruthless world. Tsui Hark [Xu Ke] made use of special effects to produce images of bodies in motion, further extending Hong Kong's unique masculinity beyond physical dimensions. Lo points out that without consideration of the socio-cultural content or intrinsic meaning of Hong Kong identity, those invented masculinities occupy an empty space.[15] Living in a commercialized city Hong Kong people are caught up in their daily lives with the reality of seeking a job and keeping it. Inventing mega-masculine images, Hong Kong filmmakers have worked within a very narrow social context. Ultra heroes have been associated with good policemen, nice gangsters, and rebellious innocent prisoners. Action plots have followed from the clichés of martial arts novels and comics. Images of masculinity have been projected according to the particular gender attitudes of male filmmakers. A scriptwriter/ production manager revealed that his senior colleague during the late 1980s often created gratuitous scenes involving the women being beaten up, and that this reflected his failures with girlfriends. In another director's action films during the 1980s, unattractive actors often played heroic roles and handsome actors played stupid and useless men, and this reflected the director's painful experiences when he was rejected for important roles because of his physical appearance.

When Hong Kong cinema began to suffer a decline during the 1990s, the industry began to realize that the surrealistic portrayals of masculinity were no longer competitive. Various attempts have been made to cultivate more alternative masculinities to enhance the competitiveness of Hong Kong films. The construction of new masculinities has included male nudity, which may be highly sensitive or even unacceptable under the dominant model of masculinity. An actress's willingness to act in nude scenes is regarded as a rational choice made to maximize her interests in the spirit of laissez-faire. According to several producers, there are actors willing to exhibit their nether regions in taboo-breaking scenes, believing that the resulting controversy may make them famous. Nevertheless, their desire to exploit their own bodies has been rejected by the reality of the market. The most Hong Kong audiences will accept, where male nudity is concerned, is a naked backside, even though the story might justify a scene showing male genitals. Chan Kam-hung [Chen Jinhong] was the first Hong Kong actor to expose his penis in a bi-sexual film, *Hold You Tight* [Yue kuaile yue duoluo], produced in 1998. The film's director Stanley Kwan [Guan Jinpeng] exhibited penises again in another gay film, *Lan Yu*, produced in 2001. Neither film appealed to the Hong Kong masses. This implies that Hong Kong cinema will not be encouraging any development of masculine sexuality, although women's bodies will continue to be exhibited in an uneven and one-sided fashion.

Another way of diversifying masculinity is to de-fantasize the ultra-hero. This genre is increasingly being adopted in Hong Kong cinema to the fascination of local audiences. Patriarchy can be explained as an authority that defines the norms of "femininity" and "masculinity," and which has the ability to enforce such gender roles. For some men, traditional masculinity may be a set of limitations akin to the restrictions on women, which alienates men from achieving their full humanity.[16] In Hong Kong, Miss Breadwinners compete with Mr Breadwinners in the workforce, with few women tending to measure men against the standards of the muscular superhero, as projected in the Hong Kong cinema of the 1980s. Presented in caricature, the male protagonist in recent Hong Kong films has often appeared selfish, discourteous and superficial. He chases girls but occasionally shows his tender side to his loved ones. Such ordinary men can be found everywhere in Hong Kong society.

The script of *Beauty and the Breast* was written by "Not A Woman." This ignominious pseudonym seems to suggest that a real man should reject any feminine quality in himself. The comedy is thus made from the perspective of traditional masculinity: men should neither reveal vulnerabilities nor express emotions. Men relate to each other as competitors in sports, work, and sexual conquest. Men assume no responsibility for housework and should regard with condescension the efforts of women to become breadwinners for the family.[17] This stereotype of masculinity is revealed in the advertising slogan for *Beauty and the Breast*: "Be a man who cannot be controlled by any woman." The selling point is that the plot focuses on two men suffering from growing breasts. The comedy wastes the opportunity to deal with the issue of a crisis in gender identity, and leaves undeveloped the interesting issue of masculine identity. Following the fad of projecting new masculinities, *Beauty and the Breast* made full use of Francis Ng's masterful acting skills to have him play a nice bastard, and featured Daniel Wu's handsome face in the role of a pathetic and useless man. In *Beauty and the Breast* the old gender codes remain firmly in place no matter how apparently different the two male leads are from the silent, unemotional, athletic, cool and traditional type man.

Sean Nixon points out that the change of masculinities corresponded to the change of femininities.[18] Lawrence Lau [Liu Guochang], a fine film director, perceives that sophisticated and professional women no longer fancy reliable and successful men because such men are likely to be pedantic, prudent, and pretentious, and thus dull and insensitive. Irrepressible, playful, and exciting men are more able to satisfy the adventurous curiosity of the "new" woman. Eason Chan [Chen Yixun], with his image of being hard to tie down, carefree, emotionally sensitive, and expressive, was the first choice for the male lead in the film projects of Lawrence Lau. But as this new masculinity becomes more and more popular in Hong Kong cinema, Eason Chan's price for playing leading roles is becoming increasingly higher, and his schedule for shooting films is becoming tighter and tighter.

La Brassiere adopts a new masculinity modeled by the two pro-feminist male characters. The masculine stereotype of a hero projected in Lau Ching-wan's previous films has been modified to that of a subservient man whose only male ambition is to win the love of a woman boss. Louis Koo portrays a lighthearted man with a masculinity similar to that of Eason Chan, whose witty flippancy is expressed when he meets several of his ex-girlfriends to discuss his weakness in maintaining relationships. The comedy seems to suggest there are two major types of men who live on women, but who do not understand them. The first is the insecure type, who tends to chase women of a higher social rank to confirm his masculinity. The second is the confident type keen to conquer arrogant women to prove his masculinity. In *La Brassiere* these two types of men are invited to design the ultimate bra, and pushed to learn what women want from not only bras but also men. Eventually, the two discover it is simply human warmth that women want most, and that men can realize their full humanity by sharing their emotions with women.

MANUFACTURERS OF GENDER IMAGES

Feminism is key to making sex a legitimate topic and to setting middle-class women free from sexual morality or pretend-conservatism. Projecting a feminist image is not new in mainstream Hong Kong cinema, although the movement has been led largely by male filmmakers. The Hong Kong film industry has only three established female directors: Ann Hui [Xu Anhua], Mabel Cheung [Zhang Wanting] and Sylvia Chang [Zhang Aijia]. Clara Law [Luo Zhuoyao] is often also included in this group, but she now lives and works in Australia. All these directors tend to be regarded as artistic or new-wave directors because they make films with a touch of realism. According to several film production managers, although Mabel Cheung and Sylvia Chang appear to be gentle women, they can talk forcefully and humorously at work, using "masculine" language. Ann Hui told me[19] that being "unfeminine" is her advantage in the industry. A woman who can free herself from typical feminine characteristics can also free her male co-workers from giving her extra consideration by making them see her as an androgynous colleague. One producer/director said in confidence that his creativity would be curbed if he were to discuss story plots with women, because he would constantly be worried about using vulgar language.

The Hong Kong film industry has fostered a handful of female scriptwriters, most of whom write for art films. As a scriptwriter, I sometimes participate in popular productions, and I have found that I have had to downplay my femininity when discussing stories and plots with filmmakers in order to adapt to the traditional practice of the "talking script" inherited from the industry's action-film production method. A film production usually starts from a proposal no longer than a page, presented to film companies by a director or a producer. This saves time that would have been required to read scripts, and projects are often presented in what can resemble a sparkling talk-show performance in order to appeal to decision makers. Many filmmakers have been trained in a storytelling technique that allows them to tell a story vividly and briefly with a full body performance, a story climax, dynamic editing, striking camera angles, symbolic inserts, and even special effects. When a film project is accepted and confirmed, the producer, director and scriptwriter hold brainstorming sessions to develop a detailed story line. After the draft of a script is agreed upon, the same storytelling technique will be employed to conduct negotiations with actors, art directors and prop providers for favorable terms. I have been warned never to write a script abstract clearly or in too much detail because the bosses would never buy it. Though the "talking script" prevails for popular productions, women in general tend to avoid profanity and racy language and thus are at a disadvantage when they have to make their talk-show performance appealing. As a result, the "talking script" has been practiced within a male-dominated industry, and this has enhanced the traditional closeness among producer, director, scriptwriter and editor. This places limits on the extent to which job duties can become independent in ways that would be beneficial for investment and product quality, and that would open opportunities to new or female professionals to participate in creative work.

Many filmmakers argue against the feminist critique that the film industry exploits female sexuality. They emphasize that many fame-seeking actresses ask to star in whatever scene is available, and that many actors are forced to play indecorous and brainless men in order to entertain female audiences. The unequal pay between female and male actors is justified by pointing to a similar policy in Hollywood. There is a tacit agreement that a leading male actor, with higher pay, is seen as a central selling point, and that his role should therefore be fully developed with interesting lines and plots. Female leads, on the other hand, are considered supporting roles to adorn "his" story. I was asked to change the leading character from a young girl to a middle-aged man in a script on Sino-Indonesian history, because no boss would feel psychologically secure about investing in a film involving expensive historical scenes led by a young girl.

Popular productions in Hong Kong's film industry offer little bargaining power to female workers. In one of my early assignments, I had designed a scene in which a supporting female character would have her breasts touched. The producer was concerned the actress might ask for more money to act in such a scene so I was required to write an alternative scene that was not used in the end. The supporting actress did not know beforehand exactly what kind of scene she would be in, and she was prepared to do whatever the director required of her. She did not dare complain or bargain while 30 crew members were waiting impatiently for her to cooperate. In Hong Kong's well-known muscular cinema, heroes are portrayed as gentlemen who tenderly protect ladies. But in the production of popular films, the industry does not in fact treat female workers in this way. I once saw another supporting actress being scolded by the whole crew because she delivered a line incorrectly. The more she was blamed for the re-takes the more nervous she felt, causing the co-actor to have to repeat his sensational acting until it was reduced to dullness. The crew insensitively continued berating her with swear words because everyone felt sorry for the innocent co-actor.

Some informants claimed that the scriptwriter who used the pseudonym, Not A Woman, for *Beauty and the Breast*, was, in fact, the famous film producer Wong Ching [Wang Jing], who has produced many pornographic films and has openly stated that the livelihoods of hundreds of local filmmakers depend on him. Obviously, his attempt to use a pseudonym in this case was to hide his pornographic reputation in order to sell a clean and upgraded sexual comedy. However, some filmmakers insist that Not A Woman is a scriptwriter who sometimes uses another pen-name, namely, Chan Number Thirteen [Chen Shisan], whose extremely strong female characters created for TV dramas have ironically been perceived as examples of feminism by local audiences. Although Not A Woman, Chan Number Thirteen and the director, Raymond Yip, could not be reached for interviews, these partners actually represent the creative team of Not A Woman under Wong's company. The story of *Beauty and the Breast* is about an adulterous man who is punished and corrected by a smart and kind-hearted woman. Overly restricting themselves within an essentially masculine identity, the creative team of Not A Woman nevertheless develops the image of the power-hungry woman. Its female protagonists easily lose their tempers over "useless" men; shout at men habitually for no particular reason; forcefully correct the wrongdoings of men; destroy the dignity of men; and enjoy seeing them suffer the pain of growing breasts. Illogically and unconvincingly, the defeated male protagonist Mario finally wins back the female protagonist Yuki. Such a deliberately politically incorrect feminist message seems to suggest that having a successful career does not bring a woman happiness unless she is loveable or conquerable by men. Because Mario's male objective in life is to meet "the right pair of breasts," Yuki finally enlarges her breasts for him.

Female producer/scriptwriter Amy Chin used her own perceptions of gender to draft the female characters in *La Brassiere*. She believes that single, economically independent women must be lonely, although they would never beg for the love of a man. Amy Chin entered the industry as a production assistant twenty years ago during the rise of action films. She was disappointed that so few opportunities were open to women to participate in creative work. One of her duties involved checking that scripts were ready in time for the shooting crews. Scriptwriters under a great deal of pressure often asked her to add content so they didn't have to do as much work themselves. This alternative route to contributing creative ideas kept her in the industry and eventually made her a talented script-talker. *La Brassiere* was orally drafted based on Amy Chin's daily observations of her career-woman friends, and organized by Chan Hing-kar, who produced and directed the film. The advertising slogan of *La Brassiere* emphasizes that every man should be given a fair chance to serve women. The two bossy women force the two male chauvinist designers to learn what it means for a woman to wear a bra. That is, the career woman changes bras every day in much the way she changes fashions or boyfriends. Women will keep changing bras until a bra that delivers feelings of LTC (love/ tenderness/care) is invented. Finally, the two men who offer LTC to women reap the benefits. As a result, a responsive chord is struck in the hearts of female viewers who are successful in their careers but emotionally insecure and lonely.

QUICK AND CHEAP

Hong Kong people are unwilling to pay to see analytical, serious or depressing movies and want to enjoy sophisticated thrillers, comedies, sensational and romantic movies made to world-class standards. This phenomenon cannot be explained by stating that Hong Kong audiences do not care about deeper issues. In the spirit of free trade, Hong Kong has imported a large variety of alternative movies, TV programs, documentaries and scientific films, and offered people with a Western education a wide range of choices to consume informative and insightful cultural products. Producing commercial action films to accentuate

"Chinese heroes" has been a practical way to overcome the problem of the domestic market. Chinese masculine images, as presented in Jackie Chan's and John Woo's movies, not only appeal to the masses, but also provide a cultural identity for the middle classes who are emotionally attached to no other place but Hong Kong. Moreover, many Asian countries in the 1980s imposed barriers against imported films containing political or religious messages. Hong Kong's commercial films were therefore in a good position to penetrate those markets. With no governmental subsidies, the cheaply made Hollywood-like films in Cantonese — a language that is not even an official language in China — successfully ruled the East Asian market and prospered until the early 1990s. During its decade of boom, this tiny industry produced more than two hundred films annually. After successfully offering mass-produced entertainment, Hong Kong cinema experienced a significant decline. This is partly because the growing film industries of Korea, Thailand, Vietnam and mainland China have affected exports of Hong Kong films, and partly because the Hong Kong films themselves have failed to satisfy people elsewhere in Asia who yearn for movies about their own cultures, and which address their own rapid social changes.

It has been observed that financial pressures have forced directors to use guerrilla tactics in their work.[20] The industry's slackness is reflected in the comments of a casting agent who complained that no client had ever given her a script requiring her to come up with suitable actors. With tight budgets and unforgiving deadlines, even the relatively simple task of providing English subtitles has been done unprofessionally, and the Chinese subtitles contain locally invented Cantonese characters impossible for non-Hong Kong Chinese to understand. Actors and actresses are reluctant to spend time studying scripts because they often have to manage several jobs at the same time. Hong Kong crewmembers only learn to say "hurry up" in different languages when they work with foreigners in overseas shoots. It is a general complaint that crews on site have to wait by the fax machine for scripts. I usually finish a script before shooting starts, but I have had to make urgent corrections because of unforeseen problems, such as budget changes or an actor falling ill. The problem of "waiting for the script by the fax machine" is less common in Western countries, where projects are preceded by a year of detailed planning. One director admitted he was addicted to rushed filmmaking, and he disliked the careful and slow pre-production work that, he claimed, would drain his creativity. Hong Kong cinema has failed to build up an infrastructure of professionalism not because of shortsightedness, but because of flexible strategies have been adopted to tackle the urgent demands of the market. Such flexibility has been seen as a cooperative work ethic in the industry.

In the midst of the problems described, which result from tight timetables and budgets, few filmmakers consider issues of gender problematic. Even fewer filmmakers are willing to deal with gender politics. Therefore, because of corporatism, gender problems have been ignored by the industry.

STRATEGIC CREATIVITY

According to Walker Percy, mankind is divided into anaesthetized consumers and satirists, who desperately try to impress the readers by selling extraordinary ideas.[21] Compared to film production, however, the writing of a novel is a more positive and reciprocal situation. Novel writing involves a novelist whose popularity depends on striking a balance between his own specific creativity and his acceptance by mainstream readers. A novelist may fail to sell his ideas if he tries too hard to please his readers, and may simply end up as a popular writer who writes made-to-order novels for commercial purposes. Film production, however, is team work and involves a much greater investment in human and financial resources, sophisticated technologies and marketing strategies, so it allows almost no room for artists to exercise any individual creativity. The criteria for a "good" film do not include whether it contains meaningful, artistic or poetic ideas, but whether it is popular and able to satisfy its investors.

In my association with Hong Kong filmmakers, I have found many to be intelligent and artistic with a consciousness of social problems, despite the fact some participate in the production of superficial and unimaginative films. I do not intend to make excuses for these filmmakers by claiming that shallow audiences or greedy investors have deprived them of the chance to use their talent properly. Rather, one might say that Hong Kong cinema has become involved in the manufacturing of socio-cultural symbols, and is manipulated by both filmmakers and audiences to explore and negotiate their problematic and paradoxical cultural space.[22] Once a symbolic norm has been created in the context of Hong Kong's social realities, both audiences and filmmakers are enticed into relating to these cultural symbols. Filmmakers supply what audiences desire, regardless of how debauched or vulgar the product may be. The result is that artistic and idealistic filmmakers are forced into unimaginative mass production, and their resistance is manifested as intentional or unintentional slackness. Hong Kong cinema has been labeled commercial, sentimental, ridiculous, bizarre and inattentive, and many local intellectuals would even be offended to be invited to "bad taste" local films. Some filmmakers have taken risks and tried to make artistic and meaningful films, but few have received support from the local intellectuals, who tend to prefer foreign movies. Thus, it is absurd to say that popular films have lowered the general aesthetic sensibility of the masses. The Hong Kong film industry has relied heavily on the working classes, so the films that are produced cater to their tastes and interests. However, these audiences now watch VCDs and DVDs at home, and this presents a major problem for the film industry. Apart from the difficulty of legal control over copying, it is also important to note that a film's revenue from copyrights on VCDs and DVDs depends on its box-office record.

Under such local market conditions, some filmmakers try to produce artistic films that win prizes and attract international attention so that they can obtain support from foreign investors to continue their filmmaking careers. Other filmmakers try to target the local market by carefully calculating what the audience likes and dislikes. Carefully calculating how to produce a hilarious joke, sensational tear or thrilling atmosphere may result in artificial and unnatural plots, thus making it more difficult to please audiences. As observed by one producer I interviewed, Hong Kong popular films have recently failed to compete with those from Korea. He blamed this on people who had swapped creativity for cautious calculation. He added that the Korean film industry has a sufficiently large domestic market to allow its filmmakers to work with their hearts, whereas the Hong Kong industry faces a tiny and fastidious domestic market. This forces local filmmakers to calculate how not only to entertain audiences but also shore up investors' feelings of psychological security. Despite the failure of other films whose makers had zealously speculated about the preferences of audiences, and thanks to women's breasts being a hot topic, both *La Brassiere* and *Beauty and the Breast* benefited from this strategy and were very creative.

UPGRADING SEX

The experiment of "upgrading" sex via these two comedies was motivated by the decline in locally made pornographic films. The massive production of low-budget pornographic films with thin plots has led to the rise of many cinemas that show movies in very poor taste. Sophisticated people feel embarrassed to walk around areas where there are "cheap porno" cinemas. In extreme cases, the proliferation of such cinemas can result in a drop in the value of real estate in the area. This has caused cinemas and theater companies to begin to refuse locally made pornographic films. According to one film distributor, the audience for pornographic films was mainly working-class men, and Hong Kong's economic recession and the boom in VCDs and websites with low-cost pornography has stopped many from patronizing cinemas.

Another factor pushing Hong Kong cinema to improve its sex-entertainment products is the Category III regulation. Young people under 18, who constitute a large percentage of cinema-goers, are strictly prohibited from viewing Category III films. The cheap locally made porn films have given Category III movies a reputation for being dirty and dull. Moreover, one aim behind the Category III regulation is to monitor films with profanity or unpleasant content as defined by the government. Several films made to reflect social realities in Hong Kong, containing swearing by characters representing poorly educated men, have been classified in the same category as pornographic films, even though the film contained no sex. Having a Category III classification thus does not necessarily mean a movie will catch the attention of those in search of sexual entertainment.

In recent years, the cinema-going population has mostly consisted of dating couples and other young people who tend to avoid pornographic films. Male companions usually let their partners decide which cinema to go to, and most women dare not suggest a sexual film for fear of being regarded as "cheap" or having "bad taste." To succeed financially, filmmakers must target those who decide which cinema to go to. Although classic romance films appeal to middle-class women, they cannot always persuade their male companions to accompany them to such "feminine" films. Furthermore, local audiences have lost their appetite for relentless, over-produced action movies. *Shaolin Soccer* (dir. Stephen Chow, 2001) was incredibly successful at the box office, but many film companies saw its enormous budget as too risky during a recession. In the process of seeking a product that could attract women and make them bring their male companions, *La Brassiere* cultivated a new product line in 2001, intending to provide educated and sexually moral people with a legitimate excuse to enjoy looking at women's breasts in a Category IIB movie. Officially, the Category IIB rating means "Not suitable for young persons and children." It subtly suggests that the movie will not be something "healthy," which basically means it is something illicitly stimulating and titillating. Its success at the box office proved there is a general craving for entertainment involving body talk among local middle-class women. Subsequently, *Beauty and the Breast* adopted this new method of packaging sex. The movie was made in 2002 with a smaller budget, and it also succeeded in gaining relatively good receipts at the box office.

In order to obtain cultural acceptance of sex as something "not dirty, but funny," it is necessary to create a "clean" image through high-class showmanship. Popular filmmakers and audiences have influenced each other intensively. As noted by Greg Dancer, an audience's enjoyment depends to some extent on their knowledge of what is involved in making a film and on who acts in it. A performance is a contract between the showman and the audience. Hardworking reporters and paparazzi constantly provide material for gossip about movie stars, and revealing a particular lifestyle or an unusual event that a movie star has encountered can increase the audience's admiration for that star and ensure his/her next film's success at the box office.[23] *La Brassiere* cast four superstars: Lau Ching-wan, Carina Lau Kar-ling, Louis Koo and Gigi Leung. The superstar status of both Lau Ching-wan and Carina Lau Kar-ling is maintained by their professionalism in acting. The star ranking of Louis Koo and Gigi Leung is maintained by their physical attractiveness, which enables them to build up an elegant image of "prince" and "princess." *Beauty and the Breast* employed only three superstars to achieve similar success. The two male leads were Francis Ng, who is considered a multi-talented actor, and the handsome Daniel Wu. The female lead was the famous beauty Michelle Reis, who has modeled for plastic-surgery clinics in Hong Kong, Taiwan and mainland China.[24] Although audiences do not see the breasts of the actresses in either *La Brassiere* or *Beauty and the Breast*, they seem to enjoy the movie stars' open discussions about sexuality.

The French title, *La Brassiere*, is a statement about taste. In Hong Kong, many refined cafes, fancy hair salons and high-fashion boutiques carry French or Italian names, and "aristocratic" shopping malls require local tenants to give their shops French-sounding names in order to maintain upmarket rents. However, the touch of class added by the French title was not enough to sell a story about bras; *La Brassiere* also needed to signal modernity and professionalism. Sophisticated qualities in Hong Kong popular culture have somehow been transmitted from Japan, despite knowledge about Paris and New York among Hong Kong's elite. The story of *La Brassiere* is therefore set in a Japanese bra company, which involved extra production expenses. The English title, *Beauty and the Breast*, seems to be an attempt to create a link to the famous European fairy-tale *Beauty and the Beast*. Both Chinese titles are expressed in *mouh leih tauh* style, in which suggestive "inside" Cantonese puns give a feeling of a private vernacular, and reinforces the linguistic boundary separating the "in-group" of Hong Kong Chinese from the "out-group" of other Chinese. The ability of *mouh leih tauh* to maintain its popularity in Hong Kong illustrates that the local media, facing a limited market, dare not stop using the Hong Kong vernacular, even though other Chinese throughout the world cannot understand it. To overcome the cheap and sub-cultural image of the *mouh leih tauh* style, the use of English words is necessary. Speaking in a mixed code of Cantonese with some English words is not only a colonial legacy in Hong Kong, but also conveys the image of a respectable social status. Hong Kong people often use English when they need to express indecent language used by comedians in Hong Kong films.

CONCLUSION

Filmmakers are touched by tensions and fantasies, and their profits are dependent on their ability to guess popular feelings and trends. A straight line cannot be drawn between the film industry and popular norms. One cannot simply conclude that films determine social values, but there is no doubt that films reflect and reinforce popular preconceptions.[25] Behind the making of *La Brassiere* and *Beauty and the Breast* is the historically specific filmmaking culture of Hong Kong cinema, which has been shaped by a predominantly male industry. Facing the need to modify gender images to create maximum box-office returns, both comedies competently employ the gender norms of Hong Kong's economically independent women. Their economic power is not matched by their cultural liberation. Their feminist struggle does not aim to transform masculinity from traditional stereotypes to pro-feminist ones. They tend to emancipate themselves by improving their appearance on the basis of the thinking promoted by slimming companies — that beauty is the major source of a woman's happiness, and the reconstruction of beauty requires that women have the willpower to pursue beauty eternally. In this sense, improving one's appearance has been advanced to a spiritual level. Understanding this trend in the empowerment of women, both films cleverly brought women's breasts into the mainstream as a natural weapon for female empowerment, in conjunction with the modified masculinities hilariously mirrored in the men's attempts to negotiate power in a situation of a changing gender culture.

Messages conveyed by popular cultural products are usually discursive, multifaceted and contradictory. The audience's reception may reproduce a second-hand message based on specific social and cultural contexts, in which misunderstandings and exaggerations may be the ingredients to constitute a more concrete ideological system.[26] The Hong Kong public apparently both responded and reacted to *La Brassiere* and *Beauty and the Breast.* Finding evidence was relatively effortless. I saw a magazine cover with the heading: "Unable to forget her womanizer boyfriend Maggie Cheung Ho-yee [Zhang Keyi] enlarged her breasts to revive the dying romance — size 31A to size 33B." Inside there were two more news items about the breasts of movie stars: "Sandra Ng [Wu Junru]'s size 31A swiftly expanded to 33C — Director Chan was mesmerized"; "Chu Yan [Zhu Yin]'s sudden confidence comes from her sudden big breasts."[27] The filmmakers did not imagine that their ambiguous and contradictory feminist messages would mobilize a fad for breast enlargement so effectively. While the two comedies desperately tried to entertain the masses, Hong Kong women have employed whatever strategies are available for their empowerment.

⊦ 10 ⊦

Post-Fordist Production and the Re-appropriation of Hong Kong Masculinity in Hollywood

Wai Kit Choi

In "The Marxism of Rosa Luxemburg," an essay in *History and Class Consciousness*, Lukacs writes that "it is not the primacy of economic motives in historical explanation that constitutes the decisive difference between Marxism and bourgeois thought, but the point of view of totality." [1]

In this chapter I will show how changes in cultural representation in the media relate to changes in the organization of capitalist production, while at the same time demonstrating the independence of the former from the latter. This chapter then is an attempt to analyze cultural representation by steering clear of both a solipsistic textual analysis and a crude economic determinism. Rather, an attempt is made to analyze cultural representation from the standpoint of *totality* — a totality in which the cultural and productive spheres are interlocked while remaining distinct from each other. I will illustrate this theoretical point with a case study of Hong Kong film professionals' recent crossover into Hollywood.

It has been argued that the crossover of Hong Kong film professionals into Hollywood signifies that there is now greater multiculturalism in the U.S. film industry, and that representation of the socially marginalized is no longer distorted. However, I will argue that despite the migration of Hong Kong film professionals, the dominant social groups in the U.S. maintain their cultural hegemony in the film industry, and their stereotypical treatment of other cultural groups continues to rein in cinematic representation. Hong Kong films have a distinctive representation of masculinity. To show how Hollywood becomes "multicultural" while maintaining its cultural hegemony, I will discuss the cases of John Woo (Wu Yusen) and Jackie Chan (Cheng Long), both of whose treatments of masculinity have become assimilated into Hollywood's system of male representation, which has a long history of subordinating Asian males.

My second argument concerns the origin of the "multicultural turn" in Hollywood. Why did U.S. film producers decide to incorporate the Hong Kong element into the U.S. film market? To understand why Hollywood undertakes the multicultural turn, I will refer to the notion of cultural industry originating in Horkheimer and Adorno. Their theory is important because it allows us to situate film production in the context of capital accumulation. However, modification of their theory is needed because they wrote about the cultural industry from the 1940s to the 1960s. To explain Hollywood's multicultural turn adequately, I will refer to the literature on economic restructuring under capitalism. I will argue that the multicultural turn can be viewed as a consequence of the cultural industry's transformation from Fordism to Post-Fordist production.

The conclusion to be drawn from these two arguments is *not* that changes in cultural representation are determined by changes in the organization of production. The two are clearly related. However, as Hollywood seeks to expand its share of the global film market, a strategy that features less stereotypical and more egalitarian representation of other cultural groups would be a sensible business decision. The absence of an egalitarian multiculturalism in Hollywood and the persistence of cultural hegemony by the socially dominant groups show precisely that cultural representation is not completely dictated by the imperative of capital accumulation, and one sees then the autonomous logic of cultural contestation.

MULTICULTURALISM AND CULTURAL DOMINATION

In recent years we have seen an exodus of Hong Kong directors, actors, and martial art choreographers to the U.S.. In addition to John Woo and Jackie Chan, the two most widely recognized Hong Kong film professionals in the U.S. film industry today, there is also Yuen Wo-ping (Yuan Heping), who choreographed *The Matrix* (dir. Andy Wachowski, Larry Wachowski, 1999) and *Crouching Tiger, Hidden Dragon* (Wohu canglong) (dir. Ang Lee, 2000), Yuen Cheung-yan (Yuan Xiangren), who choreographed *Charlie's Angels* (dir. McG, 2000), as well as Chow Yun-fat (Zhou Runfa) and Jet Li (Li Lianjie), whose Hollywood-produced films have been shown in mainstream theatres across the U.S.

There is a burgeoning debate about globalization in both academia and popular media around the world. To the critics globalization means, in the economic sphere, the formation of a global capitalist order under the auspices of the World Bank, IMF, and WTO, organizations that are under U.S. or Western control. In the cultural sphere, globalization signifies an equally unpalatable phenomenon to the critics: the homogenization of different national cultures that is a result of the ubiquitous diffusion of American popular culture. In this context the crossover of the Chinese film professionals from this tiny but culturally hybrid former British colony into the heartland of U.S. cultural imperialism raises provocative interpretive questions.

Does the incorporation of Hong Kong film professionals into the U.S. film industry merely indicate that their talents are being used to increase Hollywood's share of the global entertainment market, and that they are powerless to change, or may even perpetuate the racial, gender and political biases promulgated by U.S. films? Or does the Hong Kong professionals' assimilation signify that Hollywood is not really the ideological apparatus of the white American male capitalist hegemony, but rather has the potential to become a global cultural mosaic that promotes cultural diversity?

Analyzing Hong Kong professionals' integration into Hollywood in terms of the notion of "double negation," Lo suggests that "the transnational crossing of Hong Kong film people to Hollywood perhaps also provides alibis for the continued domination and exploitation of the Western globalizing entertainment industry," and that we "may need to see the limited 'Asianization' of Hollywood as a displacement of the old hegemony, as the West displaces itself into new representations of its own self and of the world."[2] In contrast to Lo's reservations about the ability of these Hong Kong professionals to dilute the ideological domination of Hollywood, an *L.A. Times* writer, while commenting on "the prevalence of martial arts and Hong Kong-style balletic choreography in American movies," observes that "[American] action films, which were once almost exclusively the purview of white male protagonists, have become more inclusive, featuring female actors and ethnic minorities in heroic roles."[3]

This chapter also examines the significance of Hong Kong's crossover into the U.S. film industry. I will argue that Lo's and Natale's positions are not mutually exclusive but are consistent with each other. As a result of the influx of Hong Kong film workers into the American film industry, there are now more Asians acting or involved in behind-the-scenes production in U.S. films. In that sense Natale is right that there is now greater "cultural diversity" in Hollywood. However, I will also show that Lo's observation is equally valid: the presence of Hong Kong actors and directors in Hollywood has contributed to, rather than undermined, the continued domination of mainstream U.S. cultural values and ideology propagated in U.S. films.

What this chapter will show then is that just as the radicalism of the Che Guevera icon has been absorbed into the capitalist circuit of consumption, becoming a global commodity, multiculturalism can also be co-opted and used to strengthen the "cultural imperialism" of a hegemonic group. Before I lay out my argument in detail, I will first clarify what is meant by "cultural imperialism," and how it can co-exist and even co-opt multiculturalism.

Cultural imperialism, as defined by Bourdieu and Wacquant, rests "on the power to universalize particularism linked to a singular historical tradition by causing them to be misrecognized as such."[4] The particularism with which Bourdieu and Wacquant are concerned is the particularism of U.S. society. They argue that "today numerous topics directly issuing from the intellectual confrontations relating to the social particularity of American society and of its universities have been imposed, in apparently de-historicized form, upon the whole planet."[5] While Bourdieu and Wacquant's observation on the global expansion of the American academic discourse can be questioned, the imperialistic dissemination of American popular culture as well as its political and social practices is conspicuous. It is here that Hollywood becomes a major vehicle through which the particularistic ideology of the dominant segments of the U.S. population become universalized. In many Hollywood productions, U.S. capitalist democracy is extolled as the system that best protects individual freedom while non-Western political and cultural practices are denigrated; whites are cast as fully fledged three-dimensional leading actors and actresses while actors of other races are assigned to stereotypical roles; masculine bodies and actions are glorified while women are often reduced to objects of desire for male spectators.

Suppose the cultural values and ideology propagated in some of these Hollywood productions express the particular worldview of the politically and economically dominant group, the important point here is that the cultural or ideological domination of this dominant group is not exercised by excluding or prohibiting representations of the marginalized groups in the media or the cultural arena. Rather, just as the dominant group and the marginalized groups are occupying different positions in the political and economic hierarchies in social reality, we see in Hollywood films the cinematic representation of this hierarchical order — the privileged and much more favorable representations of whites, men and American capitalism than that of people of color, women and non-Western societies.

In some of these Hollywood productions, there is then also a hierarchical differentiation in their cinematic representations that reflects and rationalizes the social and political hierarchies within both the U.S. and the world, and the presence of actors from the marginalized groups are crucial for the construction of these representations.

The dominant group exercises its cultural hegemony by maintaining, in the cultural arena, a system of representation in which different genders, classes, races, and nationalities are differentiated hierarchically. If by multiculturalism we simply mean the celebration of cultural diversity, then this is compatible with the practice of cultural hegemony, since the latter requires *difference.*

To illustrate the general claim advanced here, I will focus on how the construction and representation of masculinity in these Hong Kong professionals' productions have changed after their crossover into the U.S. film industry. With its celebration of physical prowess, muscular bodies, and male bonding, the action film is a genre in which the spectacle of masculinity figures most prominently. While not all Hong Kong film professionals who migrated to Hollywood are involved solely in the production of action films — consider Peter Chan (Chen Kexin), Stanley Tong (Tang Jili), and Chow Yun-fat — many are, including John Woo, Jackie Chan, Jet Li, and Sammo Hung (Hong Jinbao). By focusing on how some of these directors' and actors' construction of masculinity has changed in their new Hollywood productions, we can understand more clearly the sense in which Hollywood incorporates into and manages the cultural "Other" in its system of representation, while at the same time maintaining the cultural hegemony of the dominant group.

As some feminist theorists and masculinity scholars have noted, the patriarchal construction of manhood is often intersected with an individual's location in the sexual-orientation, class, and racial order. This means masculinity is not a monolithic bloc, and that there is always a plurality of masculinities. And just as the relationship among the different races and classes is not one of equality, and members from a particular racial group or class can have more privileges than members from other groups, the relationship among the different masculinities is also structured by a hierarchy.[6] The hegemonic masculinity in the U.S. regime of masculinity privileges white heterosexual men while the masculine identities of gay men and men of color, i.e. the subordinate masculinities, are marginalized. More specifically, as Cheung points out,[7] there is a long history of "emasculation" in the representation of Asian men in U.S. popular culture. The depiction of Asian men as effeminate and weak in Hollywood films can be traced back at least to the silent film era. Tori, the Japanese villain from Cecil B. DeMille's *The Cheat* (1915), and Cheng Huan, the Chinese hero from D.W. Griffith's *Broken Blossoms* (1919), both embody "the 'feminine' qualities linked in the Western imagination with a passive, carnal, occult, and duplicitous Asia."[8] This particular representation of Asian men in films then exemplifies the way in which alternative masculinity is marginalized.

To be clear, even before their arrival in Hollywood, the paradigms of masculinity as seen in the action films of these Hong Kong professionals were as patriarchal as those of their Hollywood counterparts in that "manliness" was celebrated and the woman's point of view equally excluded in both traditions. Nonetheless, insofar as it is a different kind of "manliness" being celebrated, critics still regard the Hong Kong paradigms as examples of "alternative" masculinity. However, I will argue that after their arrival in Hollywood, their alternative paradigm becomes incorporated into the U.S. regime of masculinity, and their work fails to escape from the forces of "emasculation" that have long been a dominant factor in shaping the representation of Asian men in U.S. popular culture. Whatever "destabilizing" or "emancipatory" potential these Hong Kong film workers' earlier paradigms of masculinity might have vis-à-vis the white heterosexual male paradigm, their new Hollywood productions show that their once alternative conception has become integrated into the U.S. regime of masculinity, and is helping to sustain a representation of gender relation that subordinates Asian men.

THE TRANSFORMATION OF HONG KONG MASCULINITY: JOHN WOO

Bordwell identifies John Woo as, along with Griffith, Hitchcock, and

Welles, an *auteur* in popular filmmaking.[9] It is Woo's "hyperkinetic and hyperbolic new style in action filmmaking, founded on wild extremes of firepower, body counts, camera angles and cutting patterns"[10] that brought him fame in Hollywood. However, the focus of our analysis here is not the kinetic choreography of gun battles in Woo's films. What concerns us here is the transformative process in which Woo's distinctive treatment of masculinity in his earlier Hong Kong productions becomes assimilated into Hollywood's standardized representation.

Alternative Representation of Masculinity in Woo's Hong Kong Productions

In *A Better Tomorrow* and *The Killer*, Woo's hybrid treatment of masculinity — where the masculine subject is constructed in texts that mix the gangster genre with melodrama — differs "from the 'hard bodies' tradition of 1980s US cinema in its refusal to assert phallic power through the fetishistic display of the spectacularly pumped-up male, and this opens up the possibility of a slightly different definition of masculinity."[11]

Referring to Geoffrey Nowell-Smith's genre classification of U.S. popular cinema, Stringer suggests that a distinction can be made between the men action "doing" genre and the women "suffering" genre. The first is exemplified by Westerns, war epics, and gangster and cop films, while examples of the latter include melodrama and "women's films."[12] Each of these genres plays a different role in the construction of male identity. In the "doing" genres, an ego-ideal for the male viewers is constructed through the muscular body and the daring actions of an omnipotent individual male hero. In the "suffering" genres, however, the ideal of masculinity is undermined and here one sees expressions of sorrow and fear from the male protagonists.

Woo's early works differ from Hollywood productions in that, Stringer argues, Woo combines both genres in his representation of masculinity. While most critics focus on what they call the "ballet-like" choreography of physical violence, as if this were the sole distinguishing feature of Woo's male action films, Stringer calls our attention to the interdependence between the "doing" and the "suffering" genres in Woo's films, and its importance in Woo's construction of the masculine subject.

The kind of passionate yet agnostic romantic relationship that is typical of the "suffering" genre is replaced in both *A Better Tomorrow* (Yingxiong bense) (dir. John Woo, 1986) and *The Killer* (Diexue

shuangxiong) (dir. John Woo, 1989) by an emotionally intense male
bonding. This intimate camaraderie generates much of the trauma and
suffering experienced by the male protagonists, and outbursts of violence
in these films are consequences of these emotional upheavals. As Stringer
observes:

> [Woo's films] oscillate between scenes of extreme, sadistic cruelty and
> violence (such as the beatings of Mark in *A Better Tomorrow* and
> Sydney in *The Killer*, Mark's shooting up of the Fung Lim restaurant in
> the former film, Jeff's contract hit during the opening of the latter), and
> scenes of melancholic sadness and longing (Ho's father's bedside
> decree for his son to give up the underworld, the composed, ritualistic
> deaths of Sydney and Randy). Often suffering provides the catalyst for
> the leap into violence ... In all of these examples, violations of the body
> are outward manifestations of internal traumas, while painful inner
> conflicts can only be resolved by the outward projection of feats of
> incredible heroism.[13]

Unlike Hollywood's representation, Woo's masculine subject is then
constructed, in Stringer's interpretation, by juxtaposing scenes of
emotional turmoil generated from a deeply felt male bonding with
images of extreme violence and effusive bloodshed. We see then in
Woo's pre-Hollywood production an *alternative representation of
masculinity*. Note that in referring to Woo's construction of masculinity
as "alternative," it does not imply that Woo's treatment is more
progressive or less alienating from the woman's standpoint. There is, as
Stringer suggests, both a positive and a negative side in Woo's
representation. On one hand, "the loving, anguished, pained look of one
impaired male melodramatic action hero at another embodies a same-
sex bond of intense feeling to which a heterosexist culture does not
normally permit access." But, on the other hand, "such views privilege
the male, patriarchal, masculinists, woman-excluding point of view."[14]

Woo's Construction of Masculinity in Hollywood

What we see after Woo's crossover into Hollywood is the assimilation
of his once-distinctive construction of the masculine subject into
Hollywood's dominant representation of masculinity. In his first
Hollywood production, *Hard Target* (1993), "[what] remained of Woo's
style was his choreography of the gun fights, heretofore unseen action
stunts, the injection of the action hero with Chinese knightly values, and

the portrayal of his adversaries as completely corrupted by capitalist values."[15] As for his second Hollywood film, *Broken Arrow* (1996), "while displaying a typical John Woo opening shot of two men boxing and exhibiting some of his earlier themes of friendship and betrayal between men, is very much an action-packed succession of set pieces enhanced by digital effects."[16] At most, Hanke adds, "*Broken Arrow* is a competent piece of genre that may be read as an anti-nuclear proliferation cautionary fable for the post-cold war era. But the melodramatic structure of feeling that infused Woo's pre-Hollywood films is nowhere to be felt, so that physical violence is not linked to any acknowledgment of emotions."[17]

While Hanke argues that these two films reflect Woo's assimilation into mainstream Hollywood action genre, he sees in *Face/Off* Woo's return to his original treatment of the male subject.[18] However, in contrast to Hanke, Bordwell argues that "[everything] in *Face/Off* becomes a self-conscious inflation of "Wooness." Woo's religious imagery comes to a hyperbolic climax in yet another church scene, with the doves from *The Killer* flapping through in slow motion and the villain laying a pistol at Jesus's feet."[19]

Moreover, there is another important reason to doubt Hanke's observation on *Face/Off*. Hanke is right about the centrality of the "melodramatic structure of feeling," and the link between emotion and physical actions in Woo's earlier work, but he fails to specify that this melodramatic dimension is often developed around a highly emotionally charged male bonding. But the problem of Hanke's interpretation is that the relationship between Archer (played by John Travolta) and Troy (played by Nicolas Cage) is one of complete rivalry, and it hardly resembles the kind of intense, almost homoerotic, intimacy between Jeff (played by Chow Yun-fat) and Lee (played by Danny Lee) in *The Killer*. Of all of Woo's Hollywood productions, it is only in the relationship between Joe (played by Nicolas Cage) and Ben (played by Adam Beach) in *Windtalkers* (2002) that we see a close camaraderie between the male protagonists. But even if one can make the argument here that this indicates a return to Woo's original style, it is still clear that in the majority of cases Woo must adapt his alternative treatment of the masculine subject to Hollywood's dominant representation of masculinity.

THE EMASCULATION OF HONG KONG MASCULINITY: JACKIE CHAN

Jackie Chan's crossover into Hollywood is another example of how an erstwhile alternative representation of masculinity becomes assimilated into Hollywood's dominant system of male representation. There is, however, one crucial difference between Woo and Chan. While Woo assimilates by muting the melodrama and emotional intensity characteristic of his earlier work, Chan basically remains a comical kung fu fighter in all his Hollywood films. What has changed in the case of Chan is that, unlike his previous Hong Kong productions, he is no longer a comical action hero with whom the audience, primarily Hong Kong Chinese and Asians, can identify. Instead, Chan's identity as the Other, a Chinese man, figures prominently in these Hollywood productions, and his assimilation results from his subordination into the hegemony of the Hollywood system of male representation that has a long tradition of emasculating Asian males.

Jackie Chan as an Alternative Kung Fu Hero

The construction of Chan as an alternative masculine hero in his earlier kung fu films must be seen in the context of Bruce Lee (Li Xiaolong)'s established position as the paradigm of kung fu fighter. Bruce Lee is the ultimate icon of masculinity in the martial arts genre. He is invincible and has almost superhuman strength. But unlike those Hollywood action heroes, Lee inspired many people of color with his "fearless confrontations with white power."[20] The challenge that Chan had to face then was how he could become the next Lee without being just another replica. As Bordwell points out, "Chan decided to invert Lee's heroic image. He has endlessly explained: 'Instead of kicking high like Bruce Lee, I kick low. He plays the invincible hero, I'm the underdog. His movies are intense, mine are light'."[21]

What we see in Chan's Hong Kong productions then is an alternative masculine hero, a non-threatening, non-domineering comical fighter whose heroism lies in his uncanny capacity to withstand pain and his relentless tenacity in defeating his evil opponent.

The Assimilation of Jackie Chan into Hollywood's System of Racial Representation

The popular American stereotypes of Asians, Chinese in particular, are full of contradictions. In an article titled "The Image of Overseas Chinese in American Cinema," Ng observes that in the 1930s two contradictory Chinese characters were hugely popular in American cinema. They were Fu Manchu, the arch Oriental villain, and Charlie Chan, the sage from China. These two characters represent two moments in this continuing alternation of racial stereotyping.[22]

Another contradiction can be found in the asymmetrical attitudes toward the two Asian genders. On one hand Asian women are often depicted as submissive and adorable. As Marchetti argues in her discussion of *Love is a Many-Splendored Thing* (dir. Henry King, 1955) and *The World of Suzie Wong* (dir. Richard Quine, 1960), these films:

> [U]phold both the gender and racial status quo by depicting Asian women as more truly "feminine," content at being passive, subservient, dependent, domestic, and slaves to "love." The films implicitly warn both white women and women of color to take the Western imagination's creation of the passive Asian beauty as the feminine ideal if they want to attract and keep a man.[23]

While Asian women are perceived as the "feminine ideal" to white men, Asian men present a threat to white women, and these men's sexual desires must be reined in. This anxiety over Asian men's sexual aggression is reflected in the portrayal of Fu Manchu — who has the ability to hypnotize hapless victims, white women in particular — while the need to discipline or simply to castrate and emasculate Asian men is exemplified in the creation of numerous passive and asexual Asian characters, ranging from Charlie Chan to the more recent nerdy Asian engineers. The creation of an inept Asian male character who lusts after white females as illustrated by Long Duck Dong in *Sixteen Candles* (dir. John Hughes, 1984) is another stereotype often seen in U.S. cinema.

In his original Hong Kong films, Jackie Chan represents an alternative masculine kung fu hero. However, Chan's role in more recent Hollywood productions reflects his incorporation into this established system of racial representation that has a long history of deforming the racial and sexual identities of both Asian women and men. Analyzing the representation of race in *Rush Hour* (dir. Brett Ratner, 1998), Lo observes:

Although Chan's image is by no means effeminized as many Asian men were in Hollywood films, his ethnicity has already been framed in a passive feminized space. As some critics point out, the male characters of racial minority in American cinema always fall into the category of a passive and asexual figure that is not only threatening to the white hero but also confirming his sexual domination. However, there is hardly any white hero in *Rush Hour*, let alone one with sexual appeal. Perhaps, it is the mainstream white audience that the film does not want to pose any threat to.[24]

Lo points rightly to the effeminization involved in the construction of Chan's image in *Rush Hour*. However, I would add that effeminization is part of an inherently contradictory representational schema that acknowledges, on one hand, the almost superhuman martial arts skill of the other while at the same time underscoring its subject's "primitive" or "underdeveloped" qualities. In *Rush Hour II* (dir. Brett Ratner, 2001), the asexual dimension of Chan's character is even more conspicuous when we see Carter (played by Chris Tucker) portrayed as a leering, sex-crazed American, which is a stereotype of the African-American male corresponding to the stereotype of the Asian male as devoid of libido. However, there are other features about Chan's character that are equally prominent — his child-like mannerisms as well as his inability to speak English. For instance, in an interview conducted with Jackie Chan by *The Los Angeles Times*, the reporter writes: "[Since] his 1998 international hit *Rush Hour*, Jackie Chan has become known to moviegoers around the world as that funny martial arts guy who speaks broken English and whirls around at warp speed beating villains to a pulp."[25]

Although Chan can perform impressive stunts, because he is juvenile, asexual and speaks only fractured English, he is still not, in the mainstream American system of male representation, the same kind of Hollywood masculine hero as Bruce Willis or Mel Gibson. It might seem as though *The Tuxedo* (dir. Kevin Donovan, 2002), Chan's more recent Hollywood production, contradicts this interpretation. Throughout the film, Chan is portrayed as a taxi-driver sexually interested in a female Asian shopkeeper, and at the end we see Del Blaine (played by Jennifer Love Hewitt), who has a secret interest in Chan, becoming engaged to him. In this film Chan is clearly not asexual, but his role in that film is still characterized by ineptness and a lack of autonomy. Chan's boss in the film is Clark Devlin (played by Jason Isaacs), a well-rounded playboy spy, and he is the one who coaches Chan on how to "win" women over.

Chan's role in *The Tuxedo* does have a more developed sexuality, but it is still the white master who teaches him how to express it.

In this chapter I argue that the migration of Hong Kong film professionals into the U.S. does lead to greater multiculturalism in Hollywood productions, but that this does not imply the hegemony of a long-established system of racial and sexual stereotype has in any way been weakened. There is then a paradox: the co-existence of multiculturalism and cultural domination. In both Woo's and Chan's earlier work, we see a representation of masculinity that departs from what we typically see in the American action or traditional Chinese kung fu genre. What the above analysis shows then is how, after their migration into Hollywood, their alternative representation of masculinity becomes assimilated into the mainstream American system of male representation. Their experiences illustrate how Hollywood manages multiculturalism and maintains the hegemony of a representation schema that subordinates the other.

CAPITAL ACCUMULATION AND THE MULTICULTURAL TURN

While it might now be clear how the cultural hegemony of the dominant social groups in the U.S. is maintained even after Hollywood has become more "multicultural," there is another related, and perhaps more fundamental, question: what were the factors that led to this "multicultural turn" in Hollywood? What prompted Hollywood's decision to incorporate Hong Kong film professionals into its film industry? At first glance this seems to be a straightforward question. Hollywood became multicultural because there is a market for multiculturalism in films, and it was, in other words, simply a business decision. This answer is broadly correct but we need a more refined and theoretically grounded analysis. For instance, why is the "multicultural turn" occurring now rather than fifty years ago? What is the difference between Hollywood's present business strategy and its previous one? What is the relationship between multiculturalism in Hollywood and the more general social, political and economic changes in the last several decades?

Different theoretical approaches can be used to address these issues. In this chapter I will show how the notion of "cultural industry" and its attendant theory originating in Horkheimer and Adorno's writings on the U.S. entertainment industry are relevant in this regard. Horkheimer and Adorno's analyses provide a general framework for conceptualizing the link between mass culture and the social/economic sphere. However, they mainly wrote about the cultural industry during the era of mass consumption in the 1950s and 1960s, and their focus was on the erosion of aesthetic sensibility and the standardization of taste. In order to explain adequately Hollywood's turn to multiculturalism, I will refer to the literature on economic restructuring under capitalism, and will argue that the multicultural turn is to be understood as a consequence of the cultural industry's transformation from a Fordist system to a regime of Post-Fordist production.

The Cultural Industry

Horkheimer and Adorno first introduced the term "cultural industry" in *Dialectic of Enlightenment*. This book explains the movement through which "enlightenment relapses into mythology,"[26] and "progress reverts to regression."[27] The chapter "The Cultural Industry: Enlightenment as Mass Deception" is central to the book because it shows how enlightenment thinking becomes a reified ideology in contemporary Western capitalist society. In mass culture, Horkheimer and Adorno observe, "enlightenment consists primarily in the calculation of effects and in the technology of production and dissemination; the specific content of the ideology is exhausted in the idolization of the existing order and of the power by which the technology is controlled."[28]

Because the discussion in that chapter is concerned with showing how mass culture exemplifies the self-destruction of enlightenment through standardization and the construction of "pseudoindividuality,"[29] there is no explicit statement on the relationship between mass culture and the social/economic sphere. This is in a separate essay, "Cultural Industry Reconsidered," published in 1967, which shows more explicitly how Adorno conceptualizes the link between mass culture and the capitalist mode of production. Adorno explains:

> The cultural commodities of the industry are governed, as Brecht and Suhrkamp expressed it thirty years ago, by the principle of their realization as value, and not by their own specific content and harmonious function. The entire practice of the culture industry transfers the profit motive naked onto cultural forms. Cultural entities typical of the culture industry are no longer *also* commodities, they are commodities through and through. This quantitative shift is so great that it calls forth entirely new phenomena.[30]

The production of mass entertainment in the cultural industry is driven by the principle of profit maximization. Its structuring principle is then not unlike that underlying the production of any other commodities in other industries. In fact, the products of mass entertainment are standardized commodities manufactured to be consumed by a wide range of people. What is incessantly called "new" in the cultural industry "remains the disguise for an eternal sameness; everywhere the changes mask a skeleton which has changed just as little as the profit motive itself since the time it first gained its predominance over culture."[31]

Though seeing the parallels between the cultural industry and other industries in capitalist societies, Adorno also points to their differences. The term "industry" is not "to be taken too literally" since it is primarily only in the film industry that we see mass production through a rigid division of labor while some degree of "individuality" is maintained in other entertainment sectors. But this semblance of "individuality," Adorno argues, only functions to propagate a false sense of free choice and autonomy in a mass consumer society.[32] In analyzing mass culture, the crux of Adorno's analysis is that, as Held observes:

> The conditions of labor, production and distribution must be examined, for society expresses itself through its cultural life and cultural phenomena contain within themselves reference to the socio-economic whole.[33]

Our central question here is how to account for Hollywood's "multicultural turn" that has led to Hong Kong film professionals' migration to the U.S. film industry in recent years. Horkheimer and Adorno's discussion is crucial in this connection. They emphasize that mass culture is embedded within the nexus of capital accumulation, and perhaps an answer to our question could be found by examining the integrated processes of production, distribution and marketing.

Fordism and Post-Fordist Production

However, Horkheimer and Adorno provide only the first step toward an analysis. From their writings we learn that although we can look to socio-economic factors for an answer, they still do not immediately allow us to explain *how* these factors necessitate the multicultural turn in Hollywood. One point that is under-theorized in Horkheimer and

Adorno's discussion of the cultural industry is the periodization of capitalist development. This is the idea that the historical process of capitalist production/circulation develops through different stages, and discussion of this thesis can be found as early as *Capital Vol. 1*. Marx argues there that as capitalism develops, the way in which its economic production is organized also changes over time. The historical movement of capitalism can then be demarcated into different periods depending on how economic production at a given time is organized. In his own work, Marx identifies three periods in the development of early capitalism. He examines the transformation from handicraft production to manufacturing and then to large-scale factory production.[34]

We see, in more recent times, further theoretical development of Marx's thesis that the historical process of capitalist economic development can be demarcated into distinct periods. Harvey, for instance, demarcated the post-World War II development of capitalist production in advanced Western countries into two successive regimes of accumulation. The regime of accumulation from 1945 to 1973 is referred to as the Fordist system. It is a growth regime characterized by mass production, mass consumption and a balance of power among labor unions, large corporate capital and the state. From 1973 onward, the Fordist system was replaced by a new regime of accumulation that Harvey refers to as the system of flexible accumulation. The previous labor-control practices waned in a new regime characterized by "more flexible labor processes and markets, of geographical mobility and rapid shifts in consumption practices."[35]

The periodization of capitalist development is important. It captures the historical specific character of a particular nexus of capital accumulation at a particular point in time. The culture industry described by Horkheimer and Adorno between the 1940s and the 1960s is accordingly to be understood as a historically specific way of organizing the production of mass culture — the system of Fordist production. The multicultural turn in Hollywood is then a result of the changes in the organization of production, distribution and marketing in the U.S. film industry after its transition from Fordism to a system of flexible accumulation.

Hollywood under Fordism

In the early days of the U.S. film industry there were many small enterprises, and competition was cut-throat. However, the industry gradually came to be dominated by a handful of studios. They were the Big Five: Paramount, Loew's, Fox Film, Warner Bros., and RKO; and the Little Three: Universal, Columbia, and United Artists.[36] This emerging oligopoly marked the beginning of Fordism in Hollywood. The strategy of profit accumulation during this stage was through the use of "(1) the star system, (2) the national (and international) distribution system and (3) the run-zone-clearance system of exhibition."[37]

However, in the area of production, the film industry was like other industrial sectors under Fordism at the time: the strategy was the production of standardized commodities for a mass consumer market through an assembly-line operation characterized by a rigid division of labor. As Storper observes, the organization of film production was separated into three stages.[38] First, it was "pre-production," in which movie scripts were chosen and preparation for filming was made. The second stage was "production," in which the actual filming was carried out, while the third was "post-production," in which films were edited and sound effects added. The principles of mass production structured, Storper notes, coordination within and between each of the three stages:

> For example, the major studios had permanent staffs of writers and production planners who were assigned to produce formula scripts in volume and push them through the production system. Production crews and stars were assembled in teams charged with making as many as thirty films per year. Studios had large departments to make sets, operate sound stages and film labs, and carry out marketing and distribution. A product would move from department to department in assembly-line fashion. The studios endeavoured to maximise capacity utilities and stabilise throughput. As a result, the internal organization — or technical division of labour — in each phase of the labour process became similar to that of true mass production, where routinisation and task fragmentation were the guiding principles. (201–203)

Storper's description of the Fordist system in the film industry is consistent with Horkheimer and Adorno's observations in the 1940s and 1960s that the cultural commodities in mass culture were characterized by standardization and pseudo-individuality. When a small number of studios were able to form an oligopoly in the mass entertainment market, there was little competition and hardly any need for product innovation or diversification. Multiculturalism was simply not a consideration in Hollywood because standardization of films remained a viable strategy for making profits.

Post-Fordist Production in Hollywood

By the 1950s, however, Storper points out that already visible were those institutional and technological changes that would eventually render Fordism obsolete as an effective strategy for profit maximization.

Oligopoly of the film industry by a small number of studios was one factor that led to the standardization and mass production of films in Hollywood. This oligopoly was not just confined to the sphere of production where potential producers faced barriers into the industry. Rather, oligopoly spanned almost every niche of the film market before the 1950s owing to the large studios' strategy of *vertical integration*. This means the studios not only had control of every step of the production; they also controlled distribution as well as movie theaters.

For example, in 1944, 70% of the cinemas in the ninety-two U.S. cities with populations of 100,000 or more were owned by five large studios. Half of the nation's movie box-office receipts came from these cinemas (203). The first setback to the film industry was then the U.S. Supreme Court's decision to break up these studios' control of the cinemas. The result of "The Paramount Decision" (*US* v. *Paramount Pictures*, 334 US 131, 1948), Storper observes, was that because "the assured market once enjoyed by the studios was now gone, average returns per picture declined and returns per film began to fluctuate wildly"(204).

The second event that also resulted in Hollywood's loss of earnings was the invention of television. As television became a ubiquitous household item in the U.S., Storper says, "what had been essentially a unified market for filmed entertainment, dominated by one medium, became a segmented market in which different products competed for the consumer's entertainment expenditures." The effect of television is reflected in the statistics on the changing size of the movie box office, where there was a decline from 1945 to 1955 of almost 40% in real terms. In 1960 the box office was only 39% of its real level in 1945. During this period, the profit of the top eight studios decreased by more than 50% in real terms, and this decline is to be understood in the context of the Paramount decision as well as the diffusion of television (204).

These socio-political, and technological challenges along with other market changes made it increasingly difficult for the large studios to maintain their profit margin simply through mass production of standardized products in an assembly-line operation. A result of this is the rise of a production system in which the independent producers play an important role. It is also here that the shift to the Post-Fordist production began. As Thompson and Bordwell explain:

> As the big Hollywood studios cut back on the number of films they created, independent production became more prominent. Independent producers hired the personnel needed to make a film on a one-time-only basis, creating a "package" in order to get financing. Once the film was made, it would often be released through one of the Big Five or Little distributors. These big firms discovered they could reduce overhead costs by cutting back on the number of actors and filmmakers they had under long-term contract. They increasingly filled out their regular release schedules by buying up more independently made films.[39]

The collapse of the mass-production studio system was replaced by a subcontracting system that was also a characteristic of other industries during the Post-Fordist era. The failure of the mass-production system also shows that the audience could no longer be treated as a homogenous and undifferentiated bloc. Demographic differences such as age and gender as well as the differences between domestic and foreign markets have become crucial factors shaping film production. Films were made and packaged differently to cater to different segments of the population, and there was then gradually more product differentiation. As product differentiation became a prominent strategy for accumulating profit, the old standardized mass production model was no longer viable, and the differentiation of taste led to a new type of specialization based on the use of a subcontracting system in the production process. This transformation to the Post-Fordist mode of production in the U.S. film industry, or what is sometimes called the system of *flexible specialization*,[40] is closely tied to the "multicultural turn" in Hollywood. More specifically, a strategy of product differentiation that aims to capture a greater share of two major segments of the movie audience — teenage males and the foreign market — explains Hollywood's demand for Hong Kong film professionals.

In Hollywood, the traditional "bone-crunching, bloody nature of the action genre had not only peaked creatively but its excesses were also coming under attack from Washington. Stricter enforcement of the R rating also made gore-fest films less economically viable."[41] The Hong Kong-style of action films provides an alternative to Hollywood. For example, Peter Hyams, the director of *Timecop* (1994) and *The Musketeer*

(2001), comments that "[as] with the Hong Kong films, it's breathing and cartoon-like, it allows the audience to sit back amused by the athleticism and the beauty of the choreography."[42] To Leonard Goldberg, the producer of *Charlie's Angels*, a hallmark of the Hong Kong style "is a mixture of action and comic absurdity." One reason *Charlie's Angels* was a success was precisely its "combination of humor and fluid movement."[43]

With its removal of graphic violence, and an emphasis on ballet-like choreography, Hong Kong-style action films can be rated as PG-13 rather than R, hence "enabling Hollywood to market these movies to the all-important core teenage moviegoer. At the other end, segments of the older audience turned off by hard-edged action have also become converts to this new style."[44] The importation of Hong Kong action stars and choreographers then plays a central role in revitalizing the traditional Hollywood action genre, and these action films can now reach a wider audience than before.

No less important than the domestic teenage market to Hollywood is the foreign market. About 50% of Hollywood's annual revenue comes from overseas. In some cases it can be more than that. For example, the foreign gross earnings of *Harry Potter and the Sorcerer's Stone* (dir. Chris Columbus, 2001) were $651 million, while domestic gross earning was only $317 million.[45] Commenting on the importance of the foreign market, an executive from a major studio, Tom Rothman, Co-Chairman of 20th Century Fox, points out that "[it] would be like crossing the street and not looking both ways" if the international market was not taken into consideration when planning a new film production.[46]

However, studios found it a challenge to increase its sales in the international market to the expected level that expected — 70% rather than 50% of its total revenue. As Warren Lieberfarb, president of Warner Home video, explains, "[It] isn't one world when it comes to laughing, crying or being frightened. There is not one homogeneous appetite for American movies, and that is what poses this huge challenge for the U.S. studios."[47] One solution for overcoming these cultural barriers is simply to incorporate overseas cultural elements into Hollywood's products, and the recruitment of Hong Kong film professionals, most of whom already have an Asian following, can achieve just that.

The re-organization of film production in Hollywood from Fordist to Post-Fordist production, or flexible specialization, is then a major factor prompting the multicultural turn. Under the Post-Fordist system, mass production of standardized products is replaced by a strategy of product differentiation. The differentiation of films to satisfy different audience segments requires specialized input, and major studios sub-contracted out some of their operations to independent firms that specialized in a particular domain of the production process. Crucial to Hollywood's maximization of profit are the domestic teenage market and the international market. The assimilation of Hong Kong film professionals into the U.S. film industry is a rational decision in this connection because it extends Hollywood's reach to both markets.

CONCLUSION

This chapter makes two arguments regarding multiculturalism and film production, and jointly they make a more theoretical claim. First, I argue that Hollywood is incorporating "multiculturalism" into its film industry during this new round of global capitalist expansion while the established power elites continue to exercise their cultural hegemony. The discussion about John Woo and Jackie Chan serves to illustrate this point. In both Woo's and Chan's earlier Hong Kong productions we see an alternative representation of masculinity not commonly found in Hollywood's action genre. However, after their crossover into Hollywood, their distinctive treatment of masculinity is either muted, as in the case of Woo, or, as in Chan's case, their once "alternative" masculinity becomes assimilated into a system of gender representation that has a tradition of denigrating or "castrating" Asian males. There is indeed more "multiculturalism," but this "multiculturalism" is subsumed under a hierarchical representational system that perpetuates the privileged representation of men over women, whites over non-whites, American democracy over non-western political models, etc. Cultural representation continues to "reflect" or rationalize social, political and economic domination in the non-cultural realms.

I then proceed to explain Hollywood's decision to incorporate multiculturalism into its film industry. My second argument is that the multicultural turn taken by Hollywood can be explained by a modified notion of "cultural industry" originating in Horkheimer and Adorno's writings. This concept suggests an analysis that situates cultural production within the nexus of capital accumulation — a web of social institutions along with organizations of production, distributing, marketing, etc. However, Horkheimer and Adorno wrote about the cultural industry more than 40 years ago, and capitalism has continued to develop. I argue that the organization of film production changes from one stage of capitalist development to another. The cultural industry at the time of Horkheimer and Adorno's writings was under the system of Fordist production. Studios accumulated profit through the mass production of standardized products in an assembly-line operation. In the mid 1950s, this strategy of profit maximization became ineffective under a new set of institutional and technological changes. The strategy of product differentiation was adopted, and the film market was differentiated into different segments. Under this Post-Fordist system of production, the assimilation of Hong Kong film professionals is a strategy that expands Hollywood's share in two segments of the markets, the domestic teenage and the international markets.

These two arguments jointly demonstrate a theoretical point: that cultural representation is embedded within a *social totality* constituted in part of organizations of capitalist production. While changes in cultural representation relate to changes in capitalist production process, each sphere is still autonomous and the dynamics of one cannot be reduced to that of the other.

In neo-liberal literature on globalization, it is often believed that the global expansion of the market economy will break down barriers and lead to greater cross-cultural understanding.[48] As Hollywood attempts to expand its global reach, for instance, it might feature more congenial and less stereotypical portrayals of other cultural groups in its cinematic representations. A genuine multiculturalism might result from a business strategy that aims to capture the world market.

Far from providing an analysis assuming such a crude economic determinism, this chapter shows a more intricate picture of the relationship between culture and capitalist development. While the multicultural turn in Hollywood is in part to be explained by the new strategy of profit maximization in the Post-Fordist era, the cultural hegemony of the socially dominant groups in entertainment persists. What this shows is that while the dynamics of cultural contestation are in part shaped by the imperative of capital accumulation, they still have their own logic. Rather than an egalitarian multiculturalism, we see in Hollywood a re-configuration of the technology of cultural domination. In this case, cultural representation *adapts* itself to the production process but it is not *dictated* by it. This analysis then shows how culture and capitalist production interact with each other while maintaining their own autonomous logics of development.

11

Masculinities in Self-Invention:
Critics' Discourses on Kung Fu–Action Movies and Comedies

Agnes S. M. Ku

Hong Kong cinema is known across the world for its production of muscular bodies. Among the most notable are those belonging to kung fu king Bruce Lee (Li Xiaolong), Zhang Che's martial arts heroes in his "*new wuxia pian*" (new style martial arts films) in earlier decades, stunt-performing megastar Jackie Chan (Cheng Long), and John Woo (Wu Yusen)'s gunfighters of recent memory. Just as the virile bodies of Hong Kong have made themselves the object of conspicuous display worldwide, the question of masculinity or the masculine body in Hong Kong movies is beginning to "surge" in film criticisms and scholarly discussion.[1] While these discussions generally contribute to a more variegated understanding of masculinity, there have been a few attempts to explore how specific representations of masculinity are part and parcel of the invention of identity of Hong Kong people.[2]

In the 1990s, Stephen Teo presented a nationalist reading of kung fu or action movies that equates identity with nationalism and masculinity.[3] There is little sense of a break between China and Hong Kong in such a reading. More recently, the "local" as a distinct entity has gained greater prominence in Hong Kong cultural studies. For Kwai-cheung Lo, for instance, the sublimation (or disappearance) of male bodies is a necessary condition for understanding the history of cultural formation of the Hong Kong identity.[4] He nonetheless argues that the sublime bodies of these male protagonists present a paradox, namely a failed or unpresentable representation of Hong Kong subjectivity. For "they allude to no positive, descriptive cultural features from which Hong

Kong identity can easily be drawn."[5] Interestingly, this perhaps explains why, even as a male, Lo should find himself worrying about how representative Jackie Chan is of Hong Kong when he saw the latter showing off his athleticism live on *The Late Show* on CBS. These diverse readings about the muscular bodies open up a space for us to rethink the relationships among gender, popular representations, and collective identity in Hong Kong cinema.

In the past two or three decades Hong Kong cinema has been dominated by male-centered genres.[6] Action or kung fu movies being circulated overseas and displaying virile bodies are one of two genres of this kind. Comedy that centers on the performance of male comedians like Michael Hui (Xu Guanwen) and Stephen Chow (Zhou Xingchi) is the other. In particular, since the early 1990s, Chow's style of "nonsense talk" has been widely acclaimed as representing the folk culture of Hong Kong.[7] Local film critics and analysts have given added significance to his performance by relating his style and popularity to the larger social and political context in Hong Kong. Yet these comedies have not received as much academic or serious attention as the action or kung fu movies. Why? While this reflects that the high/low or art/market distinction remains crucial in our cultural discourses, the global market under Hollywood is certainly a significant cause. Hollywood has been itself dominated by action film for nearly two decades.[8] The privileging of such action movies over the other genres in the movie industry only shows and reinforces a pattern of hierarchical ordering among different forms of masculinities, both locally and globally.

On a deeper level, while action movies are unmistakably characterized as movies for and by men, especially among American critics who like to compare Asian with Hollywood representations of masculinity,[9] the male protagonist in comedy has seldom been conceived as a gendered subject embodying a particular kind of masculinity. In this regard, the invention of Chow as representing a typical Hong Kong person by film critics and analysts can conceal a gendered overtone in the construction of local collective identity. If action-movie stars present masculinity in a readily visible form, it is because our discourses enable us to identify certain qualities as being masculine, albeit in increasingly diverse and multiple ways. On the contrary, if male comedy actors as gendered subjects are rendered both omnipresent and invisible, it perhaps shows how our culture has deeply naturalized masculinist values and assumptions.

In this chapter, I will look at the different ways film critics and analysts construct, negotiate, and silence the gendered layer of Hong Kong identity with regard to the two genres of kung fu-action movies and comedy. If we understand film criticism as a form of cultural politics, questions such as "who is representing whom?" "from what position?" and "with what ideological content?" will become pertinent as we analyze the different reading strategies by the critics. In my discussion, I will distinguish among three reading strategies by the critics, namely reflectionism, deconstructionism, and hermeneutics, and further differentiate between localism and nationalism in their ideological positions. In explaining and comparing their reading strategies, I seek to look into ways of self-invention of Hong Kong through critics' discourses, and to explore the question of how the invented identity conveys or conceals a gendered overtone.

KUNG FU–ACTION MOVIES: THE DISCOURSES OF NATIONALISM, LOCALISM, AND TRANSNATIONALISM

In the late 1960s and during the 1970s, kung fu movies with martial arts heroes — represented most distinctly by the productions of the Shaw Brothers and Golden Harvest — began to dominate Hong Kong cinema. For instance, from 1970 to 1972 almost every film in the Top 10 highest-grossing films list belonged to this genre. These included, among others, Bruce Lee's *Fist of Fury* (Tangshan daxiong) (1971) and *The Way of the Dragon* (Menglong Guojiang) (1972), and also the "New Style" martial arts films of Zhang Che and King Hu (Hu Jinquan). They were taking the place of the Cantonese cinema dominated by a group of young female stars. The female stars of the Cantonese cinema were "comparatively gentle," which reflected a continuation of the Chinese tradition of the "weak male."[10] On the contrary, the male stars of the Mandarin cinema manifested "strong emotions more suited to the restlessness of the times."[11] The rise of such kung fu movies therefore marked a double turn away from the female-led Cantonese cinema and from the traditional weak image of the male.

A number of critics read into the martial arts movies the dual element of masculinity and nationalism against the context in which they were produced. Masculinity and nationalism were perceived to go hand in hand because the latter was understood in terms of certain qualities such as assertiveness, power, strength, aggressiveness, and fierceness, which were embodied in the heroic male body. Nationalism had been a potent theme in Hong Kong cinema, but it was under the sway of director Zhang Che that a violent male-dominated genre was promoted to "help re-cultivate masculine strength in the Chinese national character which was said to have become too feminine."[12] Bruce Lee, the biggest star in the history of Hong Kong cinema, arose in such a context. For film critic Stephen Teo, Bruce Lee fused masculinity and nationalism in a way that evoked national pride:

> Bruce Lee stood for ... Chinese nationalism as a way of feeling pride in one's identity ... Kung fu films were particularly conducive to nationalism of the abstract kind ... Lee is literally putting his bravest face (and body) forward in order to show that the Chinese need no longer be weaklings.[13]

The discourse of masculine-nationalism nonetheless is not self-evident and does not speak for itself unambiguously. For example, regarding Bruce Lee, the English critic Tony Rayns believes his works are characterized more by narcissism.[14] In this light, nationalism should best be understood as an interpretive strategy in the cultural politics of self-invention, not only by filmmakers but also by film critics. Among the latter, while some writers are inclined to relate the muscular body with nationalism, diversity in their reading strategies is shown with regard to substantive focus and/or the method of interpretation.

A Unitary-Reflectionist Interpretation of Masculine-Nationalism

Stephen Teo's strategy presents a reading of nationalism that relies on a unitary discourse that encompasses the hero, the movie, the social context, and the audience within a coherent framework. On one level, Bruce Lee's nationalism is understood as a form of personal exorcism, expressing sheer xenophobia out of his own anger as "a subjugated colonial and lowly Asian immigrant" in America.[15] On another level, it is sublimated in more abstractly cultural, universalizing terms. Teo conceives a peculiar form of cultural nationalism, which is "a culturally positive, politically abstract phenomenon emerging from *tianxia* and hitting Hong Kong cinema around the late 1950s in the context of the Cold War and its Yellow-Peril rhetoric."[16] The form of Chinese nationalism expressed in Lee's movies intends to make a transnational appeal to include Chinese people living outside China and not speaking the national language. This kind of nationalism is expressed through a masculine body that shows an aura of superb martial arts. "Chinese audiences take pride in the image Lee projects as a superb fighting specimen of manhood who derives his status from 'traditional' skills."[17] For Teo, Bruce Lee is more than a kung fu hero with mere physical brawn. He embodies also a spirit or distinctive philosophy about his kung fu — a "will to succeed." He himself is the personal incarnation of such spirit, for it is the kung fu and identity of the "real" Bruce Lee behind the cinematic representation that appeals to the imagination of the people.[18] In a similar vein, Desser suggests that Chinese nationalism came to be embodied in the male body of the Chinese kung fu stars.[19] It is embodied, moreover, on "a *displaced body* in diaspora or in exile from a homeland, Hong Kong."[20]

Teo insists on a nationalist reading, which he generalizes by means of a "reflectionist" logic:

> To see Lee as a mere kung fu martial artist without taking into account his nationalist sentiments is to perceive Lee as Narcissus gazing in a mirror: the image reflected is an illusion without substance ... When the dragon looks in the mirror, it sees not Narcissus but the Chinese masses looking back. This is the substance behind the reflective theory of Hong Kong cinema — that it mirrors the aspirations of Hong Kong people, and reflects their psychological mind-set and behavior ...With death, Lee achieved true mythic status, allowing him to be all things to all men: Narcissus gazing in the mirror or Little Dragon exhorting the Chinese to stand up and be counted. Lee achieved the distinction of being both Narcissus and the Little Dragon, straddling East and West.[21]

In the reflectionist interpretation, Bruce Lee, the "Little Dragon," mirrored the hopes and desires of the people. In this connection, the masculine-nationalist reading is given a more specific historical meaning in relation to the larger socio-economic context. Teo sees that a distinctly masculinist dimension to the Mandarin martial arts hero revolved around a newly economically assertive Hong Kong: "The *wuxia* or martial hero emerged in the mid-1960s, when China was asserting its newly acquired superpower status and Hong Kong was becoming 'an Asian tiger,' while the Japanese economic expansion into East and Southeast Asia was at its most aggressive." In short, the emergence of the Mandarin martial arts film is understood to reflect a newly emergent Hong Kong consciousness of itself being a tiger or a fighter in the regional economy, which fed into a new Chinese symbolic nationalism.[22]

Martial arts films declined briefly in the mid-1970s only to become predominant again later in the decade. There emerged, for example, Jackie Chan and the successes of director Lau Kar-leung (Liu Jialiang) and star Lau Ka-fai (Liu Jiahui) in Cantonese movies. Drawing on the unitary discourse of nationalism, Teo sees it as a continuation of the earlier masculine-nationalist tradition.[23] Following this, Desser conceives of it as returning both martial arts and "a resurgent nationalism to the fore ... a Cantonese-inflected Chinese nationalism."[24] With this comes a kind of imperialism as well as a kind of pan-Asian identification, especially in Jackie Chan's films: "Hong Kong came to mean not just 'China' but 'Asia', enabling Chinese nationalism to become pan-Asian cultural nationalism.[25] In the present context, the representation of cultural nationalism is extended and reinforced, similarly through the masculine body. In this way, the masculine body is being increasingly sublimated into the discourse of nationalism, while the latter is being masculinized through the male hero (especially the male body), market expansion, and a subtle form of cultural imperialism.

Apart from filmmakers and overseas distributors, local film critics perhaps play a not insignificant role in contributing to the self-invention of a proud national identity in the industry. As observed by Bordwell, Hong Kong critics tend to treat local movies as reflecting social trends.[26] Or, putting it in a slightly different way, they seek to use the reflectionist form of criticism to explore a movie's relation to current social trends. Behind this reflectionist approach is a pervasive assumption in Hong Kong film criticism that has united writers of different generations and tastes, who agree that movies must address the community on matters of moral significance. Such an intellectual tradition has the effect of urging directors and scriptwriters to think about their role as public educators. Even though many critics find that many movies fail in their moral responsibility, they still see the movies as reflecting the moral, cultural, and psychological climate of the time.

Deconstructing Hong Kong's Self-Invention through the Male Body

Kwai-cheung Lo's deconstructionist approach offers an alternative reading of the male body in popular representations as part of the Hong Kong subject formation.[27] Ideologically or substantively, he focuses on localism rather than nationalism as his interpretive standpoint. What he picks on is nonetheless a form of localism that suggests the impossibility, fragility, and futility of a coherent representation of Hong Kong subjectivity. Methodologically, he consciously steers away from the conventional approaches to Hong Kong film criticism. On the one hand, this approach highlights the fantastic quality about the heroes that cannot be simply reduced to a historical interpretation. In this way, it marks a departure from the predominant approach of reflectionism that relates social trends, popular representations and the psychology of reception in a most coherent and linear manner. On the other hand, it avoids the ahistorical approach that reads kung fu movies as pure visual and aural spectacle. Instead it straddles a middle path between a semiotic void and historical specificity to grasp the mechanism of subject construction. For him, the body is not simply a reflection of the meaning of history, but "always already a part of the historical transformation of Hong Kong self (re)construction"(109). The analytical anchor is found in the notion of the sublime body.

"Sublime" refers to something formless, unimaginable and incommensurable. The muscular bodies on screen are sublime bodies that "occupy an empty space without any positive content or intrinsic meaning, and their void can only subsequently be filled through the specificity of their particular historical milieu"(107). It is by filling the semiotic void yet without fixing meanings in any determinate way that the Hong Kong subject is represented. For example, for Lo, Bruce Lee's body reveals a paradox of identification and hollowness about Hong Kong identity: it creates an empty space with little cultural specificity with which Hong Kong people nonetheless can identify. Lee's kung fu is superb and insurmountable. Yet it is hollow in the sense that there is little trace of Hong Kong's local culture in his movies. His onscreen image as a Chinese hero with a strong national spirit is only remotely related to a Hong Kong identity. Regarding his onscreen body, it is real yet alien, being deficiently localized and nearly superhuman. Even his famously gimmicky shrieks and wails only suggest a free-floating, disembodied life of its own without a fixed subject. As far as Chineseness is concerned, what is invoked is an imaginary and void China, which suggests the ambiguity of both attachment and distance. In this connection, his hybrid identity, his diasporic life journey, and his metropolitan profile all add up to complicate further this sense of ambiguity vis-à-vis China.

Still, despite the lack of localism, Bruce Lee becomes part of the invention of a Hong Kong subjectivity. As Lo points out, the causal mechanism does not lie in Lee's body locating or signifying a specific

Hong Kong identity. It lies, rather, with its phantasmic quality, in his body creating a hollow space for identity construction among the Hong Kong people. More specifically, the kind of Chineseness invoked is abstract and fictive enough to allow for an easy association. Lo then argues that a Hong Kong identification with Lee is possible precisely because of the lack of localism. The historical genesis of the subject is only "a retroactive reconstruction" in specific historical conditions (115).

The project of representation is nonetheless a failed and negative one, for the Hong Kong subject is itself unsignifiable. It is unsignifiable because Hong Kong culture is neither Chinese tradition nor Western influence, but one characterized by a self-awareness of "'in-betweeness,' its impurity, its difference at the origin, or its changing indeterminacy" (106). Fragility and instability are the consequent hallmarks. Thus the cultural identity of Hong Kong may be articulated not so much in positive terms as through certain negativities. As a result, Lo asserts that neither Chinese nationalist discourse nor a Western global perspective can grasp the local sense of Hong Kong identity. Likewise the sublime male body in Hong Kong movies presents "what is unpresentable of Hong Kong subjectivity" (106).

In more recent years, the action hero Jackie Chan has emerged in the context of Hong Kong becoming an international metropolis and uniting itself with China under the "one country, two systems" principle. Unlike his predecessors, he does not embrace a nationalist cause but rather carries an ambiguity of being both local and international at once. In Lo's observation, such ambiguity is perhaps manifested in his characteristic breathtaking stunts, which enact what is real and yet almost humanly impossible, and which lack any specific ideological content or inner conviction. As such, Chan's movies do not signify a Hong Kong subjectivity but only indicate a space for identification that somehow suggests its impossibility. Later martial arts movies by Tsui Hark (Xu Ke) (*Zu: Warriors from the Magic Mountain*, 1983; *Once Upon a Time in China*, 1991; *Swordsman II*, 1992) and by Wong Kar-wai (Wang Jiawei) (*Ashes of Time*, 1994) further sublimate the male body by undermining its materiality and coherence. The former virtually give up what is real and lend themselves to special technological effects that accentuate dazzling speed and flamboyant action, which suggests a sense of restlessness and dislocation. The latter empty masculine bodies of erotic desires for the impossible, which bespeaks the social atmosphere of anxiety and impotency in Hong Kong toward 1997.

Siu-leung Li's reading of kung fu movies is a variation within a deconstructionist framework similar to that of Kwai-cheung Lo, but he harps back on the theme of nationalism only to dismantle its unity.[28] He argues against any complacent nationalist interpretation of the movies as redeeming the national pride of the Chinese people. Following Lo and yet taking us further from where Lo has left us, Li agrees that Bruce Lee carries little trace of local Hong Kong culture but sees a special imaginary link between Hong Kong and his figure. Hong Kong was "a place colonized, marginalized, hybridized and yet privileged by a modernity" through a colonial encounter while Bruce Lee's image can be read as "a cosmopolitan postcolonial in the Hong Kong connection."[29] In other words, Bruce Lee's image does not just create a hollow space for identity construction, but represents significant parallels with Hong Kong whereby a mechanism of self-invention is effected.

In his reading, Li deliberately re-interprets the kung fu imaginary in a more radical way, as enacting a continuous unveiling of its own incoherence:

> Kung fu is caught in a dilemma of representation: the traditional and the modern, the mimetic and the non-mimetic modes of discourse are coexistent and coextensive in the filmic imaginary, rendering it more relevant for cultural critics to attend to the incoherence, contradictions and instabilities of its meanings in circulation.[30]

Earlier, examples of such contradictions and instability were found in the motif of kung fu being fundamentally useless in the modern world (Tsui Hark's *Once Upon a Time in China*, 1991), or of its being essentially an artistic expression of the human body rather than a sign of physical prowess (Bruce Lee). More recently, under the force of globalism, Jackie Chan and other action stars have transformed traditional kung fu into a more universal action choreography. All these would only suggest the impossibility of a unitary national imagination evoked through the kung fu body. For Li, this radical re-reading can problematize conventional assumptions of monolithic identity. In this way, it registers the latent subversiveness of the Hong Kong cultural imaginary — subversion of a unitary discourse of Chinese nationalism. Li intends his critical reading to be a "tactic of intervention" to counteract the reactionary patriotic discourse by the post-handover government. It is further suggested that the end of the kung fu genre coinciding with the start of the new "transnational action" genre around 1997 points to a more cosmopolitan Hong Kong.

For critics, the kung fu–action genre, which has been dominant in Hong Kong cinema since the mid- to late 1960s, shows the fusion of nationalism and masculinity. While both focus on the male body as the basis for identity construction, the reflectionist and deconstructionist approaches offer two ways to read this. The former assumes coherence, unity, and correspondence among individual psychology, the cinematic texts, and social currents. The latter stresses incoherence, indeterminacy, localism, and hybridity in identity formation while attributing the mechanism of identification or self-invention to symbolic processes, such as retrospective interpretation and imagined parallels. The former tends therefore to exalt nationalism as embodied in the heroic male body, from Bruce Lee to Jackie Chan, whereas the latter shows hesitations and even resistance and highlights ruptures in the masculine/ nationalist connection. Regarding identity, in the nationalist reading, cultural nationalism (including pan-Asian cultural nationalism) becomes part and parcel of a Hong Kong identity. In the deconstructionist reading by Kwai-cheung Lo, however, Hong Kong identity cannot be sufficiently signified through a nationalist, Western, or transnational representation of the male body, but remains an "impossibility" for any coherent signification. Such impossibility could perhaps best be captured in a representation that signifies in-betweenness, negativities, dislocation, impotence, instability, ambiguity, and disappearance. On this count, if Lo's analysis presents a self-reading of Hong Kong before 1997, then Siu-leung Li's article in 2001 presents a more forward-looking view of a post-handover Hong Kong developing a cosmopolitan culture as a potential counterweight against nationalism. Still, as far as the relationship between masculinity and local identity is concerned, how far have these critics' discourses taken us? We shall reflect on this further in the conclusion.

COMEDY: FOLK CULTURE AND NATURALIZATION OF MASCULINITY

Although Hong Kong's kung fu and art films are better known in the United States than its comedies, locally the latter has been the more popular genre. Records show that it has generated nine out of the top-ten best sellers in the past two decades.[31] If the heroic male bodies in the kung fu movies seem too unreal,[32] one may find Everyman in the comic hero. The Cantonese comic cinema of the 1950s and 1960s was "the comedy of the everyday man versus the Mandarin cinema of the upper-class fairyland from Shanghai."[33] In the 1970s and the 1980s, Michael Hui's comedies were able to retain and revive this tradition. His classic story is of the man in the street caught in a fast-changing modern society. More recently, Stephen Chow has been Hong Kong's most popular comedian. For most local critics, the comic characters he plays represent typical Hong Kong people. On one level, the so-called typical-person imagery refers to the community as a whole; on another, it carries clear connotations about social class and status at the lower end. Thus far, Hong Kong's comic heroes have not caught the serious attention of academics, internationally or locally;[34] yet as far as popular film criticism is concerned, Chow has certainly played a pivotal role in the identity construction of the Hong Kong person ("Heunggongyan").

Still, even if the comic hero appears more real than the kung fu hero, the question is, is the "Everyman" image in Chow's works an a-gendered subject that represents man and woman alike, or is it a gendered (male) subject made omnipresent and invisible in our construction of folk identity? I will discuss two different ways to read Chow's movies, one offered most recently as an academic piece of writing by Linda Lai,[35] the other documented from a bunch of short and fragmentary commentaries published by different local sources. I will first analyze how they construct Hong Kong identity in relation to Chow's movies, and then I will show how, in their discourses, the construction of Hong Kong folk identity conceals a deep gendered overtone in Chow's movies.

A Hermeneutical Interpretation: Slang, Parody, and Solidarity

While Chow has received little scholarly attention among academics, Linda Lai's article presents a theoretically informed and sympathetic reading of his movies using a hermeneutical approach.[36] For her, Chow entrenches himself in a culture of folk humor that defends ordinary people's creativity and that parodies power and established norms. In playing with the boundaries between the cultured and the banal, in inhabiting the space of the low, and in overthrowing established social orders, he lets shine through an aspect of humanity often condemned by social etiquette and norms. In theoretical terms, she conceives Chow's movies as a "ritualistic commemoration" of local culture through a process of enigmatization.[37]

Enigmatization refers to a process of solidarity membership through a shared history of popular culture:

the selection and reorganization of existing images from popular culture in order to distinctly select the local audience as a privileged hermeneutic community, thus facilitating a state of internal dialogue, distinguishing those within from the 'outsiders' by marking who partakes in a shared history of popular culture.[38]

More specifically, the enigmatizing power of his movies comes through with the creation of Cantonese slang — the widely acclaimed style of "nonsense talk" that has become distinctive of him. The nonsense talk seeks to overthrow established meanings and norms through puns, jokes, and allusions. Through his stylistic performance, moreover, this linguistic form is given an added "word-and-play carnivalesque" comic effect (246). In this way, his language as well as performance becomes a "rhetoric of subversion" (232) that addresses the Cantonese-speaking Hong Kong audience as the privileged viewer — the insider. In this connection, his constant parodic references to genre conventions (for example, his spoof of James Bond films in *From China with Love*, 1994), and to well-known fictional figures (for example, the opening scene with famous knights-errant in *Forbidden City Cop*, 1996) are integral to commemoration within the local community. It is in these ways that his films become a special site of identity formation among Hong Kong people.

Putting it in the historical context of the "1997" issue, Lai understands such cinematic form as reflecting a trend, in the commercial domain, of trying to capture a local culture that is believed to be on the verge of dissolution, co-optation or erasure from above. In this regard, she is inclined to believe that enigmatization not only helps preserve a textual space of freedom from below — a space that may contradict official views. It also provides a shared textual domain for identity formation that addresses such cultural and identity anxieties in society. Lai nonetheless adds that insofar as solidarity by ritualistic commemoration is effected through shared signs, images, and representations as the public stock of culture, it emphasizes the "surface" without necessarily involving "an imaginative grasp of the subjective experience" of the authors or any "intersubjective exchange of psychological signification" (233). Thus in Chow's movies, the Hong Kong collective identity shows an ephemeral and transient quality through the language used (242).

Divergent Strands of Reflectionism: Hero or Anti-Hero?

In popular film criticism, most local critics also highlight the grassroots or the folk element in Chow's movies, but the image of the comic hero in their depictions is not entirely the same as that of Lai's. While he is also playful and an anti-hero, deep down he may succumb to the dominant values. While he speaks of the voice of the common people, he can be relaxed and comforting sometimes and defeatist and anxious at others. He may appear helpless and powerless on the one hand, and he can also be competitive and successful on the other. He acts as the people's hero, but he can also play God. He is mostly clown-like, but he can also be tragi-romantic. His images are not entirely stable and coherent.[39]

Most critics adopt a reflectionist approach in their reading, but with different emphases. For some critics, Chow's voice and performance are most readily identified by people in the 1990s. His voice is the voice of the powerless. In a political context, at a time when Hong Kong people had only a small role over their future, the powerless were destined to be able to play the hero on the spur of a moment but then recede immediately.[40] For others, Chow's movies (for example, *The King of Beggars*, 1992) tell of an approach to life as well as the typical success story of Hong Kong underpinned by a distinctive kind of ethos, or a belief in the Hong Kong dream: one cannot be serious about anything, but still one can hold an optimistic attitude about oneself; the lowly can rise to the top and achieve success with shrewdness if only one affirms one's own worth and sets the right target.[41] In his most recent movie, *Shaolin Soccer* (Shaolin zuqiu) (2001), the same theme is expanded, except that the drive to achieve comes from a simple passion for the ideal rather than sheer shrewdness. Critics contextualize their interpretations with a reflectionist logic such that the movie is understood to be encouraging Hong Kong people to pick themselves up despite frustrations and to continue fighting in the face of the economic downturn in the post-1997 years.[42]

How might one explain such variegated images of Stephen Chow? While most local popular critics write commentaries on a movie-by-movie basis, Chiu-hing Lee attempts to offer an overall account of Chow's changing images in relation to the changing political contexts.[43] As a critic, Lee is conscious of his role in speaking his thoughts through Chow's movies by means of "hijacking" their meanings whereby one's identity is constructed:

> The mass public, upon their reception, encode the meanings of the popular cultural products and appropriate the use of these products in their own ways, which enable them to resist the dominant ideology, whereby to construct their identity through the popular texts and language.[44]

On one level, Lee's reading, compared with the conventional reflectionist approach, gives to both critics and audience a greater degree of agency in stressing one's interpretive role. Yet in his own reading, he still relies on a reflectionist methodology that sees in the movies a manifestation of a most direct and straightforward link between the audience's psychology and their context.

To Lee, Stephen Chow is himself a microcosm of Hong Kong people. He divides his development into four stages. First, Chow was someone with neither power nor responsibility, which reflected Hong Kong people's sense of detachment in the early transitional period beginning in 1984. Second, by 1990, his nonsensical talk represented the voice of the powerless, especially after the Tiananmen Square incident of 1989. Because people lacked the language to express their feelings of anxiety and helplessness, they then picked up the fragmented ideas offered them in the movies to help voice their feelings as a way of release. (This is where the similarity with Lai's interpretation lies.) Third, around 1995, two years before the handover, a sense of destiny was looming large, hence a shift from the happy-guy image in Chow's earlier movies to a melancholy mood as in *A Chinese Odyssey* (Xiyouji) (1995). After 1997, there was a period of transition for Chow in which he produced. *King of Comedy* (Xiju zhi wang) (1999) and *The Tricky Master* (Qianwang zhi wang 2000) (1999). In 2001, *Shaolin Soccer* signified a completion in the shift from rejection to an embrace of Greater China. The movie's subtext was how Chow, who stood for Hong Kong people, was embarking on a new start. But the irony was, in moving toward a universal language for both the Mainland audience and the global market, was Chow not also moving toward un-becoming Hong Kong? In a postmodern era, as Lee concludes, "we are all heroes, but for fifteen minutes."[45]

In sum, in Linda Lai's hermeneutical approach, Chow's movies mark out a site that addresses the Hong Kong audience as an insider within the local community, and which preserves a space of freedom from below. In relating the movies to the larger context of the "1997" issue, her reading shows a reflectionist tendency and yet moves beyond the conventional position. She sees the movies as attempts — amid a growing fad in the marketplace — to preserve local culture through the rhetoric of subversion. She analyzes the enigmatic form of Chow's movies — the internal grammar of the text such as codes, images, styles, language, genre convention, the use of parody and so on — without delving into their ideological content. Yet precisely because of her relative inattention to ideological content, while popular film critics also situate Chow in the context of the "1997" issue, Lai's construction of Hong Kong people in the person of Chow does not shed much light on the specificities of his varied images. As has been shown, popular film critics saw in Chow a set of contradictory images, ranging from folk hero to embodiment of the Hong Kong dream, and from a celebration of the purely local to a ready embrace of the national and beyond. The question is, is he an anti-hero, a postmodern hero, or a folk hero sharing the hegemonic values in society?

A further and related question about ideology is: is Chow not a gendered subject after all? Don't his characters bespeak the voice, desires, dreams, fantasies and fears of a heterosexual male subject? In his characters, we see much about the parodying of power, banality, shrewdness, playfulness, dreams about success, and a celebration of the individual. Although the tone is sometimes not without a tinge of compassion, there is comparatively less on human bonds, deep affection, understanding and emotional experiences. Although women are neither absent nor uniform in his movies, it is always Chow who stands center stage and takes the plot lead, while intermittently reminding his audience of the typical heterosexual male fantasy about women. In the same vein, jokes about male homosexuality are quite commonplace in his movies.[46] All in all, masculinity as a set of gender qualities is manifested in a hierarchical order of social relationships, which differentiates not only between men and women, and between masculinity and femininity, but also among men of different positions and masculinities of different kinds.[47] After all, doesn't the image of anti-hero or folk hero in Chow reflect the masculinist order and hierarchy in our culture? If he represents someone off the streets of Hong Kong, it is because he represents the popular as opposed to the official or the elite sector of society. The popular, however, remains a site where hegemonic values may prevail under the rhetoric of subversion: the belief in economic success, the ideology of masculinism, the talk of monumental history and so on. Since both readings by Lai and by the popular critics are framed within the narrative of "1997," they tend only to see in his image(s) a typical Hong Kong person within a hegemonic framework, rather the gender specificity of a Hong Kong man in everyday social interaction. In the present masculinist discourse, Chow is both celebrated as a folk hero (or anti-hero) and forgotten as a gendered subject. This leaves us wondering whether in the critics' conscious attempt to construct the image of a Hong Kong person they are unconsciously naturalizing, and hence further reinforcing, the deeply embedded masculinist norms in our culture.

CONCLUSION

Some further remarks on the issue of masculinism. As we have seen, the critics we have discussed are aware of the link between nationalism and masculinity in the kung fu–action genre. A deconstructionist reading, in particular, is able to highlight the gendered principles on which the discourse of nationalism operates in those movies. They are therefore able to bring to view the rupture produced in the connection between the kung fu myth and the fantasy of a strong nation in more recent movies by Tsui Hark (*Once Upon a Time in China*, 1991) and Wong Kar-wai (*Ashes of Time*, 1994). However, the critics do not take us very far beyond this apparent association as well as rupture. Stephen Teo's reading tends to reinforce a masculinist discourse of nationalism and simply embraces it as reflecting the ethos of the times. Kwai-cheung Lo focuses more on the heroic male body than on the representations of masculinity or the underlying discourse of masculinism. Although he has brought to view the theme of longing for erotic love in Wong's movies, it is not clear whether the "excessive emotional drives" as well as the accompanying sense of futility in the characters suggests a rupture or reinforcement of the masculine culture. Certainly the male body has moved a long way from an invincible hero in Bruce Lee, but the issue of masculinism in relation to different forms of masculinity does not come up in his discussion of Hong Kong subjectivity. Similarly, Siu-leung Li's radical reading of the subversiveness of the Hong Kong cultural imaginary has severed the nationalism/kung fu link only to point us to the connection between the new transnational action genre and a more cosmopolitan Hong Kong culture. What remains barely discussed is the form of masculinity and the masculinist norm underlying this transnational genre and cosmopolitan culture.[48]

In a way, despite their differences, local film critics from different camps similarly offer a politicized reading of Hong Kong movies in relation to the larger socio-political context. They tend to privilege dominant political issues such as nationalism, localism, and transnationalism. In this way, they overlook the deeper gender dimension in the self-invention of Hong Kong. If their analysis has succeeded in bringing to view the heroic male body as part of the self-invention process, film criticism of comedy would tend to submerge the issue of masculinity altogether in favor of an a-gendered reflectionist or hermeneutical approach to issues of culture and identity. As I have suggested, this reveals an under-conceptualization of masculinity in local film criticism, and also a taken-for-grantedness as well as an implicit hierarchical ordering of gender qualities in prevailing cultural discourses.

· 12 ·

Women's Reception of Mainstream Hong Kong Cinema

Day Wong

From the 1950s to the 1960s melodramas were popular in Hong Kong's film culture. A group of young female stars ruled the screen. Later, action films and comedies became the leading genres. This shift marked a phasing out of female-audience-oriented productions and their replacement with those of prominent male taste and ideology. Early media critiques, which focused primarily on image-based textual analysis, were concerned with the misrepresentation of gender and the reproduction of dominant ideologies in popular culture. However, such studies have been increasingly questioned on two grounds. First, media messages are diverse, diffuse and contradictory. It is difficult to categorize texts as purely celebratory of the dominant order or critical of it. Second, instead of being passively indoctrinated with the dominant ideologies, viewers often appropriate the media as a site of meaning construction, actively engaging and even contesting images and themes of gender domination. If we are concerned with how cultural forms work ideologically or politically, we need to understand texts as they are understood by audiences. Rather than assuming that women are passive receivers of media content, I examine the selective and creative ways in which women engage with images of gender in mainstream Hong Kong cinema. Drawing on fifteen in-depth interviews of women whose ages ranged from 25 to 50, I compare and contrast the diverse ways in which women looked at the stars and derived pleasure from movie-watching. Specifically, this chapter will focus on their experiences with two different genres: the melodramas that starred Connie Chan Po-chu (Chen Baozhu) and Josephine Siao Fong-fong (Xiao Fangfang) in the 1960s, and the action movies of Bruce Lee (Li Xiaolong) and Jackie Chan

(Cheng Long) in the 1970s and 1980s. I argue against the model of the female spectator understood solely as a textual effect, and do not take women to be a homogeneous group united by an essential womanness. I foreground the social dimension of spectatorship and offer a differentiated understanding of female spectatorship.

As I will show, women are historically specific social subjects who are situated at the points of intersection of a number of different discourses about the world. The effects of media are often mediated by the discourses surrounding them as well as their lived experiences of being females in different historical periods. In reconstructing the memories and experiences of these female audiences, I seek to demonstrate the complex interplay of text, context, and discourse.

TEXT, CONTEXT, AND DISCOURSE

When second-wave feminism hit its stride in the 1960s and 1970s, popular media culture often came under attack as a site of gender inequality. Feminist critics not only charged that the representation of gender roles in film and television reinforced the dominant beliefs that legitimate male domination of women, but also began to develop frameworks that examined audience reception. Laura Mulvey's 1975 essay "Visual pleasure and narrative cinema," which is a psychoanalytic-informed account, introduces the notion of the male gaze to explain how the audience is positioned in an inherently masculine manner.[1] She argues that in Hollywood films with the male protagonist as the controlling figure, the spectator looks with the camera that looks at the hero who looks at the woman. The woman is constructed as the object of male desire, and the ideal spectator is constructed as the voyeuristic male. Mary Ann Doane elaborates the psychoanalytic perspective by adding that the binary opposition at work is not only an opposition between passivity and activity (between the passive feminine object of the look and the active masculine control of the look), but also an opposition between proximity and distance in relation to image.[2] In her view, a reversal of the male gaze is not likely to be possible, for a precondition for voyeurism is a physical as well a psychological distance between the bearer and the object of the look. In early childhood little girls recognize sexual sameness and identify with their mothers to the extent that separation and distance become problematic. According to Doane, female specificity is characterized by proximity, and thus women lack the prerequisite of voyeurism. As a result, the female spectator can only be thought of as narcissistically immersed in the cinematic female object, or as suffering masculinization by identifying with the male protagonist.

Does the introduction of a female character as central to a story have any impact on the modes of cinematic pleasure and identification? In a postscript to the 1975 essay, Mulvey begins to question her earlier idea that identification of Hollywood films can only impose a masculine point of view on spectators.[3] In her discussion of films in which a woman central protagonist is shown to be unable to achieve a stable feminine identity, she argues that rather than simply a signifier of sexuality, the presence of the woman protagonist enables spectators to identify with the different sides of desires and aspirations of the woman protagonist. Tania Modleski can be regarded as the pioneer providing a systematic analysis of women's genres and the subject positions that are created for female audiences.[4] She points out that soap operas serve to affirm the primacy of the family not by presenting an ideal family, but by portraying a family in constant turmoil and appealing to the spectator to be understanding and tolerant of the many evils that go on within that family. Hence, in soap operas the spectator is constructed as the idealized mother who is always sympathetic, tolerant, and forgiving. Taking up the subject positions offered in these media, female spectators are socialized into identification with the very patriarchal ideologies that reproduce their subordinate status.

What must be noted is the aforementioned studies tend to assume that women are passive receivers of media and the subject positions they inhabit are problematic. Stuart Hall's essay "Encoding/decoding"[5] marks a major theoretical shift because it emphasizes context rather than text, and the active rather than passive viewer. Hall contends that readers can take a dominant-hegemonic position and decode the message in a way that reproduces dominant ideology. However, readers may also be able to adopt negotiated codes and even oppositional codes. In these cases, readers are aware of the limitations of the dominant code and choose to decode the message within alternative frameworks of reference. In light of Hall's argument, it cannot be overlooked that some women are capable of re-appropriating texts and pleasures renounced by a more pessimistic analysis of patriarchy's success. For instance, some female academics assert that through a strategy of "reading against the grain," they can adopt alternative readings and obtain marginalized pleasures within dominant media texts.[6] If female academics are also members of audiences, their experience reminds us that similar meanings and pleasures are most likely available to other women.

In a study of women's memories of female Hollywood stars, Jackie Stacey finds that audiences' identification with the stars involves not simply the passive reproduction of existing femininities, but rather an active production of desired identities.[7] She points out that in some categories of cinematic identification such as devotion, adoration and worship, the star is at the center and the audience is only included in so far as she facilitates the construction of the star's idealized image. However, in other categories of identificatory fantasies, the relationship between the star's image and the audience's identity can be rather relational and fluid. For instance, escapism or transcendence is a form of identification that allows the audience to take pleasure in escaping into the world of Hollywood cinema, and indeed in taking on the star's identity. In other forms of identification, the audience expresses a strong desire for the transformation of her own identity and may even take action to become more like the star. Hollywood stars offer not only simple role models of sexual attractiveness, but also a source of fantasy of a more powerful and confident self. Through extra cinematic identificatory practices including imitating stars' appearances, singing and dancing, a new feminine identity is produced, one that combines an aspect of the star with the audience's own self. In this light, identification can no longer be conceptualized as a process reproducing sameness and confirming existing identities. In contrast to the first form of identification, in which the audience's own identity is relatively marginal, the star in this process becomes more marginal and is only relevant in so far as the star's identity relates to the audience's own identity. This form of identification opens up diverse possibilities in the ways audiences engage and appropriate the meanings of the stars' images.

Stacey's audience study does not only draw our attention to the diverse modes of cinematic pleasure, but also highlights the importance of the historical contexts in giving rise to specific forms of identification with the star. Cinema-going in wartime Britain was a pleasurable escape from domestic womanhood into a utopian alternative represented by Hollywood stars, while the postwar expansion in consumption promoted extracinematic identificatory practices.[8] In a study of women's use of video recorders, Ann Gray also focuses on context, and this time it is the context in which viewing takes place that is under scrutiny.[9] She notes that women watching videos alone or with other women had experiences that were very different from those of women watching videos with their male partners. For instance, when women watched a video together, they talked about the genre in relation to their male partners. They experienced a sense of the "power of definition" within the partnerships, and the ways in which women themselves think of their own pleasures.

In emphasizing the importance of context, one should be careful not to abandon the textual focus entirely.[10] The split between text and context, or between spectator as the ideal viewer and social audience as the real viewer, needs to be addressed if we want to gain a full understanding of what happens when women watch films. Rather than conceiving the spectator as interpellated by text, Annette Kuhn suggests a move into theories of discourse to understand the construction of spectators.[11] Both spectators and social audience should be regarded as discursive constructs. Since the state of a discursive formation is not constant, Kuhn argues, it can be apprehended only by means of inquiring into specific instances or conjunctures.

Female spectators should therefore be seen as social subjects inscribed by various historically specific discursive formations such as gender, class, and ethnicity. Rather than constructing woman as a singular and stable category, we need to look into the differences between women. As Elizabeth V. Spelman argues in *Inessential Woman*, "Though all women are women, no woman is only a woman."[12] Much feminist work has examined the experiences of housewives in conceptualizing women's reception of popular media. Women cannot be equated with housewives: they are divided by their socio-economic status, ethnicity, sexuality, etc. Gender is not a pre-existing category that determines an individual's behavior. Rather, being a woman or a man requires continuous work. As Judith Butler pointed out, maleness and femaleness are "performative in the sense that the essence or identity that they otherwise purport to express are fabrications manufactured and sustained through corporal signs and other discursive means".[13] Gender should be conceived not as a fixed property of individuals but as an ongoing process by which gendered subjects are constituted. Movie watching should be seen in terms of an active engagement and reproduction of changing gender identities. While there are "masculine" and "feminine" positions in fantasy, Constance Penley states, men and women do not have to assume those positions according to their assigned genders.[14] They are subjects who can oscillate through a number of identificatory positions.

Women should not be seen as a homogeneous group. Media content, too, does not contain one single message. In the studies of audience reception, sometimes texts are treated as unified, reproducing hegemonic ideology without contradiction. Hall's encoding/decoding model foregrounds the diverse possibilities of reading. What the model leaves relatively intact is the notion of a text's dominant ideology. As Judith Mayne argues, individual texts cannot be any more easily categorized as purely 'dominant' than readers can.[15] It should not be overlooked that texts often display a polysemic nature, and feature competing and contradictory discourses. The subject positions that are created by a text are not only multiple, but also in a state of flux. The exact terms of the subject positions are constituted through competing discourses about femininity and masculinity. They can be transformed in historical discursive formations and among specific viewing contexts.[16]

I will now move on to the theoretically informed empirical sites to study spectatorship. Hong Kong women's reception of the melodramas of Connie Chan Po-chu and Josephine Siao Fong-fong and the action movies of Bruce Lee and Jackie Chan will be examined. Feminist critics have reclaimed melodramas as a worthwhile subject for analysis, for this genre's associations with subject matters (the family, personal relationship, and love) that are central to women's lives. However, critics are also critical of the subject position of the idealized mother created by melodramas. Mulvey's attack on the visual pleasure of Hollywood cinema raises the concern of whether the gaze in mainstream action films can only be a masculinized gaze. To gaze at and take pleasure in the images of the melodramas and action movies, are female audiences simply interpellated into the subject positions that confirm passivity as woman's lot? Do the movies construct only one, fixed position for female audiences? Could female audiences construct other positions that coincide with their own experiences, and which are at variance with dominant gender ideologies? How is women's engagement with gender images in popular media influenced by the historical discursive formations of class and ethnicity?

WATCHING FEMALE STARS AND MELODRAMAS OF THE 1960S

The film industry in Hong Kong witnessed its early period of prosperity in the 1950s and 1960s, when an influx of refugees from mainland China and an inflow of capital and entrepreneurship provided the impetus for the industrialization of the colony. To cater to growing numbers of female cinema-goers, which included factory workers and housewives who sometimes worked part-time to supplement their family incomes, a group of young female stars came to rule Cantonese cinema. Among them, Connie Chan Po-chu and Josephine Siao Fong-fong were the most prominent in the 1960s. Chan, as the girl next door, became the idol of lower-middle-class girls, while Siao, fashionably dressed and proficient in popular song and dance, attracted college girls.

It could be argued that the images of Connie Chan and Josephine Siao are constructed around a central notion — that of the dutiful daughter. The film *Eternal Love* (Qicai Hubugui), released in 1966 and directed by Lee Tit (Li Tie), is a representative example in which Chan and Siao play the characters of obedient children who win their parents over by devotion and duty. Another film, entitled *The Dutiful Daughter* (Xiaonü Zhuzhu) (dir. Qin Wantao, 1966), starring Connie Chan Po-chu, is self-explanatory. The film stresses a woman's duty not just to her mother, but also to her teacher, who represents a father figure. While the melodramas of the 1960s had happy Confucianist endings that reaffirmed traditional concepts of filial piety, the theme of filial piety, as Stephen Teo notes, often coexisted with a counter theme of the transgression of the young.[17] Chan and Siao played the role of the transgressor in such movies. Examples include Chan's character in *Young, Pregnant and Unmarried* (Yunü tianding) (dir. Chor Yuen, 1968) pretending to be pregnant out of wedlock to help her sister who really is pregnant, and Siao's acting as an alienated youth who finally resorts to violence to seek revenge in *Teddy Girls* (Feinü zhengzhuan) (dir. Long Gang, 1969). The youth movies of Chan and Siao portray the young as independent and enjoying their freedom and way of life, but at the same time call for a return of the young rebels to the filial fold.

The independence signified by Chan and Siao finds its most obvious manifestation in the characters of the woman warrior and the female Bond. Chan and Siao embody these characters with intelligence, competence, self-confidence, and strong physical traits. They are women who fight and defeat enemies, who have the power to overcome all odds. Sek Kei argues that while this is the era of the weak male and the strong female, the strong woman is at the same time a weak woman.[18] Sek explains the wide acceptance of the model of the strong woman warrior through the meritocratic system of examinations in Chinese civilization, whereby men could attain fame and profit. However, in emphasizing the civil strain over the martial, men came to be perceived as weak bookworms. The tradition of the weak male hero, Sek states, gives rise to the classic role of the ideal Chinese woman: one who is both a weak woman and a strong warrior, and one who can fight the male yet pose no threat to his authority. Sek argues that these lady knights errant fight not for female liberation but to preserve the authority of men. Arguing along the same lines, Sam Ho concludes that no matter how independent she is, no matter how superior she is to the men around her, the fighting woman must eventually return to her dutiful position in the family.[19]

Preoccupied with the conservative meanings of these films, both Sek and Ho seem to lose sight of the diverse and contradictory meanings of femininity created by the movies of the 1960s. While the woman warrior usually achieves union with her man, the love relation does not necessarily imply a defeat or a taming of the strong woman. As Lisbeth Ku points out, many films hint at the continued partnership between lovers in upholding justice in the future, and place the emphasis more on portrayals of independence than on the final resolution of love and marriage.[20] In view of the diverse meanings of the texts, different readings of the films are indeed possible. Whether these films should be condemned because of their relationship of complicity with patriarchy cannot be predetermined without listening to the voices of the social audience.

These female stars and melodramas were popular in the 1960s, when women were recruited to join the labor force in the first phase of industrialization. While it was the first time that many women could earn a wage, they could not simply keep the money for their own use. Janet Salaff points out that the centripetal family was able to gather, allocate, and use its members' contributions for the purpose of economic survival and betterment.[21] In Salaff's view, the harsh conditions of this phase of industrialization — low wages combined with the lack of welfare provisions from the government — rendered it necessary for the people to rely on family and kin for economic assistance. The family thus became the center of individuals' concern and loyalty. In a study of twenty-eight working daughters, Salaff describes how they made sacrifices in their education and career, and contributed a substantial part of their income to the well-being of the family. Under the influence of patriarchal thought, daughters usually quit school and worked to supplement the family's income and enable their brothers to continue with their education.[22] Despite their contributions, they were not expected to be the decision-makers of the family. Salaff seems to share the concern of Sek and Ho about the tyranny of patriarchy. However, I would like to highlight that, as seen from Salaff's study, employment enabled women to keep a small amount of money for their own use, and build up their own circles of friends with whom they could share their leisure activities. Far from being captive under the force of patriarchy, women could negotiate space for their own autonomy.

Lai and Wong, two of my respondents, aged 52 and 50 respectively, were typical working daughters in the 1960s. Lai was a fan of Connie Chan Po-chu, whereas Wong had a taste for Josephine Siao Fong-fong. Their schismic sentiments for the two stars can be understood in light of the historical discursive formation of class in Hong Kong society. Lai quit school and worked in an electronics factory to support her family. Wong also worked in factories, but managed to study at an evening school. Later, Wong was able to leave her blue-collar occupation and work as a salesperson and an office assistant. In the eyes of Lai and Wong, Po-chu and Fong-fong had rather different images. They did not see the two idols uniformly under the banner of the dutiful daughter. Wong, a fan of Fong-fong, described the two stars in this way:

> The fans of Po-chu were dressed in a simple way. Po-chu seemed to represent the factory girl while Fong-fong was seen by other people as belonging to the so-called higher class. I liked Fong-fong not because of this. I liked her because she was trendy; she had character. Her look was more trendy than Po-chu's. I imitated her way of dressing, wearing tight pants, growing my hair long, and wearing it in a ponytail with a big bow.

Wong did not admit that her taste for Fong-fong was directly related to the class symbolism attached to the idol. However, she also quickly claimed that she could be classified as middle-class at that time. In this way, Wong implicitly admitted that she and Fong-fong shared the same class. Fong-fong's image is indeed different to Po-chu's. Po-chu has straight and long hair and often wears trousers. Her image of an indigenous girl enabled her to gain widespread identification among working-class females. Fong-fong, being tall and slim, and occasionally wearing short skirts, presented a more sexy and elegant image. Her Westernized image, as Ku notes, provided a site for the nurturing of the middle-class dream.[23] What should be noticed is that class is in a historical process of making and remaking. In the 1960s the notion of 'the middle-class' was unpopular. Only when increasing numbers of people received university education and entered into the professional world in the 1980s did we begin to see a more common use of the term 'middle class' in describing the status and way of life of some people. After Wong completed her secondary education at evening school she left her blue-collar work and became a clerk. Wong now came to identify herself as belonging to the middle class, like many of those who worked their way up from the working class in the past few decades. In recalling her identification with the idol, Wong also recollected the memory of the realization of a middle-class dream.

Apart from imitating Fong-fong's style of dressing, Wong learnt the popular dance that Fong-fong performs in her films. "At that time I was like a film's title," said Wong, "*I love Ah-go-go*". Working daughters in those days were able to participate in leisure activities with their friends. Their allegiance to the family did not prevent them developing their own circles and hobbies. Wong was no slave. She enjoyed social dance and went to parties with her friends. Being a dutiful and yet independent daughter was not merely a theme of the melodramas of the 1960s. It was a role with meanings that Wong had to negotiate in her everyday life. She fulfilled the duties of a daughter by contributing financially to the family and avoiding open conflict. However, despite her family members' objections, she did not give up her hobbies, and neither did she change her way of thinking. It is true that Wong, as a dutiful daughter, never attempted to overthrow the patriarchal family, but she succeeded in preserving space for her leisure and for her own life. The form of femininity from Fong-fong's movies that she inhabited was one that emphasized not simply rebellion, but self-assertiveness and confidence in her own judgment:

> My elder brother scolded me for coming home late. He cut my clothes, saying "these kinds of clothes are just for *ah-fei* (delinquents)." They were short skirts. It was the fashion at that time. He thought it was dangerous to hang out late and wear short skirts … I, of course, did not agree. But I did try to come home early in the following weeks.
>
> I went to parties and made friends with some of the guys I met. My family did not approve of partygoing, but I did not let them know where I had been … It's true that there could have been bad guys, but I did not worry. We went there in a group and we had to make judgments for ourselves.

Lai, who worked in an electronics factory for eight years after quitting school, was attracted to Po-chu. While Po-chu sometimes played the male role in opera films and martial arts serials, Lai's identification did not seem to be related to any erotic fantasy of the hero. Lai said that the name Po-chu (lit. precious pearl) itself signified femininity. This was different from the case of Yam Kim-fai (Ren Jianhui) (lit. sword and brightness), a female opera star whose gender identity was disguised not just by the male role that she constantly played, but also by the masculine name she used. Lai treated Po-chu's cross-gender performance as proof of a talented performer able to play multiple roles. Instead of a trans-gender identification, what made Lai a fan of Po-chu had to do with a sense of identification Po-chu provided for working-class females. Although Po-chu was often dressed in a plain and unadorned manner, Lai commented that Po-chu was more beautiful than Fong-fong because she was more gentle and approachable. The idol, instead of being someone to be admired and gazed at from afar, seemed to have become one of them, one who shared their way of life. The identification with the star idol empowered Lai. Being a working-class woman was no longer a fact to be concealed. Rather, the life of the working class was to be affirmed and celebrated. The *Movie-Fan Princess* (Yingmi gongzhu) (dir. Wong Yiu, 1966), in which Po-chu plays a factory girl, still captured her imagination. Lai described the film enthusiastically:

> The life of factory girls was presented in a realistic way. We were like the characters in the film. We brought our own rice pots to the factory. We ate together, we chatted and laughed together. We were so happy. It made me feel that being a factory girl was not a bad thing.

Melodramas are often popular among female audiences. They provide satisfaction through placing emotions, domestic affairs, and interpersonal relationships, which are often discarded as unimportant or non-rational, on center stage. Feminists caution us that the ideological effect of melodramas reinforces the belief that family and marriage are the destiny of women. However, while love and romance are a major theme, melodramas do not focus exclusively on the relationship between women and men. Melodramas also portray strong relationships between women. The emphasis on female friendship and bonding promotes the importance of sisterhood. Whether a viewer reads melodramas in terms of the theme of sisterhood depends on the context in which the viewing is taking place.[24] Wong went to movies with her co-workers. In their factory workplace, movies were sometimes shown on television. They watched movies together even at work. Her life was intermingled with the movie texts. Her movie-watching experience and the close relationships that she had with other factory girls enabled her to identify with the sisterhood portrayed in the film.

Wong's experience as a married mother allowed her to make a comparison that further reinforced her belief that her years spent working as a factory girl were a golden era. When she was single and living without men, her life was most pleasurable and memorable. Though Wong once believed, as many women do, that marriage and motherhood were her dream, she came to realize their mythical side. While she had to fulfill her duties as mother and wife, she did not take up the subject positions of "the ideal mother" or "the dutiful wife" that were provided by melodramas. Instead, she gained pleasure from watching female bonding and friendship. The text worked side by side with her lived experience to produce a discursive effect that disrupted the romanticized, but almost mandatory, codes of marriage and family. The form of femininity that she inhabited and re-created from the film was one that emphasized sisterhood over marriage and family.

> Like other girls of my age I used to believe that marriage would bring happiness, but after I got married this turned out to be very untrue. Though I did not have to work outside, it was such hard work to take care of my first child. She was often ill and cried in the middle of the night. Because we lived in a rented room, I had to carry her outside the house so as not to wake my husband. I can't remember how many times I cried in those days.

As we have seen, being born in the 1950s, Lai and Wong were able to identify with the female stars of the 1960s. My younger respondents might have seen the movies on TV, but did not identify with the stars. May, who was 25, said that for her Chan and Siao were just two good-looking stars who danced from time to time in their movies. She did not regard the stars as symbols of independence. Her lack of any strong impression about the stars could be explained by the viewing context. May watched the movies on TV when she was doing school work at home. She was not involved in the watching. All she wanted was some noise to alleviate her boredom. The meanings of the characters or the stars, therefore, cannot be seen as fixed. The viewing of the melodramas of the 1960s by women of different generations at different historical times and in different can give rise to entirely different interpretations.

Women from the same historical period could also be divided by their socio-economic conditions or class consciousness. Middle-class symbolism bound Wong and her idol Fong-fong, whereas the working-class imagery united Lai and Po-chu. In their identification with the idols, Wong fulfilled her middle-class dream and Lai consolidated her working-class awareness. Critics may worry that the melodramas of the 1960s created the subject position of a dutiful daughter. However, Wong's and Lai's reception did not emphasize the dutiful role that confirms suffering as women's lot. Rather, the two women constructed meanings that destabilized patriarchal ideology. Wong inhabited the position of the self-confident, independent subject who never gives up the attempt to cultivate space for autonomy in an oppressive environment. Lai came to affirm that female bonding and life before marriage were treasurable. While the discourse of women's liberation was not made available to them at that time, they had appropriated notions of female independence and sisterhood to resist the workings of patriarchal force. The reception of such melodramas should be seen as a process that can be enabling rather than constraining, empowering rather than oppressive.

WATCHING THE ACTION MOVIES OF THE 1970S AND 1980S

During the 1970s, action films dominated the local screens and began to influence international markets. The popularity of this genre marked a fundamental change in Hong Kong cinema: action was valued over drama, and male stars replaced female stars as the main box-office appeal. According to Sek, the dominance of the male hero in the 1970s rescued Chinese men from a weak male destiny.[25] The male hero was exacting his revenge for decades of negative imagery, but it was overdone. Sek observes that there were many problems in the portrayal of male-female relations, with the spread of misogyny an unhealthy tendency. In the 1970s Bruce Lee's assertion of a strong, muscular Chinese hero succeeded in promoting martial arts film both locally and overseas. His movies deployed a discourse of macho Chinese nationalism and presented a powerful, asexual hero. There is little emphasis on romance or female protagonists in his films. In *The Way of the Dragon* (Menglong guojiang) (dir. Bruce Lee, 1972), a European prostitute tries to seduce Lee but he immediately leaves when he discovers her intentions. There is a traditional Chinese saying: "Heroes can hardly get through the frontier gate guarded by a beautiful woman." It follows that real heroes are those who can resist a woman's temptation.

If women were not seducers, then they were being rescued. In Jackie Chan's action movies, which became popular from the late 1970s, women are often girlish. This treatment designates women the roles of both decoration and weak victim who needs protection. In the two *Police Story* (Jingcha gushi) (dir. Jackie Chan, 1985 and 1988) films, heterosexual romance not only helps to define an adult masculine identity, but also marks the beginning of myriad problems.[26] Substantial screen time is given to the comic demonstration of women's incompetence or women-as-chaos. If women are represented as a troublesome presence, and if heterosexual romance is portrayed as the beginning of problems, then how would female audiences gain pleasure from watching these action movies?

Before answering these questions, we need to ask whether Chan's movies really contain a unified, unambiguous sexist message. Unlike Bruce Lee's invincible hero, Chan is an ordinary hero who avoids danger, expresses feelings of fear and pain, and who can be defeated, especially at the beginning. Chan often assumes a stance that parodies the convention of male heroism. When Chan briefly steps into the boastful male-hero role, a female character or a villain quickly deflates his attempt to assume the position of dominant masculinity.[27] For example, *Police Story* features a comedy sequence in which Chan tries to impress a friend with anecdotes about his controlling status in a love relationship, unaware that his girlfriend can hear every inflated word. His sweetheart suddenly reveals her presence and mashes a cake into his face. Because the messages of Chan's movies are multiple and contradictory, this may give rise to a realm of possibilities in terms of female audience reception.

How do female audiences derive meaning from Bruce Lee and Jackie Chan movies? Do they take up the position of a vulnerable feminine subject? How do they engage with the hero images in these movies? Most of my respondents had watched Lee's and Chan's movies, but they could recall little about the female characters. They referred to female characters as decorations and could hardly identify with them. Some textual analyses, when charging popular media with maintaining sexist ideas, wrongly assume that audiences will automatically be affected by sexist content. From such an assumption emerges a view of the female audience as passive individuals incapable of recognizing the force of dominant ideology. My respondents' replies demonstrate that viewers are selective in their identification, and able to contest the images of gender domination. Because female characters mainly function as foils to make heroes noticeable, the respondents chose to focus their attention on the male protagonists when they watched these movies.

Most respondents preferred Jackie Chan's movies to those of Bruce Lee. However, they considered Lee a real hero while having reservations about Chan's hero status. Two reasons were given for this. "Lee was a hero because he introduced Chinese martial arts to both local and overseas people," said May. In Lee's movies, his supremacy over Japanese karate and Western boxing symbolize a victory of Chinese kung fu in the international arena. May's interpretation went beyond the text to view Lee's popularizing of Chinese kung fu with Western audiences as heroic. "A hero should be one who has done something for the people," she added. The second reason, given by Kuen, is Lee's construction of kung fu as a philosophy and a way of life for understanding himself and his existence. The immortality of the hero Lee lies not only in his image of an invincible fighter, but also in the philosophy associated with his unique style of kung fu, Jeet Kune Do (Jiequan dao). However, recognition of his hero status was not transformed into a sense of identification.

Emily, 40, had no doubt Lee was a hero, but was critical of the nationalistic element associated with his hero image. She commented that "the image is very Mainland". Emily indicated that she tended to admire the West rather than identify with the Chinese nation. She preferred Western hero stars to their Chinese counterparts. In the last few decades, Hong Kong has rapidly transformed into an active member of the international economy and become quite Westernized. The disparity in the levels of development and standard of living between Hong Kong and the Mainland generated a sense of superiority among Hong Kong people, some of whom manifestly held mainland Chinese in contempt. This prejudice also manifested itself in the television programs of the 1970s that depicted newly arrived immigrants from the mainland as impolite and uncivilized, as objects of ridicule. The construction of local identity often involved a juxtaposition of mainland Chinese and Hongkongese. Politically, Chinese communism was repulsive to many Hong Kong people. After the June 4 incident in 1989, which saw the Chinese government using military force to crack down on student protestors, they became more mistrustful of the Chinese government. Many saw democratization as a means of bolstering Hong Kong's autonomy against Chinese interference. The resumption of Chinese sovereignty of Hong Kong in 1997 only heightened their anxiety about loss of freedom and rights. Research shows that more locals have adopted the Hongkongese identity than the Chinese identity: half of the respondents chose Hongkongese as their primary identity, while 30 percent chose Chinese. Those with higher-education backgrounds or socio-economic status were more inclined to regard themselves as Hongkongese.[28] Emily, with a middle-class background, was among them. She constructed her ethnic identity as Hongkongese rather than Chinese. The critical distance that Emily kept from Lee's heroism signifies the critical distance that she kept from Chinese nationalism.

The other reason for respondents to stay aloof from Lee's heroism had to do with the dominant masculinity embedded in it. Lee's assertion of a strong, muscular Chinese hero produces unsettling effects among Western audiences, particularly in view of a history of soft images in which both Chinese men and women have been represented as passive and compliant.[29] The image has been able to win over the hearts of Westerners owing to its congruence with the convention of Hollywood's male hero. Lee's movies glorify the beauty of muscle, physical strength, and strong masculinity. The local female audience, however, did not seem to admire this hypermasculinized form of hero. Specifically, Lai expressed her dislike for Lee's way of displaying his muscles. "He liked to shake his muscles in his chest and arms. That is disgusting." Lai also hated the voice that Lee used when fighting. Lee adopted a high-pitched whine similar to the sound made by an animal that is excited or in agony. The voice created the effect that something violent, and probably bloody, was going to happen. Most respondents did not enjoy Lee's movies. Emily's response was typical: "I don't like it because the fights are too real, too cruel." They preferred Jackie Chan's movies to those of Bruce Lee, for in their eyes the former were comic and the latter violent. Lee and Chan present two different hero images: "one glowering menacingly; the other comically cute".[30] For female audiences to take pleasure in and relate positively to the hero image, the masculinity embodied therein needs to be of a non-violent type. My female respondents refused to place themselves in any collaborated position with a violent form of masculinity. Rather than endorsing the opposition of hard male and soft female, they opted for males to be like them, soft and non-violent.

The popularity of Jackie Chan's non-violent action movies among female viewers can be understood in light of their role in family life and, more specifically, the discourses of motherhood surrounding them. As Hong Kong becomes modernized, children and youngsters are increasingly seen as not only valuable assets but also vulnerable groups in need of intensive care and protection. Mothers not only take care of their physical and emotional needs, but are also assigned the responsibility of protecting them from any bad influence. The credo that has been widely circulated is violence and sex are not suitable for children. Lee's asexual hero type does not create difficulty for mothers, yet his real kung fu and almost-real fights worry them. My respondents thought Chan's movies were suitable for children and were something the family could watch together. A contrast was made with the experience of watching Bruce's Lee's films. "When watching Lee's films on television with my children, I have to explain to them that the fights are not real; they are just special effects," Kuen said, adding that she did so to prevent them imitating the acts. Why women have no taste for Lee's films, or why "too real" is a problem, should therefore be understood in light of the historically specific discursive formation of the motherly role. It is not so much a universal psychic reaction of women to avoid Lee's kung fu movies; rather, their self-understanding of being protectors of children from dangerous influences enables them to be cautious about the movies. Kuen added that she preferred comedies now, though when she was young she enjoyed melodramas. She sometimes watched Stephen Chow (Zhou Xingchi)'s comic movies with her children. She said that this was a relaxed and happy experience, though she admitted that she did not always understand his sense of humor.

Compared with Bruce Lee's movies, Chan's movies are more able to provide pleasure to viewers. The respondents said that they enjoyed watching Chan's acrobatic feats. On the one hand, they were comic and non-violent; on the other hand, they displayed unique skill. In fight sequences, the "perpetual motion technique" can be identified.[31] Its premise is the maintenance of continuous body motion throughout the entire fight sequence to give the impression of non-stop action. In *Drunken Master 2* (Nanbei zuiquan) (dir. Yuen Wo-ping, 1979) for example, Chan demonstrated uninterrupted action for nearly five minutes, during which he leapt, punched, and kicked his way around a spacious teahouse to evade his attackers. In explaining why she liked Jackie Chan's movies, Linda said that "this is exciting, leaping up and down. It is humorous." The excitement is unlike that of Bruce Lee, which makes one feel tense and horrified. Chan's combat scenes showcase his instant reflexes and rubbery contortions. In fight scenes, Chan always comically exaggerates panic. Stunning exercises in pacing, his fights and chases avoid looking mechanical by the display of emotion. Chan's facial expression and, in general, the comic treatment of escape and flight, allow the audience to find humor in thrilling scenes. Displays of violence are transformed into enjoyable comedies.

While no respondents openly regarded Chan as a hero, some engaged with the policeman character that Chan plays in the two *Police Story* movies and showed sympathy for or admiration of the character. Processes of audience identification can therefore be examined. Some feminist work assumes that identification only confines women to the position of object of male desire or protection. In refuting this assumption, Penley, among others, argues that rather than being constrained to the position of a passive object, female spectators are able to make identifications across gender boundaries.[32] In engaging with Jackie Chan's movies, female viewers did not put themselves in the female protagonist's place; neither did they take up the position of the male gaze when they identified with the male protagonist. Instead, some viewers identified with Chan's hero position in their own, non-sexist ways.

Sammy, 28, observed that Chan's role in the two *Police Story* movies presents a form of heroism. Its premises include an untiring dedication to one's goal and mission and a willingness to uphold justice at all costs. "Starring as a policeman, Chan is very involved in the investigation of crime. Though his superior has issued him with a warning and even suspended him from work, he still continues his investigation." Sammy added, "This kind of person can hardly be found in the world." Sammy had been able to admire the character that Chan plays in the movie, but she also commented that if people like this were to exist in the real world, they would be regarded as fools. "In real life, one cannot confront one's superiors. Nor can an employee make mistakes that cost his employer, and in this case, the government." Sammy's identification with Chan's character can be traced to her role as an employee. Sammy was a clerical worker at a university. In real life, she had to avoid confronting the head of her section. With the gradual disappearance of the university's tenure system, staff no longer had job security. They had to be regularly appraised by the head. If they wanted to keep their jobs, they could not argue with the head. Sammy had to live with this oppression in her everyday life. Watching *Police Story* provided her with a kind of comfort and compensation. In the movie, when facing a formidable enemy, Chan is not afraid to strike back. The story ends with the success of the policeman-hero in capturing the criminals, which implies a combination of rewards such as admiration from peers and recognition of superiors.

The identification process that Sammy experienced did not entail worship or adoration, but rather, transcendence.[33] In a feminized, low-rank, white-collar job, her sense of control, autonomy, and satisfaction was limited. The text offered a utopia of autonomy and justice, which was utterly different from the one that Sammy inhabited. Engaging Chan's character enabled her to achieve a temporary loss of self in an ideal other. This transcends all of life's hesitations and inhibitions. The text provides a fantasy world for audiences to seek comfort from despair and revenge against the real world. While the pleasure can be regarded as escapist, it is debatable whether it should simply be conceived of as a sign of complicity with women's oppression in the workplace. In addressing the politics of pleasure, Janice Radway argues that reading romance can be seen as a hidden protest against patriarchal culture.[34] The texts offer fantasies of a utopia in which women are nurtured by men, thus compensating for the nurturing that they provide themselves. Such escapist pleasure, in Radway's view, does have potential. The task of the feminist critic is to exploit the threads of dissatisfaction that are expressed in reading romances and help readers to understand that a better world is possible in which the vicarious pleasure supplied by romance reading is unnecessary.[35] In light of Radway's argument, one should not deprive the viewer's hidden protest against the real world of its potential to change the social conditions of life.

Another respondent, Fanny, 39, experienced a rather different form of identification. For Fanny, the two *Police Story* movies depicted a hero who had a mission and strove for justice at all costs. She felt that somehow this was an ideal model for her to follow. Unlike Sammy's comment that the character would be regarded as silly in the real world, Fanny believed that this is the kind of person society needs. She recalled her social participation in the 1980s when the draft of the Basic Law[36] was underway:

> Chan's movies somehow reinforced my sense of justice … During the 80s I joined a social concern group to fight for a democratic political system in Hong Kong. We held seminars on public education and submitted our position papers to the Government. When the draft of the Basic Law appeared we were disappointed to see its failure in embodying democracy. We felt that this was a long battle; we had to fight for it.

The process of identification was articulated in relation to the similarity between the self and the ideal. The viewer imagined herself as ideal through similarity with the star with whom she identified. The identification process did not involve a denial of self in favor of praising the screen hero, nor did it give rise to escapist pleasure that resulted in a temporary loss of self. Rather, the boundary between the self and the hero-ideal was fluid and relational.[37] In confirming her identity and mission, the identification empowered the viewer to achieve her goal.

By the 1990s, Fanny was influenced by feminist discourse and became more involved in the women's movement. She then read the hero image of Chan as a kind of back-up in her fight to promote gender equality. Fanny said that while she could not remember well the stories of the movies, she felt that the hero image was close to her every time when she heard the *Police Story* theme song, which was popular at the time. The police force's public-affairs department used the song in its television programs. It seemed that Chan's hero image was everywhere, urging people to report crime. Fanny liked the song's tune and lyrics. For her, it was a work of fervent exhortation to act. Fanny enjoyed humming the song. She said that the words of the song depicted a "tough guy" who devoutly believed in the "big meaning" of life. She could identify with the song's words and imagine herself as a tough guy. "Perhaps under the influence of the feminist discourse of androgyny, I believe that there are some good human qualities that should be possessed by all people, no matter if they are regarded as feminine or masculine characters," Fanny claimed. Despite its depiction of a male hero, the song's text was interpreted in a way that supported the women's movement. In the identification process, the merging of the self and the ideal subvert the masculine/feminine and tough/soft oppositions.

It is often assumed that female audiences would naturally identify with the female protagonist, and male audiences with the male protagonist. Hence examining women's reception of melodramas is essential to the study of female spectatorship. Yet, the focus on the female audiences of certain genres such as soaps and romance runs the risk of stereotyping women. Female audiences can indeed obtain pleasure from action movies. In the psychoanalytic frameworks of Mulvey and Doane, the female spectator can either be immersed with the passive/female object of being looked at, or identify with the active/ male subject of looking. Female spectatorship entails either a masochistic identification with the female object or a transvestite position of masculinization. While allowing for trans-gender identification, it is conceived that pleasurable spectatorship is possible only when women inhabit the masculine position or adopt perspectives that are unfeminine. In this study, the trans-gender identification experienced by the female audience was not so much identification with the male subject of looking. Rather, it was recognition of the heroic qualities of a fighter. Yet, such identification should not be conceptualized in terms of the active/male/masculine code. A fundamental problem of the psychoanalytic frameworks lies in the dichotomous definition of gender as either masculine and active, or feminine and passive. Women's own voices and reception experiences call for an abandonment of an essentialist understanding of sexual difference and the dichotomy underlying definitions of gender.

To summarize, the action movies of the 1970s and 1980s are often seen as representing prominent male taste and ideology. However, my study shows that Chan's action comedies were understood very differently from Lee's action movies. In general, my respondents did not enjoy watching Lee's movies. Some watched them at the invitation of their male partners; some watched them in their childhood when their fathers took them to the cinema; more watched them simply because they were on television. Though they admitted that Lee was a hero and had achievements in both the local and international arenas, they disliked the violent, cruel image that he represented. In refusing to identify with Lee's hero image, they protested against the hypermasculinized form and placed their concern for non-violence at center stage.

Lee's nationalistic image also put Emily off any identification. Locally born in the 1960s and with a middle-class background, Emily identified herself as Hongkongese rather than Chinese. Her rejection of Chinese nationalism may perhaps not be shared by women of the older generation who migrated from the Mainland to settle in Hong Kong during the 1950s, or by women who migrated from the Mainland in recent decades. Rather than a homogeneous group, Hong Kong women are divided in terms of class, age, and ethnicity. What is shared by women, at least this group of women, seems to be a rejection of what they perceive to be violence. The perception that Chan's movies are not violent enabled respondents not only to enjoy watching them, but also to identify with the male protagonist.

The identification of the policeman-hero did not place women in a feminine subject position that awaited the hero's protection. Far from confirming existing identities that serve only the interests of the patriarchy, women's identification can represent a hidden or even open protest against the oppression. In Fanny's case, the confirmation of an existing identity was, ironically, a feminist one. Coming from a feminist who took pleasure in Hong Kong action movies, the identification did not necessarily imply any self-denial, but rather a highlighting of the heroic qualities of the feminist viewer. A resemblance of personality or life goal connected the viewer and the character. The trans-gender identification did not imply any worship of the male protagonist. Both the male protagonist and his hero image were marginal and only relevant in so far as the image related to the viewer's own identity. This re-appropriation of the hero image in action movies displayed the diverse potentials of the texts, as well as the agency of the social audience.

Instead of assuming that women are mere receptacles for the ideologies disseminated through mainstream local cinema, I have shown that reception is a gendered social practice that is active rather than passive, and that can be empowering rather than constraining. Nevertheless, this is not to say that viewers are completely free and autonomous agents. Nor does it imply a denial of any power of dominant ideologies. Rather, the effects of cinema have to be assessed in relation to other discourses that are at the disposal of the viewers. As discourses exist in hierarchical relations with one another, they are, of course, not in a struggle on equal terms.

If viewers can and do respond to films in ways that contradict or reject the presumably ideal spectator structured into the text, then the value of textual analysis needs to be seriously rethought and reevaluated. In refusing the notion of the ideal spectator prescribed by a text, one must not privilege the context over the text or ignore how the text works on viewers. Such an opposition of text and context is highly problematic and unnecessary, for texts are themselves discursive products. The subject positions that texts create are multiple and fluid. They are subject to change in different historical discursive formations. Instead of posing text and context as either-or options, the interplay between social reader and social text must be kept in focus in our future discussion and conceptualization of spectatorship.

Notes

INTRODUCTION

I need to thank Day Wong, who provided wonderful insights into and critical comments about my earlier draft.

1. International film criticism of Hong Kong cinema is too voluminous to cite, but some examples of scholarly books include Stephen Teo's *Hong Kong Cinema: The Extra Dimensions* (London: British Film Institute, 1997); Lisa Odham Stokes's *City on Fire: Hong Kong Cinema* (London: Verso, 1999); David Bordwell's *Planet Hong Kong: Popular Cinema and the Art of Entertainment* (Harvard: Harvard University Press, 2000); Poshek Fu and David Desser, eds., *The Cinema of Hong Kong: History, Arts, Identity* (Cambridge and New York: Cambridge University Press, 2000); and Esther Yau, ed., *At Full Speed: Hong Kong Cinema in a Borderless World* (Minneapolis: University of Minnesota Press, 2001).

2. The two terms borrow from the titles of two recent books, Aida Hozic's *Hollyworld: Space, Power, and Fantasy in the American Economy* (Ithaca: Cornell University Press, 2001) and Bordwell's *Planet Hong Kong*.

3. Esther C. M. Yau, "Introduction: Hong Kong Cinema in a Borderless World," in Esther C. M. Yau, ed., *At Full Speed: Hong Kong Cinema in a Borderless World*, 2.

4. See, for example, Patricia Brett Erens, "Crossing Borders: Time, Memory, and the Construction of Identity in *Song of the Exile*," *Cinema Journal* 39. 4 (Summer 2000): 43–59; and Shuqin Cui, "Stanley Kwan's *Center Stage*: (Im)possible Engagement between Feminism and Postmodernism," *Cinema Journal* 39.4 (Summer 2000): 60–80.

5. Steven Cohan, *Masked Men: Masculinity and the Movies in the Fifties* (Bloomington and Indianapolis: Indiana University Press, 1997), 35.

6. Chris Holmlund, *Impossible Bodies: Femininity and Masculinity at the Movies* (London and New York: Routledge, 2002), 5.

7. Kwai-cheung Lo, this volume, 140.

8. Bordwell, 8.

9. Michael Kimmel, *Manhood in America: A Cultural History* (New York: Free Press, 1996), 7.

10. John Ellis, *Visible Fictions* (London: Routledge, 1982).

11. See, for example, Laura Mulvey, "Visual Pleasure and Narrative Cinema" *Screen* 16. 3 (1975): 6–18; and Mary Ann Doane, *The Desire to Desire: The Woman's Film of the 1940s* (Blooming: Indiana University Press, 1987).

12. See Sek Kei's "The War between the Cantonese and Mandarin Cinemas in the Sixties or How the Beautiful Women Lost to the Action Men," in Law Kar, ed., *The Restless Breed: Cantonese Stars of the Sixties (The 20th Hong Kong International Film Festival)* (Hong Kong: The Urban Council, 1996), 26–33.

13. There are exceptions, of course, such as some of the action films featuring Michelle Yeoh, which demonstrate a complex intertwining of femininity and masculinity. See Kwai-cheung Lo's chapter in this volume.

14. See Zhang Jian, *Jiushi niandai gangcanpian gongyi yipie* (A glance at Hong Kong's film productions in the 1990s) (Hong Kong: Guanzi Xianggang dianying gongyi fazheng yanjiu hui, 1998), and Grace Leung and Joseph Chan, "The Hong Kong Cinema and Its Overseas Market: A Historical Review, 1950–1995," in Law Kar, ed., *Fifty Years of Electric Shadows: The 21st Hong Kong International Film Festival* (Hong Kong: Urban Council, 1997), 136–51.

15. Ding-Tzann Lii, "A Colonized Empire: Reflections on the Expansion of Hong Kong Films in Asian Countries," in Kuan-Hsing Chen, ed., *Trajectories: Inter-Asia Cultural Studies* (London and New York: Routledge, 1998), 122–41.

CHAPTER 1

I would like to thank Prof. Cheuk Pak-tong of Hong Kong Baptist University for inviting me to participate in a conference on the Shaw Brothers on the International Movie Stage, where I presented an earlier version of this chapter. I would also like to thank Prof. Lo Wai-luk of HKBU for his help with translations from the Chinese and providing a deeper understanding of the critical discourse surrounding these films. And a special thanks to Dhugal Meachem, graduate assistant extraordinaire, for more help than I can even remember.

1. Winnie Fu, ed., *The Making of Martial Arts Films — As Told by Filmmakers and Stars* (Hong Kong Film Archive, 1999), 43.

2. Ibid., 90.

3. Tony Rayns, "King Hu: Shall We Dance?" in *A Study of the Hong Kong Martial Arts Film* (Hong Kong: Urban Council, 1980), 103.

4. See Hector Rodriguez, "Questions of Chinese Aesthetics: Film Form and Narrative Space in the Cinema of King Hu," *Cinema Journal* 38.1 (1998): 73–97.

5. Zhang Zhen, "Bodies in the Air: The Magic of Science and the Fate of the Early 'Martial Arts' Film in China," *Post Script* 20. 2–3 (2001): 44.

6. A glimpse of what King Hu-inspired martial arts movies look like can be gleaned from the swordplay films made at Cathay in the late 1960s, with stars like Tian Qing, better suited to light comedy than hard-edged martial arts (e.g. *The Smiling Swordsman*, dir. Jiang Nan, 1968; *Mad, Mad Sword*, dir. Wang Tianlin, 1969). Perhaps only Roy Chiao (Qiao Hong) starring in *Escorts over Tiger Hills* (Hushan xing) (dir. Wang Xinglei, 1969), approximates the kind of *yanggang* Zhang Che demanded. Chiao, of course, would go on to star in Hu's *A Touch of Zen* and *The Fate of Lee Khan* (1973), the latter, however, best remembered as a veritable Who's Who of female *wuxia* stars: Xu Feng, Li Lihua, Angela Mao and Helen Ma (Ma Hailun). See also Stephen Teo, "Cathay and the Wuxia Movie" for a discussion of the problems Cathay had in making *wuxia* movies in the late 1960s (Stephen Teo, "Cathay and the Wuxia Movie," in *The Cathay Story: The 26th International Hong Kong Film Festival* [Hong Kong: Hong Kong Film Archive, 2002].) It is arguable that had King Hu directed a film from 1966 to 1969 his influence in Hong Kong cinema might have been greater. *Dragon Inn* was a huge hit in Hong Kong and the most influential film in Taiwan during this period. The lengthy production process of *A Touch of Zen* and its subsequent commercial failure (generally attributed to mishandling of its release) gave Zhang the opportunity to release films in Hu's absence. By the time *A Touch of Zen* was released, with its female action star and non-action male lead, it was out of touch with the emerging martial arts genre. *A Touch of Zen*, to be sure, would have some impact on martial arts choreography and stunt scenes, with its brilliant use of trampolines and (re)construction of action through fragments and eye-line matches, but the themes of the films all derive from Zhang.

7. David Desser, "Diaspora and National Identity: Exporting China Through the Hong Kong Cinema," *Post Script* 20.2 & 3 (2001): 126.

8. Sek Kei, "The Development of 'Martial Arts' in Hong Kong Cinema," in *A Study of the Hong Kong Martial Arts Film* (Hong Kong Urban Council, 1980), 29.

9. Fu, 21.

10. Ibid., 43.

11. David A. Cook, *Lost Illusions: American Cinema in the Shadow of Watergate and Vietnam, 1970–1979 (History of the American Cinema, volume 9)* (New York: Charles Scribner's Sons, 2000), 339.

12. Sek Kei, 29.

13. Fu, 21.

14. *A Study of the Hong Kong Martial Arts Film*, 2.

15. Wendy Siuyi Wong, *Hong Kong Comics: A History of Manhua* (New York: Princeton Architectural Press, 2002).

16. Fu, 21. Ibid., 32.

17. Fu, 32.

18. http://changcheh.Ocatch.com/yang.htm.

19. Desser, 126–7.

20. The quote is from an essay by Zhang Che in *The Making of Martial Arts Films — As Told by Filmmakers and Stars*, 19.

21. Zhang Che continued to work unabated throughout the 1970s, averaging five or six films a year, though never again putting a film in the top ten. Yet it is in this period of the resurgent masculinist martial arts film, 1978–79, that Zhang directed some of his most favored films: *The Five Deadly Venoms* (Wudu) (1978) and *Ten Tigers from Kwantung* (Guangtong shihu) (1979).

22. I have not undertaken an analysis of 1960s box-office figures yet to see exactly when and how immediately Zhang's films began their dominance. It is generally acknowledged that *One-Armed Swordsman* became the first Hong Kong movie to gross HK$1,000,000. (See, for instance, Wong Yan, "Chang Cheh's Directorial Journey" *Influence Magazine* no. 13 [April 1976]). Retrieved from: http://changcheh.Ocatch.com/ch-bio2.htm). Shaw Brothers Studio certainly had faith in Zhang's films thereafter: in 1969 he directed six, all with some combination of stars Lo Lieh, Wang Yu, David Chiang, and Ti Lung.

23. *Yang ± Yin: Gender in Chinese Cinema* [Nansheng nuxiang: Zhongguo dianying de xingbie]. Transcription of the opening fifteen minutes. http://changcheh.Ocatch.com/yang.htm.

24. Interview with Lau Kar-leung, http://changcheh.Ocatch.com/lau-int.htm.

25. Ibid.

26. See Desser, "The Kung Fu Craze: Hong Kong Cinema's First American Reception," in Poshek Fu and David Desser, eds., *The Cinema of Hong Kong: History, Arts, Identity* (New York: Cambridge University Press, 2000).

27. A user comment on the Internet Movie Database is particularly revealing of how the film reproduces Zhang Che's favored motifs, with the writer claiming that Zhang in fact, directed the film! "There is a certain charm to a Chang Cheh film. It's a sense of futility and dread. You just know things are going to go bad, and when you think it won't get more brutal, somehow, Chang Cheh can always make it worse. *Five Fingers of Death* (aka *King Boxer*) is a classic film in two ways. First it is your usual Chang Cheh grindhouse film with the master director in top form. Second, *Five Fingers* is one of the films that helped Western audiences gain exposure to kung fu flicks in the early 1970s. It may not be the greatest Chang Cheh work or even the greatest kung fu film, but it is certainly not without its gruesome eye gouging, hand smashing, hot coal training, disemboweling, supernatural-glowing-fist-power charms." This would be a neat summation of Zhang's films, were it not for the fact that he did not direct this one! See: http://us.imdb.com/Title?0070800.

28. *Five Fingers of Death* lifts a number of scenes from the classic Hollywood Western *Shane* (George Stevens, 1951). To the extent that *Shane* is a virtual

paradigm of masculinist mythmaking, it is interesting to think that such overt borrowings from a Hollywood Western further helped this film achieve its international breakthrough. It is something of a cliché to compare kung fu films to Westerns, but recognizing these borrowings on the part of *Five Fingers of Death* allows us to think more fully about what such comparisons mean and their significance in terms of worldwide appeal and ideologies of masculinity.

CHAPTER 2

1. Julian Stringer, "'Your Tender Smiles Give me Strength': Paradigms of Masculinity in John Woo's *A Better Tomorrow* and *The Killer*," *Screen* 38.1 (1997): 40.
2. Interview with author, 1 October 2000.
3. Tania Modleski, *Feminism without Women: Culture and Criticism in a "Postfeminist" Age* (New York, London: Routledge, 1991), 7.
4. John Beynon, *Masculinities and Culture* (London: Open University, 2002), 90.
5. Clearly the patriarchy has been under constant challenges from all directions, and it is not able to deal with them with the same degree of success. See, for example, the several studies on the crisis of masculinity quoted in R. W. Connell, *Masculinities* (Berkeley, Los Angeles: University of California Press, 1995), 84.
6. Stephen Teo, "Sinking into Creative Depths," in Law Kar, ed., *Hong Kong Panorama 97–98: The Twenty-second Hong Kong International Film Festival* (Hong Kong: Provisional Urban Council, 1998), 11.
7. David Bordwell, *Planet Hong Kong: Popular Cinema and the Art of Entertainment* (Cambridge, MA: Harvard University Press, 2000), 269.
8. Athena Tsui and C. Fong, "Too Many Ways to be a Filmmaker: Interview with Johnnie To," in Law Kar, ed., *Hong Kong Panorama 98–99: The Twenty-third Hong Kong International Film Festival* (Hong Kong: Provisional Urban Council, 1999), 64.
9. Bordwell, 269.
10. Wai Kar-fai, however, denies in an interview any direct relation between his film and *Young and Dangerous* (Tsui, 24–5).
11. Connell, 76–81.
12. Steven Cohan, *Masked Men: Masculinity and the Movies in the Fifties* (Bloomington and Indianapolis: Indiana University Press, 1997), 34–9.
13. In another paper I discuss more specifically how the gangster formula is interrupted in this film. See Laikwan Pang, "Death and Hong Kong Cinema," *Quarterly Review of Film and Video* 18.1 (Spring 2001): 15–29.
14. Esther C. M. Yau, "Border Crossing: Mainland China's Presence in Hong

Kong Cinema," in Paul U. Pickowicz, et. al., eds., *New Chinese Cinemas: Forms, Identities, Politics* (Cambridge, New York: Cambridge University Press, 1994), 180–201.

15. Wai-luk Lo, "Xianggang dianying zhong de daluren—xiangxiang, xianshi yu yuwang" [Mainlanders in Hong Kong films: Imaginations, Reality, and Desire], paper presented to the Conference on Hong Kong Culture, Hong Kong, 1999.

16. Yau, "Border Crossing."

17. Susan Jeffords, *Hard Bodies: Hollywood Masculinity in the Reagan Era* (New Brunswick, New Jersey: Rutgers University Press, 1994), 176.

18. Among the annual top ten most popular films, there were two action films in 1992, five in 1993, two in 1994, three in 1995, four in 1996, six in 1997, and six in 1998. See annual box-office records published in the annual publications of MPIA (Hong Kong, Kowloon and New Territories Motion Picture Industry Association Ltd).

19. Jitao, "*Mission,*" http://www.filmcritics.org.hk/mission/reviewC.html/ (2000).

20. See Bordwell, 248–60; Law Kar, ed., *Transcending the Times: King Hu and Eileen Chang (Hong Kong International Film Festival 1998)* (Hong Kong: Provisional Urban Council, 1998).

21. Jillian Sandell, "Reinventing Masculinity: The Spectacle of Male Intimacy in the Films of John Woo," *Film Quarterly* 49.4 (1996): 23.

22. Eve K. Sedgwick, *Between Men: English Literature and Male Homosocial Desire* (New York: Columbia University Press, 1985).

23. Johnny To, Post-screening discussion of *The Mission*, Hong Kong Baptist University, Hong Kong, November, 1999.

24. Peter Krämer, "A Powerful Cinema-going Force? Hollywood and Female Audiences since the 1960s," in Melvyn Stokes and Richard Maltby, eds., *Identifying Hollywood's Audiences: Cultural Identity and the Movies* (London: BFI, 1999), 103–4.

25. Ibid., 104. Quoting Anne Thompson, "Studios Stick to their Guns over Sex Appeal of Pics," *Variety* 7 (January 1991): 111.

CHAPTER 3

1. "Glbt" means "gay, lesbian, bisexual and transsexual," but it is also an umbrella term that includes other sexual minorities such as transvestites, sadomasochists, paedophiles, etc.

2. By post-structuralism, I refer to a loose interdisciplinary movement that originated in France during the 1960s. Its members primarily (re-) appropriated Saussure's theory of language. The prominent figures in the movement included Jacques Lacan, Roland Barthes, Michel Foucault, Julia

Kristeva and Jacques Derrida. Their divergent paths of thought cannot or should not be treated as a unified perspective, or even as a coherent paradigm. What unites all these scholars, however, seems to be their attempt to problematize the traditional epistemologies by arguing that we have no way of accessing the reality in which our theory can be grounded without some form of conceptual and linguistic ordering with which to understand experiences, and thus that there is a need for discourse to be analyzed if the social world is to be understood (Chantal Mouffe, "Feminism, Citizenship, and Radical Democratic Politics," in Linda Nicholson and Steven Seidman, eds., *Social Postmodernism: Beyond Identity Politics* (Cambridge: Cambridge University Press, 1995): 315–31; Steven Seidman and David G. Wagner, eds., *Postmodernism and Social Theory* (Oxford: Basil Blackwell, 1992); Steven Seidman, ed., *The Postmodern Turn: New Perspectives on Social Theory* (New York: Cambridge University Press, 1994)). Post-structuralism per se is thus the social thought that rejects the stable structure of fixed binary pairs through which meanings can be found and suggests that the production of meaning is always deferred, both in process and intertextually (Chris Barker, *Cultural Studies: Theory and Practice* [London: Sage, 2000]).

3. The following works of queer theory are emblematic: Eve Kosofsky Sedgwick, *Between Men: English Literature and Male Homosexual Desire* (New York: Columbia University Press, 1985); Eve Kosofsky Sedgwick, *Epistemology of the Closet* (Berkeley: University of California Press, 1990); Diana Fuss, *Essentially Speaking: Feminism, Nature and Difference* (London: Routledge, 1989); Diana Fuss, ed., *Inside/Out: Lesbian Theories, Gay Theories* (London: Routledge, 1991); Judith Butler, *Gender Trouble: Feminism and the Subversion of Identity* (London: Routledge, 1990); Michael Warner, ed., *Fear of A Queer Planet: Queer Politics and Social Theory* (Minneapolis: University of Minnesota Press, 1993).

4. Andrea Cornwall and Nancy Lindisfarne, "Dislocating Masculinity: Gender, Power and Anthropology," in Andrea Cornwall and Nancy Lindisfarne, eds., *Dislocating Masculinity: Comparative Ethnographies* (London: Routledge, 1994), 12.

5. First, the rise of women's liberation at the end of the 1960s provided a powerful critique of the exaggerated differences between men and women. The growing body of feminist research on gender and sex roles since then has critically examined the male/female dichotomy, and has provided new ways of understanding gender (Elizabeth Grosz, *Volatile Bodies: Towards a Corporeal Feminism* [Bloomington: Indiana University Press, 1994]; Thomas W. Laqueur, *Making Sex: Body and Gender from the Greeks to Freud* [Cambridge, Mass.: Harvard University Press, 1990]; Carol S. Vance, "Social Construction Theory and Sexuality," in Berger Maurice, Wallis Brian, and Watson Simon, eds., *Constructing Masculinity* [London: Routledge, 1995]).

Second, the conflation of masculinity with heterosexuality has been severely criticized by lesbian and gay academics and activists since the late 1960s (Lynne Segal, *Slow Motion: Changing Masculinities, Changing Men* [London: Virago, 1990]; Sedgwick, 1990).

Third, historians, anthropologists, ethnographers and post-colonial theorists have provided valuable materials with which to dismantle a unifying but Eurocentric notion of masculinity by showing how masculinity changes over time in a society as well as how it is perceived differently in different cultural settings. A more recent understanding of masculinity can be gained by recognizing its global dimension (R. W. Connell, *Masculinities* (Cambridge: Polity Press, 1995); Roger N. Lancaster, "Subject Honour and Object Shame: The Construction of Male Homosexuality and Stigma in Nicaragua," *Ethnology* 27.2 (1988): 111–25; Dennis Altman, "Rupture or Continuity? The Internationalization of Gay Identity," *Social Text* 48: 14.3 (1996): 77–94; Cornwall and Lindisfarne, 1994).

6. Connell, 1995.

7. Kenneth Plummer, ed., *Modern Homosexualities: Fragments of Lesbian and Gay Experience* (London: Routledge, 1992), 19, (italics original).

8. Adrienne Rich, "Compulsory Heterosexuality and Lesbian Existence," *Signs* 5 (1980): 631–60.

9. Rice (1980), 648.

10. Butler, 1990.

11. George Weinberg, *Society and the Healthy Homosexual* (New York: Doubleday, 1973); Rich, (1980); Butler, (1990); Gayle S. Rubin "Thinking Sex: Notes for a Radical Theory of the Politics of Sexuality," in Henry Abelove, Michele Aina Barale and David M. Halperin, eds., *The Lesbian and Gay Studies Reader* (London: Routledge, 1993): 3–44.

12. Lan Kwai Fong is the name of a small street in Central, the business district of Hong Kong, but Hong Kong people use it to refer to the surrounding area as well. The area is characterized by new, bright and trendy Western-style bars, restaurants, cafés, saloons and other entertainment venues. It thus signifies an "up-town" atmosphere and the glorification of the Western-values of hedonism and consumption. It is also alleged to be a "gay ghetto."

13. W. S. Chou and M. C. Chiu, *The Closet Sexual History* (Chinese Edition) (Hong Kong: Comrade Research Centre, 2000).

14. Roland Barthes, *Image-Music-Text*, trans. S. Heath (Glasgow: Collins-Fontana, 1977); Barthes, "From Work to Text," in Josué V. Harari, ed., *Textual Strategies: Perspectives in Post-structural Criticism* (Ithaca, NY: Cornell University Press, 1979), 73–81.

15. Pierre Bourdieu, *In Other Words: Essays Towards a Reflexive Sociology* (Cambridge: Polity, 1990).

16. Bourdieu, (1990), 63.

17. Michel Foucault, *The History of Sexuality, Volume One: An Introduction*, trans. Robert Hurley (New York: Vintage, 1980).

18. Michel Foucault, *Discipline and Punish: The Birth of the Prison*, trans. Alan Sheridan (London: Penguin Books, 1977).

19. Sandra Lee Bartky, "Foucault, Femininity and the Modernisation of Patriarchal Power," in Irene Diamond and Lee Quinby, eds., *Feminism and Foucault: Reflections on Resistance* (Boston: Northeastern University Press, 1989), 61–86.

20. Frantz Fanon, *Black Skin, White Masks* (New York: Grove Press, 1967).

21. Travis S. K. Kong, "The Seduction of the Golden Boy: The Body Politics of Hong Kong Gay Men," *Body & Society* 8.1 (2002): 29–48.

22. Foucault, (1980), 86.

23. Stuart Hall, "Culture, Media, and the 'Ideological Effect,'" in J. Curran, M. Gurevitch, and J. Woollacott, eds., *Mass Communication and Society* (London: Edward Arnold, 1977), 333.

24. Jeffrey Weeks, *Sexuality and Its Discontents: Meanings, Myths and Modern Sexualities* (London: Routledge, 1985); Steven Seidman, "Identity and Politics in a 'Postmodern' Gay Culture: Some Historical and Conceptual Notes," in Michael Warner, (1993), 105–42; Annamarie Rustom Jagose, *Queer Theory: An Introduction* (New York: New York University Press, 1996).

25. Barthes, 1977.

26. Foucault, *The Archaeology of Knowledge* (New York: Pantheon, 1972); Foucault, (1977); Jacques Derrida, *Of Grammatology* (Baltimore: Johns Hopkins University Press, 1976); Pierre Bourdieu, *Outline of a Theory of Practice* (Cambridge: Cambridge University Press, 1977); Stuart Hall et al., *Culture, Media, and Language: Working Papers in Cultural Studies, 1972–79* (London: Hutchison, 1980); see also Charles C. Lemert, "Post-structuralism and Sociology," in Seidman (1994): 265–81.

27. Foucault, (1980), 86.

28. Alexander Doty, *Flaming Classics: Queering the Film Cannon* (London: Routledge, 2000); see also James R. Keller, *Queer (Un)Friendly Film and Television* (London: McFarland & Company, Inc, 2002).

29. Walter Benjamin, *Illuminations* (London: Fontana Press, 1992 [1968]).

30. Aspasia Kotsopoulos, "Reading Against the Grain Revisited," in *Jump Cut: A Review of Contemporary Media*, no. 44 (2001).

31. Gayatri Chakravorty Spivak, *In Other Worlds: Essays in Cultural Politics* (London: Methuen, 1987): 241–68.

32. For example, Brett Farmer, *Spectacular Passions: Cinema, Fantasy, Gay Male Spectatorships* (London: Duke University Press, 2000).

33. Linda Nicholson and Steven Seidman, eds., *Social Postmodernism: Beyond Identity Politics* (Cambridge: Cambridge University Press, 1995); Steven Seidman, ed., *Queer Theory/Sociology* (Oxford: Basil Blackwell, 1996); Jagose, 1996.

34. Fuss, 1989; Sedgwick, 1990; Butler, 1990.
35. Butler, (1990), 31.
36. Butler, (1990), 6.
37. Rosemary Hennessy, "Queer Visibility in Commodity Culture," in Nicholson and Seidman, (1995), 142–83.
38. Diane Raymond, "Popular Culture and Queer Representation: A Critical Perspective," in Dines, Gail and Jean, M. Humez, eds., *Gender, Race, and Class in Media: A Text-Reader* (London: Sage, 2003).
39. S. G. Epstein "Gay Politics, Ethnic Identities: The Limits of Social Constructionism" *Socialist Review* 17.3–4 (1987): 9–50.
40. Butler, 1990.
41. Raymond, (2003), 104.
42. Travis S. K. Kong, "Queer at Your Own Risk: Marginality, Community and the Body Politics of Hong Kong Gay Men," *Sexualities* 7.1 (2004): 5–30.
43. C. Lee Harrington and Denise D. Bielby, eds., *Popular Culture: Production and Consumption* (Malden, Mass.: Blackwell Publishers, 2001), Introduction.
44. Lam, *Fake Sexual Politics*. (Chinese Edition) (Hong Kong: Big Camp, 1993).
45. Frank Mort, *Cultures of Consumption: Masculinities and Social Space in Late-Twentieth Century Britain* (London: Routledge, 1988).
46. Chang Hsiao-hung, "Taiwan Queer Valentines," in Chen Kuan-Hsing, ed., *Trajectories: Inter-Asia Cultural Studies* (London: Routledge, 1998), 283–298.
47. Chang (1998), 294.
48. Ibid.
49. Caroline Evans and Lorraine Gamman, "The Gaze Revisited, or Revisiting Queer Viewing," in Paul Burston and Colin Richardson, eds., *A Queer Romance: Lesbians, Gay Men and Popular Culture* (London: Routledge, 1995), 32.
50. Emig Rainer, "Queering the Straights: Straightening the Queers: Commodified Sexualities and Hegemonic Masculinity," in Russell West and Frank Lay, eds., *Subverting Masculinity: Hegemonic and Alternative Versions of Masculinity in Contemporary Culture* (Amsterdam: Rodopi, 2000), 223; see also Brian McNair, *Striptease Culture: Sex, Media and the Democratisation of Desire* (London, New York: Routledge, 2002).
51. Alan Sinfield, *Gay and After* (London: Serpent's Tail, 1998), 168.
52. D. Kellner, *Media Culture: Cultural Studies, Identity, and Politics Between the Modern and the Postmodern* (London: Routledge, 1995), 40.
53. bell hooks, "Eating the Other," in S. HesseBiler, C. Gilmartin, and R. Lydenberg, eds., *Feminist Approaches to Theory and Methodology* (New York: Oxford University Press, 1999).
54. Helen Leung Hok-sze, "Queerscapes in Contemporary Hong Kong Cinema," *positions: east asia cultures critique* 9.2 (2001): 423–47.

55. Samshasha [Xiaomingxiong], *History of Homosexuality in China*. (Chinese Edition) (Hong Kong: Ng, Siuming and Rose Winkel Press, 1997).

56. The *dan* character in Peking Opera might be less a culturally determined phenomenon than the result of a specific policy of the puritan Qing government, which banned all public appearances by females. Joshua Goldstein's discussion of Mei Lanfang is a good example to look at the political implications of men's playing *dan* characters in Peking Opera (Joshua Goldstein, "Mei Lanfang and the Nationalization of Peking Opera, 1912–1930," *positions: east asia cultures critique* 7.2 [1999]: 377–420).

57. Kam Louie and Edwards Louise, "Chinese Masculinity: Theorizing Wen and Wu," *East Asian History* 8 (1994): 135–48; see also Susan Brownell and Jeffrey N. Wasserstrom, "Introduction" of *Chinese Femininities/Chinese Masculinities: A Reader* (London: University of California Press, 2002), 1–46.

58. Lam, (1993); Lenuta Giukin, "Boy-Girls: Gender, Body, and Popular Culture in Hong Kong Action Movies," in Murray Pomerance, ed., *Ladies and Gentleman, Boys and Girls: Gender in Film at the End of the Twentieth Century* (New York: State University of New York Press, 2001).

59. Kong, 2004.

60. See Helen Chan's discussion of the same movie in this collection.

61. Stanley Kwan, *Yang ± Yin: Gender in Chinese Cinema*. (Video Format) (London: Connoisseur Video, 1995).

62. Kong, 2004.

63. The *Butterfly Lovers* (Liangshanbo yu Zhuyingtai) is a famous Chinese legend of two lovers, Liang Shanbo and Zhu Yingtai. Liang was a boy who had been sent away to school. Disguised as a boy, Zhu went to school as well. They met at school, became good friends and lived together for three years. During this time, Liang never knew that Zhu was a girl, although she tried many times to reveal her true identity. Zhu was later sent back to her family and forced to marry a rich neighbour. When Liang discovered that Zhu was a girl and in love with him, he fell sick and died of sorrow. On her wedding day, when Zhu was taken in a bridal chair to the house of her future husband, she passed the grave of Liang. She descended in bitter despair and begged the grave to open up. There was a clap of thunder, the tomb opened and Zhu leapt in. They then became two butterflies and flew away, which symbolized the union of their long-awaited love.

   The story has been played many times in operas, TV, films and plays, and the music has become one of the most famous pieces in classical Chinese music. But the story could be read from a queer perspective. For example, Lam, (1993); Lam, *The Male Boundary* (Chinese Edition) (Hong Kong: Big Camp, 1994). The fact that Liang had not realized that Zhu was a girl is quite unbelievable if they had been living together for three years. It is more difficult to believe that Liang actually knew that Zhu was a girl but was such a gentleman who strictly followed Confucian teachings that he refrained from engaging in any "acts" of intimacy. It is thus more believable that Liang was a closet gay and thus did not want to admit that Zhu was a girl.

64. Butler, 1990.

65. Eve Kosofsky Sedgwick, "Gosh, Boy George, You Must Be Awfully Secure in Your Masculinity," in Maurice Berger, Brian Wallis and Simon Watson, eds., *Constructing Masculinity*, (London: Routledge, 1995), 12.

66. Sedgwick, (1995), 16.

67. Many films use the same logic but focus on "women to women" relationships: *Intimate Confessions of a Chinese Courtesan* (Ainu) (dir. Chor Yuen, 1972); *An Amorous Woman of the Tang Dynasty* (Tangdai haofangnü) (dir. Fong Ling-Ching, 1984); *Twin Bracelets* (Shuangzhuo) (dir. Wong Yuk-Saan, 1991); *Intimates* (Zishu) (dir. Cheung Chi-Leung, 1997); *Portland Street Blues* (Hongxing shisan mei) (dir. Raymond Yip, 1998); *Peony Pavilion* (Youyuan jingmeng) (dir. Yonfan, 2001).

68. Butler, 1990.

69. David Forrest, "We're Here, We're Queer, and We're Not Going Shopping: Changing Gay Male Identities in Contemporary Britain," in Cornwall and Lindisfarne, (1994), 97–110; Segal, (1990); Sedgwick, (1989), (1990).

70. Jachinson W. Chan, "Bruce Lee's Fictional Models of Masculinity," *Men and Masculinities* 2.4 (2000): 371–87.

71. Chan (2000), 376, brackets added.

72. Kwan, 1995.

73. Julian Stringer, "Your Tender Smiles Give Me Strength: Paradigms of Masculinity in John Woo's *A Better Tomorrow* and *The Killer*," *Screen* 38.1 (1997): 25–41.

74. Jillian Sandell, "Reinventing Masculinity: The Spectacle of Male Intimacy in the Films of John Woo," *Film Quarterly* 49.4 (Summer, 1996): 23–34.

75. Kong, 2002; Chris Berry, "Sexual DisOrientations: Homosexual Rights, East Asian Films, and Postmodern Postnationalism," in Xiaobing Tang and Stephen Snyder, eds., *In Pursuit of Contemporary East Asian Culture* (Colorado, US: Westview Press, 1996): 157–82.

76. Stephen Whittle, ed., *The Margins of the City: Gay Men's Urban Lives* (Aldershot: Arena, 1994); Plummer, 1999.

77. William L. Leap, ed., *Public Sex/Gay Space* (New York: Columbia University Press, 1999); David Woodhead "'Surveillant Gays': HIV, Space and the Constitution of Identities," in David Bell and Gill Valentine, eds., *Mapping Desire: Geographies of Sexualities* (London: Routledge, 1995): 231–44.

78. Emig Rainer, (2000), 223.

79. Kong, 2002; c.f. Connell, 1995.

80. Doty, *Making Things Perfectly Queer: Interpreting Mass Culture* (Minneapolis: University of Minnesota Press, 1993), xvii.

CHAPTER 4

Earlier drafts of this article were presented during 2002 at Inside Out: The 12th Toronto Gay and Lesbian Film and Video Festival, the "Intersecting Asian Sexualities" conference at the University of British Columbia, and the "Queer Visualities" conference at SUNY-Stony Brook. I have benefited enormously from the thoughtful responses to my work at these events. I am also grateful to Kam Wai-kui, whose rich experience in transgender activism and continual love of Hong Kong cinema have illuminated endless conversations that ultimately shaped many of my best ideas.

1. Susan Stryker, "The Transgender Issue: An Introduction," *GLQ* 4.2 (1998): 149.

2. In addition to the works cited in the article, the growing scholarship that is defining the emergent field of transgender theory includes, among others, the works of Kate Bornstein, Jacob Hale, Kate More, and Riki Wichins. See Susan Stryker and Stephen Whittle, ed., *The Transgender Reader* (New York: Routledge, 2003) for a comprehensive review.

3. One of the earliest critiques of transphobia in feminism is Sandy Stone's now classic rebuttal to Janice Raymond in "The Empire Strikes Back: A Posttranssexual Manifesto," revised 1993 version, http://www. sandystone. com/empire-strikes-back. See also Pat Califia, *Sex Changes: The Politics of Transgenderism* (San Francisco: Cleis, 1997), 86–119.

4. For an account of gay studies' relation to transgender theory, see Califia, 120–62. For works that intersect lesbian gender practices and transgender theory, see Minnie Bruce Pratt, *S/he* (New York: Firebrand, 1995) and Joan Nestle, *A Fragile Union* (San Francisco: Cleis, 1998). For the intersection between transgender theory and bisexuality, see Claire Hemmings, *Bisexual Spaces: A Geography of Sexuality and Gender* (New York: Routledge, 2002), 99–144.

5. In 1997, the Harry Benjamin International Gender Dysphoria Association (HBIGDA), the professional organization of health specialists in transgender care, elected transgender individuals to sit on its board of directors for the first time. See Stryker, 146.

6. For a description of the aims and activities of the centre, as well as links to recent scholarly works on transgender issues in Asia, visit the centre's web site at http://web.hku.hk/~sjwinter/TransgenderASIA/.

7. Jin Yong (Louis Cha), *Xiao'ao Jianghu* (The smiling, proud wanderer) Vol. 4 (Hong Kong: Minghe she, 1980), 1690. Subsequent references to this text will be given parenthetically after quotations. All translations of Chinese that appears in the chapter is my own.

8. Dongfang Bubai has also been variously translated as "Master Asia" or "Asia the Invincible" in the film's English subtitles and other English-language publications on the film.

9. For a discussion of this historiographic "use" of the eunuch, see Samshasha

(Xiaomingxiong), *Zhongguo tongxing'ai shilu* (History of homosexuality in China), revised ed. (Hong Kong: Rosa Winkel Press, 1997), 348–9.

10. For a discussion of the role of the hero-hermit in martial arts fiction, see Chen Pingyuan, *Qiangu wenren xiakemeng: wuxia xiaoshuo leixing yanjiu* (The literati's chivalric dreams: narrative models of Chinese knight-errant literature) (Taipei: Rye Field Publishing, 1995), 187–228. See, also, Kam Louie's study of the archetypes of masculinity in Chinese culture, *Theorising Chinese Masculinity: Society and Gender in China* (Cambridge: Cambridge University Press, 2002).

11. I am indebted to one of the anonymous reviewers of the book for pointing out this intriguing relation between feminization and freedom from female sexuality in the martial arts genre.

12. For an analysis of the relationship between the decriminalization debates and the emergence of gay identity in the 1980s-1990s, see Petula Sik-ying Ho, "Policing Identity: Decriminalisation of Homosexuality and the Emergence of Gay Identity in Hong Kong" (Ph.D. Diss., University of Essex, 1997).

13. See Stanley Kwan's documentary *Yang ± Yin: Gender in Chinese Cinema* (*Nansheng Nuxiang*) (1996) for a provocative look at transgressive gender representations throughout Chinese cinema.

14. The description of the film in the festival catalogue celebrates Dongfang Bubai's "ease with this newly acquired gender identity as a woman." http://www.transgenderfilmfestival.com/2001/_GB/article_swordsman.html.

15. Jay Prosser, *Second Skins: The Body Narratives of Transsexuality* (New York: Columbia University Press, 1998), 23.

16. Chou Wah-shan (Zhou Huashan), *Tongzhi lun* (On tongzhi) (Hong Kong: Tongzhi yanjiu she, 1995), 300.

17. Yau Ching (You Jing), *Lingqi luzao* (Starting another stove) (Hong Kong: Youth Literary Bookstore, 1996), 165.

18. Ibid., 166.

19. Chou, *Tongzhi,* 300.

20. Didier Anzieu, *The Skin Ego: A Psychoanalytic Approach to the Self,* trans. Chris Turner (New Haven: Yale University Press, 1989). For a discussion of Anzieu's notion of the "self" in the context of the development of psychoanalytic theory, see Barbara Socor, *Conceiving the Self: Presence and Absence in Psychoanalytic Theory* (Madison and Connecticut: International Universities Press, 1997), 253–60.

21. Prosser, 65.

22. Ibid., 77.

23. Ibid.

24. Ibid., 84.

25. Updated versions of the Harry Benjamin International Gender Dysphoria Association Standards of Care for Gender Identity Disorders are available from http://www.hbigda.org/soc.html/.

26. For an account of transgender activism that challenges the medical discourse of transsexuality, see Califia, 221–44.

27. Leslie Feinberg, *Stone Butch Blues* (Milford, CT: Firebrand, 1992), 301.

28. See, especially, Leslie Feinberg, *Trans Liberation: Beyond Pink or Blue* (Boston: Beacon, 1998), Kate Bornstein, *My Gender Workbook* (London: Routledge, 1998), and Joan Nestle, Clare Howell, and Riki Wilchins, eds., *Genderqueer: Voices from Beyond the Sexual Binary* (Los Angeles: Alyson, 2002).

29. For a detailed analysis of the *Young and Dangerous* series in relation to the gangster genre in Hong Kong cinema, see Lisa Odham Stokes and Michael Hoover, *City on Fire: Hong Kong Cinema* (London: Verso, 1999), 79–86.

30. Judith Halberstam, *Female Masculinity* (Durham: Duke University Press, 1998), 142–73.

31. Sek Kei, *Shi Qi yinghua ji* (Collected Reviews of Sek Kei), Vol. 4 (Hong Kong: Subculture, 1999), 39.

32. Shelly Kraucer, email correspondence, 28 May 2002.

33. David Bordwell, *Planet Hong Kong* (Cambridge, MA: Harvard University Press, 2000), 108–9.

34. Jillian Sandell, "A Better Tomorrow: American Masochism and Hong Kong Action Film," *Bright Lights Film Journal* 13 (1994). Reprinted on http://www.brightlightsfilm.com/31/hk_better1.html/.

35. Mikel J. Koven, "My Brother, My Lover, My Self: Traditional Masculinity in the Hong Kong Action Cinema of John Woo," *Canadian Folklore* 19.1 (1997): 55–68.

36. Ibid., 56.

37. For a beautifully written account of the homoerotic tradition (*nanfeng*) in pre-modern Chinese literature and culture, see Kang Zhengguo, *Chongshen fengyue jian* (*Aspects of Sexuality and Literature in Ancient China*) (Taipei: Rye Field Publishing, 1996), 109–66.

38. Natalia Chan (Luo Feng), *Shengshi bianyuan* (*City on the Edge of Time*) (Hong Kong: Oxford University Press [China], 2002), 41–2.

39. The Gender/Sexuality Rights Association in Taiwan has created a memorial website for Lin. See http://www.gsrat.org/.

CHAPTER 5

1. Hector Rodriguez argues in "Hong Kong Popular Culture as an Interpretive Arena: the Huang Feihong Film Series" that the Huang films of the 1950s are situated at the intersection of "overseas capital," and search for "ethnic identity" of Cantonese emigrants, and filmmakers' "self–proclaimed goal of promoting patriotism, social responsibility and a sense of ethnic identity"

(*Screen* 38.1 [1997]: 2). With some qualification, Rodriguez's commentaries can be applied to explain my and my fellow expatriates' interest in Hong Kong films.

2. What Sheldon Hsiao-peng Lu asserted about Chinese mainland films, particularly Zhang Yimou and Chen Kaige's "art films," is equally valid with respect to King Hu and Ang Lee: " 'transnational' films [are] primarily targeted to non-Mainland audiences and international film festivals and are distributed outside of China" (9) and these films are "funded by foreign capital (Hong Kong, Taiwan, Japan, Europe), produced by Chinese labor, distributed in a global network, and consumed by an international audience." (Sheldon Lu, "Historical Introduction: Chinese Cinemas [1896–1996] and Transnational Film Studies," in Sheldon Lu, ed., *Transnational Chinese Cinemas: Identity, Nationhood, Gender* (Honolulu: University of Hawaii, 1997), 1–31).

3. Stefan Hammond makes the same observation that "many of HK's [sic] action heroines like Michelle Yeoh, Cynthia Khan, and Moon Lee were ballet-trained prior to stepping in front of the camera, and many action heroes had Peking opera or acrobatic training" (Stefan Hammond, *Hollywood East: Hong Kong Movies and the People Who Make Them* [Lincolnwood : Contemporary Books, 2000], 78); Lenuta Giukin, in addition, attributes the rise of untrained martial arts performers — Maggie Cheung (Zhang Manyu), Brigitte Lin, Anita Mui — to technology: "Another major feature of the eighties and nineties martial arts movies is the presence of modern techonology — such as cars, motor bikes, explosives, guns, and automatic weapons — which, combine with special effects and fast editing techniques, was at the base of a new modality of making and viewing martial arts films" (Lenuta Giukin, "Boy-Girls: Gender, Body, and Popular Culture in Hong Kong Action Movies," in Murray Pomerance, ed., *Ladies and Gentlemen, Boys and Girls: Gender in Film at the End of the Twentieth Century* [Albany: SUNY Press, 2001], 57).

4. Evidence even links the assassination with Chiang Ching-kuo's second son. For details, visit http://www.taiwandc.org/twcom/tc19-int.pdf/.

5. David Bordwell, *Planet Hong Kong: Popular Cinema and the Art of Entertainment* (Cambridge, MA: Harvard University Press, 2000), 224.

6. Citing *Swordsman II* (1991) and *The East Is Red* (1992), Lenuta Giukin argues that in the fin de siecle Hong Kong action movies, "the strong masculinization of the heroine often creates a break with the classical representation of feminine passivity in cinema, a transformation that affects her body representation to a degree that questions the received notion of gender" (55). However, Giukin totally ignores the titillating effect of lesbian love. By turning a well-known actress like Brigitte Lin into a male engaged in implied love-making with another actress does not question gender divisions at all. It strengthens the worst of gender divisions, namely, a

pornographic use of gender. More specific to Hu's use of eunuch antagonist, Giukin believes that "the presence of eunuchs, castrated men in the service of the emperor, prepared society for ... another gender: the neutral ... In action films, eunuchs are often evil presences" (Giukin, 66).

7. David Bordwell in "Richness Through Imperfection: King Hu and the Glimpse" maintains that King Hu "stress[es] certain qualities of these feats; their abruptness, their speed, their mystery. And he chooses to do so by treating these feats as only partly visible" (in Poshek Fu and David Desser, eds., *The Cinema of Hong Kong: History, Arts, Identity* [Cambridge: Cambridge University Press, 2000], 118). To illustrate, Bordwell analyzes Hu's leaping stunts: "Hu gives us only phase 1 or 2 or 3 — launch or leap or landing, or only two of them. ... Hu teases us with mere glimpses of the action" (120). Bordwell terms this "constructive editing."

8. Stefan Hammond comments on the Wong Fei-hong myth as used by Tsui Hark: "A turn-of-the-century hero renowned for his abilities as both a martial artist and a herbalist/physician, Wong [Fei-hong]'s defense of Chinese culture against Western encroachment, while opposing internal political corruption, continues to be seen as an atypical manifestation of Confucian values in a practical, modern setting" (152). Hammond continues to dissect the irony: "A Beijing native [Jet Li] and an American-educated Vietnamese immigrant [Tsui Hark] coming together on a Hong Kong production about a legendary hero [Wong Fei-hong]" (Hammond, 155).

9. Qu Yuan's *Zu Ci*: *"Ju Qing Ming er shu hung xi"* ("Leaning against the sky [or the ultimate realm], I arrange a rainbow"). *"Qing Ming"* signals "the sky" or "the ultimate level one could hope to approach."

10. In *The Sacred Wood* (1920), T. S. Eliot uses "objective correlative" to describe an artistic approach whereby a situation or a set of objective materials is presented to evoke a certain effect.

11. The middle-aged Chow Yun-fat who plays Li is obviously too heavy for such wirework and looks rather clumsy, especially on landing. Another flaw in the digital manipulation comes when a long shot shows Li and Jen flying on top of bamboo before reaching the boulder by a pool of water. They hold their swords in their left hand in the distance, only to reemerge from bamboo with swords in their right hands.

12. Georges Bataille writes in *Death and Sensuality: A Study of Eroticism and the Taboo* (New York: Arno Press, 1977) that the major cause of transgression is the desire to eliminate a felt discontinuity in life. The erotic form of violation, intercourse, eases the sense of isolation in each individual. Sometimes called "little death," love or lust in consummation, due to the magnitude of the act, propels the participants to a state of temporary cessation of life.

13. To Lo (played by the Taiwanese actor/singer Chang Chen), there is no ambiguity. Jen asks him to make a wish and Lo replies: "Bring you back

to Xin Jiang." As Jen leaps into the ravine, Lo holds back his tears. The homeward longing is shared by any immigrant or exile, one increasingly intensified with the passage of time, since there is no way to return home.

CHAPTER 6

1. Stanley Kwan's *Lan Yu* won best actor and best director; Fruit Chan's *Durian Durian* won best picture and best actress.
2. The Golden Horse had about 17 Taiwan entries and 28 Hong Kong entries in 2002.
3. Consider Peter Chan (Chen Kexin)'s *Comrades: Almost a Love Story* (Tianmimi, 1996) and Ann Hui's *Ordinary Heroes* (Qianyan wanyu, 1998).
4. Ping Lu's 2002 novel, *He-je chiun tsai-lai* (Heri jun zailai) (Whence shall you visit again) (Taipei: INK Publishing), explores Teresa Teng's death through the investigations of a defunct Taiwan secret agent.
5. The film's sculpted figure clearly resembles the statue erected in Tiananmen Square in May 1989, which was modeled after America's Statue of Liberty; the protesting Chinese students at the square named their statue Goddess of Democracy.
6. Sheldon Lu, in his article "Filming Diaspora and Identity: Hong Kong and 1997," Poshek Fu and David Desser, eds., *The Cinema of Hong Kong: History, Arts, Identity* (Cambridge: Cambridge University Press, 2000): 273–88, analyzes *Farewell China*, but does not mention "Ssu Hsiang Ch'i." Lu, however, does pay a lot of attention to the Mainland song "My Motherland" (Wo de zuguo) in the same film.
7. See Lan Tsu-wei, *Film Music Composers* (Taipei: Rye Field Publishing Company, 2001): 243–5. Shen Sheng-te, also known as Jim Shum, is presented by Lan Tsu-wei as a music person "from Hong Kong, but who has fallen in love with Taiwan" (238).
8. Ibid., 243–4.
9. Lan Tsu-wei, in his eight-page interview with Shen Shen-te, adamantly takes three pages to question Shen on his choice of "Ssu Hsiang Ch'i." *Farewell China* took part in Taiwan's Golden Horse Award in 1990, and garnered awards for best actor, editing, and sound (not music); it was also awarded a special jury prize. It is recorded that the award judges heatedly debated *Farewell*'s music choice; some thought it to be a stroke of genius, some, a cheap trick (Lan, 51).
10. *A Barthes Reader*, ed. Susan Sontag (New York: Hill & Wang, 1983), 317–33.
11. Ibid., 320.
12. Ibid., 319.
13. Ibid., 320.

14. Even today, when reporting the death of Taiwan's musicologist Hsu Chang-hui, *Taipei Times* (7 September 2001) would cite his discovery of Chen Ta, "the true voice of Taiwan," in 1970 as one of his major cultural contribution. "Ssu Hsiang Ch'i" was made popular when the Cloud Gate dance troupe chose it for their Hsin Chuan dance.

15. Barthes, 331–2.

16. Ibid., 318.

17. Clara Law and Eddie Fong, aside from their continued interest in subjects of migration (Law's first work, *The Other Half and the Other Half* (1988), was a comedy about immigration to Canada), moved to Australia in the 1990s and produced works such as *Floating Life* (1996) and *The Goddess of 1967* (2000) from Down Under.

18. In Hong Kong, the Chinese translation of *Chinese Box* is precisely "Zhongguo he." Although many films have different Chinese titles when released in different Chinese markets, the case of *Chinese Box* is particularly evident in how the political and cultural is linked with the commercial when considering the Taiwan and Hong Kong markets.

19. Articles in *City Entertainment* and *1998 Xianggang dian ying hui gu* all deride *Chinese Box* as a film that spectacularizes Hong Kong at the time of its handover. However, positive reviews can be found in English publications: in "Chinese Box," *Film Quarterly* 52.1:(Fall 1998) 31–4, Wena Poon finds the film "reflective, timely, encyclopedic" when compared to works such as *Pillow Book* or *Irma Vep*. More recently, *Chinese Box* has become a film text academics find much to write about: three papers analyze Wayne Wang's film in *Before and After Suzie: Hong Kong in Western Film and Literature* (part of the *New Asia Academic Bulletin* Series, No. 18), an anthology based on the essays from a symposium on Western Images of Hong Kong in Film and Literature, held on May 4–5, 2000 at the Chinese University of Hong Kong.

20. See Kristin Hohenadel, "A Human Face for Hong Kong's Identity Crisis," *The New York Times* (19 April 1998), 38.

21. Ibid., 29.

22. For readers who have not yet viewed *Chinese Box*, Maggie Cheung's character actually has a facial scar; the history of the intriguing scar is never explained in the film (neither in the theater nor the DVD version released in Taipei). However, one cannot help but infer that her scar might be related to her love and loss of her past colonial lover. In a way, this somewhat parallels the two females in the film — Gong Li as a Chinese woman with a shady past (the character worked as an up-market prostitute when she first arrived in Hong Kong) and Maggie Cheung as the Hong Kong local with a scarred past. I have also been informed that in the 110-minute version of Wayne Wang's film (shown at the 1997 Toronto International Film Festival), Maggie Cheung's scar might have something to do with the

character's attempt to escape from the clutches of an incestuous father; but she probably gave this explanation to the Jeremy Irons character, the voyeuristic Western journalist, to shock him. Whichever way we might want to speculate, Wayne Wang cleverly keeps the scar unexplained, thereby conferring it more allegorical potential.

23. Dadawa's 1997 album was named "Voices from the Sky." In 2000, she named her concert "Heavenly Music for Sentiment Beings — Dadawa@2001" (yes, it uses "sentiment," not "sentient"). In the musical theater "The Riddler," the part she plays is identified as the Celestial Spirit.

24. "*Chinese Box.*" http://www.geocities.com/hungry_ghost_2000/box-kit.htm/.

25. Barthes, 323–4.

26. Wena Poon identifies *Chinese Box* as a thinking picture, and as a picture with thought-out intelligence, 32.

27. It is curious how the number three functions so prominently in *Happy Together*. In Chris Doyle's journal about the film's making, he mentions the insistent emergence of the number during filming ("To the End of the World" *Sight and Sound* [May 1997] 16): "There's something ominous about the number three in this film. It comes before 'four', which is homonym for death in Chinese. Outside the 3 Amigos bar/cabaret, bus number 33 is about to stop … They dance to a song called 'Milonga for Three'. Now Wong is talking about adding a third character to the story … . It's all getting a little too 'mystical' for me, with all these threes …" Doyle's *Happy Together* shooting diary appears in more extended form as "Don't Try for Me, Argentina" in John Boorman and Walter Donohue, eds., *Projections 8: Film-makers on Film-making* (London: Faber and Faber, 1998).

28. "News of the Week," *Hong Kong Cinema*, 21 May 1997, Internet edition (http://egreto.stanford.edu/hk/reports/97may21.html#7/).

29. Marc Siegel analyzes the spaces in *Happy Together* in his "The Intimate Spaces of Wong Kar-Wai," in Esther C. M. Yau, ed., *At Full Speed: Hong Kong Cinema in a Borderless World* (Minneapolis: University of Minnesota Press, 2001).

30. Production material about *Happy Together*, such as Chris Doyle's shooting journal, reveals that the film's story started out with only the two male roles played by Tony Leung Chui-wai and Leslie Cheung. The film's shooting began mid-August in Argentina, Chang Chen and Shirley Kwan (Guan Shuyi) were called to join the picture at around mid-November; according to Doyle, these two actors "idle in their rooms waiting for their roles to materialize while WKW hides in nearby coffee shops hoping for the same" ("Don't Try for Me," 176). Scenes with Shirley Kwan were discarded in the final editing while those with Chang Chen have become integral to this very rare happy-ended Wong Kar-wai film.

31. In the many existing writings about *Happy Together*, Rey Chow, in her "Nostalgia of the New Wave: Structure in Wong Kar-Wai's *Happy Together*"

Camera Obscura 42 (1999): 31–48, observes the Taiwan Chang as a character who provides an alternative kind of relationship for Fai (41). Helen Hok-sze Leung, in her "Queerscapes in Contemporary Hong Kong Cinema" *Positions* 9.2 (Fall 2001): 423–47, goes further and reads Chang as signifying the possibility of reinventing the boundaries of sexual and political identity (439). In "What's So Queer about *Happy Together*? A.k.a. Queer (N)Asian: Interface, Community, Belonging" *Inter-Asia Cultural Studies* 1.2 (2000): 251–64, Audrey Yue notes that Chang has become "the emergent third space in the Hong Kong transnational and diasporic imaginary" (261).

32. Chu's article has been published both in Chinese and English. *Chung-Wai Literary Monthly* 29.10 (March 2001): 6–18; *Post Script* 20.2 & 3 (Summer 2001): 147–58.

33. Huang Wu-lan, ed., *Dang-tai chung-guo tian-ying, 1995–1997* (Contemporary Chinese Cinema, 1995–1997) (Taipei : Shihpao, 1998), 142.

34. In her *City Entertainment* (521 [April 1999], 27–9) interview, Ann Hui talks a lot about the actual figure — Li Siu-tung — who inspired the story of *Ordinary Heroes*. Hui specifically stated that she wanted "an outsider" to play the role of Li Siu-tung.

35. Lee Kang-sheng had a part in TV drama *Boys* (also translated as *The Kid*), directed by Tsai Ming-liang in 1991, before making his film debut in Tsai's 1992 *Rebels of the Neon God*.

36. In his 1997 *The River*, Tsai's probing went as far as examining the taboo of taboos — father-son incest.

37. I use "Taiwan Lee Kang-sheng" rather than "Taiwanese Lee Kang-sheng" to accommodate the entangled identity-language situation in Taiwan: "Taiwanese" is often still used to refer to people of Fukien descent; my use of "Taiwan" keeps the origins more open.

38. This song was often sung by the students at Tiananmen Square before June Fourth.

CHAPTER 7

1. Judith Halberstam, *Female Masculinity* (Durham: Duke University Press, 1998), where she looks at films and theater in order to trace the many distinctive characteristics of such masculinity without men. However, she is not interested in the "sexy" kind of female masculinity portrayed in mainstream Hollywood movies, those muscular female leads such as Sigourney Weaver in *Aliens* (dir. James Cameron, 1986), Linda Hamilton in *Terminator 2: Judgment Day* (dir. James Cameron, 1991) and Demi Moore in *G. I. Jane* (dir. Ridley Scott, 1997), who are all heterosexual though transgressing gender in various senses especially through their muscular look and manly behavior. What Halberstam argues for is a more threatening

kind of female masculinity engaging in different types of masculine performance and relating primarily to same-sex desire.

2. I have serious doubts about Halberstam's view that "female masculinity seems to be at its most threatening when coupled with lesbian desire," *Female Masculinity*, 28. To whom is it threatening? To men or feminine women? Eve Kosofsky Sedgwick also argues that male homosexuality is far more threatening than the female version to a male-dominated society. See her *Between Men: English Literature and Male Homosocial Desire* (New York: Columbia University Press, 1985). But I have to admit that, for some people, the two kinds of threat co-exist.

3. The full quotation from Lacan's *Encore* is: "Woman precisely, except that Woman can only be written with a bar through it. There's no such thing as Woman, Woman with a capital *W* indicating the universal. There's no such thing as Woman because, in her essence — I've already risked using that term, so why should I think twice about using it again? — she is not-whole." See Jacques Lacan, *Encore: The Seminar of Jacques Lacan, Book XX: On Female Sexuality, the Limits of Love and Knowledge 1972–1973*, trans. Bruce Fink (New York: W. W. Norton, 1998), 72–3.

4. For a similar argument that masculinity does not exist, see John MacInnes, *The End of Masculinity: The Confusion of Sexual Genesis and Sexual Difference in Modern Society* (Buckingham: Open University Press, 1998).

5. I am of course reiterating here the famous line from George Orwell's *Animal Farm*: "All animals are equal, but some animals are more equal than others."

6. The concepts of deterritorialization and reterritorialization have played a significant role in the works of Deleuze and Guattari. They see capitalism as a force that decodes and deterritorializes according to its tendency. See *Anti-Oedipus: Capitalism and Schizophrenia* (Minneapolis: University of Minnesota Press, 1977).

7. The term, of course, is taken from Laura Mulvey's classic article, "Visual Pleasure and Narrative Cinema," originally published in *Screen* 16.3 (1975), reprinted in Bill Nichols, ed., *Movies and Methods*, vol.2 (Berkeley and Los Angeles: University of California Press, 1985), 303–15.

8. Sek Kei, "Achievement and Crisis: Hong Kong Cinema in the 80s," in Law Kar, ed., *Hong Kong Cinema in the Eighties: A Comparative Study With Western Cinema* (Hong Kong: Urban Council, 1991), 59.

9. David Bordwell, *Planet Hong Kong: Popular Cinema and the Art of Entertainment* (Cambridge: Harvard University Press, 2000), 153.

10. See Stefan Hammond and Mike Wilkins, *Sex and Zen & A Bullet in the Head: The Essential Guide to Hong Kong's Mind-Bending Films* (New York: Fireside, 1996), 49.

11. See Bey Logan, *Hong Kong Action Cinema* (London: Titan Books, 1995), 153.

12. Detailed depictions of the swordswoman character can be traced back to the fictions and legends of the Tang Dynasty (618–907 AD). One of the earliest

Tang swordswoman characters was Hong Xian (Red Thread), whose previous life was as a male doctor being punished for malpractice: he is reincarnated as a woman. Meanwhile, the first woman warrior on Chinese screens was played by the actress Xuan Jinglin in the silent film *The Nameless Hero* (Wuming yingxiong) (dir. Zhang Shichuan, 1926). See Law Kar, ed., *A Study of the Hong Kong Swordplay Film 1945–1980* (Hong Kong: Urban Council, 1981). For more discussion on the female subgenre of martial arts film in early Chinese cinema, see Zhang Zhen, "Bodies in the Air: The Magic of Science and the Fate of the Early 'Martial Arts' Film in China," *Post Script: Essays in Film and the Humanities* 20.2 & 3 (2001): 52–5.

13. Halberstam, *Female Masculinity*, 4.
14. In the action comedy *My Lucky Stars* (1985), directed by Sammo Hung, the orphanage buddies are obsessed with smirking at long-suffering policewoman Sibelle Hu in the scenes that are typically a gang rape joke. In another scene, one of these buddies who does not speak Japanese tries to get a sausage by underhandedly displaying a part of his anatomy to a Japanese waiter, who brings him a plate with a tiny mushroom.
15. For a detailed chronicle of Michelle Yeoh's filmography from the 1980s to date, see Tony Williams, "Michelle Yeoh: Under Eastern Eyes," *Asian Cinema* 12.2 (2001): 119–31.
16. Logan, *Hong Kong Action Cinema,*157.
17. For a brief history of D & B Films, see Chen Qingwei, *Xianggang dianying gongye ji shichang fenxi* (The Structure and Marketing Analysis of the Hong Kong Film Industry), (Hong Kong: Film Biweekly, 2000), 654–60.
18. Halberstam, *Female Masculinity*, 24.
19. As Morpheus tells Neo in the sci-fi movie *The Matrix* (dir. Andy Wachowski, Larry Wachowski, 1999): "It is the world that has been pulled over your eyes, to blind you from the truth … that you are a slave, Neo. Like everyone else, you were born into bondage, born into a prison that you cannot smell or taste or touch. A prison for your mind." The most powerful ideology is one that makes you do something without your being aware of it.
20. Rothrock was initially offered a chance to play the main fighting villain in Jackie Chan's *Armour of God*. But she made the smart choice by accepting a co-starring role, opposite Yuen Biao, in *Righting Wrongs*.
21. The action sequence of the mahjong parlor scene — in which Rothrock displays great martial arts skills by hand- and foot-cuffing four guys together with only a chair and one pair of cuffs — is so impressive that Bordwell has analyzed it frame by frame to illustrate Hong Kong action cinema's versatility and inventiveness in cutting. See Bordwell, *Planet Hong Kong*, 238–43.
22. David Desser, "The Martial Arts Film in the 1990s," in Wheeler Winston Dixon, ed., *Film Genre 2000: New Critical Essays* (Albany: State University of New York Press, 2000), 81.

23. There is a parallel development in Hollywood. Desser points out that "[m]ore than any other genre, it has been the martial-arts film, while co-opting an Asian genre and remaking it for white, mainstream cultural needs, that has nevertheless opened up a space for Chinese directors and Asian and Asian American stars," "The Martial Arts Film in the 1990s," 108.

24. Tasker, *Spectacular Bodies: Gender, Genre and the Action Cinema* (New York: Routledge, 1993), 24–5.

25. Even in *The Inspector Wears a Skirt* (Baiwang hua), produced by Jackie Chan, a mixed genre of comedy and female-cop action, in which every Chinese policewoman in the film is romantically paired with a cop, Rothrock is left alone. She disappears in the middle of the film, filled with alleged comic relief, and shows up again in time for the final fight scene, and is only given opportunities to show off her kung fu fighting skills in a duet with a Caucasian robber that may be symbolically understood as a virtual coupling act.

26. For further elaboration on the traditional Chinese concepts of chivalry that emphasize the desexualization of the heroes, see James J. Y. Liu, *The Chinese Knight-Errant* (Chicago: University of Chicago Press, 1967) and Kam Louie, *Theorizing Chinese Masculinity: Society and Gender in China* (New York: Cambridge University Press, 2002). It is indeed not difficult to find asexual portrayals of the heroes in Bruce Lee's (Li Xiaolong) and Jackie Chan's kung fu movies.

CHAPTER 8

1. Ackbar Abbas, *Hong Kong: Culture and the Politics of Disappearance* (Minneapolis: University of Minnesota Press, 1997), 23. Page numbers of citations from this work are henceforth noted parenthetically in the main text.

2. We might trace this distrust back to Plato and Aristotle, but I would probably emphasize the critique of the spectacular by French theorists such as Guy Debord and Michel Foucault. See Martin Jay's engaging study *Downcast Eyes: The Denigration of Vision in 20th-Century French Thought* (Berkeley: University of California Press, 1993).

3. This perceived maleness requires that we overlook or at least argue around the simple fact that women have frequently played important roles in Hong Kong action films (the heroic bloodshed genre strikes me as somewhat of an exception in this regard). I might simply mention as standout examples Cheng Pei-pei (Zheng Peipei)'s swordplay in *Come Drink with Me* (Da zuixia) (dir. King Hu, 1966) or the derring-do of Maggie Cheung (Zhang Manyu), Michelle Yeoh (Yang Ziqiong) and Anita Mui (Mei Yanfang) in *The Heroic Trio* (Dongfang sanxia) (dir. Johnnie To, 1992).

4. A deeper look into the question of "maleness" in the work of Woo would have to take into account the issue of masochism, the strong presence of which runs counter to the obviously sadistic side of many action films. See the following: Julian Stringer, "'Your tender smiles give me strength': Paradigms of Masculinity in John Woo's *A Better Tomorrow* and *The Killer*," *Screen* 38.1 (Spring 1997): 25–40; and Anthony Enns, "The Spectacle of Disabled Masculinity in John Woo's 'Heroic Bloodshed' Films," *Quarterly Review of Film and Video* 17.2 (2000): 137–45.

5. Concerning postcoloniality and the spectral woman (including a reading from Hong Kong cinema), see Bliss Cua Lim's "Spectral Times: The Ghost Film as Historical Allegory," *positions: east asia cultures critique* 9.2 (Fall 2001): 287–329.

6. There is some confusion in the secondary material as to whether producer Danny Lee (Li Xiuxian), who also has major role in the film, is to be given partial directorial credit as well. Most sources, however, including Tai Seng, the film's distributor, simply credit Yau.

7. For readers unfamiliar with the Hong Kong rating system, Category III is similar to the NC-17 designation in the United States or the British X in that sexually explicit content and violence are primary considerations.

8. See Darrel W. Davis and Yeh Yueh-yu, "Warning Category III: The Other Hong Kong Cinema," *Film Quarterly* 54.4 (Summer 2001): 12–26. This engaging essay will no doubt serve as a prolegomenon to any future study of this aspect of the rating system.

9. See Darrell W. Davis and Yeh Yueh-yu, 20–1.

10. Paul Fonoroff, *At the Hong Kong Movies: 600 Reviews from 1988 Till the Handover* (Hong Kong: Film Biweekly Publishing House, 1998), 299.

11. Ibid., 299.

12. David Bordwell, *Planet Hong Kong: Popular Cinema and the Art of Entertainment* (Cambridge, MA: Harvard University Press, 2000), 189–90.

13. On the film's success in Hong Kong as well as in the overseas market, see Bordwell, 77 and 155.

14. See Daniel Dayan, "The Tutor-Code of Classical Cinema," *Film Quarterly* 28.1 (Fall 1974): 22–31. On "suture," see also: Jean-Pierre Oudart, "La Suture," *Cahiers du Cinéma* 211 (April 1969): 36–9; Jean-Pierre Oudart, "La Suture" (part two), *Cahiers du Cinéma* 212 (May 1969): 50–5; Steven Heath, "Notes on Suture," *Screen* 18.2 (1977–78): 48–76. The concept and its reception are nicely summed up and explained in Kaja Silverman, *The Subject of Semiotics* (Oxford: Oxford University Press, 1983), 194–236. For a postcolonial take on the concept and its limitations, see Rey Chow, "Film and Cultural Studies," in John Hill and Pamela Church Gibson, eds., *The Oxford Guide to Film Studies* (Oxford: Oxford University Press, 1998): 169–75. I might add that the concept of "suture" as originally put forward by

Lacanian psychoanalyst Jacques-Alain Miller was not a theory of how the Imaginary is stitched to the Symbolic (as it became in its film-studies reception). Rather, Miller is interested in how lack becomes constitutive of the subject (Frege's set theory and specifically the generation of the series of natural numbers from zero serve as a model). This puts Miller's work somewhat more in line with the theories of identity formation discussed below.

15. See Julia Kristeva, "L'abjet d'amour," *Tel Quel* 91 (Spring 1982): 17–32. See also, Julia Kristeva, *Pouvoirs de l'horreur* (Paris: Editions du Seuil, 1980), 9–39 in particular. One might compare in this regard Darrell Davis and Yeh Yueh-yu's discussion of extreme "objectification" in Category III horror, including *The Untold Story* (Davis and Yeh, 19–20).

16. See Jacques Lacan, *Le Séminaire VII: L'éthique de la psychanalyse* (Paris: Seuil, 1986), 55–86, passim. Lacan's notion of *das Ding* gets an explanation and political spin in Slavoj Zizek, *For They Know Not What They Do: Enjoyment as a Political Factor* (London: Verso, 1991), 229–77.

17. A historical genealogy of such psychoanalytic notions would also include Freud's *Beyond the Pleasure Principle* at the very least — there are many affinities with Nietzsche's *Birth of Tragedy* and Artaud's "theater of cruelty" as well.

18. See Bordwell, 97.

19. For a French example, one need go no further than Monléon's grimly theatrical adaptation — severed limbs and heads are revealed onstage by suddenly pulling back curtains — of Seneca's aforementioned work: *Thyeste* (1638). Similar works from the German Baroque have gained academic recognition thanks to Walter Benjamin's *The Origin of German Tragic Drama*, trans. John Osbourne (London: Verso, 1998).

20. Notable commentaries on *Bullet in the Head* include: Stephen Teo, *Hong Kong Cinema: The Extra Dimensions* (London: British Film Institute, 1997), 178–9; Kenneth E. Hall, *John Woo: The Films* (Jefferson, NC: McFarland & Company, Inc., 1999), 135–47; Lisa Odham Stokes and Michael Hoover, *City on Fire: Hong Kong Cinema* (London: Verso, 1999), 183–4; and Bordwell, 109–11. See also, my essay "Bullet in the Head: Trauma, Identity, and Violent Spectacle," in Chris Berry, ed., *Chinese Films in Focus: 25 New Takes* (London: British Film Institute, 2003): 23–30.

21. See Laikwan Pang, "Death and Hong Kong Cinema," *Quarterly Review of Film and Video* 18.1 (2001): 15–29.

22. On the separation of place and space as a fundamental feature of modernity, see Anthony Giddens, *The Consequences of Modernity* (Stanford: Stanford University Press, 1990), 17–21.

23. See Rey Chow, *Primitive Passions* (New York: Columbia University Press, 1995), 176–202.

24. I borrow the expression from Clifford Geertz's classic explanation and

defense of hermeneutic anthropology: "Notes on the Balinese Cockfight," *The Interpretation of Cultures: Selected Essays* (New York: Basic Books, 1973), 452.

25. Thomas Weisser, *Asian Trash Cinema: The Book* (Miami: ATC/ETC Publications, 1994), 110.

26. Thomas Weisser, *Asian Trash Cinema: The Book (Part 2)* (Miami: Vital Sounds Inc. and ATC Publications, 1995), 58.

27. Ibid, 130.

28. Weisser (1994), 52.

29. Stefan Hammond and Mike Wilkins, *Sex and Zen & A Bullet in the Head* (New York: Fireside, 1996), 239. The authors also note the galvanizing effect that the success of *The Silence of the Lambs* had on Category III production (v. 227). I should remark that although Hammond and Wilkins are given as the primary authors of this book, much of the writing is done by "contributing writers." Thus, for the entry on *The Untold Story*, the author is Jim Morton. Of the nine additional contributors, eight are men.

30. Ibid., 237.

31. Bordwell, "Aesthetics in Action: *Kungfu*, Gunplay, and Cinematic Expressivity," in Esther C. M. Yau ed., *At Full Speed: Hong Kong Cinema in a Borderless World* (Minneapolis: University of Minnesota Press, 2001), 73. See Bordwell's similarly appreciative and ambivalent comments on fandom in *Planet Hong Kong,* 82–97.

32. Specifically, Abbas objects to Hong Kong cinema being labeled "'a cinema of blazing passions', which was how one popular festival of Hong Kong films was billed in the United States" (16). This disdain for the popular — neither intellectual nor subaltern — might be further looked into. As for the local-versus-foreign issue, Abbas states: "When the Hong Kong cinema is praised (interestingly enough, more often by foreign than by local critics), it is for its action sequences, its slick editing, its mastery of special effects [...] as if the mere downplaying of dialogue, narrative structure, or even intelligence somehow made Hong Kong cinema more immediate, more like 'pure cinema'" (18). Note how this polarizing and charged binary is sneaked in the back door, appearing offhandedly within parentheses.

33. We are here reminded that when it comes to information theory, analysis of the parasite/host relationship often leads to the discovery of unexpected ambiguities (see Michel Serres, *Le Parasite* [Paris: Éditions Grasset et Fasquette, 1980]), and a discovery shared by deconstruction (J. Hillis Miller, "The Critic as Host," in Gregory S. Jay, ed., *Modern American Critics Since 1955, Dictionary of Literary Biography*, vol. 67 [Detroit: Gale Research Company, 1988]: 327–32).

34. A point nicely made by Jinsoo An in "*The Killer*: Cult Film and Transcultural (Mis)Reading," *At Full Speed*: 95–113. An's intervention makes several interesting gestures in the direction of the breaking apart of traditional

hermeneutics (the cultural unity of producer, product and consumer), but ultimately falls back on a sort of nativism (q.v. the essay's title).

35. On the ways in which mass media simultaneously engender the notion of "culture" and render it largely irrelevant, see Niklas Luhmann's *The Reality of the Mass Media*, trans. Kathleen Cross (Stanford: Stanford University Press, 2000), 85–7.

36. On the return of the native, see the chapter of Rey Chow's *Writing Diaspora: Tactics of Intervention in Contemporary Cultural Studies*, entitled "Where Have All the Natives Gone?" (Bloomington: Indiana University Press, 1993), 27–54. See also Chow's more recent analysis of the topic in her *The Protestant Ethnic and the Spirit of Capitalism* (New York: Columbia University Press, 2002), 95–127.

CHAPTER 9

1. Some interviewees criticized other films and filmmakers. To avoid conflicts and problems that could result from their comments, the names of many informants have been withheld in this chapter.

2. This trend is even more pronounced in Hong Kong.

3. The Chinese titles and names of actors, scriptwriters and directors are given in the corresponding Chinese characters and Mandarin pinyin romanization in the following section. The English names and titles of other persons and movies that appear throughout the text employ the spellings chosen by the individuals involved because Hong Kong-style English names and titles convey specific meanings and cultural symbols.

4. Although some recent international-award-winning artistic films have attracted the attention of academics, they received little popular support in Hong Kong. This makes them of limited use in any coherent cultural analysis of local society. I therefore selected these two comedies, which were popular locally, to develop a cultural analysis of gender in Hong Kong.

5. Clifford Geertz, *The Interpretation of Culture* (NY: Basic Books, 1973), 5.

6. Several filmmakers shared the observation, based on their experiences in East Asia, that although Hong Kong women live in a modern, international city, their sexual attitudes seem to be more traditional than those of women in other Confucian-influenced societies, such as South Korea, Japan, mainland China and Taiwan.

7. Category III refers to X-rated publications and films that are approved for exhibition only to persons in Hong Kong who are at least 18 years of age.

8. Robin Lakoff, *Talking Power: The Politics of Language in Our Lives* (NY: Basic Books, 1990), 203.

9. Nancy Bonvillain, *Language, Culture, and Communication: the Meaning of Messages* (NJ: Prentice Hall, 1993), 145–241.

10. Kingsley Bolton and Christopher Hutton, "Bad Boys and Bad Language: Chou Hau and the Sociolinguistics of Swearwords in Hong Kong Cantonese," in Grant Evans and Maria Tam, eds., *Hong Kong: The Anthropology of a Chinese Metropolis* (Surrey: Curzon, 1997), 304.

11. S. I. Hayakawa, *Language in Thought and Action* (San Diego: Harcourt Brace, 5th edition, 1990), 191.

12. The survey was conducted by the Psychology Department of the Chinese University of Hong Kong in 2002, and reported by many local newspapers. Please also refer to *Oriental Daily*, 8 June 2002.

13. Stuart Ewen, "Marketing Dreams," in Alan Tomlinson, ed., *Consumption, Identity & Style* (Routledge, 1990), 43.

14. Michel Foucault, *Discipline and Punish: The Birth of the Prison*, trans. Alan Sheridan (London: Penguin Books, 1997).

15. Kwai-cheung Lo, "Muscles and Subjectivity: A Short History of the Masculine Body in Hong Kong Popular Culture," in *Camera Obscura* 39 (September 1996): 106–7.

16. Kenneth Clatterbaugh, *Contemporary Perspectives on: Masculinity* (Westview Press, 1990), 40–5.

17. Ibid.

18. Sean Nixon, "Exhibiting Masculinity," in Stuart Hall, ed., *Representation: Cultural Representations and Signifying Practices* (Sage Publications, 1997), 298.

19. Ann Hui also said this to Winnie Chung, a reporter with the *South China Morning Post*, 14 March 2002, 5.

20. David Bordwell, *Planet Hong Kong: Popular Cinema and the Art of entertainment* (Massachusetts and London: Harvard University Press, 2000), 123–4.

21. Walker Percy, *The Message in the Bottle* (NY: Straus & Giroux, 1983), 115.

22. Ackbar Abbas, "The New Hong Kong Cinema and the Deja Disparu," *Discourse* 16.3 (1994): 66.

23. Greg Dancer, "Film Style and Performance: Comedy and Kung Fu from Hong Kong," *Asian Cinema* 10.1 (Fall 1998): 44.

24. I discovered that Michelle Reis had modeled for plastic surgery when she appeared in a Taiwanese TV program during the summer of 2001. I missed the title of the program, which was a show inviting members of the audience to guess who among several women had had plastic surgery.

25. Leonard Quart and Albert Auster, *American Film and Society Since 1945* (London and Basingstoke: Macmillan, 1984), 2–3.

26. Liesbet van Zooner, *Feminist Media Studies* (Sage Publications, 1994), 8.

27. Please refer to *Oriental Sunday Magazine* [Dongfang xindi], issue 287, 11 June 2003. Maggie Cheung Ho-yee is an actress.

CHAPTER 10

1. Georg Lukacs, *History and Class Consciousness; Studies in Marxist Dialectics*, Translated by Rodney Livingstone, Cambridge: MIT Press, 1971), 27.

2. Lo Kwai-cheung, "Double Negations: Hong Kong Cultural Identity in Hollywood's Transnational Representations," *Cultural Studies* 15.3 & 4 (2001): 465.

3. Richard Natale, "Springing to Action; Adopting Hong Kong's Style of Martial Arts Scenes, with Their Ballet-Like Moves, Has Helped Movie Makers Revive a Genre with Less Graphic Violence," *The Los Angeles Times* (8 January 2002).

4. Pierre Bourdieu and Loic Wacquant, "On the Cunning of Imperialist Reason," *Theory, Culture and Society* 16.1 (1999): 41.

5. Ibid.

6. John Beynon, *Masculinities and Culture* (Buckingham; Philadelphia: Open University Press, 2002): 16; Judith Kegan Gardiner, "Introduction," in Judith Kegan Gardiner ed., *Masculinity Studies and Feminist Theory: New Directions* (New York: Columbia University Press, 2002), 11.

7. King-kok Cheung, "Art, Spirtuality, And the Ethic of Care: Alternative Masculinities in Chinese American Literature," in Judith Kegan Gardiner, ed., *Masculinity Studies and Feminist Theory: New Directions* (New York: Columbia University Press, 2002), 263.

8. Gina Marchetti, *Romance and the "Yellow Peril": Race, Sex and Discursive Strategies in Hollywood Fiction* (Berkeley: University of California Press, 1993), 35.

9. David Bordwell, *Planet Hong Kong: Popular Cinema and the Art of Entertainment* (Harvard: Harvard University Press, 2000), 98.

10. (Kehr, 2002: 1)

11. Julian Stringer, "'Your Tender Smiles Give Me Strength': Paradigms of Masculinity in John Woo's *A Better Tomorrow* and *The Killer*," *Screen* 38.1 (1997): 32.

12. Ibid., 29.

13. Ibid., 30.

14. Ibid., 32.

15. Robert Hanke, "John Woo's Cinema of Hyperkinetic Violence: From *A Better Tomorrow* to *Face/Off* (Critical Essay)," *Film Criticism* 24.1 (1999): 7.

16. Ibid., 8.

17. Ibid., 9.

18. Ibid.

19. Bordwell, 113.

20. Ibid., 50.

21. Ibid., 55.

22. Paul Ng Chun-ming, "The Image of Overseas Chinese in American Cinema,"

in Kar Law, ed., *Overseas Chinese Figures in Cinema* (Hong Kong: Urban Council, 1992), 84.

23. Marchetti, 116.
24. Lo, 475.
25. Hugh Hart, "Fall Sneaks; His Career Is No Stunt; Comedy may be his forte, but Jackie Chan is quite serious about which movies he chooses," *The Los Angeles Times* (8 September 2002): 9.
26. Max Horkheimer and Theodor W. Adorno, *Dialectic of Enlightenment: Philosophical Fragments* (Stanford: Stanford University Press, 2002), xvi.
27. Ibid., xviii.
28. Ibid., xviii-xix.
29. Ibid., 125.
30. Theodor W. Adorno, *The Cultural Industry* (London: Routledge, 2002), 99–100.
31. Ibid., 100.
32. Ibid., 100–1.
33. David Held, *Introduction to Critical Theory* (Berkeley and Los Angeles: University of California Press: 1980), 77.
34. Karl Marx, *Capital, Vol. 1* (London: Penguin Books, 1990), 439–636.
35. David Harvey, *The Condition of Postmodernity* (Oxford: Blackwell, 1989), 124.
36. Douglas Gomery, *Movie History: A Survey* (Belmont: Wardworth, 1991), 169–81.
37. Robert Allen and Douglas Gomery, *Film History: Theory and Pracrice* (New York: Alfred Knopf, 1985), 143.
38. Michael Storper, "The Transition to Flexible Specialization in the US Film Industry: External Economies, the Division of Labour and the Crossing of Industrial Divides," in Ash Amin, ed., *Post-Fordism: A Reader* (Oxford: Blackwell, 1994), 201.
39. Kristin Thompson and David Bordwell, *Film History: An Introduction* (New York: McGraw-Hill, 1994), 380.
40. Storper, 196.
41. Natale.
42. Ibid.
43. Ibid.
44. Ibid.
45. Claudia Eller and Lorenza Munoz, "The Plots Thicken in Foreign Markets," *The Los Angeles Times* (6 October 2002), A26.
46. Ibid.
47. Ibid.
48. See Kenichi Ohmae, *The End of the Nation State: The Rise of Regional Economies* (New York: Free Press, 1995); Jean-Marie Guehenno, *The End of the Nation State* (Minneapolis: University of Minnesota Press, 1995);

Walter Wriston, *The Twilight of Sovereignty* (New York: Charles Scribners Press, 1992).

CHAPTER 11

The author would like to express thanks to Thomas Yui-choi Chan for his helpful research assistance.

1. Jachinson W. Chan, "Bruce Lee's Fictional Models of Masculinity," *Men and Masculinities* 2.4 (2000): 371–87; David Desser, "The Kung Fu Craze: Hong Kong Cinema's First American Reception," in Poshek Fu and David Desser, eds., *The Cinema of Hong Kong: History, Arts, Identity*, (Cambridge: Cambridge University Press, 2000), 19–43; Mark Gallagher, "Masculinity in Translation: Jackie Chan's Transcultural Star Text," *The Velvet Light Trap* 39 (1997): 23–40; Philippa Gates, "The Man's Film: Woo and the Pleasure of Male Melodrama," *Journal of Popular Culture* 35.1 (2001): 59–79; Siu-Leung Li, "Kung Fu: Negotiating Nationalism and Modernity," *Cultural Studies* 15.3 & 4 (2001): 515–42; Kwai-Cheung Lo, "Muscles and Subjectivity: A Short History of the Masculine Body in Hong Kong Popular Culture," *Camera Obscura* 39 (1996): 105–25; Laikwan Pang, "Masculinity in Crisis: Films of Milkyway Image and Post-1997 Hong Kong Cinema," *Feminist Media Studies* 2.3 (Fall 2002), 325–40; Barbara Ryan, "Blood, Brothers, and Hong Kong Gangster Movies: Pop Culture Commentary on 'One China,'" in John A. Lent, ed., *Asian Popular Culture* (Boulder: Westview Press, 1995), 61–77; Jillian Sandell, "Reinventing Masculinity: The Spectacle of Male Intimacy in the Films of John Woo," *Film Quarterly* 49.4 (1996): 23–34; Julian Stringer, "'Your Tender Smiles Give Me Strength': Paradigms of Masculinity in John Woo's *A Better Tomorrow* and *The Killer*," *Screen* 38.1 (1997): 25–41.

2. Li, "Kung Fu," 515–42; Lo, "Muscles and Subjectivity," 105–25; Stephen Teo, *Hong Kong Cinema: The Extra Dimension* (London: BFI, 1997), 97–8, 110–22; Stephen Teo, "The True Way of the Dragon: The Films of Bruce Lee," in *Overseas Chinese Figures in Cinema (The 16th Hong Kong International Film Festival)* (Hong Kong: Urban Council, 1992), 70–80.

3. Teo, *Hong Kong Cinema*, 97–8, 110–22; Teo, "The True Way of the Dragon," 70–80.

4. Lo, "Muscles and Subjectivity," 105–25.

5. Ibid., 106.

6. Sek Kei, "The War between the Cantonese and the Mandarin Cinemas in the Sixties, or How the Beautiful Women Lost to the Action Men," in Law Kar, ed., *The Restless Breed: Cantonese Stars of the Sixties (The 20th Hong Kong International Film Festival)* (Hong Kong: The Urban Council, 1996), 26–33.

7. Linda Chiu-Han Lai, "Film and Enigmatization: Nostalgia, Nonsense, and Remembering," in Esther Yau, ed., *At Full Speed: Hong Kong Cinema in a Borderless World* (Minneapolis: University of Minnesota Press, 2001), 231–50.

8. Gallagher, "Masculinity in Translation," 23–40.

9. Gates, "The Man's Film," 59–79; Sandell, "Reinventing Masculinity," 23–34; Stringer, "Your Tender Smiles," 25–41.

10. Sek, "The War between."

11. Ibid., 30.

12. Li, "Kung Fu," 525.

13. Teo, *Hong Kong Cinema*, 110–4.

14. Tony Rayns, "Bruce Lee: Narcissism and Nationalism," in *A Study of the Hong Kong Martial Arts Film, Hong Kong International Film Festival Catalogue* (Hong Kong: Urban Council, 1980). On this issue, one reviewer kindly shares the information that Stephen Teo's "The True Way of the Dragon" (1992) was partially written to answer Rayns's comments.

15. Teo, *Hong Kong Cinema*, 116.

16. Ibid., 111–2.

17. Ibid., 114.

18. Li, "Kung Fu," 515–42; Lo, "Muscles and Subjectivity," 105–25.

19. David Desser, "Diaspora and National Identity: Exporting 'China' Through the Hong Kong Cinema," *Post Script* 20.2 & 3 (2001): 124–36.

20. Desser, "Diaspora and National Identity," 124.

21. Teo, *Hong Kong Cinema*, 124.

22. Desser, "Diaspora and National Identity," 124–36.

23. Teo, *Hong Kong Cinema*, 122.

24. Desser, "Diaspora and National Identity," 127.

25. Ibid., 134.

26. David Bordwell, *Planet Hong Kong: Popular Cinema and the Art of Entertainment* (Cambridge, MA: Harvard University Press, 2000), 46–7.

27. Lo, "Muscles and Subjectivity," 105–25.

28. Li, "Kung Fu," 515–42.

29. Ibid., 528–9.

30. Ibid., 522.

31. Jenny Kwok-wah Lau, "Besides Fists and Blood: Hong Kong Comedy and Its Master of the Eighties," *Cinema Journal* 37.2 (1998): 18–34.

32. Lo, "Muscles and Subjectivity," 105–25.

33. Lau, "Besides Fists and Blood," 26.

34. In the early 1990s there was some local discussion in Chinese on the culture of "nonsense talk" epitomized by Stephen Chow's movies, but it remained brief, sketchy, and impressionistic. Perhaps one exception is that in recent years Chow's movies have aroused some phenomenal discussion among the young intellectuals in China.

35. Linda Chiu-han Lai, "Film and Enigmatization: Nostalgia, Nonsense, and Remembering," in Esther Yau, ed., *At Full Speed: Hong Kong Cinema in a Borderless World* (Minneapolis: University of Minnesota Press, 2001), 231–50.

36. Lai, "Film and Enigmatization," 231–50.

37. Besides Chow's cinema of nonsense, ritualistic commemoration is also found in nostalgic films.

38. Lai, "Film and Enigmatization," 232.

39. Hong Kong Film Critics Society, *Review on Hong Kong Movies (1994, 1995, 1996, 1997, 1998, 1999)* (Hong Kong: Hong Kong Film Critics Society); Zhuotao Li (Cheuk-to Li), *Guan Ni Ji* (Hong Kong: Ci Wan Hua Tang, 1993); Zhuotao Li , *Linli Yingxiang Guan — Paozhuan Pian* (Hong Kong: Ci Wan Hua Tang, 1996); Zhuotao Li, *Linli Yingxiang Guan — Jingshui Pian* (Hong Kong: Ci Wan Hua Tang, 2000); Chiu-hing Lee, *Hong Kong Postmodern* (Hong Kong: Compass Corporation Ltd, 2002); Sek Kei, *Shiqi Yinghua Ji* (Hong Kong: Ci Wan Hua Tang, 1999); W. Wang, *Hong Kong Cinema POV* (Taipei: Yang Zhi Wen Hua Shi Ye Gu Fen You Xian Gong Si., 2002); see also website: http://filmcritics.org.hk/.

40. Hong Kong Film Critics Society, *Review on Hong Kong Movies (1996)*, 282.

41. Wang, *Hong Kong Cinema POV*, 364.

42. Ibid., 365.

43. Lee, *Hong Kong Postmodern*.

44. Ibid., 86.

45. Ibid., 42.

46. This contrasts quite interestingly with the representation of male homoeroticism in some of the action films, especially those by John Woo.

47. Stephen Whitehead and Frank Barrett, *The Masculinities Reader* (Cambridge: Polity Press, 2001).

48. Among Western critics there is increasing attention to the question of different forms of masculinity in Hong Kong cinema (Gallagher, "Masculinity in Translation," 23–40; Gates, "The Man's Film," 59–79; Sandell, "Reinventing Masculinity," 23–34). For discussion by a local scholar, see Pang, "Masculinity in Crisis."

CHAPTER 12

1. Laura Mulvey, "Visual pleasure and narrative cinema," *Screen*, 16.3 (1975): 6–18. Reprinted in P. Erens, ed., *Issues in Feminist Film Criticism* (Bloomington, IN: Indiana University Press, 1990), 28–71.

2. Mary Ann Doane, "Film and masquerade: theorizing the female spectator," *Screen* 23.3–4 (1982). Reprinted in Mary Ann Doane, *Femmes Fatales* (New York & London: Routledge, 1991), 17–32.

3. Laura Mulvey, "Afterthought on 'Visual Pleasure and Narrative Cinema'

inspired by *Duel in the Sun*," in Constance Penley, ed., *Feminism and Film Theory* (New York: Routledge, 1988), 69–79.

4. Tania Modleski, *Loving with a Vengeance: Mass Produced Fantasies for Women* (London: Methuen, 1984).

5. Stuart Hall, "Encoding/Decoding," in Stuart Hall, Dorothy Hobson, Andrew Lowe and Paul Willis, eds., *Culture, Media, Language* (London: Hutchinson,1980), 128–38.

6. Janet Bergstrom and Mary Ann Doane, "The female spectators: contexts and directions," *Camera Obscura*, 20–21(1989): 5–27.

7. See Jackie Stacey's discussion of different forms of cinema identification in *Star Gazing: Hollywood Cinema and Female Spectatorship* (London & New York: Routledge, 1994), 126–75.

8. See Stacey, 1994, 176–223, for a discussion of how female spectators related to Hollywood stars through consumption practices in different historical periods.

9. Ann Gray, "Behind closed doors: video recorders in the home," in H. Baehr and G. Dyer, eds., *Boxed in: Women and Television* (London: Pandora Press, 1987), 38–54.

10. Annette Kuhn makes a distinction between a social-audience approach that emphasizes the context of the actual viewing process, and a psychoanalytic approach that is concerned with the ideal spectator provided by a text. See Kuhn's criticism of the either-or approach in Annette Kuhn, "Women genres," *Screen* 25.1 (1984):18–28. Reprinted in Graeme Turner, ed., *The Film Cultures Reader* (London & NY: Routledge, 2002), 20–7.

11. Kuhn, ibid.

12. Elizabeth V. Spelman, *Inessential Woman: Problems of Exclusion in Feminist Thought* (London: Women's Press, 1990).

13. Judith Butler, *Gender Trouble: Feminism and the Subversion of Identity* (New York: Routledge, 1990), 136.

14. Constance Penley, Untitled, *Camera Obscura* 20–21(1989): 256–60.

15. Judith Mayne, "Paradoxes of spectatorship," in Graeme Turner, ed., *The Film Cultures Reader* (London & New York: Routledge, 2002), 28–45.

16. Janet Staiger, "Reception studies in film and television," in Graeme Turner, ed., *The Film Cultures Reader* (London & NY: Routledge, 2002), 46–72.

17. Stephen Teo, "The decade with two faces: Cantonese cinema and the paranoid Sixties," in *The Restless Breed: Cantonese Stars of the Sixties* (Hong Kong: The Urban Council of Hong Kong, 1996), 18–25.

18. Sek Kei, "The war between the Cantonese and Mandarin Cinemas in the Sixties, or how the beautiful women lost to the action men," in The 20th Hong Kong International Film Festival, ed., *The Restless Breed: Cantonese Stars of the Sixties* (Hong Kong: The Urban Council of Hong Kong, 1996), 30–3.

19. Sam Ho, "Licensed to kick man: the Jane Bond films," in The 20th Hong

Kong International Film Festival, ed., *The Restless Breed: Cantonese Stars of the Sixties* (Hong Kong: The Urban Council of Hong Kong,1996), 34–6.

20. Lisbeth Ku, "Mass-mediated images of women: Connie Chan Po-chu and Josephine Siao Fong-fong as desired cultural images," in *Hong Kong Cultural Studies Bulletin*, 819.8–9 (Spring/Summer 1998): 31–40.

21. Janet Salaff, *Working Daughters of Hong Kong* (Cambridge: Cambridge University Press, 1981).

22. The situations of working daughters are recounted in the autobiographical parts of Allen Fong's *Father and Son* (Fuzi qing) (1981) and Stanley Kwan's *Yang ± Yin: Gender in Chinese Cinema* (Nansheng nuxiang: Zhongguo dianying de xingbie)(1996).

23. Ku, 1998.

24. Ref. Gray, 1987.

25. Sek, 1996.

26. Yvonne Tasker, "Fists of Fury: Discourses of Race and Masculinity in the Martial Arts Cinema," in Harry Stecopoulos and Michael Uebel, eds., *Race and the Subject of Masculinities* (Durham: Duke University Press, 1997), 315–36.

27. Mark Gallagher, "Masculinity in transition: Jackie Chan's transcultural star text," in *The Velvet Light Trap* 39 (Spring 1997): 23–41.

28. Lau Siu-kai, *Hongkongese or Chinese: the Problem of Identity on the Eve of Resumption of Chinese Sovereignty over Hong Kong* (Hong Kong: Hong Kong Institute of Asia-Pacific Studies, the Chinese University of Hong Kong, 1997). Also see Kuan Hsin-chi and Lau Siu-kai, *Political Attitudes in a Changing Context* (Hong Kong: Hong Kong Institute of Asia-Pacific Studies, the Chinese University of Hong Kong, 1997) for a discussion of the identity of Hong Kong Chinese.

29. Tasker, 1997.

30. David Bordwell, *Planet Hong Kong: Popular Cinema and the Art of Entertainment* (Cambridge: Harvard University Press, 2000), 60.

31. Gallagher, 1997, 29.

32. Penley, 1989, 256.

33. Ref. Stacey, 1994, 145–50.

34. Janice Radway, *Reading the Romance: Women, Patriarchy, and Popular Literature* (Chapel Hill, NC: University of North Carolina Press, 1984).

35. Ibid., 222.

36. In the Sino-British Joint Declaration signed by the Chinese and British governments in 1984, it is stated that the socialist system and policies of China shall not be practised in Hong Kong after China resumes her sovereignty in 1997. A committee was formed in 1985 to draft the Basic Law. The Basic Law is a constitutional document that enshrines the concept of "one country, two systems" and that prescribes the various systems to be practised in Hong Kong.

37. Ref. Stacey, 1994, 145ff.

Glossary

Name as it appears in the text	Pinyin	Chinese
PEOPLE		
Ah Fa	A Hua	阿花
Ah Yee	A Yi	阿儀
Baak Suet-sin	Bai Xuexian	白雪仙
Bai Ying	Bai Ying	白鷹
Booi Dai	Bei Di	貝蒂
Chan, Eason	Chen Yixun	陳奕迅
Chan, Evans	Chen Yaocheng	陳耀成
Chan, Fruit	Chen Guo	陳果
Chan Hing-kar	Chen Qingjia	陳慶嘉
Chan, Jackie	Cheng Long	成龍
Chan, Jordan	Chen Xiaochun	陳小春
Chan Kam-hung	Chen Jinhong	陳錦鴻
Chan Kwok-bong	Chen Guobang	陳國邦
Chan, Natalia	Luo Feng	洛楓
Chan Number Thirteen	Chen Shisan	陳十三
Chan, Pauline	Chen Baolian	陳寶蓮
Chan, Peter	Chen Kexin	陳可辛
Chan Po-chu, Connie	Chen Baozhu	陳寶珠
Chan Sing	Chen Xing	陳星
Chang Chen	Zhang Zhen	張震
Chang, Grace	Ge Lan	葛蘭

Chang, Sylvia	Zhang Aijia	張艾嘉
Chen, Bobby	Chen Sheng	陳昇
Chen Chen	Zhen Zhen	甄珍
Chen Chi-li	Chen Qili	陳啟禮
Chen Kaige	Chen Kaige	陳凱歌
Chen Kuan-tai	Chen Guantai	陳觀泰
Chen Ta	Chen Da	陳達
Cheng Chang-ho	Zheng Changhe	鄭昌和
Cheng Dan-shui	Zheng Danrui	鄭丹瑞
Cheng Dieyi	Cheng Dieyi	程蝶衣
Cheng, Ekin	Zheng Yijian	鄭伊健
Cheng Ka-wing	Zheng Jiaying	鄭嘉穎
Cheng Pei-pei	Zheng Peipei	鄭佩佩
Cheng, Sammi	Zheng Xiuwen	鄭秀文
Cheung Chang-chak	Zhang Zengze	張曾澤
Cheung Chi-leung	Zhang Zhiliang	張之亮
Cheung Hok-yau	Zhang Xueyou	張學友
Cheung, Leslie	Zhang Guorong	張國榮
Cheung, Mabel	Zhang Wanting	張婉婷
Cheung, Maggie Ho-yee	Zhang Keyi	張可頤
Cheung, Maggie (Man-yuk)	Zhang Manyu	張曼玉
Cheung Yiu-yeung	Zhang Yaoyang	張耀揚
Chia Ling	Jia Ling	嘉凌
Chiang Ching-kuo	Jiang Jingguo	蔣經國
Chiang, David	Jiang Dawei	姜大衛
Chiao, Roy	Qiaao Hong	喬宏
Chin, Amy	Qian Xiaohui	錢小惠
Chin Ping	Qin Ping	秦萍
Chin, Wellson	Qian Shengwei	錢升瑋
Ching Gong	Cheng Gang	程剛
Ching Siu-tung	Cheng Xiaodong	程小東
Chiu, Derek	Zhao Chongji	趙崇基
Chiu Mei	Zhao Wei	趙薇

Chor Yuen	Chu Yuan	楚原
Chou Wah-shan	Zhou Huashan	周華山
Chow Man-kin	Zhou Wenjian	周文健
Chow, Matt	Zhou Kaiguang	鄒凱光
Chow, Raymond	Zhou Wenhuai	鄒文懷
Chow (/Chiau), Stephen	Zhou Xingchi	周星馳
Chow Yun-fat	Zhou Runfa	周潤發
Chu Yan	Zhu Yin	朱茵
Chui Chang-wang (Sui Jang Hung)	Xu Zenhong	徐增宏
Cui Zi'an	Cui Zi'en	崔子恩
Dadawa	Zhu Zheqin	朱哲琴
Deng Xiaoping	Deng Xiaoping	鄧小平
Ding Sin-saai	Ding Shanxi	丁善璽
Dongfang Bubai (Invincible Asia)	Dongfang Bubai	東方不敗
Duan Xiaolou	Duan Xiaolou	段小樓
Fok, Clarence	Huo Yaoliang	霍耀良
Fong, Alex	Fang Zhongxin	方中信
Fong, Allen	Fang Yuping	方育平
Fong Ling-ching	Fang Lingzheng	方令正
Fong Min	Fang Mian	房勉
Fu, Alexander	Fu Sheng	傅聲
Fung, Patrina	Feng Baobao	馮寶寶
Fung Tak-lun	Feng Delun	馮德倫
Gam Kei-chu	Jin Qizhu	金琪珠
Gau Goo-leung	Jiu guniang	九姑娘
Gong Li	Gong Li	鞏俐
Goo Man-chung	Gu Wenzong	顧文宗
Ha, Pat	Xia Wenxi	夏文汐
Han Bin	Han Bin	韓賓
Han Yingjie	Han Yingjie	韓英杰
Hau Wing-choi	Hou Yongcai	侯永財
Heung, Charles	Xiang Huaqiang	向華強

Ho, Cheri	He Peiyi	何佩儀
Ho-nam	Haonan	浩南
Ho Po-wing	He Baorong	何寶榮
Hoh Mung-wa	He Menghua	何夢華
Hsu Feng	Xu Feng	徐楓
Hu Jin-gwan	Xu Yanjun	許彥鈞
Hu Jun	Hu Jun	胡軍
Hu, King	Hu Jinquan	胡金銓
Hui, Ann	Xu Anhua	許鞍華
Hui, Michael	Xu Guanwen	許冠文
Hung, Sammo	Hong Jinbao	洪金寶
Jade Fox	Yu Huli (Biyan Huli)	玉狐狸
Jen	Yu Jiaolong	玉嬌龍
Jiang Nan	Jiang Nan	姜南
Jiangnan He	Jiangnan He	江南鶴
Jin Yong (Louis Cha)	Jin Yong	金庸
Jitao	Jitao	紀陶
Kang Zhengguo	Kang Zhengguo	康正果
Kawashima Yoshiko	Chuandao Fangzi	川島芳子
Ko Chi-sum	Gao Zhisen	高志森
Koo Ka-ming	Gu Jiaming	顧家明
Koo, Louis	Gu Tianle	古天樂
Kot Man-fai, Eric	Ge Minhui	葛民輝
Kuo Nam-hong	Guo Nanhong	郭南宏
Kwan, Shirley	Guan Shuyi	關淑儀
Kwan, Stanley	Guan Jinpeng	關錦鵬
Kwan Tak-hing	Guan Dexing	關德興
Lai Ming, Leon	Li Ming	黎明
Lai Yiu-fai	Li Yaohui	黎耀輝
Lam Chi-cheung	Lin Zixiang	林子祥
Lam Chi-wing	Lin Ziying	林子穎
Lam Chiu-yin	Lin Chaoxian	林超賢
Lam Kar-sing (Lam Kau)	Lin Jiao	林蛟

Lam, Ringo	Lin Lingdong	林嶺東
Lan Tsu-wei	Lan Zuwei	藍祖蔚
Lau, Andy	Liu Dehua	劉德華
Lau Ching-wan	Liu Qingyun	劉青雲
Lau, Jeff	Liu Zhenwei	劉鎮偉
Lau Ka-fai	Liu Jiahui	劉家輝
Lau Kar-leung	Liu Jialiang	劉家良
Lau Kar-ling, Carina	Liu Jialing	劉嘉玲
Lau, Lawrence	Liu Guochang	劉國昌
Lau Siu-ming	Liu Shaoming	劉紹銘
Lau Wai-keung	Liu Weiqiang	劉偉強
Law, Clara	Luo Zhuoyao	羅卓瑤
Law Ka-sing	Luo Jiasheng	羅家聲
Law Ma	Luo Ma	羅馬
Law Wing-cheong	Luo Yongchang	羅永昌
Lee, Ang	Li An	李安
Lee, Bruce	Li Xiaolong	李小龍
Lee Chi-ngai	Li Zhiyi	李志毅
Lee, Chris	Li Jiansheng	李健生
Lee, Daniel	Li Rengang	李仁港
Lee, Danny	Li Xiuxian	李修賢
Lee, Julian	Li Zhichao	李志超
Lee Kang-sheng	Li Kangsheng	李康生
Lee Lai-chen	Li Lizhen	李麗珍
Lee Lik-chi	Li Lichi	李力持
Lee Tit	Li Tie	李鐵
Lee Wai-man	Li Huimin	李惠民
Leung, Gigi	Liang Yongqi	梁詠琪
Leung Hong-man	Liang Hanwen	梁漢文
Leung, Patrick	Liang Baijian	梁柏堅
Leung Chiu-wai, Tony	Liang Chaowei	梁朝偉
Leung Ka-fai, Tony	Liang Jiahui	梁家輝
Leung, Raymond	Liang Benxi	梁本熙

Liang Shanbo	Liang Shanbo	梁山伯
Li Bihua	Li Bihua	李碧華
Li Ching	Li Qing	李菁
Li Han-hsiang	Li Hanxiang	李翰祥
Li, Jet	Li Lianjie	李連杰
Li Li-hua	Li Lihua	李麗華
Li Mu-bai	Li Mubai	李慕白
Lin, Brigitte	Lin Qingxia	林青霞
Lin Guohua	Lin Guohua	林國華
Lin, Jeanette	Lin Cui	林翠
Lin, Linda	Lin Dai	林黛
Ling, Ivy	Ling Bo	凌波
Linghu Chong	Linghu Chong	令狐沖
Liu, Henry	Jiang Nan	江南
Lo Lieh	Luo Lie	羅烈
Lo Wei	Luo Wei	羅維
Loh, Betty	Le Di	樂蒂
Long Gang	Long Gang	龍剛
Loui, Simon	Lei Yuyang	雷宇揚
Lung Kim-sun	Long Jiansheng	龍劍笙
Ma, Helen	Ma Hailun	馬海倫
Ma, Joe	Ma Weihao	馬偉豪
Ma, Victor	Ma Caihe	馬才和
Ma, Yo Yo	Ma Youyou	馬友友
Mak, Johnny	Mai Dangxiong	麥當雄
Mang Hoi	Meng Hai	孟海
Mao, Angela	Mao Ying	茅瑛
Mao Zedong	Mao Zedong	毛澤東
Mei Lanfang	Mei Lanfang	梅蘭芳
Mo, Teresa	Mao Shunjun	毛舜君
Mui, Anita	Mei Yanfang	梅艷芳
Murong Yan, Ms	Murong Yan	慕容嫣
Murong Yan, Mr	Murong Yan	慕容燕

New Formosa Fun Park Band	Xin baodao kangle dui	新寶島康樂隊
Ng, Francis	Wu Zhenyu	吳鎮宇
Ng Man-tat	Wu Mengda	吳孟達
Ng Min-kan	Wu Mianqin	吳勉勤
Ng Ngai-cheung	Wu Yijiang	吳毅將
Ng, Sandra	Wu Junru	吳君如
Ng See-yuen	Wu Siyuan	吳思遠
Ng Wing-mei	Wu Yongwei	伍詠薇
Not A Woman (English pen name)	Bushi nüren	不是女人
Ping Lu	Ping Lu	平路
Poon, Dickson	Pan Disheng	潘迪生
Qin Wantao	Qin Wantao	秦晚濤
Reis, Michelle	Li Jiaxin	李嘉欣
Samshasha	Xiaomingxiong	小明雄
Sek Kei	Shi Qi	石琪
Sek Yin-tsi (Sek Kin)	Shi Jian	石堅
Shangguan Lingfeng	Shangguan Lingfeng	上官靈鳳
Shaw, Run Run	Shao Yifu	邵逸夫
Shen Sheng-te	Shen Shengde	沈聖德
Shih Jun	Shi Jun	石雋
Shu Kei	Shu Qi	舒琪
Shu Qi	Shu Qi	舒淇
Shum, John	Cen Jianxun	岑建勳
Siao Fong-fong, Josephine	Xiao Fangfang	蕭芳芳
Siqin Gaowa	Siqin Gaowa	斯琴高娃
Sister Thirteen	Shisan mei	十三妹
Sit, Nancy	Xue Jiayan	薛家燕
Siu Kwok-wah	Shao Guohua	邵國華
Sun Mak-tse	Xin Mazai	新馬仔
Sun Yat-sen	Sun Chongshan	孫中山
Tam Lei-chuen	Tan Liquan	譚麗泉
Tan Dun	Tan Dun	譚盾

Tang, Billy	Deng Yancheng	鄧衍成
Tang Gei-chan	Deng Jichen	鄧寄塵
Teresa Teng	Deng Lijun	鄧麗君
Ti Lung	Di Long	狄龍
Tian Qing	Tian Qing	田青
Tin Fung	Tian Feng	田丰
To, Johnnie	Du Qifeng	杜琪峯
To Man-chat	Du Wenze	杜汶澤
To Tsung-hua	Tuo Zonghua	庹宗華
Tong, Stanley	Tang Jili	唐季禮
Tree Demon	Laolao	姥姥
Tsai Ming-liang	Cai Mingliang	蔡明亮
Tsang, Eric	Zeng Chiwei	曾志偉
Tsang, Ken-cheung	Zeng Jinchang	曾謹昌
Tsang, Kenneth	Zeng Jiang	曾江
Tse Kwan-ho	Xie Junhao	謝君豪
Tse, Patrick	Xie Xian	謝賢
Tsui Hark	Xu Ke	徐克
Tung Lam	Dong Lin	佟林
Wai Ka-fai	Wei Jiahui	韋家輝
Wang Dulu	Wang Dulu	王度廬
Wang Tianlin	Wang Tianlin	王天林
Wang, Wayne	Wang Ying	王穎
Wang Xinglei	Wang Xinglei	王星磊
Wang Yu	Wang Yu	王羽
Wei Tong	Wei Tong	偉同
Wong, Anthony	Huang Qiusheng	黃秋生
Wong, Arthur	Huang Yuetai	黃岳泰
Wong, Barbara	Huang Zhenzhen	黃真真
Wong Ching	Wang Jing	王晶
Wong Chi-wah	Huang Zihua	黃子華
Wong, Faye	Wong Fei	王菲
Wong Fei-hong	Huang Feihong	黃飛鴻

Wong Gam-fung	Wang Jinfeng	王金鳳
Wong Hei	Wang Xi	王喜
Wong, Joey	Wang Zuxian	王祖賢
Wong Kar-wai	Wang Jiawei	王家衛
Wong, Kirk	Huang Zhiqiang	黃志強
Wong Man-wan	Huang Wenyun	黃文雲
Wong, Melvin	Huang Jinshen	黃錦燊
Wong, Michael	Wang Minde	王敏德
Wong Tai-loi	Huang Tailai	黃泰來
Wong, Wyman	Huang Weiwen	黃偉文
Wong Yiu	Huang Yao	黃堯
Wong Yuk-saan	Huang Yushan	黃玉珊
Woo, John	Wu Yusen	吳宇森
Woo Wai-chung	Hu Huizhong	胡慧中
Wu, Daniel	Wu Yanzu	吳彥祖
Wu, Jacqualine	Wu Qianlian	吳倩蓮
Wu Ma	Wu Ma	午馬
Xuan Jinglin	Xuan Jinglin	宣景琳
Xue Qianxun	Xue Qianxun	雪千尋
Yam Kim-fai	Ren Jianhui	任劍輝
Yam, Simon	Ren Dahua	任達華
Yang, Peter	Yang Qun	楊群
Yau Ching	You Jing	游靜
Yau, Herman	Qiu Litao	丘禮濤
Yau, Patrick	You Dazhi	游達志
Yeh, Julie	Ye Feng	葉楓
Yen, Donnie	Zhen Zidan	甄子丹
Yeoh, Michelle	Yang Ziqiong	楊紫瓊
Yeung Choi-nei	Yang Caini	楊采妮
Yeung, Kristy	Yang Gongru	楊恭如
Yeung, Miriam	Yang Qianhua	楊千嬅
Yilin	Yilin	儀琳
Yingying	Yingying	盈盈

Yip Kam-hung	Ye Jinhong	葉錦鴻
Yip, Raymond	Ye Weimin	葉偉民
Yongfan	Yang Fan	楊凡
Yu Hoi	Ru Hai	如海
Yu, Lucilla	You Min	尤敏
Yu Shu-lien	Yu Xiulian	俞秀蓮
Yu Suqiu	Yu Suqiu	于素秋
Yu Zhanyuan	Yu Zhanyuan	于占元
Yuan Biao	Yuan Biao	元彪
Yue Feng	Yue Feng	岳楓
Yue Lingshan	Yue Lingshan	岳靈珊
Yuen, Anita	Yuan Yongyi	袁詠儀
Yuen Cheung-yan	Yuan Xiangren	袁祥仁
Yuen Kwai	Yuan Kui	元奎
Yuen Wo-ping	Yuan Heping	袁和平
Zhang Che	Zhang Che	張徹
Zhang Shichuan	Zhang Shichuan	張石川
Zhang Xinyan	Zhang Xinyan	張鑫炎
Zhang Ziyi	Zhang Ziyi	章子怡

FILMS

18 Bronze men	*Shaolinsi shiba tongren*	《少林寺十八銅人》
36th Chamber of Shaolin (Master Killer)	*Shaolin sanshiliu fang*	《少林三十六房》
Accident, The	*Xinyuan yima*	《心猿意馬》
All's Well Ends Well	*Jiayou xishi*	《家有囍事》
Amorous Woman of the Tang Dynasty, An	*Tangdai haofangnü*	《唐朝豪放女》
Angel	*Tianshi xingdong*	《天使行動》
Anonymous Heroes, The	*Wuming yingxiong*	《無名英雄》
Armour of God	*Longxiong hudi*	《龍兄虎弟》
As Tears Go By	*Wangjiao kamen*	《旺角卡門》
Ashes of Time	*Dongxie xidu*	《東邪西毒》

Assassin, The	Da cike	《大刺客》
Autumn Moon	Qiuyue	《秋月》
Beauty and the Breast	Fengxiong mi "Cup"	《豐胸秘 Cup》
Better Tomorrow, A	Yingxiong bense	《英雄本色》
Beyond Hypothermia	Sheshi sanshi'er du	《攝氏 32 度》
Big Boss, The	Tangshan daxong	《唐山大兄》
Bishonen ...	Mei shaonian zhi lian	《美少年之戀》
Black Cat	Heimao	《黑貓》
Black List	Heiming dan	《黑名單》
Black Mask	Heixia	《黑俠》
Blood Brothers	Cima	《刺馬》
Bloody Fists, The	Dangkou tan	《蕩寇灘》
Boxer from Shantung, The	Ma Yongzhen	《馬永貞》
Boys (Kid, The)(TV)	Xiaohai	《小孩》
Boy's?	Jianan jianü	《假男假女》
Brothers Five	Wuhu tulong	《五虎屠龍》
Bugis Street	Yaojie huanghou	《妖街皇后》
Bullet in the Head	Diexue jietou	《喋血街頭》
Butterfly Murders, The	Diebian	《蝶變》
Center Stage	Ruan Lingyu	《阮玲玉》
C'est la Vie, Mon Chérie	Xin buliao qing	《新不了情》
Cheap Killers	Yue duoluo yue yingxiong	《愈墮落愈英雄》
Chinese Box	Zhongguo xia / Qingren hezi	《中國匣》 / 《情人盒子》
Chinese Boxer, The	Longhu men	《龍虎門》
Chinese Ghost Story, A	Qiannü youhun	《倩女幽魂》
Chinese Odyssey	Tianxia wushuang	《天下無雙》
Chinese Odyssey, A	Xiyouji	《西遊記》
Chung King Express	Chongqing senlin	《重慶森林》
Come Drink with Me	Da zuixia	《大醉俠》
Comeuppance	Tian youyan	《天有眼》
Comrades: Almost a Love Story	Tianmimi	《甜蜜蜜》

Conjugal Affairs	*Xin tongju shidai*	《新同居時代》
Crazy	*Siji sharenkuang 2 chi nanfeng*	《四級殺人狂 2 — 男瘋》
Crouching Tiger Hidden Dragon	*Wohu canglong*	《臥虎藏龍》
Days of Tomorrow	*Tianchang dijiu*	《天長地久》
Deadful Melody	*Liuzhi qinmo*	《六指琴魔》
Deadly Duo, The	*Shuangxia*	《雙俠》
Dr. Lamb	*Gaoyang yisheng*	《羔羊醫生》
Dragon Gate Inn	*Longmen kezhan*	《龍門客棧》
Dragon Inn	*Xin longmen kezhan*	《新龍門客棧》
Dragon Lord	*Longshaoye*	《龍少爺》
Drunken Master	*Zuiquan*	《醉拳》
Drunken Master 2	*Nanbei zuiquan*	《南北醉拳》
Duel of Fists	*Quanji*	《拳擊》
Duel, The	*Da Juedou*	《大決鬥》
Durian Durian	*Liulian piaopiao*	《榴槤飄飄》
Dutiful Daughter, The	*Xiaonü Zhuzhu*	《孝女珠珠》
Eagle Shooting Hero, The	*Shediaoyingxiongzhuan zhi dongcheng xijiu*	《射鵰英雄傳之東成西就》
Eastern Condors	*Dongfang tuying*	《東方禿鷹》
Enter the Clowns	*Choujiao dengchang*	《丑角登場》
Escorts over Tiger Hills	*Hushan xing*	《虎山行》
Eternal Love	*Qicai Hubugui*	《七彩胡不歸》
Expect the Unexpected	*Feichang turan*	《非常突然》
Farewell China	*Ai zai taxiang de jijie*	《愛在他鄉的季節》
Farewell My Concubine	*Bawang bieji*	《霸王別姬》
Fat Choi Spirit	*Liguligu xinniancai*	《嚦咕嚦咕新年財》
Fate of Lee Khan, The	*Yingchunge de fengbo*	《迎春閣的風波》
Father and Son	*Fuzi qing*	《父子情》
Feel 100%	*Baifenbai ganjue*	《百分百感覺》
Feel 100% Once More	*Baifenbai "ngam feel"*	《百分百啱 Feel》
Final Justice	*Zuihou panjue*	《最後判決》
Fists of Fury	*Jing wumen*	《精武門》

Five Deadly Venoms, The	Wudu	《五毒》
Five Fingers of Death (King Boxer)	Tianxia diyi quan	《天下第一拳》
Flag of Horror	Fenghuo jiaren	《烽火佳人》
Fong Sai Yuk	Fang Shiyu	《方世玉》
Forbidden City Cop	Danei mitan linglingfa	《大內密探零零發》
Fourteen Amazons, The	Shisi nüyinghao	《十四女英豪》
From China with Love	Guochan linglingqi	《國產凌凌漆》
From the Highway	Luke yu daoke	《路客與刀客》
Full Contact	Xiadao gaofei	《俠盜高飛》
Full Moon in New York	Ren zai niuyue	《人在紐約》
Fulltime Killer	Quanzhi shashou	《全職殺手》
Gimme Gimme	Aishang wo ba	《愛上我吧》
Goddess of 1967, The	Yushang 1967 de nüshen	《遇上1967的女神》
Golden Swallow, The	Jin yanzi	《金燕子》
Good and the Bad, The	Ehu kuanglong	《餓虎狂龍》
Handsome Siblings	Juedai shuangjiao	《絕代雙驕》
Happy Together	Chun'guang zhaxie	《春光乍洩》
He and She	Jiemei qingshen	《姊妹情深》
He's a Woman, She's a Man	Jinzhi yuye	《金枝玉葉》
Help!!!	Lashou huichun	《辣手回春》
Hero Never Dies, A	Zhenxin yinxiong	《真心英雄》
Heroic Ones, The	Shisan taibao	《十三太保》
Heroic Trio, The	Dongfang sanxia	《東方三俠》
Hold You Tight	Yue kuaile yue duoluo	《愈快樂愈墮落》
House of 72 Tenants	Qishi'er jia fangke	《七十二家房客》
I'm Your Birthday Cake	Budaode de liwu	《不道德的禮物》
In the Line of Duty 3	Huangjia shijie san cixiong dadao	《皇家師姐 3 雌雄大盜》
In the Line of Duty 5: Middle Man	Huangjia shijie zhi zhongjianren	《皇家師姐之中間人》
In the Mood for Love	Huayang nianhua	《花樣年華》
Inspector Wears a Skirt, The	Bawang hua	《霸王花》

Intimate Confessions of a Chinese Courtesan	Ainu	《愛奴》
Intimates	Zishu	《自梳》
Intruder	Kongbu ji	《恐怖雞》
Invincible Eight, The	Tianlong bajiang	《天龍八將》
Jiang Hu: The Triad Zone	Jianghu gaoji	《江湖告急》
July Rhapsody	Nanren sishi	《男人四十》
Justice, My Foot!	Shensi guan	《審死官》
Kawashima Yoshiko	Chuandao Fangzi	《川島芳子》
Killer Clans	Liuxing hudie jian	《流星蝴蝶劍》
Killer, The	Diexue shuangxiong	《喋血雙雄》
Killing Me Tenderly	Aini aidao shasini	《愛你愛到殺死你》
King of Beggars, The	Wuzhuangyuan Suqi'er	《武狀元蘇乞兒》
King of Comedy	Xiju zhi wang	《喜劇之王》
La Brassiere	Jueshi hao "Bra"	《絕世好Bra》
Lady General Hua Mulan	Hua Mulan	《花木蘭》
Lady Hermit, The	Zhongkui niangzi	《鍾馗娘子》
Lady of Steel	Huangjiang nüxia	《荒江女俠》
Lan Yu	Lan Yu	《藍宇》
Lavender	Xunyi cao	《薰衣草》
Legends of Cheating	Pianshu qitan	《騙術奇譚》
Legends of Lust	Fengyue qitan	《風月奇譚》
Let's Sing Along	Nange nuchang	《男歌女唱》
Long Arm of the Law	Shenggang qibing	《省港旗兵》
Longest Nite, The	Anhua	《暗花》
Love Eterne	Liang Shanbo yu Zhu Yingtai	《梁山伯與祝英台》
Love on a Diet	Shoushen nannü	《瘦身男女》
Lovers, The	Liangzhu	《梁祝》
Mad Mad Sword	Shenjin dao	《神經刀》
Magic Blade, The	Tianya mingyue dao	《天涯明月刀》
Map of Sex and Love, The	Qingse ditu	《情色地圖》
Mission, The	Qianghuo	《鎗火》
Movie-Fan Princess	Yingmi gongzhu	《影迷公主》

My Left Eye Sees Ghosts	*Wo zuoyan jiandao gui*	《我左眼見到鬼》
My Lucky Stars	*Fuxing gaozhao*	《福星高照》
Naked Killer	*Chiluo gaoyang*	《赤裸羔羊》
Nameless Hero, The	*Wuming yingxiong*	《無名英雄》
Needing You	*Gunan gua'nü*	《孤男寡女》
New One-Armed Swordsman	*Xin dubi dao*	《新獨臂刀》
Night Corridor	*Yaoye huilang*	《妖夜迴廊》
Odd One Dies, The	*Liangge zhineng huo yige*	《兩個只能活一個》
Oh! My Three Guys	*Sange xiang'ai de shaonian*	《三個相愛的少年》
Once Upon a Time in China	*Huang Feihong*	《黃飛鴻》
Once Upon a Time in China II	*Huang Feihong er zhi nan'er dang ziqiang*	《黃飛鴻 II 之男兒當自強》
One-Armed Boxer	*Dubi quanwang*	《獨臂拳王》
One-Armed Swordsman	*Dubi dao*	《獨臂刀》
Ordinary Heroes	*Qianyan wanyu*	《千言萬語》
Owl vs. Dumbo	*Maotouying yu xiaofeixiang*	《貓頭鷹與小飛象》
Pantyhose Hero	*Zhifen shuangxiong*	《脂粉雙雄》
Peking Opera Blues	*Daomadan*	《刀馬旦》
Peony Pavilion	*Youyuan jingmeng*	《遊園驚夢》
Police Story	*Jingcha gushi*	《警察故事》
Portland Street Blues	*Hongxing shisan mei*	《洪興十三妹》
Queer Story, A	*Jilao sishi*	《基佬40》
Rebels of the Neon God	*Qingshaonian nazha*	《青少年哪咤》
Righting Wrongs (Above the Law)	*Zhifa xianfeng*	《執法先鋒》
River, The	*Heliu*	《河流》
Rouge	*Yanzhi kou*	《胭脂扣》
Royal Warriors	*Huangjia zhanshi*	《皇家戰士》
Running Out of Time	*Anzhan*	《暗戰》
Running Out of Time 2	*Anzhan 2*	《暗戰 2》

Sacred Knives of Vengeance, The	Da shashou	《大殺手》
Sausalito	Yijian zhongqing	《一見鍾情》
Sealed with a Kiss	Tianyan miyu	《甜言蜜語》
Second Time Around	Wuxian fuhuo	《無限復活》
Shadow Whip, The	Yingzi shenbian	《影子神鞭》
Shaolin Soccer	Shaolin zuqiu	《少林足球》
Shaolin Temple	Shaolin si	《少林寺》
She Shoots Straight	Huangjia nüjiang	《皇家女將》
Singing Killer, The	Xiao shaxing	《小煞星》
Smiling Swordsman, The	Xiaomian xia	《笑面俠》
Song of the Exile	Ketu qiuhen	《客途秋恨》
Spacked Out	Wuren jiashi	《無人駕駛》
Sting, The	Xiasheng	《俠聖》
Story of a Gun	Heixing fengyun	《黑星風雲》
Sword and the Lute, The	Huoshao hongl013nsi zhi qinjian enchou	《火燒紅蓮寺之琴劍恩仇》
Swordsman II	Xiao'ao jianghu II zhi Dongfang Bubai	《笑傲江湖 II 之東方不敗》
Swordsman III: The East Is Red	Dongfang Bubai zhi fengyun zaiqi	《東方不敗之風雲再起》
Teddy Girls	Feinü zhengzhuan	《飛女正傳》
Temple of the Red Lotus	Jianghu qixia	《江湖奇俠》
Temptation of a Monk	Youzeng	《誘僧》
Ten Tigers from Kwantung	Guangtong shihu	《廣東十虎》
Three Swordsmen, The	Daojianxiao	《刀劍笑》
Tiger Boy	Huxia jianchou	《虎俠殲仇》
Tom, Dick and Hairy	Fengchen sanxia	《風塵三俠》
Too Many Ways to Be Number One	Yige zitou de dansheng	《一個字頭的誕生》
Touch of Zen, A	Xianü	《俠女》
Tricky Master, The	Qianwang zhi wang 2000	《千王之王 2000》
Truth or Dare: 6th Floor Rear Flat	Liulou houzuo	《六樓后座》

Twelve Gold Medallions, The	Shi'er jinpai	《十二金牌》
Twin Bracelets	Shuangzhuo	《雙鐲》
Twin Swords	Huoshao hongliansi zhi yuanyang jianxia	《火燒紅蓮寺之鴛鴦劍俠》
Twinkle, Twinkle Lucky Stars	Zuijia fuxing	《最佳福星》
Untold Story, The	Baxian fandian zhi renrou chashaobao	《八仙飯店之人肉叉燒包》
Valiant Ones, The	Zhonglie tu	《忠烈圖》
Valley of the Fangs	Elang gu	《餓狼谷》
Vengeance	Baochou	《報仇》
Vive l'Amour	Aiqing wansui	《愛情萬歲》
Wandering Swordsman, The	You xia'er	《遊俠兒》
Warlord, The	Da junfa	《大軍閥》
Water Margin, The	Shuihu zhuan	《水滸傳》
Way of the Dragon, The	Menglong Guojiang	《猛龍過江》
Wedding Banquet, The	Xiyan	《喜宴》
Wheels on Meals	Kuaican che	《快餐車》
Where a Good Man Goes	Zaijian Alang	《再見阿郎》
Who's the Woman, Who's the Man	Jinzhi yuye 2	《金枝玉葉 2》
Winners and Sinners	Qimou miaoji wufuxing	《奇謀妙計五福星》
Wu Yen	Zhong Wuyen	《鍾無艷》
Yes, Madam! (In the Line of Duty)	Huangjia shijie	《皇家師姐》
Yang ± Yin: Gender in Chinese Cinema	Nansheng nuxiang: Zhongguo dianying de xingbie	《男生女相：中國電影的性別》
Young and Dangerous	Guhuo zai	《古惑仔》
Young, Pregnant and Unmarried	Yunü tianding	《玉女添丁》
Zu: Warriors from the Magic Mountain	Xin shushan jianxia zhuan	《新蜀山劍俠傳》

BOOKS AND SONGS

1998 Xianggang dian ying hui gu	*1998 Xianggang dian ying hui gu*	《1998 香港電影回顧》
Aspects of Sexuality and Literature in Ancient China	*Chongshen fengyue jian*	《重審風月鑑》
Butterfly Lovers	*Liang Shanbo yu Zhu Yingtai*	《梁山伯與祝英台》
Ch'ian yen wan yu (song)	*Qianyan wanyu*	「千言萬語」
City Entertainment	*Dianying shuangz houkan*	《電影雙周刊》
City on the Edge of Time	*Shengshi bianyuan*	《盛世邊緣》
Collected Reviews of Sek Kei	*Shi Qi yinghua ji*	《石琪影話集》
Dang-tai chung-guo tian-ying	*Dangdai zhongguo dianying*	《當代中國電影》
Guan Ni Ji	*Guan Ni Ji*	《觀逆集》
He-je chiun tsai-lai	*Heri jun zailai*	《何日君再來》
Hetie Wubu Qu	*Hetie Wubu Qu*	《鶴鐵五部曲》
History of Homosexuality in China	*Zhongguo tongxing'ai shilu*	《中國同性愛史錄》
Jiushi niandai gangcanpian gongyi yipie: kunjing de tantao ji chulu	*Jiushi niandai gangcanpian gongyi yipie: kunjing de tantao ji chulu*	《九十年代港產片工業一瞥：困景的探討及出路》
Linli Yingxiang Guan — Jingshui Pian	*Linli Yingxiang Guan — Jingshui Pian*	《淋漓影像館・井水篇》
Linli Yingxiang Guan — Paozhuan Pian	*Linli Yingxiang Guan — Paozhuan Pian*	《淋漓影像館・拋磚篇》
Literati's Chivalric Dreams, The	*Qiangu wenren xiake meng*	《千古文人俠客夢》
My Motherland (song)	*Wo de zuguo*	《我的祖國》
On Tongzhi	*Tongzhi lun*	《同志論》
Oriental Sunday Magazine	*Dongfang xindi*	《東方新地》
Shiqi Yinghua Ji	*Shiqi Yinghua Ji*	《石琪影話集》
Smiling, Proud Wanderer, The	*Xiao'ao jianghu*	《笑傲江湖》
Ssu Hsiang Ch'i (song)	*Sixiang qi*	《思想起》

Starting Another Stove	*Lingqi luzao*	《另起爐灶》
Xianggang dianying gongye ji shichang fenxi	*Xianggang dianying gongye ji shichang fenxi*	《香港電影工業及市場分析》
Xue ran de fengcai (song)	*Xue ran de fengcai*	《血染的風采》
Zu Ci	*Chuci*	《楚辭》

FILM COMPANIES

Cathay	Guo Tai	國泰
Cinema City	Xin Yi Cheng	新藝城
Empire	Fu Guo	富國
Golden Harvest	Jia He	嘉禾
Kai Fa	Kai Fa	開發
Milkyway Image	Yinhe Yingxiang	銀河映像
Shaw Brothers/Shaws	Shao Shi	邵氏

OTHER TERMS*

ah-fei	阿飛
anqi	暗器
ban	板
chuguan	出關
dan	旦
fei gei cheung	飛機場
fuxing	福星
Guomingtang	國民黨
Jeet Kune Do (Jiequan dao)	截拳道
jian	奸
Ju Qing Ming er shu hung xi	據青冥而攄虹兮
jueh paah	豬扒

---

* This section contains both standard pinyin and other non-standard romanizations, corresponding to individual authors' usages.

liang hsiang (*lianghsiang*)	亮相
manhua	漫畫
mouh leih tauh	無厘頭
qi	氣
qigong	氣功
Qingming (*jian*)	青冥(劍)
sheng	生
shifu	師傅
wen	文
wo jiu gen ni zou	我就跟你走
wu	武
Wudang pai	武當派
wu shu	武術
wuxia pian	武俠片
wuxia xiao shuo	武俠小說
xincheng ze lin	心誠則靈
xinjue	心訣
yanggang	陽剛
yi	義
yinrou	陰柔
zhong	忠
Zhu Lian Bang	竹聯幫
zui xia	醉俠

Bibliography

Abbas, Ackbar. *Hong Kong: Culture and the Politics of Disappearance*. Minneapolis: University of Minnesota Press, 1997.

———. "The New Hong Kong Cinema and the Deja Disparu." *Discourse* 16.3 (1994): 66.

Adorno, Theodor W. *The Cultural Industry*. London: Routledge, 2002.

Allen, Robert and Gomery, Douglas. *Film History: Theory and Practice*. New York: Alfred Knopf, 1985.

Altman, Dennis. "Rupture or Continuity? The Internationalization of Gay Identity." *Social Text* 48 14(3) (1996): 77–94.

An, Jinsoo. "*The Killer*: Cult Film and Transcultural (Mis)Reading." In *At Full Speed: Hong Kong Cinema in a Borderless World*, edited by Esther C. M. Yau, 95–113. Minneapolis: University of Minnesota Press, 2001.

Anzieu, Didier. *The Skin Ego: A Psychoanalytic Approach to the Self*. Translated by Chris Turner. New Haven: Yale University Press, 1989.

Barker, Chris. *Cultural Studies: Theory and Practice*. London: Sage, 2000.

Barthes, Roland. "From Work to Text." In *Textual Strategies: Perspectives in Post-structural Criticism*, edited by Josué V. Harari, 73–81. Ithaca, NY: Cornell University Press, 1979.

———. *Image-Music-Text*. Translated by S. Heath. Glasgow: Collins-Fontana, 1977.

Bartky, Sandra Lee. "Foucault, Femininity and the Modernisation of Patriarchal Power." In *Feminism and Foucault: Reflections on Resistance*, edited by Irene Diamond and Lee Quinby, 61–86. Boston: Northeastern University Press, 1989.

Bataille, Georges. *Death and Sensuality: A Study of Eroticism and the Taboo*. New York: Arno Press, 1977.

Benjamin, Walter. *The Origin of German Tragic Drama*. Translated by John Osbourne. London: Verso, 1998.

Bergstrom, Janet and Doane, Mary Ann. "The Female Spectators: Contexts and Directions." *Camera Obscura* 20–21 (1989): 5–27.

Beynon, John. *Masculinities and Culture*. London: Open University, 2002.

Bolton, Kingsley and Hutton, Christopher. "Bad Boys and Bad Language: Chou

Hau and the Sociolinguistics of Swearwords in Hong Kong Cantonese." In *Hong Kong: The Anthropology of a Chinese Metropolis*, edited by Grant Evans and Maria Tam, 304. Surrey: Curzon, 1997.

Bonvillain, Nancy. *Language, Culture, and Communication: The Meaning of Messages*. NJ: Prentice Hall, 1993.

Bordwell, David. "Aesthetics in Action: *Kungfu*, Gunplay, and Cinematic Expressivity." In *At Full Speed: Hong Kong Cinema in a Borderless World*, edited by Esther C. M. Yau, 73–93. Minneapolis: University of Minnesota Press, 2001.

———. *Planet Hong Kong: Popular Cinema and the Art of Entertainment*. Cambridge, MA: Harvard University Press, 2000.

Bornstein, Kate. *My Gender Workbook*. London: Routledge, 1998.

Boudieu, Pierre. *In Other Words: Essays Towards a Reflexive Sociology*. Cambridge, MA: Polity, 1990.

———. *Outline of a Theory of Practice*. Cambridge: Cambridge University Press, 1977.

Boudieu, Pierre and Wacquant, Loic. "On the Cunning of Imperialist Reason." *Theory, Culture and Society* 16.1 (1999): 41–58.

Brownell, Susan and Wasserstrom, Jeffrey N. *Chinese Femininities/Chinese Masculinities: A Reader*. Introduction: 1–46. Berkeley: University of California Press, 2002.

Burston, Paul and Richardson, Colin, eds. *A Queer Romance: Lesbians, Gay Men and Popular Culture*. London: Routledge, 1995.

Butler, Judith. *Gender Trouble: Feminism and the Subversion of Identity*. New York: Routledge, 1990.

Califia, Pat. *Sex Changes: The Politics of Transgenderism*. San Francisco: Cleis, 1997.

Chan, Natalia (Luo Feng). *Shengshi bianyuan* (City on the edge of time). Hong Kong: Oxford University Press [China], 2002.

Chan, Jachinson W. "Bruce Lee's Fictional Models of Masculinity." *Men and Masculinities* 2.4 (2000): 371–387.

Chang, Hsiao-hung. "Taiwan Queer Valentines." In *Trajectories: Inter-Asia Cultural Studies*, edited by Chen Kuan-hsing, 283–298. London: Routledge, 1998.

Chen, Pingyuan. *Qiangu wenren xiakemeng: wuxia xiaoshuo leixing yanjiu* (The literati's chivalric dreams: Narrative models of Chinese knight-errant literature). Taipei: Rye Field Publishing, 1995.

Chen Qingwei. *Xianggang dianying gongye ji shichang fenxi* (The structure and marketing snalysis of Hong Kong film industry). Hong Kong: Film Biweekly, 2000.

Cheung, King-kok. "Art, Spirituality, And the Ethic of Care: Alternative Masculinities in Chinese American Literature." In *Masculinity Studies and Feminist Theory: New Directions*, edited by Judith Kegan Gardiner. New York: Columbia University Press, 2002.

Chou, Wah-shan. *Tongzhi lun* (On tongzhi). Hong Kong: Tongzhi yanjiu she, 1995.

Chou, W. S. and Chiu, M. C. *The Closet Sexual History*. (Chinese Edition). Hong Kong: Comrade Research Centre, 1995.

Chow, Rey. *The Protestant Ethic and the Spirit of Capitalism*. New York: Columbia University Press, 2002.

———. "Nostalgia of the New Wave: Structure in Wong Kar-Wai's *Happy Together*." *Camera Obscura* 42 (1999): 31–48.

———. "Film and Cultural Studies." In *The Oxford Guide to Film Studies*, edited by John Hill and Pamela Church Gibson, 169–175. Oxford: Oxford University Press, 1998.

———. *Primitive Passions*. New York: Columbia University Press, 1995.

———. "Where Have All the Natives Gone?" In *Writing Diaspora: Tactics of Intervention in Contemporary Cultural Studies*, 27–54. Bloomington: Indiana University Press, 1993.

Chu, Yiu Wai. "(In)Authentic Hong Kong: The '(G)Local' Cultural Identity in Postcolonial HK Cinema." *Post Script* 20.2 & 3 (summer 2001): 147–58.

Clatterbaugh, Kenneth. *Contemporary Perspectives on Masculinity*. Westview Press, 1990.

Cohan, Stephen. *Masked Men: Masculinity and the Movies in the Fifties*. Bloomington and Indianapolis: Indiana University Press, 1997.

Connell, R. W. *Masculinities*. Berkeley, Los Angeles: University of California Press, 1995.

Cook, David A. *Lost Illusions: American Cinema in the Shadow of Watergate and Vietnam, 1970–1979*. Volume 9, History of the American Cinema. New York: Charles Scribner's Sons, 2000.

Cornwall, Andrea and Lindisfarne, Nancy. "Dislocating Masculinity: Gender, Power and Anthropology." In *Dislocating Masculinity: Comparative Ethnographies*, edited by Andrea Cornwall and Nancy Lindisfarne, 11–47. London: Routledge, 1994.

Cui, Shuqin. "Stanley Kwan's *Center Stage:* (Im)possible Engagement between Feminism and Postmodernism." *Cinema Journal* 39.4 (Summer 2000): 60–80.

Dancer, Greg. "Film Style and Performance: Comedy and Kung Fu from Hong Kong." *Asian Cinema* 10.1 (Fall 1998): 44.

Davis, Darrell W. and Yeh, Yueh-yu. "Warning Category III: The Other Hong Kong Cinema." *Film Quarterly* 54.4 (Summer 2001): 12–26.

Dayan, Daniel. "The Tutor-Code of Classical." *Film Quarterly* 28.1 (Fall 1974): 22–31.

Deleuze, Gilles and Guattari, Felix. *Anti-Oedipus: Capitalism and Schizophrenia*. Minneapolis: University of Minnesota Press, 1977.

Derrida, Jacques. *Of Grammatology*. Baltimore: Johns Hopkins University Press, 1976.

Desser, David. "Diaspora and National Identity: Exporting China Through the Hong Kong Cinema." *Post Script* 20.2 & 3 (2001): 124–136.

———. "The Kung Fu Craze: Hong Kong Cinema's First American Reception." In *The Cinema of Hong Kong: History, Arts, Identity*, edited by Poshek Fu and David Desser, 19–43. New York: Cambridge University Press, 2000.

———. "The Martial Arts Film in the 1990s." In *Film Genre 2000: New Critical Essays*, edited by Wheeler Winston Dixon. Albany: State University of New York Press, 2000.

Doane, Mary Ann. *The Desire to Desire: The Woman's Film of the 1940s*. Blooming: Indiana University Press, 1987.

———. (1982) "Film and Masquerade: Theorizing the Female Spectator." *Screen* 23.3–4 (1982). Reprinted in Mary Ann Doane, *Femmes Fatales*. New York & London: Routledge, 1991.

Doty, Alexander. *Flaming Classics: Queering the Film Cannon*. London: Routledge, 2000.

———. *Making Things Perfectly Queer: Interpreting Mass Culture*. Minneapolis: University of Minnesota Press, 1993.

Doyle, Chris. "Don't Try for Me, Argentina." In *Projections 8: Film-makers on Film-making*, edited by John Boorman and Walter Donohue. London: Faber and Faber, 1998.

———. "To the End of the World." *Sight and Sound* (May 1997), 16.

Eliot, T. S. *The Sacred Wood: Essays on Poetry and Criticism*. London: Methuen & Co. ltd. 1920.

Eller, Claudia and Munoz, Lorenza. "The Plots Thicken in Foreign Markets." *The Los Angeles Times,* 6 October 2002.

Ellis, John. *Visible Fictions*. London: Routledge, 1982.

Enns, Anthony. "The Spectacle of Disabled Masculinity in John Woo's 'Heroic Bloodshed' Films." *Quarterly Review of Film and Video* 17.2 (2000): 137–45.

Erens, Patricia Brett. "Crossing Borders: Time, Memory, and the Construction of Identity in *Song of the Exile.*" *Cinema Journal* 39.4 (Summer 2000): 43–59.

Evans, Caroline and Gammon, Lorraine. "The Gaze Revisited, or Revisiting Queer Viewing." In *A Queer Romance: Lesbians, Gay Men and Popular Culture,* edited by Paul Burston and Colin Richardson, 13–56. London: Routledge, 1995.

Ewen, Stuart. "Marketing Dreams." In *Consumption, Identity & Style: Marketing, Meanings, and the Packaging of Pleasure,* edited by Alan Tomlinson, 43. New York: Routledge, 1990.

Fanon, Frantz. *Black Skin, White Masks*. New York: Grove Press, 1967.

Farmer, Brett. *Spectacular Passions: Cinema, Fantasy, Gay Male Spectatorships*. London: Duke University Press, 2000.

Feinberg, Leslie. *Stone Butch Blues*. Milford, CT: Firebrand, 1992.

———. *Trans Liberation: Beyond Pink or Blue*. Boston: Beacon, 1998.

Fonoroff, Paul. *At the Hong Kong Movies: 600 Reviews from 1988 Till the Handover.* Hong Kong: Film Biweekly Publishing House, 1998.

Forrest, David. "We're Here, We're Queer, and We're Not Going Shopping: Changing Gay Male Identities in Contemporary Britain." In *Dislocating Masculinity: Comparative Ethnographies*, edited by Andrea Cornwall and Nancy Lindisfarne, 97–110. London: Routledge, 1994.

Foucault, Michel. *Discipline and Punish: The Birth of the Prison.* Translated by Alan Sheridan. London: Penguin Books, 1997.

———. *The History of Sexuality, Volume One: An Introduction.* Translated by Robert Hurley. New York: Vintage, 1980.

———. "What is an Author?" In *Language, Counter-Memory, Practice: Selected Essays in Interviews by Michel Foucault*, edited by Donald F. Bouchard. Ithaca, New York: Cornell University Press, 1977.

———. *Discipline and Punish: The Birth of the Prison.* Translated by Alan Sheridan. London: Penguin Books, 1977.

———. *The Archaeology of Knowledge.* New York: Pantheon, 1972.

Fu, Poshek and Desser, David, eds. *The Cinema of Hong Kong: History, Arts, Identity.* Cambridge and New York: Cambridge University Press, 2000.

Fu, Winnie, ed. *The Making of Martial Arts Films — As Told by Filmmakers and Stars.* Hong Kong: Hong Kong Film Archive, 1999.

Fuss, Diana, ed. *Inside/Out: Lesbian Theories, Gay Theories.* London: Routledge, 1991.

———. *Essentially Speaking: Feminism, Nature and Difference.* London: Routledge, 1989.

Gallagher, Mark. "Masculinity in Translation: Jackie Chan's Transcultural Star Text." *The Velvet Light Trap* 39 (1997): 23–40.

Gardiner, Judith Kegan. "Introduction." In *Masculinity Studies and Feminist Theory: New Directions*, edited by Judith Kegan Gardiner. New York: Columbia University Press, 2002.

Gates, Philippa. "The Man's Film: Woo and the Pleasure of Male Melodrama." *Journal of Popular Culture* 35. 1 (2001): 59–79.

Geertz, Clifford. *The Interpretation of Cultures: Selected Essays.* New York: Basic Books, 1973.

Giddens, Anthony. *The Consequences of Modernity.* Stanford: Stanford University Press, 1990.

Giukin, Lenuta. "Boy-Girls: Gender, Body, and Popular Culture in Hong Kong Action Movies." In *Ladies and Gentlemen, Boys and Girls: Gender in Film at the End of the Twentieth Century*, edited by Murray Pomerance, 55–69. Albany: SUNY Press, 2001.

Gomery, Douglas. *Movie History: A Survey.* Belmont: Wardworth, 1991.

Gray, Ann. "Behind Closed Doors: Videorecorders in the Home." In *Boxed in: Women and Television*, edited by H. Baehr and G.. Dyer. London: Pandora, 1987.

Grosz, Elizabeth. *Volatile Bodies: Towards a Corporeal Feminism.* Bloomington: Indiana University Press, 1994.

Guehenno, Jean-Marie. *The End of the Nation State.* Minneapolis: University of Minnesota Press, 1995.

Halberstam, Judith. *Female Masculinity.* Durham: Duke UP, 1998.

Hall, Kenneth E. *John Woo: The Films.* Jefferson, NC: McFarland & Company, Inc., 1999.

Hall, Stuart. "Encoding/decoding." In *Culture, Media, Language*, edited by S. Hall, D. Hobson, A. Lowe and P. Willis, 128–38. London: Hutchinson, 1980.

Hanke, Robert. "John Woo's Cinema of Hyperkinetic Violence: From *A Better Tomorrow* to *Face/Off.* (Critical Essay)." *Film Criticism* 24.1 (1999): 39.

Hart, Hugh. "Fall Sneaks; His Career Is No Stunt; Comedy May Be His Forte, But Jackie Chan Is Quite Serious About Which Movies He Chooses." *The Los Angeles Times,* 8 September 2002.

Harvey, David. *The Condition of Postmodernity.* Oxford: Blackwell, 1989.

Held, David. *Introduction to Critical Theory.* Berkeley and Los Angeles: University of California Press: 1980.

Hobson, A. Lowe and P. Willis. London: Hutchinson, 1980.

———. et al. *Culture, Media, and Language: Working Papers in Cultural Studies, 1972–79.* London: Hutchison, 1980.

———. "Culture, Media, and the 'Ideological Effect'." In *Mass Communication and Society*, edited by J. Curran, M. Gurevitch, and J. Woollacott. London: Edward Arnold, 1977.

Hammond, Stefan. *Hollywood East: Hong Kong Movies and the People Who Make Them.* Lincolnwood, Illinois: Contemporary, 2000.

Hammond, Stefan and Wilkins, Mike. *Sex and Zen & A Bullet in the Head: The Essential Guide to Hong Kong's Mind-Bending Films.* New York: Fireside, 1996.

Harrington, C. Lee and Bielby, Dennise D., eds. *Popular Culture: Production and Consumption.* Malden, MA: Blackwell Publishers, 2001.

Hayakawa, S. I. *Language in Thought and Action.* San Diego: Harcourt Brace, 5th edition, 1990.

Heath, Steven. "Notes on Suture." *Screen* 18.2 (1977–78): 48–76.

Hemmings, Claire. *Bisexual Spaces: A Geography of Sexuality and Gender.* New York: Routledge, 2002.

Hennessy, Rosemary. "Queer Visibility in Commodity Culture." In *Social Postmodernism: Beyond Identity Politics*, edited by Linda Nicholson and Steven Seidman, 142–83. Cambridge: Cambridge University Press, 1995.

Ho, Petula Sik-ying. *Policing Identity: Decriminalisation of Homosexuality and the Emergence of Gay Identity in Hong Kong.* Ph.D. Diss., University of Essex, 1997.

Ho, Sam. "Licensed to Kick Man: The Jane Bond Films." In *The Restless Breed: Cantonese Stars of the Sixties (The 20th Hong Kong International Film*

Festival), edited by Law Kar, 34–36. Hong Kong: Urban Council, 1996.

Hohenadel, Kristin. "A Human Face for Hong Kong's Identity Crisis." *The New York Times,* 19 April 1998.

Holmlund, Chris. *Impossible Bodies: Femininity and Masculinity at the Movies.* London and New York: Routledge, 2002.

Hong Kong Film Critics Society. *Review on Hong Kong Movies (1994, 1995, 1996, 1997, 1998, 1999).* Hong Kong: Hong Kong Film Critics Society.

Hong Kong International Film Festival. *A Study of Hong Kong Cinema in the Seventies.* Hong Kong: Urban Council, 1984.

hooks, bell. "Eating the Other." In *Feminist Approaches to Theory and Methodology,* edited by S. HesseBiler, C. Gilmartin, and R. Lydenberg. New York: Oxford University Press, 1999.

Horkheimer, Max and Adorno, Theodor W. *Dialectic of Enlightenment: Philosophical Fragments.* Stanford: Stanford University Press, 2002.

Hozic, Aida. *Hollyworld, Space, Power, and Fantasy in the American Economy.* Ithaca: Cornell University Press, 2001.

Huang, Wu-lan, ed. *Dang-tai chung-guo tian-ying, 1995–1997* (Contemporary Chinese Cinema, 1995–1997). Taipei : Shihpao, 1998.

Jagose, Annamarie Rustom. *Queer Theory: An Introduction.* New York: New York University Press, 1996.

Jay, Martin. *Downcast Eyes: The Denigration of Vision in 20th-Century French Thought.* Berkeley: University of California Press, 1993.

Jeffords, Susan. *Hard Bodies: Hollywood Masculinity in the Reagan Era.* New Brunswick, New Jersey: Rutgers University Press, 1994.

Jin Yong (Louis Cha). *Xiao'ao Jianghu* (The smiling, proud wanderer) Vol. 4. Hong Kong: Minghe she, 1980.

Keller, James R. *Queer (Un)Friendly Film and Television.* London: McFarland & Company, Inc, 2002.

Kellner, D. *Media Culture: Cultural Studies, Identity, and Politics Between the Modern and the Postmodern.* London: Routledge, 1995.

Kimmel, Michael. *Manhood in America: A Cultural History.* New York: Free Press, 1996.

Kong, Travis S. K. "The Seduction of the Golden Boy: The Body Politics of Hong Kong Gay Men." *Body & Society* 8.1 (2002): 29–48.

———. *The Voices In-Between ... : The Body Politics of Hong Kong Gay Men.* Ph.D. Dissertation, Department of Sociology, University of Essex, UK, 2000.

Koven, Mikel J. "My Brother, My Lover, My Self: Traditional Masculinity in the Hong Kong Action Cinema of John Woo." *Canadian Folklore* 19.1 (1997): 55–68.

Krämer, Peter. "A Powerful Cinema-going Force? Hollywood and Female Audiences since the 1960s." In *Identifying Hollywood's Audiences: Cultural Identity and the Movies,* edited by Melvyn Stokes and Richard Maltby, 103–4. London: BFI, 1999.

Kristeva, Julia. "L'abjet d'amour." *Tel Quel* 91 (Spring 1982): 17–32.

———. *Pouvoirs de l'horreur.* Paris: Editions du Seuil, 1980.

Ku, Lisbeth. "Mass-mediated Images of Women: Connie Chan Po-Chu and Josephine Siao Fong-Fong as Desired Cultural Images." *Hong Kong Cultural Studies Bulletin* 819. 8–9 (Spring/Summer, 1998): 31–40.

Kuan, Hsin-chi and Lau, Siu-kai. *Political Attitudes in a Changing Context,* Hong Kong: Hong Kong Institute of Asia-Pacific Studies, the Chinese University of Hong Kong, 1997.

Kuhn, Annette. "Women Genres." *Screen* 25.1 (1984):18–28. Reprinted in *The Film Cultures Reader,* edited by G. Turner. London and New York: Routledge, 2002.

Lacan, Jacques. *Le Séminaire VII: L'éthique de la psychanalyse.* Paris: Seuil, 1986.

Lai, Linda Chiu-Han. "Film and Enigmatization: Nostalgia, Nonsense, and Remembering." In *At Full Speed: Hong Kong Cinema in a Borderless World,* edited by Esther Yau, 231–50. Minneapolis: University of Minnesota Press, 2001.

Lakoff, Robin. *Talking Power: The Politics of Language in Our Lives.* NY: Basic Books, 1990.

Lam, Michael. *The Male Boundary.* (Chinese Edition). Hong Kong: Big Camp.

———. *Fake Sexual Politics.* (Chinese Edition). Hong Kong: Big Camp, 1993.

Lan, Tsu-wei. *Film Music Composers.* Taipei: Rye Field Publishing Company, 2001.

Lancaster, Roger N. "Subject Honour and Object Shame: The Construction of Male Homosexuality and Stigma in Nicaragua." *Ethnology* 27.2 (1988): 111–25.

Laqueur, Thomas W. *Making Sex: Body and Gender from the Greeks to Freud.* Cambridge, MA.: Harvard University Press, 1990.

Lau, Jenny Kwok-Wah. "Besides Fists and Blood: Hong Kong Comedy and Its Master of the Eighties." *Cinema Journal* 37.2 (1998): 18–34.

Lau, Siu-kai. *Hongkongese or Chinese: The Problem of Identity on the Eve of Resumption of Chinese Sovereignty over Hong Kong.* Hong Kong: Hong Kong Institute of Asia-Pacific Studies, the Chinese University of Hong Kong, 1997.

Law Kar, ed. *Transcending the Times: King Hu and Eileen Chang (Hong Kong International Film Festival 1998).* Hong Kong: Provisional Urban Council, 1998.

———. ed. *Overseas Chinese Figures in Cinema.* Hong Kong: Urban Council, 1992.

Leap, William L., ed. *Public Sex/Gay Space.* New York: Columbia University Press, 1999.

Lee, Chiu-hing. *Hong Kong Postmodern.* Hong Kong: Compass Corporation Ltd, 2002.

Lemert, Charles C. "Post-structuralism and Sociology." In *The Post-modern Turn:*

New Perspectives on Social Theory, edited by Steven Seidman, 265–81. New York: Cambridge University Press, 1994.

Leung, Grace and Chan, Joseph. "The Hong Kong Cinema and its Overseas Market: A Historical Review, 1950–1995." In *Fifty Years of Electric Shadows: The 21st Hong Kong International Film Festival*, edited by Law Kar, 136–51. Hong Kong: Urban Council, 1997.

Leung, Helen Hok-Sze. "Queerscapes in Contemporary Hong Kong Cinema." *Positions* 9.2 (Fall 2001): 423–47.

Li Bihua. *Farewell to My Concubine*. (Chinese Edition) Hong Kong: Cosmos Books Ltd, 1986.

Li, Siu-leung. "Kung Fu: Negotiating Nationalism and Modernity." *Cultural Studies* 15.3 & 4 (2001): 515–42.

Li, Zhuotao. *Linli Yingxiang Guan — Jingshui Pian*. Hong Kong: Ci Wan Hua Tang, 2000.

———. *Linli Yingxiang Guan — Paozhuan Pian*. Hong Kong: Ci Wan Hua Tang, 1996.

———. *Guan Ni Ji*. Hong Kong: Ci Wan Hua Tang, 1993.

Lii, Ding-tzann. "A Colonized Empire: Reflections on the Expansion of Hong Kong Films in Asian Countries." In *Trajectories: Inter-Asia Cultural Studies*, edited by Kuan-Hsing Chen, 122–141. London and New York: Routledge, 1998.

Lim, Bliss Cua. "Spectral Times: The Ghost Film as Historical Allegory." *Positions: East Asia Cultures Critique* 9.2 (Fall 2001): 287–329.

Liu, James J. Y. *The Chinese Knight-Errant*. Chicago: University of Chicago Press, 1967.

Lo, Kwai-cheung. "Double Negations: Hong Kong Cultural Identity in Hollywood's Transnational Representations." *Cultural Studies* 15 (3/4) (2001): 464–85.

———. "Muscles and Subjectivity: A Short History of the Masculine Body in Hong Kong Popular Culture." *Camera Obscura* 39 (September 1996): 105–25.

Logan, Bey. *Hong Kong Action Cinema*. London: Titan Books, 1995.

Louie, Kam. *Theorising Chinese Masculinity: Society and Gender in China*. Cambridge: Cambridge UP, 2002.

Louie, Kam and Louise, Edwards. "Chinese Masculinity: Theorizing Wen and Wu." *East Asian History* 8 (1994): 135–48.

Lu, Sheldon Hsiao-peng. "Filming Diaspora and Identity: Hong Kong and 1997." In *The Cinema of Hong Kong: History, Arts, Identity*, edited by Poshek Fu and David Desser, 273–88. Cambridge: Cambridge UP, 2000.

———. "Historical Introduction: Chinese Cinemas (1896–1996) and Transnational Film Studies." In *Transnational Chinese Cinemas: Identity, Nationhood, Gender*, edited by Sheldon Hsiao-peng Lu, 1–31. Honolulu: University of Hawaii Press, 1997.

Lukacs, Georg. *History and Class Consciousness; Studies in Marxist Dialectics.* Translated by Rodney Livingstone. Cambridge: MIT Press, 1971.

Luhmann, Niklas. *The Reality of the Mass Media.* Translated by Kathleen Cross. Stanford: Stanford University Press, 2000.

MacInnes, John. *The End of Masculinity: The Confusion of Sexual Genesis and Sexual Difference in Modern Society.* Buckingham: Open University Press, 1998.

Marchetti, Gina. *Romance and the "Yellow Peril": Race, Sex and Discursive Strategies in Hollywood Fiction.* Berkeley: University of California Press, 1993.

Marx, Karl. *Capital, Vol. 1.* London: Penguin Books, 1990.

Mayne, Judith. "Paradoxes of Spectatorship." In *The Film Cultures Reader,* edited by G. Turner. London and New York: Routledge, 2002.

McNair, Brian. *Striptease Culture: Sex, Media and the Democratisation of Desire.* London, New York: Routledge, 2002.

Miller, J. Hillis. "The Critic as Host." In *Modern American Critics Since 1955,* *Dictionary of Literary Biography,* vol. 67, edited by Gregory S. Jay, 327–32. Detroit: Gale Research Company, 1988.

Miller, V. Jacques-Alain. "La Suture (Élements de la logique du signifiant)." *Les Cahiers pour l'analyse* 3.1 & 2 (January-April, 1966): 37–49.

Modleski, Tania. *Feminism without Women: Culture and Criticism in a "Postfeminist" Age.* New York, London: Routledge, 1991.

———. *Loving with a Vengeance: Mass Produced Fantasies for Women.* London: Methuen, 1984.

Mort, Frank. *Cultures of Consumption: Masculinities and Social Space in Late-Twentieth Century Britain.* London: Routledge, 1996.

MPIA (Hong Kong, Kowloon and New Territories Motion Picture Industry Association Ltd). *Xianggang dianying* (Hong Kong Films: Yearbooks). Hong Kong: MPIA, 1992–1998.

Mulvey, Laura. "Afterthought on 'Visual Pleasure and Narrative Cinema' Inspired by *Duel in the Sun.*" In *Feminism and Film Theory,* edited by Constance Penley, 69–79. New York: Routledge, 1988.

———. "Visual Pleasure and Narrative Cinema." *Screen* 16. 3 (1975): 6–18. Reprinted in *Issues in Feminist Film Criticism,* edited by P. Erens, 28–71. Bloomington, IN: Indiana University Press, 1990.

Natale, Richard. "Springing to Action; Adopting Hong Kong's Style of Martial Arts Scenes, with Their Ballet-Like Moves, Has Helped Movie Makers Revive a Genre with Less Graphic Violence." *The Los Angeles Times,* 8 January 2002.

Nestle, Joan. *A Fragile Union.* San Francisco: Cleis, 1998.

———. Howell, Clare and Wilchins, Riki, eds. *Genderqueer: Voices from Beyond the Sexual Binary.* Los Angeles: Alyson, 2002.

Ng, Paul Chun-ming. "The Image of Overseas Chinese in American Cinema." In *Overseas Chinese Figures in Cinema,* edited by Law Kar. Hong Kong: Urban Council, 1992.

Nicholson, Linda and Seidman, Steven, eds. *Social Postmodernism: Beyond Identity Politics*. Cambridge: Cambridge University Press, 1995.

Nixon, Sean. "Exhibiting Masculinity." In *Representation: Cultural Representations and Signifying Practices*, edited by Stuart Hall, 298. Sage Publications, 1997.

Ohmae, Kenichi. *The End of the Nation State: The Rise of Regional Economies*. New York: Free Press, 1995.

Oudart, Jean-Pierre. "La Suture." Part one of two. *Cahiers du Cinéma* 211 (April 1969): 36–9.

———. "La Suture." Part two of two. *Cahiers du Cinéma* 212 (May 1969): 50–5.

Pang, Laikwan. "Masculinity in Crisis: Films of Milkyway Image and Post-1997 Hong Kong Cinema." *Feminist Media Studies* 2.3 (Fall 2002): 325–40.

———. "Death and Hong Kong Cinema." *Quarterly Review of Film and Video* 18.1 (Spring 2001): 15–29.

Penley, Constance. *The Future of an Illusion: Film, Feminism, and Psychoanalysis*. Minneapolis: University of Minnesota Press, 1989.

Percy, Walker. *The Message in the Bottle*. NY: Straus & Giroux, 1983.

Perlmutter, Howard. "On the Rocky Road to the First Global Civilization." *Human Relations* 44.1 (1991): 902–6.

Ping Lu. *He-je chiun tsai-lai* (Whence shall you visit again). Taipei: INK Publishing, 2002.

Plummer, Kenneth. "The Lesbian and Gay Movement in Britain — Schisms, Solidarities, and Social Worlds." In *The Global Emergence of Gay and Lesbian Politics: National Imprints of a Worldwide Movement*, edited by Barry D. Adam, Jan Willem Duyvendak and André Krouwel, 133–57. Philadelphia: Temple University Press, 1999.

———. ed. *Modern Homosexualities: Fragments of Lesbian and Gay Experience*. London: Routledge, 1992.

Poon, Wena. "*Chinese Box*." *Film Quarterly* 52.1(Fall 1998): 31–4.

Pratt, Minnie Bruce. *S/he*. New York: Firebrand, 1995.

Prosser, Jay. *Second Skins: The Body Narratives of Transsexuality*. New York: Columbia UP, 1998.

Quart, Leonard and Auster, Albert. *American Film and Society Since 1945*. London and Basingstoke: Macmillan, 1984.

Radway, Janice. *Reading the Romance: Women, Patriarchy, and Popular Literature*. Chapel Hill, NC: University of North Carolina Press, 1984.

Rainer, Emig. "Queering the Straights: Straightening the Queers: Commodified Sexualities and Hegemonic Masculinity." In *Subverting Masculinity: Hegemonic and Alternative Versions of Masculinity in Contemporary Culture*, edited by Russell West and Frank Lay. Amsterdam: Rodopi, 2000.

Raymond, Diane. "Popular Culture and Queer Representation: A Critical Perspective." In *Gender, Race, and Class in Media: A Text-Reader*, edited by Gail Dines and Jean, M. Humez. London: Sage, 2003.

Rayns, Tony. "King Hu: Shall We Dance?" In *A Study of the Hong Kong Martial Arts Film*. Hong Kong: Urban Council, 1980.

———. "Bruce Lee: Narcissism and Nationalism." In *A Study of the Hong Kong Martial Arts Film, Hong Kong International Film Festival Catalogue*. Hong Kong: Urban Council, 1980.

Rich, Adrienne. "Compulsory Heterosexuality and Lesbian Existence." *Signs* 5 (1980): 631–60.

Rodriguez, Hector. "Questions of Chinese Aesthetics: Film Form and Narrative Space in the Cinema of King Hu." *Cinema Journal* 38. 1 (1998): 73–97.

———. "Hong Kong Popular Culture as an Interpretive Arena: the Huang Feihong Film Series." *Screen* 38.1 (1997): 1–24.

Rubin, Gayle S. "Thinking Sex: Notes for a Radical Theory of the Politics of Sexuality." In *The Lesbian and Gay Studies Reader*, edited by Henry Abelove, Michele Aina Barale and David M. Halperin, 3–44. London: Routledge, 1993.

Ryan, Barbara. "Blood, Brothers, and Hong Kong Gangster Movies: Pop Culture Commentary on 'One China'." In *Asian Popular Culture*, edited by John A. Lent, 61–77. Boulder: Westview Press, 1995.

Salaff, Janet. *Working Daughters of Hong Kong*. Cambridge: Cambridge University Press, 1981.

Samshasha (Xiaomingxiong). *Zhongguo tongxing'ai shilu* (History of homosexuality in China), revised ed. Hong Kong: Rosa Winkel Press, 1997.

Sandell, Jillian. "Reinventing Masculinity: The Spectacle of Male Intimacy in the Films of John Woo." *Film Quarterly* 49.4 (1996): 23.

———. "A Better Tomorrow: American Masochism and Hong Kong Action Film." *Bright Lights Film Journal* 13 (1994). Reprinted on http://www.brightlightsfilm.com/31/hk_better1.html/.

Sedgwick, Eve Kosofsky. "Gosh, Boy George, You Must Be Awfully Secure in Your Masculinity." In *Constructing Masculinity*, edited by Maurice Berger, Brian Wallis and Simon Watson, 11–20. London: Routledge, 1995.

———. *Epistemology of the Closet*. Berkeley: University of California Press, 1990.

———. *Between Men: English Literature and Male Homosocial Desire*. New York: Columbia University Press, 1985.

Segal, Lynne. *Slow Motion: Changing Masculinities, Changing Men*. London: Virago, 1990.

Seidman, Steven. *Difference Troubles: Queering Social Theory and Sexual Politics*. Cambridge: Cambridge University Press, 1997.

———. ed. *Queer Theory/Sociology*. Oxford: Basil Blackwell, 1996.

———. "Identity and Politics in a 'Postmodern' Gay Culture: Some Historical and Conceptual Notes." In *Fear of a Queer Planet: Queer Politics and Social Theory*, edited by Michael Warner, 105–42. Minneapolis: University of Minnesota Press, 1993.

Sek Kei. *Shi Qi yinghua ji (Collected Reviews of Sek Kei)*. Hong Kong: Subculture, 1999.

———. "The War between the Cantonese and Mandarin Cinemas in the Sixties or How the Beautiful Women Lost to the Action Men." In *The Restless Breed: Cantonese Stars of the Sixties (The 20th Hong Kong International Film Festival)*, edited by Law Kar, 26–33. Hong Kong: Urban Council, 1996.

———. "Achievement and Crisis: Hong Kong Cinema in the 80s." In *Hong Kong Cinema in the Eighties: A Comparative Study with Western Cinema*, edited by Law Kar, 59. Hong Kong: Urban Council, 1991.

Sek Kei, with Rolanda Chu and Grant Foerster. "The HK Martial Arts Film." *Bright Lights Film Journal* 13 (1991), http://www.brightlightsfilm.com/31/hk_brief2.html/.

———. "The Development of 'Martial Arts' in Hong Kong Cinema." In *A Study of the Hong Kong Martial Arts Film*. Hong Kong: Urban Council, 1980.

Serres, Michel. *Le Parasite*. Paris: Éditions Grasset et Fasquette, 1980.

Siegel, Marc. "The Intimate Spaces of Wong Kar-Wai." In *At Full Speed: Hong Kong Cinema in a Borderless World*, edited by Esther C. M. Yau. Minneapolis: University of Minnesota Press, 2001.

Silverman, Kaja. *The Subject of Semiotics*. Oxford: Oxford University Press, 1983.

Sinfield, Alan. *Gay and After*. London: Serpent's Tail, 1998.

Socor, Barbara. *Conceiving the Self: Presence and Absence in Psychoanalytic Theory*. Madison and Connecticut: International Universities Press, 1997.

Sontag, Susan, ed. *A Barthes Reader*. New York: Hill & Wang, 1983.

Spelman, Elizabeth V. *Inessential Woman: Problems of Exclusion in Feminist Thought*. London, Women's Press, 1990.

Stacey, Jackie. *Star Gazing: Hollywood Cinema and Female Spectatorship*. London and New York: Routledge, 1994.

Staiger, Janet. "Reception studies in film and television." In *The Film Cultures Reader*, edited by G. Turner. London and New York: Routledge, 2002.

Stokes, Lisa Odham and Hoover, Michael. *City on Fire: Hong Kong Cinema*. London: Verso, 1999.

Stone, Sandy. "The Empire Strikes Back: A Posttranssexual Manifesto." Revised 1993 version, http://www.sandystone.com/empire-strikes-back/.

Storper, Michael. "The Transition to Flexible Specialization in the US Film Industry: External Economies, the Division of Labour and the Crossing of Industrial Divides." In *Post-Fordism: A Reader*, edited by Ash Amin. Oxford: Blackwell, 1994.

Stringer, Julian. "'Your Tender Smiles Give Me Strength': Paradigms of Masculinity in John Woo's *A Better Tomorrow* and *The Killer*." *Screen* 38.1 (1997): 40.

Stryker, Susan. "The Transgender Issue: An Introduction." *GLQ* 4:2 (1998): 149.

Tasker, Yvonne. *Spectacular Bodies: Gender, Genre and the Action Cinema*. New York: Routledge, 1993.

Teo, Stephen. "Cathay and the Wuxia Movie." In *The Cathay Story (The 26th International Hong Kong Film Festival)*, 108–23. Hong Kong: Hong Kong Film Archive, 2002.

———. "Sinking into Creative Depths." In *Hong Kong Panorama 97–98: The Twenty-second Hong Kong International Film Festival*, edited by Law Kar, 11. Hong Kong: Provisional Urban Council, 1998.

———. *Hong Kong Cinema: The Extra Dimensions*. London: British Film Institute, 1997.

———. "The Decade with Two Faces: Cantonese Cinema and the Paranoid Sixties." In *The Restless Breed: Cantonese Stars of the Sixties (The 20th Hong Kong International Film Festival)*, edited by Law Kar, 18–25. Hong Kong: Urban Council, 1996.

———. "The True Way of the Dragon: The Films of Bruce Lee." In *Overseas Chinese Figures in Cinema (The 16th Hong Kong International Film Festival)*, 70–80. Hong Kong: Urban Council, 1992.

Thompson, Kristin and Bordwell, David. *Film History: An Introduction*. New York: McGraw-Hill, 1994.

Tsui, Athena, and C. Fong. "Too Many Ways to be a Filmmaker: Interview with Johnnie To." In *Hong Kong Panorama 98–99: The Twenty-third Hong Kong International Film Festival*, edited by Law Kar, 64. Hong Kong: Provisional Urban Council, 1999.

van Zooner, Liesbet. *Feminist Media Studies*. Sage Publications, 1994.

Vance, Carol S. "Social Construction Theory and Sexuality." In *Constructing Masculinity*, edited by Berger Maurice, Wallis Brian, and Watson Simon. London: Routledge, 1995.

Wang, W. *Hong Kong Cinema POV*. Taipei: Yang Zhi Wen Hua Shi Ye Gu Fen You Xian Gong Si, 2002.

Warner, Michael, ed. *Fear of a Queer Planet: Queer Politics and Social Theory*. Minneapolis: University of Minnesota Press, 1993.

Weeks, Jeffrey. *Sexuality and Its Discontents: Meanings, Myths and Modern Sexualities*. London: Routledge, 1985.

Weinberg, George. *Society and the Healthy Homosexual*. New York: Doubleday, 1973.

Weisser, Thomas. *Asian Trash Cinema: The Book*. Miami: ATC/ETC Publications, 1994.

———. *Asian Trash Cinema: The Book (Part 2)*. Miami: Vital Sounds Inc. and ATC Publications, 1995.

Whitehead, Stephen and Barrett, Frank. *The Masculinities Reader*. Cambridge: Polity Press, 2001.

Whittle, Stephen, ed. *The Margins of the City: Gay Men's Urban Lives*. Aldershot: Arena, 1994.

Williams, Tony. "Michelle Yeoh: Under Eastern Eyes." *Asian Cinema* 12.2 (2001): 119–31.

Wong, Wendy Siuyi. *Hong Kong Comics: A History of Manhua*. New York: Princeton Architectural Press, 2002.

Wong, Yan. "Chang Cheh's Directorial Journey." *Influence Magazine* 13 (April 1976). Retrieved from: http://changcheh.Ocatch.com/ch-bio2.htm/.

Wriston, Walter. *The Twilight of Sovereignty*. New York: Charles Scribner's Sons, 1992.

Yau, Ching. *Lingqi luzao* (Starting another stove). Hong Kong: Youth Literary Bookstore, 1996.

Yau, Esther C. M., ed. *At Full Speed: Hong Kong Cinema in a Borderless World*. Minneapolis: University of Minnesota Press, 2001.

———. "Border Crossing: Mainland China's Presence in Hong Kong Cinema." In *New Chinese Cinemas: Forms, Identities, Politics*, edited by Paul U. Pickowicz, et al, 180–201. Cambridge, New York: Cambridge University Press, 1994.

Yue, Audrey. "What's So Queer about *Happy Together*? A.k.a. Queer (N)Asian: Interface, Community, Belonging." *Inter-Asia Cultural Studies* 1.2 (2000): 251–64.

Zhang, Jian. *Jiushi niandai gangcanpian gongyi yipie: kunjing de tantao ji chulu*. (A glance at Hong Kong's film productions in the 1990s). Hong Kong: Guanzi Xianggang dianying gongyi fazheng yanjiu hui, 1998.

Zhang, Zhen. "Bodies in the Air: The Magic of Science and the Fate of the Early 'Martial Arts' Film in China." *Post Script* 20.2 & 3 (2001): 43–60.

Zizek, Slavoj. *For They Know Not What They Do: Enjoyment as a Political Factor*. London: Verso, 1991.

Index

1997 (handover of Hong Kong), 9, 35, 36, 44, 53, 124, 125, 129, 132, 134, 141, 155, 167, 168, 228, 229, 230, 232, 234, 235, 253, 296n36

Abbas, Ackbar, 155–157, 158, 161, 164–165, 167, 171–172, 173, 287n32
  Hong Kong: Culture and the Politics of Disappearance, 155

action films, 8, 13, 35, 45, 46–47, 50, 66, 72, 73, 96, 102, 140–143, 149, 150, 151–152, 153–154, 155, 156–157, 161, 165, 190–191, 203, 217–218, 222, 223, 230, 239, 244,251, 252, 258, 259, 260, 266n18
  homosociality /homoeroticism in, 46–49, 72, 73, 95–96, 144
  and masculinity and nationalism, 13, 221, 222–223, 230, 236
  women fighters in, 11, 137, 139–144, 145–146, 151–152, 154

Adorno, Theodor, 200, 211–213, 214, 215, 219, 220
  "Cultural Industry Reconsidered," 212
  Dialectic of Enlightenment, 212

"Aesthetics in Action: Kung fu, Gunplay, and Cinematic Expressivity" (Bordwell), 171

Ai zai taxiang de jijie. See *Farewell, China*

Anti-Oedipus (Deleuze, Guattari), 139

Anzieu, Didier, 88, 274n20

As Tears Go By (Wong), 73, 155, 164–165

Ashes of Time (Wong), 71 167, 228, 236

Asian Trash Cinema, 171

Baak Suet-sin (Bai Xuexian), 70

Bai Ying, 19, 29, 109

Barthes, Roland, 61, 62 121–122, 123, 128
  "The Third Meaning: Research Notes on Some Eisenstein Stills," 121–122, 123

Bartky, Sandra Lee, 61

Bataille, Georges, 115, 277n12

Baxian fandian zhi renrou chashaobao. See *Untold Story, The*

Beauty and the Breast (Yip), 177, 179, 182–83, 186, 189–190, 193, 195, 196, 197

Better Tomorrow, A (Woo), 73, 97, 205–206

Black Mask (Lee), 110

Bolton, Kingsley, 181

Bonvillain, Nancy, 180

Bordwell, David, 5, 38, 94, 108, 109, 141–142, 161–162, 163, 165–166, 171, 173, 204, 207, 208, 217, 226, 277n7, 283n21
  "Aesthetics in Action: Kung fu, Gunplay, and Cinematic Expressivity," 171

Planet Hong Kong: Popular Cinema and the Art of Entertainment, 108, 162

Bourdieu, Pierre, 61, 202

Broken Arrow (Woo), 73, 207

Bronson, Charles, 23

Bullet in the Head (Woo), 168, 286n20

Butler, Judith, 60, 64, 138, 243
   Gender Trouble, 60

Cathay (MP & GI) Company, 21, 22, 24, 27, 263n6

Center Stage (Kwan), 156

Chan, Eason (Chen Yixun), 66, 186

Chan, Jackie (Cheng Long), 3, 8, 13, 20, 26, 28, 45, 101, 102, 117, 118, 140, 141, 146, 152, 167, 184, 191, 200, 203, 219, 221, 222, 226, 228, 229, 230, 239, 244, 252–254, 255–258, 259
   comparisons with Lee, 208, 252, 255, 259
   films, pre-Hollywood vs. Hollywood, 200, 208–211, 219
   Police Story, 252, 256, 258

Chan, Jacinson W., 72

Chan, Jordan (Chen Xiaochun), 76, 92

Chan Kam-hung (Chen Jinhong), 73, 185

Chan, Natalia, 82, 96, 97

Chan Number Thirteen (Chen Shisan), 189

Chan Po-chu, Connie (Chen Baozhu), 22, 69, 239, 244, 245, 247, 248–249, 250, 251

Chan, Yeeshan, 4, 5, 12, 13

Chang Chen (Zhang Zhen), 112, 129, 130, 132

Chang, Grace (Ge Lan), 21

Chang Hsiao-hung, 65

Chang, Sylvia (Zhang Aijia), 129, 187

Chen Kuan-tai (Chen Guantai), 25, 26, 27

Chen Ta (Chen Da), 120–121, 123, 279n14

Cheng Dan-shui (Zheng Danrui), 66

Cheng, Ekin (Zheng Yijian), 92, 97

Cheng Pei-pei (Zheng Peipei), 19, 21, 25, 27, 69, 140

Cheng, Sammi (Zheng Xiuwen), 39, 49, 50, 51, 52, 75

Cheung Hok-yau (Zhang Xueyou), 73

Cheung King-kok, 204

Cheung, Leslie (Zhang Guorong), 57, 69, 70, 71, 77, 86, 98, 130

Cheung, Mabel, 187

Cheung, Maggie (Zhang Manyu), 124, 125, 126, 127

Chia Ling (Jia Ling), 25

Chiang, David (Jiang Dawei), 25, 26, 27, 28, 31

Chiao Hsiung-ping, Peggy, 25

Chin, Amy (Qian Xiaohui), 190

Chin Ping (Qin Ping), 21

Chinese Box (Wang), 120, 124–129, 134, 135, 279n18, 279nn18–19, 278n22

Choi Wai-kit, 12

Chor Yuen (Chu Yuan), 28, 32

Chou Wah-shan, 87, 88

Chow Man-kin (Zhou Wenjian), 66

Chow, Raymond (Zhou Wenhuai), 24

Chow, Rey, 170
   Primitive Passion, 170

Chow, Stephen (Zhou Xingchi), 3, 8, 13, 222, 231–236, 255, 293n34
   and Hong Kong identity, 231–232, 233–234, 235
   Shaolin Soccer, 39, 194, 233, 245

Chow Yun-fat (Zhou Runfa), 73, 92, 94, 97, 102, 112, 115, 117, 201, 203, 277n11

Chu Yiu-wai, 132, 133

Chun'guang zhaxie. See *Happy Together*

Cinema City, 8

Cohan, Steven, 3, 4, 42
Connell, R. W., 42, 59–60
Connery, Sean, 23
Crouching Tiger, Hidden Dragon (Lee), 10, 20, 38, 69, 101, 111–117, 112, 200
"Cultural Industry Reconsidered" (Adorno), 212
D & B Films, 146, 283n17
Dadawa, 125–126, 127, 128
Dancer, Greg, 195
Davis, Darrell, 158
Deleuze, Gilles, 139, 282n6
Anti-Oedipus, 139
Desser, David, 8, 9, 151, 225, 226, 284n23
Dialectic of Enlightenment (Adorno, Horkheimer), 212
Diexue jietou. See *Bullet in the Head*
Diexue Shuangxiong. See *Killer, The*
Doane, Mary Ann, 240–241, 258
Doyle, Christopher, 280n27, 280n30
Dongxie xidu. See *Ashes of Time*
Dr. Lamb (Lee, Tang), 169, 171
Eastwood, Clint, 23
Evans, Caroline, 65
Expect the Unexpected (Yau), 38, 43, 44, 45
Face/Off (Woo), 73, 207
Fanon, Frantz, 61
Farewell China (Law), 120–124, 128, 134, 135, 278n5, 278n9
Feichang turan. See *Expect the Unexpected*
Feinberg, Leslie, 91
female audiences, 8, 22, 49–50, 52, 87, 188, 239, 240–244, 252, 258, 259
action films, reception of, 13, 239, 244, 252–255, 258
Beauty and the Breast, reception to, 182–183
melodramas, reception of, 13, 239, 244, 258

"female masculinity," 11, 137–139, 143
in action films, 140–141, 143, 146–147, 154
Female Masculinity (Halberstam), 137
feminist theory/feminist criticism, 6, 19, 82, 240, 249, 256, 257
Fengxiong mi "Cup." See *Beauty and the Breast*
Fong, Alex (Fang Zhongxin), 73, 93
Fonoroff, Paul 158–159, 169
Foucault, Michel, 61, 62, 184
Fu, Alexander (Fu Sheng), 25, 26
Fung, Patrina (Feng Baobao), 22
Freud, Sigmund, 88
Full Moon in New York (Kwan), 129
Gammon, Lorraine, 65
Gaoyang yisheng. See *Dr. Lamb*
"gay visibility," 9, 58, 67
gay films as, 58, 67, 74–77, 79
gender-bending in films as, 58, 67–71, 79
homosociality in films as, 58, 67, 72–74, 79
Geertz, Clifford, 177, 286n24
Gender Trouble (Butler), 60
Golden Harvest Limited, 223
Gong Li, 78, 124, 125, 126, 128, 129
Gramsci, Antonio, 59
Gray, Ann, 242–243
Gunan gua'nü. See *Needing You*
Guattari, Félix, 139, 282n6
Halberstam, Judith, 92–93, 137, 140, 143, 147, 281n1
Female Masculinity, 137
Hall, Stuart, 62, 241, 244
Hammond, Stefan, 171, 276n3, 277n8, 287n29
Sex and Zen & A Bullet in the Head, 171
Hanke, Robert, 207
Happy Together (Wong), 57, 77, 78 120, 129–132, 134, 135, 157, 280n27, 280nn30–31

Hard Target (Woo), 206–207
hegemonic masculinity, 3, 4, 42, 58, 59–61, 69, 74, 79, 139, 140, 142, 204
and gay masculinity, 58, 59–61, 69, 74, 143, 204
and heterosexism, 58, 60
See also masculinity
Heixia. See *Black Mask*
Hennessy, Rosemary, 64
History and Class Consciousness (Lukacs), 199
Ho, Sam, 246
Hoffman, Dustin, 23
Hold You Tight (Kwan), 75, 185
Hollywood, 1, 4, 23, 24, 25, 42, 45, 46, 52, 73, 102, 103–104, 105, 141, 142, 151, 152, 163, 169, 172, 173, 177, 188, 202–203, 204, 205–207, 222, 240, 241, 244
and Jackie Chan, 200, 203, 208, 209–211, 219
Hong Kong film professionals in, 12–13, 199, 200–202, 219, 220
"multicultural turn" in, 12–13, 199–200, 211–220
and John Woo, 200, 203, 205, 206–207, 219
Holmlund, Chris, 4
Hong Kong: Culture and the Politics of Disappearance (Abbas), 155
Hong Kong, post–1997, 129, 132, 134, 229, 230, 233, 234
"Hongllywood" films, 101, 103, 117
Chineseness, stylization of, in, 102, 103, 110, 117
bamboo, disappearance of, in, 103, 105–107, 118
body exudations, disappearance of, in, 103, 104–105, 107–108
traditional kung fu, disappearance of, in, 103–104
Hongxing shisan mei. See *Portland Street Blues*

hooks, bell, 66
Horkheimer, Max, 200, 211–212, 213, 214, 215, 219, 220
Dialectic of Enlightenment, 212
Hsu Feng (Xu Feng), 19, 25, 29, 140
Hu Jin-gwan (Xu Yanjun), 66
Hu, King (Hu Jinquan), 3, 8, 17–21, 22, 25–26, 28, 29, 30, 32, 46, 101, 103, 108–109, 113, 117, 140, 223, 263n6, 276n2, 276n6, 277n7
Huang Feihong. See *Once Upon a Time in China*
Huang Feihong er zhi nan'er dang ziqiang. See *Once Upon a Time in China II*
Huangjia shijie. See *Yes, Madam!*
Huangjia zhanshi. See *Royal Warriors*
Hui, Ann (Xu Anhua), 2, 132, 133, 135, 155, 157, 187, 281n34, 289n19
July Rhapsody, 135
Ordinary Heroes, 120, 129, 132–134, 135, 281n34
Song of the Exile, 155, 157
Hung, Sammo (Hong Jinbao), 29, 140, 141, 144, 146, 29, 140, 141, 144, 146, 152, 203
Hutton, Christopher, 181
identity, 5, 173–174
Chinese, 6, 11, 101 102, 153
gay, 58, 61, 63, 64, 75, 76, 79, 85
Hong Kong, 6, 11, 53, 155, 159, 168, 174, 184, 191, 221, 222, 223, 227, 228, 230, 253, 254, 259
transgender, 90, 91
Inessential Woman (Spelman), 243
Irons, Jeremy, 124, 125, 128
Jeffords, Susan, 45
Jin Yong, 83–85, 96
Jingcha gushi. See *Police Story*
Jitao, 46
Jueshi hao "Bra." See *La Brassiere*
July Rhapsody (Hui), 135
Kellner, Douglas, 65–66

Ketu qiuhen. See *Song of the Exile*
Killer, The (Woo), 73, 94, 205–206
Kingston, Maxine Hong, 105
Kong, Travis S. K., 5, 6, 9
Koo, Louis (Gu Tianle), 178, 186, 195
Kot Man-fai, Eric (Ge Minhui), 74, 76, 77
Koven, Mikel J., 95–96
Kraucer, Shelly, 94
Kristeva, Julia, 122, 163–164
Ku, Agnes S., 13
Ku, Lisbeth, 246, 247
Kuhn, Annette, 243, 295n10
kung fu films, 10, 28, 101, 102, 103, 107, 108, 117, 156, 167, 222, 223, 227, 228, 230, 264n28
   bamboo, as Chineseness, in, 10 109–111, 112, 113, 114, 115, 116, 117
   and nationalism and masculinity, 221, 223–224, 230, 236
Krämer, Peter, 52
Kwan, Stanley (Guan Jinpeng), 2, 82, 129, 155–156, 185, 278n1
   Center Stage, 156
   Full Moon in New York, 129
   Hold You Tight, 75, 185
   Lan Yu, 57, 185, 278n1
   Rouge, 155
   Yin ± Yang: Gender in Chinese Cinema, 82, 296n22
Kwan Tak-hing (Guan Dexing), 26, 28, 110
La Brassiere (Chan, Leung), 177, 178, 182, 183, 186–187, 190, 193, 194, 195, 196–197
Lacan, Jacques, 88, 138, 164, 282n3
Lai, Linda, 231–233, 234–235
Lai Ming, Leon (Li Ming), 74
Lam Kar-sing (Lin Jiao), 26
Lam, Ringo (Lin Lingdong), 20
Lan Tsu-wei (Lan Zuwei), 121, 278n9
Lan Yu (Kwan), 57, 185, 278n1

Lau, Andy (Liu Dehua), 49, 51, 73
Lau Ching-wan (Liu Qingyun), 51, 76, 77, 178, 186, 195
Lau Ka-fai (Liu Jiahui), 25, 26, 226
Lau Kar-leung (Liu Jialiang), 20, 25, 28, 30, 103, 226
Lau Kar-ling, Carina (Liu Jialing), 70, 178, 195
Lau, Lawrence (Liu Guochang), 188
Lau Siu-ming (Liu Shaoming), 71
Lau Tai-muk, 25
Law, Clara (Luo Zhuoyao), 120, 122, 187, 279n17
   Farewell China, 120–124, 128, 134, 135, 278n5, 278n9
Lee, Ang (Li An), 20, 38, 75, 101, 109 111, 112, 113, 114, 115, 116, 117, 276n2
   Crouching Tiger, Hidden Dragon (Lee), 10, 20, 38, 69, 101, 111–117, 112, 200
   Wedding Banquet, The, 75–76, 78
Lee, Bruce (Li Xiaolong), 8, 13, 18, 20, 25, 26, 27, 30, 31, 46, 72, 184, 208, 221, 223, 224, 227, 236, 239, 244, 251, 252, 253–254, 255, 259
   and Hong Kong identity, 227–228
   and masculinity and nationalism, 72, 224–225, 245–246, 251, 230, 251, 254, 259
Lee, Chiu-hing, 233–234
Lee, Danny (Li Xiuxian), 45
Lee Kang-sheng (Li Kangsheng), 132, 133, 134, 281n35, 281n37
Leung Chiu-wai, Tony (Liang Chaowei), 57, 70, 77, 130
Leung Hok–sze, Helen, 6, 9, 11
Leung, Gigi (Liang Yongqi), 178, 183, 195
Li, Jet (Li Lianjie), 68, 85, 101, 102, 110, 201, 203
Li Li-hua (Li Lihua), 21
Li Siu-leung, 228–229, 230, 236

Lin, Brigitte (Lin Qingxia), 68, 69–70, 71, 86, 87, 88, 276n6
Lin, Jeanette (Lin Cui), 21
Lin, Linda (Lin Dai), 21
Ling, Ivy, (Ling Bo), 21, 22
Lo Kwai-cheung, 5, 6, 11, 184, 201–202, 209–210, 221–222, 226–228, 229, 230, 236
Lo Lieh (Luo Lie), 22, 25, 26, 28, 31, 32
Loh, Betty, (Le Di), 21
Loui, Simon (Lei Yuyang), 66
Lu Hsiao-peng, Sheldon, 121, 276n2, 278n6
Lukacs, Georg, 199
    History and Class Consciousness, 199
Lung Kim-sun (Long Jiansheng), 69
Mang Hoi (Meng Hai), 144, 145, 147
Mao, Angela (Mao Ying), 25, 140
Marchetti, Gina, 209
martial arts
    and nationalism, 151
    in new style martial arts films, 25
martial arts films, 10, 11, 17, 18, 23, 24, 26–27, 28, 69, 140, 151, 152, 223, 226, 276n3
    and masculinity, 83, 85, 96
    and nationalism, 151, 223
    resurgence of, 23–24
    shift from swordplay to kung fu, 28, 29, 102
    See also kung fu films
Marx, Karl, 214
masculinity
    alternative forms of, 3–5, 6, 7
    and female masculinity, 137, 138, 140, 143–144
    and femininity, 59, 71–72
    and maleness, 137–138
    and nationalism, 13, 72, 223, 224, 226
Ma Sheng–mei, 6, 10, 11
Ma, Yo Yo (Ma Youyou), 117

Mayne, Judith, 244
Mei Lanfang, 67, 271n56
melodramas, 8, 67, 239, 244, 245, 246, 248, 249, 250, 251, 255
    female audiences, reception of, 13, 239, 244, 258
McGraw, Ali, 23
McQueen, Steve, 23
Milkyway Image, 9, 35–53
    development of 37–39
    masculinity,　　　post–1997, representation of, 9, 36, 37, 39–43, 44–46, 47, 53
    in first-phase films, 36, 39–49
    in second-phase films, 36, 49, 51–52
    shift to romance comedies, 36, 38–39, 49, 52, 53
Mission, The (To), 38, 45–46, 47–49
Modleski, Tania, 37, 241
Mui, Anita (Mei Yanfang), 70, 71, 86
Mulvey, Laura, 240, 241, 244, 258
    "Visual pleasure and narrative cinema," 240, 282n7
Nanren sishi. See *July Rhapsody*
Nansheng nüxiang: Zhongguo dianying de xingbie. See *Yin ± Yang: Gender in Chinese Cinema*
Natale, Richard, 201–202
Needing You (To, Wai), 49, 50, 51
New Formosa Fun Park Band, 126–127
new style martial arts films, 17, 21, 22, 23, 25, 26, 221, 222, 223
    appeal of, 23–26
    box office dominance of, 26–27
    and *yanggang* (masculinity), 23, 24–25
    See also Shaw Brothers Studio
Newman, Paul, 23
Ng Chun-ming, Paul, 209
Ng, Francis (Wu Zhenyu), 179, 186, 195

Ng, Sandra (Wu Junru), 92, 93, 97, 197
Nicholson, Jack, 23
Nixon, Sean, 186
Once Upon a Time in China (Tsui), 18, 109–110, 111, 167, 228, 229, 236
Once Upon a Time in China II (Tsui), 110–111
O'Neal, Tatum, 23
Ordinary Heroes (Hui), 120, 129, 132–134, 135, 281n34
Pang, Laikwan, 168
Penley, Constance, 243, 256
Percy, Walker, 192
Planet Hong Kong: Popular Cinema and the Art of Entertainment (Bordwell), 108, 162
Police Story (Chan), 252, 256, 258
Portland Street Blues (Yip), 9, 57, 90, 91–92, 93–95, 96–98
postcolonial theory/postcolonial criticism, 6, 10–11, 157, 165, 167, 169–170, 172, 173, 174, 266n2
post–structuralism/post–structuralist theory, 58, 62, 63, 88, 157, 173
Primitive Passion (Chow), 170
Prosser, Jay, 86–87, 88–89, 90
   Second Skins: The Body Narratives of Transsexuality, 86
Psycho (Hitchcock), 160
Qianghuo. See Mission, The
Qianyan wanyu. See Ordinary Heroes
Qingren hezi. See Chinese Box
queer theory/queer criticism, 9, 58, 62, 63–64, 86, 87, 267n3
   and transgender subjectivity, 9, 86–87, 90
Radway, Janice, 257
Rainer, Emig, 77–78
Raymond, Diane, 64
Rayns, Tony, 18, 224
Redford, Robert 23
Reis, Michelle (Li Jiaxin), 179, 195, 289n24

Ren zai niuyue. See Full Moon in New York
Reynolds, Burt, 23
Rich, Adrienne, 60
Righting Wrongs (Yuen), 150–151, 153, 283nn20–21
Rodriguez, Hector, 101, 275n1
Rothrock, Cynthia 11, 144, 145, 146, 147, 150, 151, 152–154, 283n20, 284n25
Rouge (Kwan), 155
Royal Warriors (Tsang), 141, 147–150
Ruan Lingyu. See Center Stage
Rush Hour (Ratner), 209–210
Rush Hour 2 (Ratner), 118, 210
Sacks, Oliver, 89
Salaff, Janet, 246, 247
Sandell, Jillian, 46, 95–96
Second Skins: The Body Narratives of Transsexuality (Prosser), 86
Sedgwick, Eve Kosofsky, 48, 71
Sek Kei, 22, 23, 24, 93, 141, 245–246, 251
Sek Yin-tsi (Shi Jian), 26
Sex and Zen & A Bullet in the Head (Hammond and Wilkins), 171
Shaolin Soccer (Chow), 39, 194, 233, 245
Shaolin zuqiu. See Shaolin Soccer
Shaw Brothers Studio, 17, 18, 21, 22, 24–25, 26, 27, 28, 223
   and new style martial arts film, 17, 26
Shaw, Run Run (Shao Yifu), 24
Shen Sheng-te (Shen Shengde), 121, 278n7, 278n9
Shen Shiao–Ying, 6, 10, 11
Shih Jun (Shi Jun), 19
Shum, John (Cen Jianxun), 144, 147
Siao Fong-fong, Josephine (Xiao Fangfang), 22, 71, 239, 244, 245, 247, 248, 249, 250, 251

Silence of the Lambs (Demme), 159, 169, 172

Siqin Gaowa, 129

Sit, Nancy (Xue Jiayan), 22

Song of the Exile (Hui), 155, 157

Spelman, Elizabeth V., 243
  Inessential Woman, 243

Stacey, Jackie, 242

Steintrager, James A., 6, 7, 10–11

Streisand, Barbra, 22

Stringer, Julian, 35, 72, 205, 206

Stryker, Susan, 81

subjectivity, transgender, 83, 85–86, 87–90, 91–92, 93–95, 96, 97, 98

Swordsman II (Ching), 19, 68, 69, 70, 83, 85–86, 87–90, 96, 98, 274n14, 276n6

"Taiwan factor," 10
  in *Chinese Box*, 120, 124–129
  in *Farewell, China*, 120–124
  in *Happy Together*, 129–132
  in *Ordinary Heroes*, 132–135

Tasker, Yvonne, 152

Taylor, Elizabeth, 22

Teng, Teresa (Deng Lijun), 119, 134, 278n4

Teo, Stephen, 37, 221, 224, 245, 226, 236, 293n14

"Third Meaning: Research Notes on Some Eisenstein Stills, The" (Barthes), 121–122, 123

Thompson, Kristin, 217

Ti Lung (Di Long), 25, 26, 27, 28, 31, 73, 97

Tiananmen Square incident (June 4, 1989), 44, 120, 123, 129, 167, 168, 234, 253, 278n5, 281n38

Tin Fung (Tian Feng), 22

To, Johnnie (Du Qifeng), 36, 37, 38, 39, 46, 49, 52
  Mission, The, 38, 45–46, 47–49
  Needing You, 49, 50, 51

To Man-chat (Du Wenze), 57

Too Many Ways to Be Number One (Wai), 37–38 in, 40–43, 45

transgender theory, 81–82, 86–87, 88–89, 90, 93, 97, 273n2, 273n4

transnational appeal, 1–2, 10 ,14, 141, 224–225
  of Lee, 224–225

Tsai Ming-liang (Cai Mingliang), 133, 281n36

Tsui Hark (Xu Ke), 18, 32, 46, 101, 103, 109, 111, 113, 144, 167, 184, 228, 236, 277n8
  Once Upon a Time in China, 18, 109–110, 111, 167, 228, 229, 236
  Once Upon a Time in China II, 110–111

Tucker, Chris, 118, 210

Tuxedo, The (Donovan), 210–211

Untold Story, The (Yau), 10, 157–159, 160–63, 164, 165–166, 167, 168–169, 170–171, 172, 173–174, 285n6, 285n13

"Visual pleasure and narrative cinema" (Mulvey), 240, 282n7

Wacquant, Loic, 202

Wai Ka-fai (Wei Jiahui), 37, 38, 39, 49, 5
  Needing You, 49, 50, 51
  Too Many Ways to Be Number One, 37–38, 40–43, 45

Wayne, John, 23

Wang, Wayne (Wang Ying), 120, 124, 125, 128, 129
  Chinese Box, 120, 124–129, 134, 135, 279n18, 279nn18–19, 278n22

Wang Yu, 22, 25, 26, 27, 30

Wangjiao kamen. See *As Tears Go By*

Wedding Banquet, The (Lee), 75–76, 78

Weisser, Thomas, 171

Wilkins, Mike, 171, 286n20
  Sex and Zen & A Bullet in the Head, 171

Windtalkers (Woo), 207

Wohu canglong. See *Crouching Tiger, Hidden Dragon*

Wong, Anthony (Huang Qiusheng), 133, 134, 157, 168

Wong Ching (Wang Jing), 2, 8, 189

Wong, Day, 6, 13

Wong Kar-wai (Wang Jiawei), 19, 38, 57, 71, 129, 132, 155, 156, 164, 167, 171, 228, 236

  As Tears Go By, 73, 155, 164 –165

  Ashes of Time, 71, 167, 228, 236

Wong, Joey (Wang Zuxian), 71

Wong, Michael (Wang Minde), 66, 147

Wong, Wyman (Huang Weiwen), 66

Woo, John (Wu Yusen), 8, 19–20, 35, 41–42, 46, 72–73, 92, 94, 95–96, 102, 104, 105, 117, 141, 156–157, 158, 165, 168, 184, 191, 200, 203, 204–207, 208, 211, 129 220, 285n4

  Better Tomorrow, A (Woo), 73, 97, 205–206

  Broken Arrow, 73, 207

  Bullet in the Head, 168, 286n20

  Face/Off, 73, 207

  films, pre-Hollywood vs. Hollywood, 200, 204–207, 211, 219

  Killer, The, 73, 94, 205–206

Woo Wai-chung (Hu Huizhong), 71

Wu, Daniel (Wu Yanzu), 77, 186, 195

Wu Ma, 22

Xiao'ao jianghu II zhi Dongfang Bubai. See *Swordsman II*

Xiyan. See *Wedding Banquet, A*

yanggang, 22, 23, 24–25, 96

  and new style martial arts film, 23, 24–25

Yanzhi kou. See *Rouge*

Yam Kim-fai (Ren Jianhui), 22, 67, 69, 70, 96, 249

Yam, Simon (Ren Dahua), 66

Yau Ching, 82, 87

Yau, Esther, 2

Yau, Herman, 10, 160, 161

  Untold Story, The, 10, 157–159, 160–63, 164, 165–166, 167, 168–169, 170–171, 172, 173–174, 285n6, 285n13

Yeh, Julie (Ye Feng), 21

Yeh Yueh-yu, 158

Yen, Donnie (Zhen Zidan), 111

Yeoh, Michelle (Yang Ziqiong), 11, 20, 102, 112, 115, 144, 145–146, 147, 262n13, 283n15

Yes, Madam! (Yuen), 141, 144–147

Yeung, Miriam (Yang Qianhua), 52

Yige zitou de dansheng. See *Too Many Ways to Be Number One*

Yin ± Yang: Gender in Chinese Cinema (Kwan), 82, 296n22

Yingxiong bense. See *Better Tomorrow, A*

Yu, Lucilla (You Min), 21

Yu Suqiu, 140

Yu Zhanyuan, 140

Yue kuaile yue duoluo. See *Hold You Tight*

Yuen, Anita (Yuan Yongyi), 70, 71, 78, 86

Yuan Biao, 110, 150, 151, 152

Yuen Wo-ping (Yuan Heping), 101, 105, 200

Zhang Che, 3, 8, 17–18, 20–21, 22–23, 24–26, 27, 28, 29–31, 72, 102, 104, 221, 223, 224, 263n6, 264nn21–22, 264n27

  impact/legacy of, of, 8, 18, 20, 31–32

  and new style martial arts films, 17, 22, 23, 221

  and rise of male–centred films, 22–23, 24–25

  and *yanggang* (masculinity), 17, 20–21, 22, 23, 24–25

Zhang Zhen, 20, 282n12
Zhang Ziyi, 69, 112, 114
Zhifa xianfeng. See *Righting Wrongs*
Zhongguo xia. See *Chinese Box*